THE BATTLE OF LISSA 1866

The Battle of Lissa 1866

How the Industrial Revolution Changed the Face of Naval Warfare

Quintin Barry

Helion & Company

Helion & Company Limited
Unit 8 Amherst Business Centre
Budbrooke Road
Warwick
CV34 5WE
England
Tel. 01926 499 619
Email: info@helion.co.uk
Website: www.helion.co.uk
Twitter: @helionbooks
Visit our blog at blog.helion.co.uk

Published by Helion & Company 2022
Designed and typeset by Mach 3 Solutions Ltd (www.mach3solutions.co.uk)
Cover designed by Paul Hewitt, Battlefield Design (www.battlefield-design.co.uk)

ISBN 978-1-914059-92-6

British Library Cataloguing-in-Publication Data.
A catalogue record for this book is available from the British Library.

Contents

List of Illustrations

Plate section can be found between pages 86 and 87.

List of Maps

In colour section:

Acknowledgements

As indicated in the preface, the early history of the ironclad has been explored in depth by a number of outstanding historians, whose work has been of the greatest assistance. I should like also to take this opportunity of acknowledging, as always, the unfailing support of my publisher Duncan Rogers, and the patient and helpful work of my editor Christopher Brice. I am also very grateful to George Anderson for the maps which he has produced; and to Laurence Townsend for his assistance in overcoming my computer illiteracy. I should also like to thank Tim Readman, who read the book in draft; Katie Proctor, for all her help with the texts; the Heeresgeschichtliches Museum in Vienna, which provided the cover illustration, and to Paul Hewitt of Battlefield Design who produced the front cover for Helion; and, of course, my wife Diana for her great tolerance of my prolonged disappearances into the nineteenth century.

Preface

In this book I have endeavoured to trace the way in which the Industrial Revolution comprehensively changed the nature of naval warfare, a process which culminated in the battle of Lissa on July 20 1866. At the end of the Napoleonic wars, navies still fought each other in much the same way as they had done for more than three centuries. Wooden warships, dependent on sail power, firing solid shot from broadside batteries, had dominated naval warfare. Although the oared galley was still to be found, it had ceased to have a decisive influence on the outcome of a sea battle since not long after the battle of Lepanto.

The coming of the Industrial Revolution brought with it a complex set of challenges not only to naval architects, but also to those decision-makers responsible for the way in which warships operated. With so many generations of practical experience and tradition behind them, it is not surprising that there was some reluctance to recognise the irresistible change that was about to overtake them. If anything, it is rather more surprising to find how quickly change was actually embraced by a profession that had tended to be very conservative.

Newcomen's steam engine of 1712 predated the start of the Industrial Revolution, which is generally put at about 1760. By 1733 some 110 engines had been built, and by 1800 the number had risen to 1,454; by then Boulton and Watt had constructed 496 examples of James Watt's original steam engine, and machine tools were coming increasingly into use. The introduction of puddled iron after 1800, and the high-pressure steam engine at about the same time, made railways a practical proposition. Engines that could drive trains could also drive ships.

In mainland Europe the Industrial Revolution came somewhat later. Much of the technological know-how there was obtained directly from British pioneers. Elsewhere, progress in Belgium was particularly rapid; German and Russian governments also supported new industries with state funding. The growth of industrialisation in France, however, was somewhat slower.

It was about half a century before the Industrial Revolution began to make an impact on naval warfare, but the next half-century saw it change out of all recognition. Professor JP Baxter, in his seminal study *The Introduction of the Ironclad Warship*, wrote of 'the five great naval revolutions of the nineteenth century – steam, shell guns, the screw propeller, rifled ordnance and armour.'[1] Admiral Ballard, in his review of Baxter's book, was inclined to think that 'only three of these were revolutionary in the fullest sense, namely steam, shells and armour.'

1 James P. Baxter, *The Introduction of the Ironclad Warship* (Cambridge, Massachusetts: Harvard University Press 1933), p. 3.

He suggested that 'if the screw had never been invented, paddles in some form would have remained and the side armour would have been extended to enclose them,' while rifling the shell was merely 'an evolutionary advance adding to its accuracy and penetration without altering its essential nature.'[2]

The British navy's policy had generally been to leave radical innovations in design to other Powers, but then to adopt these improvements and to retain its superiority by applying them on a large scale. This led historians for many years to depict the British Admiralty as resistant to change, taking action when it was almost too late. It is a view that has been effectively demolished by more recent historians, who have demonstrated that in fact the Admiralty followed closely the rapid advances in technological development. In the event, Britain soon took the lead, though it is certainly true that initially it was prompted to do so by developments in France.

In this book I have not attempted to match the hugely important work of those historians such as Oscar Parkes, DK Brown, Andrew Lambert, and Basil Greenhill and Anne Giffard, who have so clearly recorded the transition from the sailing battle fleet of the Napoleonic wars to the steam battle fleet of the 1850s. Their analysis of the development of the British navy is essential for an understanding of the ships which fought at Lissa and the tactics which they employed. Although the British and French navies and their warship designers had made the running, and the use of armour played a major part in the American Civil War, it was to be a war between European powers that saw the first fleet action between steam driven ironclads, when the Austrian and Italian fleets met off the island of Lissa in the Adriatic in July 1866.

2 Admiral George A. Ballard, 'Some Observations on Professor Baxter's book on *The Introduction of the Iron Warship*' in *The Mariner's Mirror* 19.4 (1933) p. 406.

Prologue
Lissa 1811

In 1811 the island of Lissa was crucial to the British Navy's command of the Adriatic. Lying some forty miles off the Dalmatian coast, its excellent harbour of Porto San Giorgio provided a base for the British frigate squadron of Captain William Hoste, a former protégé and devoted disciple of Nelson. From there, he had for a considerable time been able to prey on the shipping that served the needs of the French army, which at that time occupied the coastline on both sides of the Adriatic.

Hoste's continual raiding of that coastline, in the course of which he had destroyed French occupied forts, batteries, and signal stations, alongside capturing a large number of merchant vessels, had become more than merely an annoyance to the Emperor Napoleon; it disrupted the grandiose plans which he had conceived to operate with a large army in Dalmatia. He was extremely dissatisfied, with good reason, with the failure of his navy to do anything much about British naval activity in the Adriatic. For much of the time in which Hoste had been operating there, he had only one frigate and a sloop to carry on his war with the French. He was himself extremely surprised at the extent to which he had been allowed to do so. As early as December 1809 we find him writing to his father:

> Can there be a greater proof of the pusillanimity of our enemies in this part of the world, than to allow one frigate and one sloop to annoy the trade in the manner we do? I will give you their force. At Ancona, three frigates, two brigs and two schooners; at Venice, one frigate, three brigs, two schooners and gunboats innumerable; at Trieste, four Russian line of battleships, two frigates, and six French gunboats and one galley. What think you of their enterprise after that? The truth is, they are afraid of the weather, and are very badly manned; we are all well manned and do not care a fig about the weather.[1]

It was to put a stop to this that Napoleon, in 1810, appointed Captain Bernard Dubourdieu, one of the most promising officers in the French navy, to take command of the Adriatic squadron. Dubourdieu, born in 1772, had enjoyed a very successful career, in the course of which he had been taken prisoner when the ship in which he was serving was captured by the British. After 18 months in a prison hulk he succeeded in making his escape, and by capturing a transport was able to make his way back to France. In appointing him as commodore, Napoleon had high

1 Tom Pocock, *Remember Nelson* (London: Williams Sons & Co, 1977) p. 151.

hopes of putting an end to the nuisance of Hoste and his squadron. He sent Dubourdieu in the first instance to visit Venice, by now under French rule, where there were a number of vessels available to join his squadron, which was based at Ancona.

William Hoste, whom Dubourdieu was to face, was aged 31 in 1811. He enjoyed the patronage of Lord Collingwood, the British commander-in-chief of the Mediterranean fleet, and before him that of Horatio Nelson, who had taken him under his wing when the 12-year-old Hoste had joined his ship *Agamemnon*. Thereafter Nelson did all he could to further Hoste's career, seeing in him an outstandingly promising young officer, of whom Emma Hamilton remarked: 'I say he will be a second Nelson.' Collingwood had continued to foster his career, and in 1810 appointed him to command the frigate squadron based at Lissa. At the beginning of 1811 it consisted of four frigates: *Amphion*, of 32 guns, (flag), *Active*, 38, *Cerberus*, 32 and *Volage*, 22.

The island of Lissa was protected by a number of defence works constructed by the British, which would still be there fifty five years later to play a vital role for the Austrians in the repulse of the attacks of the Italian fleet. Dubourdieu had made an early move against the island; in September 1810 he had taken advantage of the absence from Lissa of Hoste's squadron to plan a raid. With two French and three Venetian frigates, and two French brigs he embarked a battalion of French infantry, and on October 22 sailed into the harbour of Porto San Giorgio, and landed his troops to occupy the port. There was some considerable dispute about what he achieved there – he claimed to have captured 30 vessels and burnt another 64, while Hoste subsequently reported that he had taken only three prizes and burnt five other vessels. However, later that day, news came that the British squadron had been sighted on its way back to Lissa, and Dubourdieu wasted no time in re-embarking his troops, and putting to sea before Hoste appeared. Dubourdieu returned to Ancona, where Hoste, who followed him there, found to his frustration that the French squadron was safely moored under the guns of the citadel.

For Hoste, it was a difficult time. Collingwood, worn out by the duties of his exacting post, had handed over his command to Sir Charles Cotton; he died on his way home. Hoste could not expect the same kind of personal support and encouragement from the new commander-in-chief, of whom he wrote: 'Sir C Cotton is very civil but he is not, like my Lord Collingwood, *in my way*.'[2]

In March 1811 Hoste decided to take his squadron across the Adriatic to Ancona, in the hope of provoking an engagement with Dubourdieu, and on the evening of March 12 assembled his four ships off the north coast of Lissa, intending to sail at first light on the following morning. At 3.00 pm next day the *Active*, the furthest to windward of the squadron, in a brisk north northwest breeze, close hauled on the port tack, sighted and reported enemy ships in the offing, and sent up a blue flare, before turning to rejoin the other ships of the squadron, at that time about a mile offshore.

Dubourdieu had saved Hoste the trouble of going to look for him. In response to an explicit order from the Emperor he had sailed from Ancona with a force consisting of three French frigates (*Favorite*, 44 (flag), *Flore*, 44 and *Danae*, 44) and three Venetian frigates (*Corona*, 44, *Bellona*, 32 and *Carolina*, 32). Accompanying his squadron there were a number of smaller Venetian vessels: the brig *Principessa Augusta*, 18, the *Principessa di Bologna*, 10, the *Eugenio*, 10,

2 Pocock, *Remember Nelson*, p. 162.

and the *Lodola*, 2.[3] Dubourdieu's squadron carried 276 guns, with a total complement of over 2000 men; he also took with him a force of 500 infantry to occupy the island.

As dawn broke, the two squadrons came in sight of each other. The French were formed in two columns; to starboard the *Favorite* led the *Flore*, *Bellona* and *Principessa Augusta*, while the port column consisted of the *Danae*, *Corona*, *Carolina* and the smaller vessels. At about 6.00 am the French began to bear down on the British ships. William James described the British squadron as it cleared for action:

> The British ships immediately formed in line ahead with, besides the customary red ensign at their respective peaks, union jacks and ensigns, blue and red, at their foremastheads and at their different stays. Thus nobly decorated, the four ships continued working to windward to close the enemy.[4]

When the two squadrons had closed to distance of about 2 miles, Hoste made the signal for which he became famous: 'Remember Nelson,' which brought cheers from the ships' companies of all his squadron. Captain Phipps Hornby of the Volage remarked: 'Never again so long as I live shall I see so interesting or so glorious a moment.'[5]

By 9.00 am the leading French vessels had come within range, and the British ships opened fire. Dubourdieu's intention was to break the line in two places, but the fierce broadsides of Hoste's squadron, and the compactness of its line, frustrated this attempt. Dubourdieu now sought to round the *Amphion*, leading the British line, to attack from leeward. As the *Favorite* closed with Hoste's ship, a mass of men, led by Dubourdieu himself, was preparing to board. At this moment a 5 ½ inch howitzer, containing 750 musket balls, was fired at them from the *Amphion*'s quarterdeck at a range of ten yards. The devastation was fearful; as the smoke cleared practically all the boarders were down, dead or wounded; among them was Dubourdieu. It was 9:40 am. The officer who took command of the *Favorite* made another attempt to wear and get to leeward of the *Amphion*, but as he put up her helm the French frigate struck firmly on the rocks. The *Amphion* narrowly escaped joining her as the British line wore round, which put the flagship at the end of the line.

The remaining ships of the French starboard column passed under the stern of the British line, engaging it to leeward, while the column led by the *Danae* tacked and remained to windward. The two squadrons continued to exchange a heavy fire, and went on pounding each other until at about 11.20 am the *Flore* was seen to have struck her colours, followed at noon by the *Bellona*. With this, the French began to retreat; Hoste endeavoured to follow, but was hampered by the considerable damage which his ships had suffered. At 3.00 pm the *Active* and the *Cerberus* were able to catch up with the sternmost enemy vessel, the *Corona*, and compelled her to strike. Meanwhile the crew of the wrecked *Favorite* had set her on fire and at 4.00 pm she blew up.

Aboard the *Amphion*, most of her boats had been smashed by the intense gunfire, and Hoste was finding difficulty in getting prize crews across to take possession of the *Flore* and *Bellona*. At this point Peridier, the captain of the *Flore*, who had been below, injured, at the time her

3 William Laird Clowes, The Royal Navy: *A History from the Earliest Times to the Present* ((London: Sampson Low Marston, 1897-1903) vol V p. 478.
4 William James, *A Naval History of Great Britain* (London: Richard Bentley, 1859), V p. 234.
5 Pocock, *Remember Nelson*, p. 167.

colours came down, ordered them to be re-hoisted, and made his escape. Hoste was outraged; he and Peridier subsequently exchanged correspondence in which the French captain denied that his ship had struck, saying that the colours had been shot away. Hoste later reflected that he could have sunk her, but for the fact that her colours had come down, and that he and Captain Gordon of the *Active* 'considered her as our own.' The time taken to secure the *Bellona* had enabled Peridier 'to steal off, till too late for our shattered ships to come up with him; his rigging and sails apparently not much injured; but, by the laws of war, I shall ever maintain he belongs to us.'[6]

In spite of this, it had been a remarkable victory. With a greatly inferior force, Hoste had taken two enemy frigates and destroyed a third. Out of his total complement of 886 men, he had lost 45 killed and 145 wounded. The total of French casualties was much higher. Apart from the death of Dubourdieu and his flag captain Meillerie, the *Favorite* had over 150 men killed and wounded. The *Corona* lost a total of over 200, and the *Bellona* 140; the losses of the other French ships are not recorded. Clowes, noting the great superiority enjoyed by the French squadron, called the victory 'one of the most creditable in British annals,' while the *Naval Chronicle* observed that 'for its extent the engagement was unquestionably one of the most severe, and, for us, one of the most brilliant, that has taken place during the war.'[7] It left the British in undisputed control of the Adriatic, and in possession of the island of Lissa, which would later come to be described as the 'Gibraltar of the Adriatic.'

6 Clowes, *Royal Navy*, V p. 481.
7 Nicholas Tracy, (ed.), *The Naval Chronicle* (London: Chatham Publishing. 1999) vol V, p. 17.

1

The Sailing Battlefleet

The end of the Napoleonic Wars in 1815 left Great Britain in a position of unassailable naval supremacy. The only other navies with which the Admiralty need be concerned to any extent were those of France and Russia. The navies of Spain and the Netherlands had been effectively wrecked during the course of the war. Sweden and Denmark possessed modest navies, but those of Prussia, Austria, and the individual states of Italy, scarcely existed at all.

For the Royal Navy, the immediate threat came from domestic politics. The British government and people looked for sweeping financial retrenchment after more than two decades of war. A reduction in the cost of the navy as well as that of the army was an obvious and immediate target for cutbacks in public expenditure. With the necessity for making urgent economies the Admiralty could not argue; but the process of carrying these out was undertaken against a background of the declining influence of the Admiralty in political affairs. Professor N.A.M. Rodger, in his history of the Admiralty, remarked that 'the nineteenth century was the age in which the Navy and the nation grew further apart than ever before,' as the power of the British Empire grew and the size of its fleet contracted.[1]

When the war ended the navy was possessed of 214 ships of the line and 792 frigates and smaller vessels of all types, although many of these were worn out and must in any case soon be disposed of.[2] By the end of 1815 the Admiralty had been able to arrive at its own view of the proper size of the fleet, and how many of the huge number of ships of the line should be retained. In its instruction to the Navy Board on December 8, it was stated:

> The first object of their Lordships' attention is the force which it may be proper to keep in readiness for sea and actual service. This force, my Lords are of opinion should be about one hundred sail of the line (exclusive of ships building) fourteen of which are to be in commission as Guard and Flag ships.[3]

1 Professor N.A.M. Rodger, *The Admiralty* (Lavenham: Terence Dalton, 1979), p. 93.
2 C.J. Bartlett, *Great Britain and Sea Power 1815-1853* (Oxford: Oxford University Press 1963), p. 22.
3 Bartlett, *Sea Power*, p. 23.

The rest would be laid up in ordinary, kept in good enough order to be brought into service in the event of an emergency. It was an ambitious target, and a costly one, and in the event it could not be met.

At the same time the French navy, badly damaged at the battle of Trafalgar, had been in the process of rebuilding, and at the war's end had some 50 ships of the line built and building, together with a large number of smaller vessels. But the restored Bourbon dynasty was not much interested in the navy, and a large part of the fleet was laid up. Nor did the French people hold the navy in high esteem:

> Few recalled the victories of the American War: to most the navy presented only a long tale of failure and of defeat. There were no colonies worth mention to protect, for France had lost almost all of them: there was no seaborne commerce to speak of: the troops could guard the coasts.[4]

The Russian navy possessed some forty ships of the line at the peace, divided between the Baltic and the Black Sea, but in the post-war years it was allowed to fall into a state of inactivity, and its effectiveness as a fighting force declined rapidly.[5]

The post-war demobilisation and the scrapping of the Royal Navy's oldest and least efficient ships got under way at once, though by no means fast enough for the politicians. A huge fleet still remained; by 1820 the rundown still left 149 ships of the line built, building or ordered; only 14 of these were in commission. Of the total of 613 other ships on the Navy List at that date, 127 were in commission.[6] While the process of reducing the size of the fleet had not gone particularly quickly, the condition of many of those laid up in ordinary was steadily deteriorating. As C.J. Bartlett has pointed out, 'neither the eradication of the useless ships nor the maintenance of the above numbers in a first class condition was attained.' The task of scaling down the fleet was huge, and was itself costly. Between 1814 and 1820, 374 ships were sold out of the service, and 178 were broken up. Although the process continued throughout the 1820s it was still found in 1832 that of the 572 ships on the Navy List there were many that were useless.[7] With so many vessels still at its command, it was inevitable that the Admiralty found it difficult to persuade governments of the need to order new ships.

Certainly the size of the fleet was such that it was not difficult in the post-war years to attain the two-power standard enunciated by Castlereagh in 1817, which was 'to keep up a navy equal to the navies of any two powers that can be brought against us.'[8] The Admiralty, of course, had to work with less money; annual naval expenditure fell steeply in the years following the end of the war.

In 1815 the ship of the line remained the most powerful weapon of war that mankind had yet produced. Built of wood, powered by sail, with a massive broadside firing solid shot, its design had been steadily refined over centuries of sea warfare. For generations the improvement in the

4 E.H. Jenkins, *A History of the French Navy* (London: Macdonald & Janes, 1973), p. 282.
5 Donald W. Mitchell, *A History of Russian and Soviet Sea Power* (London: Andre Deutsch, 1974), pp. 134-136.
6 William James, *The Naval History of Great* Britain (London: Richard Bentley, 1859), vol VI, p. 402.
7 Bartlett, *Sea Power*, p. 24.
8 David. K. Brown, *Before the Ironclad* (Barnsley: Seaforth Publishing, 1990), p. 27.

building of each new ship of the line had been gradual, so that there had effectively been little change in basic design. The most important innovation had been the introduction of coppering during the War of American Independence, which had brought with it significant increases in speed. However, the work of Sir Robert Seppings did bring about important changes in the way in which wooden hulls were designed, which enabled a substantial increase in size of the largest ships of the line. D.K. Brown wrote of Seppings' scientific approach to structural design that 'he was the first to understand fully the nature of the loading on a ship at sea and he developed a light and durable structure to meet those loads.'[9] Brown pointed out that in facilitating technical advances of this kind, the British Admiralty was far from reactionary.

Brown also addressed the question of whether British built ships were inferior to those built elsewhere, regarding it as strange, in the light of the superiority of the Royal Navy in battle, that British writers should have insisted on that inferiority. Naval officers took the view that captured French ships were larger and faster and had gun decks that were not too close to the waterline. Nelson told the First Lord that the *San Joseph*, briefly his flagship, was the finest ship in the world. The historian Edward Brenton wrote of her:

> The *San Joseph*, of 112 guns, taken in the battle off Cape Saint Vincent in 1797, was long admired in the British Navy, uniting all the superior qualities of a ship of the line with the sailing of the fastest frigate; her lower deck ports were higher out of the water with all her sea stores in than was ever known in any other ship of the line; she could carry her guns run out when few British ships would have ventured to open a port; she stowed 500 tons of water and we had nothing that compared with her as a ship of war.[10]

Brown, who made a detailed study of the evidence, was not convinced, noting that 'English builders, who were not in any way reluctant to copy the best of foreign designs, chose *Victory* as the model for the smaller three deckers.' He quoted a French writer who suggested that the French vessels were not good seaboats, and took the view that there were merely very small differences in design between the ships of the two countries. This was the view of two members of the Admiralty's Surveyors' Department who recorded in 1848 that 'the experience of late years has brought the best form of ships within a comparatively narrow compass, so that educated naval architects generally differ but little from each other.'[11]

Seppings became Surveyor of the Navy in 1813, and carried on his innovatory work on the structure of the wooden warship. His reforms included a system of diagonal framing, the use of iron knee pieces and iron straps, a round bow and later a round stern. Andrew Lambert has described his improvements as amounting to 'the first major breakthrough in the construction of warships since the introduction of carvel planking.'[12]

After 1815 the building of 74 gun ships of the line was discontinued, and the new ships ordered bore at least 80 guns; their design was based on well-established models such as the *Caledonia* and the *Victory*. By 1826, however, it had become clear that the smaller ships of the

9 Brown, *Before the Ironclad*, p. 8.
10 Brown, *Before the Ironclad*, p. 13.
11 Quoted C[harles]. I[ain]. Hamilton, *Anglo-French Naval Rivalry 1840-1870* (Oxford: Clarendon Press, 1993), p. 15.
12 Andrew Lambert, *Battleships in Transition* (London: Conway Maritime Press, 1984), p. 13.

line coming into service were not powerful enough to match ships being built for the French and American navies. In response to this the Navy Board, led by Sir Thomas Byam Martin, ordered the building of larger vessels, the first examples being those of the *Rodney* class of 91 guns. During Seppings' time as Surveyor 21 new ships of the line were ordered, of which six were first rates. In 1830 the Tory government, which had been in office for almost three decades, was replaced by a Liberal administration. This brought to an end the term of office of Lord Melville, who had been First Lord of the Admiralty since 1812, save for a brief period when the board was replaced by the appointment of the King's brother William, Duke of Clarence, as Lord High Admiral between 1827 and 1828. Melville was generally regarded as a very good First Lord; this is a view not shared, though, by Professor Rodger, who has suggested that he possessed 'only moderate talents.' He had, however, taken a particular interest in the development of naval architecture, and professional opinion felt that with him at the head of the Board the navy was in safe hands.

His departure ushered in a reformer who was to have a very considerable effect on the Admiralty and the way in which the navy was run. The Admiralty's political influence had continued to decline, and it was in no position to resist the sweeping reforms that were introduced by the new First Lord, Sir James Graham. He had no previous experience to bring to the task, but he did bring a mandate for change. Among the first casualties of his reforms was Sir Robert Seppings, who was replaced by Sir William Symonds, who had carried out several designs before his appointment as Surveyor in 1832 and was one of the British naval officers who believed in the inferiority of British design.[13]

Graham's primary concern was to reduce cost. Soon after he took office he quarrelled with Sir Thomas Byam Martin, who was another early casualty, being replaced as Comptroller of the Navy Board. It soon appeared to Graham that the Navy Board itself should go. He intended thereby to achieve 'a just division of labour, an undivided control and a due responsibility on the one hand, and, on the other, that unity and simplicity which he held to be the very essence and life of public business.'[14] Graham succeeded in reducing naval expenditure between 1830 and 1834 by about £1 million per year, a reduction of about one sixth compared to the last years of the Tory administration. C.J. Bartlett has observed that his time at the Admiralty, in spite of some considerable professional suspicion, 'was almost wholly advantageous to the navy.' Although he did not come to the office with a great reputation or considerable political influence, 'both in and out of office Graham was to prove himself one of the most forceful spokesmen for the navy among politicians.'[15]

Symonds' term of office as Surveyor proved to be controversial. The ships which he designed were severely criticised by naval officers, not least by Admiral Sir George Cockburn, the Senior Naval Lord. Of the largest group of ships of the line for which Symonds was responsible, the *Vanguard* class, it was said that they had 'all the virtues and faults of the Symondite ships. They were fast in moderate winds but rolled quickly and heavily, making them poor gun platforms.'[16] Notwithstanding the views of contemporary naval officers, William Laird Clowes expressed a much more favourable opinion of Symonds'work:

13 Brown, *Before the Ironclad*, p. 39.
14 Quoted Rodger, *Admiralty*, p. 98.
15 Bartlett, *Sea Power*, p. 50.
16 Brown, *Before the Ironclad*, p. 42.

> His ships owed their superior speed and stability chiefly to the improved form of their bottom, which he made much less heavy and full than had previously been usual. They were also broader, roomier and loftier between decks than their forerunners, and in them the sailing navy of England undoubtedly found its highest development.[17]

Recent, more thorough and more technical writers have not shared this view. D.K. Brown, for instance has noted that the increased rise of floor in Symonds' ships tended to increase leeway, that greater beam and less ballast was a move in the right direction; but that 'because he was incapable of making the necessary calculations and would not take advice from those who could, Symonds overdid both aspects.'[18] A glimpse of how Symonds was perceived in the service comes from a letter written by Alexander Milne in 1841: 'I hear he is very crusty with anyone who gives an opinion about his ships. He may do himself harm by it as his squadrons are not as popular as they were.'[19]

Symonds' ships were the subject of repeated complaints in Parliament. One of his strongest critics there was Rear Admiral Sir Charles Napier, who was always ready to speak his mind on any subject which concerned him. Professional comment of this kind led Lord Auckland, then First Lord, to establish a panel of expert contributors, the Committee of Reference on Shipbuilding. Issues raised there about the need to adopt a new hull form led Symonds to resign in 1846, ostensibly on the grounds of ill-health. Apart from design issues of this kind, his time as Surveyor coincided with an entirely new, and very difficult, set of problems with which he had to deal. The coming of steam would very soon change everything.

17 Sir William. L. Clowes, *The Royal Navy: A History from the Earliest Times to the* Present(London: Sampson Low Marston, 1901)VI, p. 192.
18 Brown, *Before the Ironclad*, p. 43.
19 John. D. Beeler (ed.), *The Milne Papers* (Aldershot: Navy Records Society, 2004), vol I, p. 153.

2

The Advent of Steam

Consideration of the possibility of powering a vessel by means of a steam engine had begun early in the eighteenth century, but it was not until the development of steam engines had reached a point at which they could be fitted to a ship that the idea became a practical proposition. This was towards the end of the century, but thereafter a number of inventors produced designs, in France, Britain, and the United States, the vessels to be driven by means of paddles. The first such steamer that could be said to have sailed under its own steam was a vessel that appeared on the River Seine in 1779. This was followed by a much larger vessel, the *Pyroscaphe*, that took to the water on the River Sâone four years later. Pioneers elsewhere were also developing paddle steamers; in Scotland in 1789 Patrick Miller designed a vessel that attained seven knots on the Forth-Clyde canal, and this was followed by the *Charlotte Dundas*. 56 feet long, she was able to tow two barges each with a 70 ton load, which gave the prospect of commercial viability.[1] In the United States Robert Fulton, who had previously worked in France, produced the first commercially successful steamer in America, known as the North River Steam Boat.

Mercantile viability was essential, if the necessary capital for the construction of steamers was to be raised. In Scotland on the Clyde, Henry Bell launched the *Comet*, which carried passengers between Glasgow and Greenock from 1812 for a fare of four shillings first class, and three shillings second class. She was 44 feet long and 12 feet in the beam. Although the *Comet* was ultimately not a great commercial success, she paved the way for others that were, and by 1815 there were ten steamers operating on the Clyde, and fifteen elsewhere in Great Britain, while the development of steamers was beginning in Europe, almost entirely on inland waterways.[2]

In 1793 the British Admiralty encouraged the Earl of Stanhope to build a paddle steamer, *Kent*, at his own expense. This was a short lived experiment, and a proposal by Henry Bell in 1800 for a steam warship was not taken up. Nevertheless, the possibilities of such a vessel were obvious. It was in the United States, however, that the first steam warship took to the water. This was the *Demologos*, designed by Robert Fulton for the defence of New York during the war of 1812. She was a catamaran, with a paddle wheel placed between her twin hulls, which were 156 feet in length. Her total breadth was 56 feet, and she drew 11 feet of water, with a displacement

1 George W. Hilton and others, *The Illustrated History of Paddle Steamers* (Lausanne: Patrick Stephens Ltd, 1976), pp. 12-13.

2 Hilton, *Paddle Steamers*, p. 20.

of about 2,475 tons; she was powered by a one cylinder engine located in one of the hulls, with a bore of 48 inches and a 5 foot stroke, and a boiler in the other hull. She was to be armed with thirty 32 pounders (in the event only 24 were fitted) firing red hot shot, and was protected by wooden bulwarks nearly five feet thick. She was built at a cost of $320,000. Her completion was delayed by the death of Robert Fulton, and she only began her trials in June 1815. She appears to have attained speeds of between three and six knots. As it turned out, she was never called upon to fight, the war coming to an end before her completion, and she spent the rest of her life as a receiving ship at Brooklyn.[3] A twentieth century historian favourably commented on the design of the *Demologos*, which considering her size was well ahead of her time:

> The design of this vessel was perfectly rational; the guns and the paddlewheel were exceedingly well protected, and the steam power gave her a decided advantage over all sailing ships, especially in channels and estuaries. The extravagant coal consumption of steam engines of that time, which was a serious drawback in the case of seagoing ships, was of small importance in a vessel built for harbour defence.[4]

In these early days, the British Admiralty did not see the need to make its own commitment to the steamship, preferring to wait and see how it developed. Isambard Kingdom Brunel was asked to advise on the practicability of using steamers to tow warships out of harbour, but the Admiralty's instructions were cautious: 'the Board deem it unnecessary to enter at the present into the consideration of the question as to how far the power of the steam engine may be made applicable to the general purposes of navigation.'[5] After some early experiments using hired vessels the Admiralty purchased its first steamer in 1821. This was the *Monkey*, of 212 tons, powered by an 80 hp engine. She was followed by the *Comet*, built in Deptford in 1822, of 238 tons. She was 115 feet long; her engines developed 80 hp, but she also had a full sailing rig. She was employed on a wide variety of duties, though most often used in towing large sailing vessels.

At this time the interest of the Admiralty was in acquiring reliable steamers, capable of undertaking reasonably long passages, but primarily suited for towing duties. Commercial interest, however, was on the other hand particularly in vessels capable of making fast and reliable short passages that would attract sufficient numbers of fare paying passengers to make them commercially viable.[6] It was suggested by a number of historians, most notably William Laird Clowes, that the Admiralty was slow to respond to the opportunities created by the advent of steam. He wrote that the Admiralty, in adopting steamers at all, 'did so half-heartedly and with a bad grace,' adding that for a time the vessels acquired did not even appear in the Navy List.[7] Actually, the Admiralty was keeping a watchful eye on the developing technology, but in the early days was content to let the commercial sector bear the cost of making the running. Otherwise conservatively minded admirals, such as Sir George Cockburn, who was Senior

3 James P. Baxter, *The Introduction of the Ironclad Warship* (Cambridge, Mass: Harvard College, 1933), p. 47.
4 William Hovgaard, *Modern History of Warships* (London: Conway Maritime Press, 1928), pp. 1-2.
5 Bartlett, *Sea Power*, p, 199.
6 Basil Greenhill and Ann Giffard, *Steam, Politics and Patronage* (London: Conway Maritime Press, 1994), p. 33.
7 Clowes, *Royal Navy*, vol.VI, p. 194.

Naval Lord on a number of occasions between 1828 and 1846, and Sir Thomas Byam Martin, as Comptroller of the Navy Board, recognised the potential of the steamship. They may not have liked it much; and along with a lot of naval officers may have considered it to be ugly as well as dirty, but they did not obstruct its development. One of the most distinguished Senior Naval Lords of the time, Sir Thomas Hardy, believed that 'happen what will, England's duty is to take and keep the lead.' Professor Rodger has noted that Hardy 'believed strongly in scientific analysis as a basis for policy, and looked forward to fundamental changes in naval warfare, which few of his contemporaries foresaw, let alone welcomed.'[8]

It was not long before steamers were engaged in action. In the West Indies, the USS *Seagull* took part in the hunt for the last remaining pirates, while the East India Company's *Diana* and *Enterprise* were employed in the First Burmese War in 1824-1825. Three steamers were completed for the Greeks during their War of Independence, of which one, the *Karteria*, saw a good deal of action under the command of Captain Frank Hastings. Although it appears that her exploits were somewhat exaggerated, she soon terrorised all who came within range of the heated shot fired from her four 68 pounder guns. It was claimed for her that she had captured or destroyed four small Turkish vessels, and had bombarded several coastal positions as well as serving as a transport.[9]

It was the bold and experimentally minded Lord Cochrane, who had previously ordered in 1821 a steam warship for use in South America, who now persuaded the London Committee for Greek Independence to purchase steamers for use in the naval war against the Turks. Although the fleet of six heavily armed steamers for which Cochrane pressed did not materialise, the exploits of the *Karteria* in particular attracted much attention, and Admiral Lord Exmouth is reputed to have said that steamers such as Cochrane envisaged might destroy all the navies of the world.[10] A historian of the War of Greek Independence has written that 'if only Cochrane could have had a flotilla of six reliable and well armed steam vessels he could probably have freed Greece in a matter of weeks.'[11]

Thus although the British navy, which by 1830 had 12 steamers in service or building, had not commissioned steam powered warships as such, the progressive introduction of more and more steam vessels meant that it was inevitable that sooner rather than later they would be armed for war. In due course two of the first dozen were in fact armed, each with two guns. But a well-known comment alleged to emanate from the Admiralty on the subject of steam has suggested that although some individuals might see the way ahead, the collective view of the Navy was negative:

> Their Lordships feel it their bounden duty to discourage to the utmost of their ability the employment of steam vessels, as they consider that the introduction of steam is calculated to strike a fatal blow at the naval supremacy of the Empire.[12]

8 Rodger, *Admiralty*, p. 100.
9 Brown, *Before the Ironclad*, p. 51.
10 Bartlett, *Sea Power*, p. 201.
11 D Dakin, *British and American Philhellenes during the War of Greek Independence* (Thessaloniki: Institute for Balkan Studies, 1955), p. 124.
12 Bartlett, *Sea Power*, p. 12.

However, this statement, attributed to Lord Melville, appears never to have been made. Captain Peter Hore, in a closely reasoned defence of Melville's attitude to the coming of steam, effectively demolished the suggestion that this represented his view, or indeed, that the statement ever existed.[13] The source of the alleged quotation was Sir John Briggs, a former clerk in the Admiralty, who wrote a book entitled *Naval Administration 1827-1892,* published posthumously in 1897 by his wife. Although the provenance of the quotation has been accepted by some historians, Hore shows that many others have either ignored it or dismissed it altogether. These include Rodger, who wrote that Briggs was 'a secondary source of marked unreliability ... only one thing need be said about this ... that it was never said;' and Greenhill and Giffard, who wrote that it appeared to be a fabrication. They concluded that in the light of the many developments that could be attributed to Melville's administration, 'it seems a most unlikely statement for him to have made.'[14]

In dealing with this, Bartlett reviewed the general attitude of the Admiralty to the development of steam, and suggested the possibility that the Admiralty knew what it was doing, and simply wished to postpone the evil day for good reason. In his analysis, Bartlett set out all the motives that might justify the avoidance, during the 1820s, of taking steps that would assist a hostile navy to cancel out the existing supremacy of the Royal Navy. He concluded that 'the ultra-cautious introduction of steamers in the decade could thus be justified – in no small measure – on grounds of expediency, economy and technical ignorance, but only as long as no other power took the lead.'[15]

During the 1820s there was no significant indication of any other Power pressing on with the development of steam powered warships. The Americans did not follow up their early progress, while the French, although a good deal of interest had been aroused there, took a cautious view similar to that of the British Admiralty. The Minister of Marine wrote: 'France will, perhaps, hereafter regret having remained so long inactive. It is not, however, possible yet to know what influence this powerful engine may have in the chances of warfare.'[16] He did think, however, that it was quite certain that steamers would be valuable for harbour defence, for protecting the coasting trade, and for towing. In 1830 the French employed seven steamers in their invasion of Algeria. They were used in covering the landing of troops, and were considered to have been very successful. Conservative French naval opinion was no more enthusiastic about the aesthetic qualities of paddle steamers than their British counterparts, and their vulnerability in combat was recognised; but nevertheless it was seen that steamers had an important future.

The possibility that this situation might change, and that France or the United States might take up the opportunities provided by steam, was one which was the subject of a warning from Sir John Ross, who wrote a treatise on steam navigation in 1828. In this he addressed the possibility that

> other nations conscious from experience of their inferiority as to naval warfare on the old system, and hopeless of attaining, in an equal degree, that management of large vessels

13 Captain Peter Hore, 'Lord Melville and the Coming of Steam Navigation', *Mariner's Mirror*, vol 86 (2000), p 157.
14 Greenhill and Giffard, *Steam, Politics and Patronage*, p. 37.
15 Bartlett, *Sea Power*, pp. 202-205.
16 Bartlett, *Sea Power*, p. 206.

> and fleets ... will gladly resort to a system more practicable and more economical, and one, which from its requiring far less of what is called nautical knowledge, will bring their means to that equality which may render their future enmity at sea most hazardous to our superiority.[17]

This farsighted work predicted the end of the line of battle, and the end of dependence on sail power, which meant that there was no longer need to be concerned about the weather gauge. Ross saw how steamers could tow ships of the line into action, and how they would be better able to prevent invasion than any fortifications, and he saw the need for coaling stations across the Empire. He was well known to Melville, and to Byam Martin.

Before leaving Hore's penetrating review of Lord Melville and the coming of steam, it must be observed that he by no means accepted that the Admiralty was deliberately dragging its feet, even for the good reasons identified by Bartlett. He shows that the Admiralty had entirely grasped that one brake on the introduction of steamships was the lack of large stockpiles of coal, which they needed to replenish their supplies, due to their extravagant consumption. In key minutes from Melville, he shows that there was no suggestion of any opposition to steam, but that on the contrary he kept himself well informed of the technological progress of all aspects of steam navigation, and as soon as the technology was ripe he devised, with Byam Martin and Seppings, a secret plan to enable the Royal Navy to 'outsteam' all Europe.

This plan was set out in a series of letters exchanged between Melville and Byam Martin, in the first of which, dated February 22, 1823, Melville observed that it was 'desirable and proper' that steps should be taken to ensure that the navy was possessed of the ships that would be needed at once if war broke out, even though that was at that time very improbable:

> There is every reason to believe from the purposes to which steam vessels are now applied that they would be found very useful in the protection of our trade in the Channel; but I understand that several months must elapse before proper steam engines could be provided, even if any of our small vessels can be fitted to receive them. I think it probable by what I learnt in conversation with Sir R Seppings that the ordinary class of 10 gun brigs will be found well adapted for this service, and it will be satisfactory for me to know, on further investigation, that this is the case. At any rate it will be proper now to provide steam engines for at least six vessels, in addition to those constructing and intended for the use of the dockyards, and I have therefore to desire that you will take the necessary steps for that purpose.[18]

In the following year Melville wrote to the Duke of Wellington on the same subject, addressing him in his capacity as Master General of the Ordnance:

> Though there is no prospect of this country being engaged in war at an early period, I deem it nevertheless my duty to request your attention (in case you shall think it right to bring the matter under the notice of government) to the present state of the defences of some of our

17 Quoted Hore,'Melville,' p. 161.
18 Hore, 'Melville', pp. 161-162.

> principal naval arsenals. A full consideration of this subject seems to be necessary, not only from the present condition of those defences, but from the novel mode of warfare to which we are exposed in the Channel by the employment of steam vessels ... There can be no question that, if Bonaparte had at one period been possessed of such means, we should have considered that so much of our security as was derived from the great difficulties which the wind and tides opposed to his schemes against this country would have been materially diminished. If we are tolerably alert, and with our command of machinery and fuel, we ought to *outsteam* all Europe ... I believe that we are only in the infancy of our skill and knowledge in regard to the application of those vessels to the purpose of naval warfare.[19]

Letters such as these make clear that Melville was fully alive to the possibilities of steam; and perhaps provide a riposte to the judgment of Professor Rodger that Melville possessed only 'moderate talents.' Rodger was being equally unfair when dismissing Byam Martin as 'an aged and reactionary Tory.'

The Admiralty was heavily involved in the use of steamships for the mail service, and appears to have encouraged the Post Office in the building of steam packets, of which 29 had been constructed by 1830. At the same time the Admiralty was starting to build its own ships expressly as warships, loosely based on the design of the sailing brigs identified by Melville. At first they were treated as auxiliaries, armed only with two brass 6 pounders, but they were added to the Navy List in 1828, and their armament was substantially increased. One of these, *Alban*, had three 32 pounders; but her bunker could carry only sufficient coal for four days' steaming, and she was obliged to carry 4 tons on deck. In a voyage which she made from Barbados to Falmouth of 51 days in July 1834, only seven were under steam.

As a warship, the paddle steamer may have lacked the elegance of the sailing ship, but her functional design was developing a certain grace. The fall of the Tory government in 1830, which had brought in Sir James Graham and Sir Thomas Hardy as First Lord and Senior Naval Lord respectively marked, if anything, an increase in the commitment of the Admiralty to acquire new steamers. In particular, this was indicated by the immediate order for four larger steamers, the *Rhadamanthus* class, the first three of which were laid down in 1831. Of over 800 tons, their engines developed 220 hp. Graham made his views clear in a letter to Byam Martin on January 22, 1831: 'Steam, also, must change the character of the next war with France, and if we have not a superior force of armed steamboats in the Channelour own shores will be unprotected – and our homeward bound trade will be exposed to constant and inevitable danger.'[20]

He asked to know how many steamers would be available for service in the Channel; in reply, Byam Martin sent him a list, remarking that Britain had 'a greater command of steam vessels (and many of large size) than perhaps all other nations together,' adding that in the event of war a sufficient number could be hired and armed for the protection of trade. Three months later, remarking that he was 'far from underestimating the growing importance of steam,' Byam Martin was warning also of the need to maintain the supremacy of the navy in all classes of ships, writing to Graham: 'Whatever may be the means of warfare persisted in or adopted by other nations, the safety of this empire depending as it does upon our superiority at sea, requires

19 Navy Records Society, *British Naval Documents 1204-1960* (London: Navy Records Society1993) pp. 574-575.

20 Greenhill and Giffard, *Steam, Politics and Patronage*, p. 50.

that we should take the lead so as to be capable of meeting the united force of the world of whatever description that force may be.'[21] The time had arrived, he said, for increasing the navy's force of steamers, having until then built only a few such 'while steam, as regards the navy was in its infancy.' He was confident in Britain's ability to maintain a superiority over others in steam.

The *Rhadamanthus* and her sisters *Medea*, *Salamander* and *Phoenix*, were highly praised as beautiful ships by contemporary writers, 'sylph-like' with sharp bows and fine in calm weather. Captain W.H. Henderson thought *Rhadamanthus*, which was the first steamer of the Royal Navy to cross the Atlantic, 'an excellent sea boat and a very serviceable vessel.'[22] In 1833-1834 four more were built, the *Falcon* class, followed by the *Hermes*, the first steamship design by Symonds after he took over as Surveyor. She was at first considered unsatisfactory, as she was underpowered, but she was later re-engined and also rearmed, and formed the basis for several later classes. Symonds was unenthusiastic about such ships; Lambert wrote that 'having dedicated his professional life to improving the performance of sailing ships it was not surprising that Symonds adopted the most hostile attitude towards steam.'[23]

Among the many voices that were heard by the Admiralty recommending a wide range of ideas for the development of steam warships, one of the loudest was that of Sir Charles Napier. In July 1827 he put forward his proposals for the ideal steam warship, which would have a steaming range of twenty days' duration. He suggested abandoning the broadside, and the rigging of the vessel as a schooner. 'In another war,' wrote Napier, 'steam will become to the Navy what the cavalry is to the Army – it will be the post of honour.'[24] All his professional life Napier would be an enthusiastic supporter of steam vessels and would, when Britain next went to war, be in command of one of her major fleets. For the present, however, it was the design of the current vessels with which he was concerned, criticising the expense, for instance, of the boilers of the *Dee* and the *Rhadamanthus*. When in command of the *Galatea* he had experimented with manually propelled paddles and he continued to offer advice on a wide range of issues concerning the design of warships both built and ordered for the Royal Navy. In 1840 he was to distinguish himself in operations in the eastern Mediterranean off the Syrian coast against Mehemet Ali.

In spite of his lack of enthusiasm for steamships, Symonds was responsible for the *Gorgon*, which he designed in 1835 as a slightly enlarged version of the *Medea*. She was ultimately fitted with engines producing 350 hp, and was enabled to carry 380 tons of coal. She was more heavily armed than any of her predecessors, and has been described as 'the first true fighting steamship.' She has also been called 'the first steam frigate,' but this was not really the case, 'because a frigate by definition had her principal battery on the main deck with a deck over and was shiprigged. *Gorgon*, apparently rigged as a schooner and later as a brig, carried her six 32 pounders on the weather deck.'[25]

Thereafter the larger paddle frigates which followed the *Gorgon* continued to be designated 'paddle frigates.' It is worth noting what the term 'frigate' actually implied, or had done in the

21 Greenhill and Giffard, *Steam, Politics and Patronage*, p. 52.
22 Brown, *Before the Ironclad*, p. 55.
23 Lambert, *Battleships*, p. 28.
24 E.A.M. Laing, 'The Introduction of Paddle Frigates into the Royal Navy', *The Mariner's Mirror* 66.4 (1980), pp. 331-343.
25 Greenhill and Giffard, *Steam, Politics and Patronage*, p. 53.

past. It has been said that over the centuries the term has had six distinct meanings, in each case relating to smaller, faster vessels. The name was first applied to the Mediterranean 'fregata,'a tender to the galley. Next, in Elizabethan days, it described a smaller version of the galleon. In the seventeenth century the term was used of the smaller fighting ships such as the *Constant Warwick,* and these morphed into the frigates of Nelson's day; vital for reconnaissance and as convoy escorts, he never had enough of them. It was this class of ship which gave its name to the paddle frigate, a term intended to define its functions in the steam navy. It was, however, also used to describe much larger vessels, especially in the navies of other Powers. Finally, the term reappeared during the Second World War to describe a ship much like a destroyer, but less speedy.[26]

The *Gorgon* was of 1,110 tons, 178 feet long and 37 ½ feet in the beam. In favourable conditions she attained a speed of between 9 ½ and 10 knots. Captain Henderson, her first captain, thought her 'powerful, easy and a first rate sea boat.' In 1836 Symonds ordered a sister ship, the *Cyclops*; fitted with larger engines and copper boilers, she was just over 12 feet longer, and was able to carry somewhat more coal. The two ships were apparently designed to carry a main deck armament, but never did so. They were however prototypes for the large number of classes of frigate which followed in their footsteps.

In one respect in particular *Gorgon* and *Cyclops* differed from all their predecessors, which had been powered by side lever engines. These were heavy, and insufficiently compact. The two ships were instead fitted with direct acting engines, which reduced the length of the engine room by about one third and the total weight of machinery by about two fifths. The ships had apparently been intended to have side lever engines, and it is unclear why this was not the case, save that the engines originally intended were installed in other vessels. The direct acting engine, which became known as the 'Gorgon' engine, consisted of a vertical cylinder mounted underneath the paddlewheel crankshaft and connected to it by a short connecting rod. In the following years, despite criticism from other manufacturers, the Admiralty concentrated on engines of this design, many of which were supplied by Seward and Capel.

In June 1838, even before the final acceptance of the *Gorgon's* engines as fitted, the Admiralty decided to proceed with the *Cyclops*. After the *Gorgon's* sea trials were concluded, it was decided that the *Cyclops*' engines should be of 300 hp.[27] Both vessels were engaged in the operations off the Syrian coast in 1840, and gave excellent service, together with other steamers. At the bombardment of Acre, Admiral Stopford commanded the operation from the steamer *Phoenix*. He ordered that the steamers operate at long range, a decision commented on by a junior officer in a letter to his brother. Because 'steamers were the only things to trust to, to tow the line of battleships off shore, there not being much wind, and a single shot might have disabled them, I think the Admiral was quite right in giving the order to keep at long balls.'[28]

Lord Minto, who had been First Lord until September 1841, reviewed what he considered the correct policy which the new Board of Admiralty should pursue. He and the retired Byam Martin had had a conversation, at a dinner to celebrate Queen Victoria's coronation, when they agreed that 'victory in future wars at sea would be secured by the nation with the most powerful steam force.' Minto now suggested that the creation of a powerful force of steamers 'ranked

26 Philip Cowburn, *The Warship in History* (London: Macmillan, 1966), p. 152.
27 Laing, 'Paddle Frigates', p. 336.
28 Bartlett, *Sea Power*, p. 214.

second only, and perhaps even equal to the maintenance of the superiority of the British battle fleet over the combined navies of France, Russia and the United States.'[29] He still advocated a huge number of ships of the line, recommending that the Navy should have at least 70, with 10 ready for launching, 10 more building and another 10 in frame. At that time Britain actually possessed 73 afloat; the combined total of France, Russia and the USA was 68, but no less than 31 of the British vessels were the obsolescent 74s.

The change of government in September 1841 brought in Lord Haddington as First Lord, while Cockburn returned as Senior Naval Lord. As has been seen, Cockburn had considerable reservations about Symonds and his influence, and he encouraged the bringing forward of designs from a wide range of sources. One of these was the inveterate opponent of the government, Sir Charles Napier, with whom Cockburn cooperated in the acceptance of a proposal for a paddle steamer, later called the *Sidon* in a nice acknowledgement of Napier's achievements on the Syrian coast. Cockburn told the House of Commons in 1844 that the government was trying everything it possibly could to improve the design of steamships. As for Napier, he claimed in 1845 that there had been no material improvement in the steamship since the *Gorgon* and the *Cyclops* a decade earlier. Cockburn still saw ships of the line as Britain's first line of defence, with steamers subsidiary to them, but he did not have a closed mind, and he briefed the First Lord in June 1845 on the situation in order to enable him to reply to a further criticism from Napier:

> From the period when the first large seagoing steam vessel was successfully completed, it became evident to everybody that a facility, never before existing, must be afforded thereby for sudden invasion of this country from the opposite shores of France, and … it is quite clear that the whole line of coast from Dover to the Lizard cannot be secured, and it is equally clear that an enemy intending a hostile landing would and could by means of steam select a spot for landing where no important fortifications exist.[30]

It was still his belief, though, that naval command of the Channel was the best defence, and for this he relied upon a greater fleet of ships of the line.

Napier's complaint that there had been no improvement in the design of steamers since the *Gorgon* and *Cyclops* was not entirely justified. Soon after the new government took office, a steamer of 1,640 tons was authorised, 50% larger than anything that had gone before. This was the *Retribution*, designed by Symonds in 1844 as the first paddle frigate to carry a main deck armament, although it appears that this was not mounted until 1850. The rate of building of new steamers, however, was not considerable. Nineteen sloops were laid down between 1837 and 1846, together with seven frigates.[31] There seems to have been a general assumption that in the event of war the relatively large British merchant fleet of paddle steamers would provide all that was needed to supplement those on the Navy List.

In February 1845 the *Terrible* was launched, and she perhaps represented the high water mark of the paddle frigate. When completed, she displaced 3,189 tons; she carried four 56 pounders, four 68 pounders and three 12 pounders on her main deck, and four 56 pounders and four 68

29 Bartlett, *Sea Power*, pp. 212-214.
30 Roger Morriss, *Cockburn and the British Navy in Transition* (Exeter: University of Exeter Press, 1997), p. 246.
31 Brown, *Before the Ironclad*, p. 71.

pounders on her upper deck. Her engines provided 800 hp. She was a handsome ship, with four funnels; 226 feet long, she was the largest paddle frigate completed. Napier, in 1846, wrote to Lord Ellenborough, Haddington's successor, with a wide-ranging denunciation of the stability of some of the sailing ships of the Royal Navy; the steamers, he wrote, were still worse. His criticism extended to the whole class of vessels 'miscalled frigates' in respect of their armament and their vulnerability to shot.[32] The *Terrible* did good work, however, remaining in service until the 1860s.

Napier did concede, however, that the *Terrible* was an improvement over her predecessors, even if he took the view that she had not been properly constructed; but for this, (he instanced the omission of her stern ports on the main deck) she would have been a most efficient ship. In 1847 he had a report from Captain Sir William Ramsay on the lessons to be learned from voyage in the *Terrible* from Lisbon to Luanda and back, which led Napier to conclude that her sailing qualities might have been better had she not been under mastered and under sailed.[33]

But the day of the paddle steamer was coming to an end. Five more vessels classed as paddle frigates were built, though none was as large as the *Terrible.* The last of them was the *Valorous*, of the *Magicienne* class, which remarkably remained in service until 1891. For a while the paddle steamer had offered the possibility of being the way forward. From the start, it had had many enthusiasts, including the redoubtable General Henri Paixhans, who was to revolutionise naval gunnery, and in spite of its obvious defects did good service in a number of naval campaigns. One such was the operation of a joint Franco-British squadron in the Parana River in 1845-1846, in which a number of British paddle steamers, notably the *Gorgon* and the *Firebrand,* did excellent work. In spite of the vulnerability of paddle steamers so often pointed out, they survived a considerable number of damaging hits, including to the paddle wheels. Captain Bartholomew Sulivan described in considerable detail the experiences of the squadron, giving one example of the amount of punishment that a paddle steamer could absorb:

> There was one remarkable case there to show what a steam vessel could stand. The French steam boat *Fulton* (six or seven hundred tons) went up to cover her chief, who was suffering dreadfully, and anchored between him and the batteries. The boom not being cut, she was detained there for, I think, three hours. They put fifty six heavy round shot into her paddle wheels and sponsons; they destroyed every particle of the wheel nearest the side … and yet, when the chains were cut, she was the first that went through with her one remaining wheel.[34]

This was given in evidence by Sulivan to the Royal Commission on Coast Defences in 1860, and illustrated just how difficult it was to stop vessels passing batteries.

By now, the genie was out of the bottle. Steam power was the greatest of all the elements which would transform naval warfare. Its effects were concisely summarised by Bernard Brodie:

32 Laing, 'Paddle Frigates', p. 340.
33 Laing, 'Paddle Frigates,' p. 341.
34 Henry Norton Sulivan (ed.), *Life and Letters of Admiral Sir Bartholemew James Sulivan* (London: John Murray, 1896), p. 89.

> It completely revised the conditions governing naval tactics; it modified the whole geography of position and distance, thus profoundly affecting strategy; it enhanced the potential military power of industrialised states; and it injected the all-important factor of fuel into the problem of naval supplies, thus affecting the range of fleets and the strategic importance of stations abroad. In short, the steam warship was the most important development since the fifteenth century, when the discovery of the art of tacking inaugurated the era of the sailing ship.[35]

35 Bernard Brodie, *Sea Power in the Machine Age* (Princeton NJ: Princeton University Press, 1941), p. 18.

3

Screw Ships

In the nineteenth century the screw propeller could claim a number of fathers, but its original inventor was Archimedes of Syracuse, who discovered the principle in the third century BC. It was only the arrival of the steam engine, however, which provided the means by which the screw propeller could drive a ship through the water.

By 1836 both the value of steamships and the serious shortcomings of paddle steamers as warships were becoming clear. Commercially, they were beginning to enjoy considerable success; designed principally for carrying mail and passengers, the powerful paddle steamers were not built to take heavy cargoes, and did not have to provide the guns, stores, and large crews. The problems inherent in the design have been previously referred to, and no entirely satisfactory warship had been produced. The difficulties fundamentally arose from the concept of the paddlewheel. Other than in the exceptional design of a vessel built as a catamaran, when the paddlewheel could be located between twin hulls, it was seriously exposed to shot. It took up so much space that only a limited broadside was possible, reducing its fire power substantially. Located well above the waterline, the paddle shaft and most of the machinery, including in most cases the boilers as well, were dangerously exposed to enemy fire.[1] The problem of reduced firepower was only partly compensated for by the fitting of very heavy guns to the later designs of paddle steamers. Another difficulty, for which no solution was found, was that the existence of the paddlewheel seriously impaired the vessel's performance under sail. The use of sail power wherever possible was necessary to eke out the fuel so voraciously consumed by the engines, but its poor performance under sail meant that the paddle steamer could not operate effectively with the rest of the sailing fleet. The need to conserve fuel meant that her operational range was severely limited. Thus inventors putting forward a different mode of propulsion were pushing at an open door.

Before 1836 at least 40 inventors had proposed designs for screw propellers, none of which achieved any significant success. In that year, however, two men, working entirely independently but in parallel, produced designs which at last indicated the way forward. One of these was John Ericsson, born on July 31, 1803, the son of the Swedish inspector of mines. As a child, he was of an enquiring mind, with a great interest in mechanical toys. It is said that by the age of ten years he was producing his own designs. Joining the Swedish army, he served in

1 Bartlett, *Sea Power*, pp. 211-212.

the corps of mechanical engineers, and worked on the building of the Gota Canal. He rose to the rank of captain before resigning in 1826, when he travelled to England. There, he became a partner in a machine manufacturing firm. He produced a large number of designs, including a steam railway engine, the *Novelty*, which competed against Stephenson's *Rocket* in the Rainhill trials of 1829.[2] The essential limitations of the paddle steamer led him to turn his mind to the possibility of devising a workable screw propeller. It appears that he had been working on the problem since before 1833. At all events, on July 13, 1836 he took out a patent for an improved propeller suitable to be driven by a steam engine, and during the rest of the year experimented with a model to test his design.

Ericsson was not, though, the first to file a patent for a screw propeller that year. Francis Pettit Smith was born in Kent in 1808. He started work as a farmer on Romney Marsh, before moving to a farm at Hendon. As a boy, he had built many model boats, and took a particular interest in their means of propulsion. When he grew up, he maintained this interest, and by 1835 had built a model boat which was propelled by a screw driven by a spring. This was so successful that Smith became convinced that it was feasible for a screw propeller to drive a ship, and on May 31, 1836 he took out his patent. Having obtained technical assistance from an engineer, Thomas Pilgrim, and financial backing from Wright's Bank, Smith continued to work on his model on the pond at his farm at Hendon. Taking it to London, he demonstrated it to Sir John Barrow, the Secretary of the Admiralty. Meanwhile he had become friends with John Ericsson, with whom he exchanged ideas.

Importantly, Smith's design was different from that of Ericsson and other inventors in one particular; 'he had realised the essential problem of efficient screw propulsion and found a solution for it.'[3] The problem was the effect of the propeller on the steering of the vessel; the solution was to locate the propeller forward of the rudder, which enabled the propeller to gain the advantage of the water slowed down by friction with the hull. At the same time the propeller directed a stream of water on to the rudder, which thereby became much more responsive in the steering of the vessel. As he worked on this design, Smith obtained the influential support of Lord Sligo, who was in due course to be one of the initial subscribers to the private company subsequently formed to exploit Smith's invention.

The results of his early experiments were sufficiently encouraging for Smith to build a six ton vessel, 30 feet in length, powered by a 4.5 hp engine. Named the *Francis Smith*, she was demonstrated on the Paddington Canal between November 1836 and September 1837. A fortunate accident damaged the wooden propeller, which was of two turns. This revealed that the broken screw, now of only one turn, effectively doubled the boat's speed to 8 miles per hour.

Meanwhile Ericsson was also making progress. In April 1837 a steam launch, named the *Francis B Ogden* for his friend, the American consul at Liverpool, took to the water on the Thames. She was fitted with twin propellers, and was 45 feet long and 8 feet in the beam. On her first trial she attained a speed of 10 knots. Subsequently she succeeded in towing a schooner of 140 tons at 7 knots, and then the American packet *Toronto* at 4 knots. This was followed by a crucially important trial, to be witnessed by a number of senior officials of the Admiralty, including the Senior Naval Lord, Sir Charles Adam, and Sir William Symonds, the Surveyor

2 Baxter, *Introduction*, p. 12; Brown, *Before the Ironclad*, p. 102.
3 Greenhill and Giffard, *Steam, Politics and Patronage*, p. 137.

of the Navy. They were passengers in the Admiralty barge, which was towed by the *Francis B Ogden* at 10 knots from Somerset House to Limehouse Reach and back. On the face of it the trial was a complete success.

To Ericsson's dismay, however, this proved not to be the case. D.K. Brown gives a detailed account of the reasons for this which were given by John O. Sergeant in a lecture in Boston some years later. Apparently, throughout the trip Symonds' body language conveyed all too clearly his scepticism about the project, which he had approached with an entirely closed mind. The reason for this was not immediately apparent, but Ericsson discovered it later when a friend of his attended a dinner at which Symonds was also present. In the course of this the Surveyor remarked that 'even if the propeller had the power of propelling a vessel, it would be found altogether useless in practice because, the power being applied in the stern, it would be absolutely impossible to make the vessel steer.'[4]

This deluded opinion appears to have been based on the experiences of a number of paddle steamers in which the paddle box was located well aft of amidships, as a result of having been lengthened in the bows. Symonds apparently jumped to the conclusion that if moving the power source near the stern in this way could render a vessel difficult to steer, moving it to the stern itself would make that impossible. Undaunted by this setback, and encouraged by Ogden, and by Captain Robert Stockton, his successor as US consul at Liverpool, Ericsson decided to take his invention to the United States. A propeller of his design was fitted to a small iron steamer built by Lairds of Birkenhead. Named the *Robert F Stockton*, she was some 70 feet long, and was powered by a 50 hp engine. She was successfully demonstrated to a group of scientists in January 1839 on the Thames, and then in April crossed the Atlantic under sail. Once in the United States she was sold to the Delaware and Raritan Canal Company, which renamed her *New Jersey*, and she served as a river tug there for many years.[5]

It was Smith who was to break down the Admiralty's resistance to the screw propeller. In September 1837 he took the *Francis Smith* to sea. She was now fitted with an iron propeller of a single turn, and she steamed successfully from Blackwall to Gravesend, where she took on a pilot before proceeding first to Ramsgate and then to Dover, where Smith showed her to his banker, Wright. He then took her on to Hythe, and then back to Folkestone, from where she set off for the voyage to London in stormy weather. She performed well, and coastguards who observed her progress reported favourably on her. News of this successful trip reached the Admiralty, and kindled fresh interest in the possibilities of the screw propeller. In March 1838 the Admiralty asked that the *Francis Smith* undergo a series of trials under official supervision. After she had performed these satisfactorily, the Admiralty was sufficiently encouraged to call for screw propulsion to be tested on a much larger vessel.

In response to this, Smith founded the Screw Propeller Company, with the object of building such a ship. This was the *Archimedes*, designed by Edward Pascoe and laid down by Henry Wimshurst in 1838. Of 237 tons, she was 125 feet overall, with a beam of 26 ½ feet, and was driven by a direct acting steam engine of 80 hp. She was fitted with a wrought iron screw of a single turn and was completed in 1839. She made her first seagoing voyage from Gravesend to Portsmouth, and there underwent a trial against the *Vulcan*, a paddle steamer belonging to the

4 Brown, *Before the Ironclad*, pp. 102-103.
5 Brown, *Before the Ironclad*, pp. 103-104.

navy of 720 tons. Following this, the *Archimedes* received a favourable report. Subsequently, her trials were interrupted by accidents to her boiler and to her crankshaft. Experience had shown that the diameter of her propeller was too great, and it was progressively reduced to 4 feet 9 inches, and she was then fitted with a propeller of two blades, each forming a half turn.[6]

It was still possible, however, for more than one opinion to be formed about the success of the *Archimedes.* There was evidently still some reserve felt on the part of some Admiralty officials who were very conscious that the *Archimedes* was being assiduously promoted as a commercial venture. On October 16, 1839 she was demonstrated to a senior group which, though no member of the Board of Admiralty was present, included Symonds, Peter Ewart, the Chief Engineer and Inspector of Machinery at Woolwich, Captain Sir Edward Parry, the Comptroller of Steam Machinery, and Captain George Evans, who had been an early witness to the success of the *Francis Smith.* Parry's report to the Secretary of the Admiralty cast grave doubts on the reliability of the machinery of the *Archimedes.* He also remarked on 'the abominable annoyance created both by the sound and vibration. It is like the most noisy flour mill as regards the former, and the shaking very great.' The problem with the engine, which was unable to keep up steam, meant in Parry's view 'therefore, as the principle of the screw is concerned, it must be considered no experiment at all.'[7] On the other hand, Evans expressed a very different opinion in his report to Sir William Parker, the Second Naval Lord. This has been described as 'perhaps the most important single document in the history of the screw steamship.' Evans listed eleven separate advantages of the screw over the paddle, adding what he considered the crucial factor: 'namely its effect on the steerage. The screw being placed immediately before the stern post, forces the water against the rudder with such velocity, that the slightest motion of the helm is sufficient to turn the vessel.' Evans concluded his report:

> When I take into consideration the probability that ere long an engine will be adapted to give the screw any velocity required (such as Lord Dundonald's rotary engine now in the course of trial at Portsmouth), I have no hesitation in declaring it to be my firm conviction that the screw will supersede every other means hitherto adopted for propelling vessels, except in 'very shoal water.'[8]

With an endorsement as favourable as this, it is not surprising that the Screw Propeller Company lost little time in preparing a prospectus to raise capital, seeking the consent of both Evans and Parker to incorporate the former's letter into the document. It is worth remarking at this point that it was Smith's understanding that if the *Archimedes* was a success, the Admiralty had agreed to purchase her but unfortunately for him, and for the company, this proved to be a misapprehension.

In 1840 the *Archimedes* was subjected to a fresh series of trials against a number of mail packets in the Channel, including in particular the *Widgeon*, said to be the fastest packet on the service. These trials were conducted on the Admiralty's behalf by Captain E. Chappell, for thirteen years the Superintendent of the Packet Service, and Thomas Lloyd, Assistant Chief Engineer and Inspector of Machinery at Woolwich. Most importantly, their findings included

6 Brown, *Before the Ironclad*, p. 105.
7 Greenhill and Giffard, *Steam, Politics and Patronage*, pp. 139-140.
8 Greenhill and Giffard, *Steam, Politics and Patronage*, pp. 141-142.

the opinion that the *Archimedes* would answer her helm and obey all necessary movements when advancing, stopping or backing, as well as any paddle steamer. This finally laid to rest Symonds' curious belief that such a vessel could not be steered.

The trials were a complete success. In their report, Chappell and Lloyd dealt with the question of noise and vibration, and explained that Smith intended to substitute spiral gearing in place of the existing cogs:

> It is, however, in propelling ships of war that the value of Mr Smith's invention will probably be experienced. In such cases the rumbling noise in the ship made by the spur wheels is of no great moment, even if it cannot be overcome; for outside this vessel, the noise is not so audible to so great a distance as that made by the common paddle vessel.[9]

They also reported that a ship fitted with a screw propeller could be used either as a sailing or steaming vessel, or as both if required, since the engine could be connected or disconnected in any weather in two or three minutes. Lloyd's opinion carried particular weight; he had a wide-ranging role, surveying the machinery of all mail packets, and conducting inspections on behalf of the Admiralty of some of the principal engineering establishments in Great Britain, advising in particular on their capabilities.

In October 1840 Brunel produced a report on the trials of the *Archimedes*, which was entirely favourable. This followed a visit of the vessel to Bristol where Brunel was building the *Great Britain*. He had become an enthusiastic convert to the principle of screw propulsion, and in his report he addressed its advantages, which were particularly relevant to the navy's concerns about the shortcomings of paddle steamers. Following this, there was considerable debate within the Admiralty as to the next step to be taken, and ultimately it was decided to order a much larger vessel, constructed on much the same lines as the paddle steamer *Alecto* in order that a proper comparison might be made, the two ships having engines of a similar power.

The tide was now running strongly in favour of screw propulsion. In May 1840 Admiral Sir Edward Codrington, victor of the battle of Navarino, wrote to the Board to say that 'the screw is well adapted for ships of the line.' Considering how early in the process of the screw's evaluation this opinion was offered, it was a powerful endorsement; there had never been any serious contemplation that a ship of the line could be powered by paddles. In March 1841 Parry suggested that the advice of Brunel should be obtained. This regrettably led to a good deal of friction, since Smith had already been appointed as consultant, and disputes arose not only between the two men but also with Thomas Lloyd at Woolwich as well. Brunel complained bitterly to Parry of interference, objecting in particular to his plans going to Lloyd. At the end of 1841 there was an abortive proposal to save money by converting an existing vessel rather than building from scratch; Brunel was indignantly opposed to this, complaining that it would not in fact achieve any reduction in cost, and in January 1842 he wrote to the new Senior Naval Lord Sir George Cockburn to explain why a new vessel was essential.[10]

Brunel's relationship with Cockburn did not get off to a good start. He had been strongly supported by Codrington, with whom Cockburn had been at odds since Navarino; and when he

9 Brown, *Before the Ironclad*, p. 108.
10 Brown, *Before the Ironclad*, p. 111.

met the Senior Naval Lord for the first time, a serious misunderstanding arose over a cutaway model of a three decker which had been supplied by Symonds labelled 'Mr Brunel's mode of applying the screw to Her Majesty's ships.' Cockburn indignantly demanded of Brunel: 'Do you mean to suppose that we shall cut up Her Majesty's ships after this fashion, Sir?' Brunel, who must been taken aback, denied the charge, but it was not a helpful encounter.[11]

However, the plans for the new vessel were soon approved, and the screw sloop *Rattler*, as she was named, was launched on April 13, 1843. Of 888 tons, she was 176 ½ feet long by just under 33 feet in the beam, fitted with the Maudslay four-cylinder engine producing 360 hp designed to achieve just over 9 knots. She was completed in October 1843, and at once was sent on a trial run from Blackwall to Greenhithe and back, when she attained a speed of 8 knots. On November 5 Brunel, Smith, and Lloyd, who were still not working cooperatively, were on board the *Rattler* when she commenced a number of trials, in the course of which various adjustments were made to her propeller. That was that for 1843; during the winter, her bottom was coppered, and further adjustments made.

During the period that the *Rattler* was under construction, the Admiralty had in March 1842 bought the 164 ton steam yacht *Mermaid*, which was renamed *Dwarf*, to be utilised as a test bed for trials of the screw propeller. These began in May 1843 and continued until 1846, when Lloyd conducted a series of tests to determine the effect of changes to the stern lines on the efficiency of the screw propeller.

Cockburn, meanwhile, had made a considerable contribution to the process of introducing screw propulsion. His biographer has described how, during the building of the *Rattler*, he acted as a coordinator between the disputing designers, 'endorsing recommendations, authorising action, even concerning himself with trials of pressure acting upon a safety valve. He was fully informed of what was being done and commanded a position that gave control over the whole procedure.'[12] Aware that the process raised technological problems outside his own competence, he enlisted the help of a steam enthusiast, Lieutenant John Hoseason, as his personal adviser. His concern to see the project succeed was sharpened by the knowledge that the French were building a screw frigate, the *Pomone*, based on Ericsson's design for her screw. Even before the *Rattler*'s trials were completed, Cockburn was confidently telling the House of Commons that his impression was that proof that a screw would be better than paddle wheels would soon be obtained. Although in commissioning the *Pomone* the French were ahead of the British in recognising the value of the screw, a historian of the French navy has pointed out that though France had more than once taken the lead in matters of steam, 'she did not long retain it; for the British ship building programme with each development was always the larger.'[13]

Across the Atlantic, John Ericsson had continued to develop his designs. His connection with Captain Stockton brought him into contact with the Navy Department, and in 1842-1843 he supervised the building at Philadelphia of a fully rigged ship of 954 tons displacement, designed as a screw frigate. She was fitted with a six bladed propeller, and her machinery lay below the waterline. She had a telescopic funnel, boilers designed to burn anthracite coal, and fan blowers

11 Morriss, *Cockburn*, p. 250.
12 Morriss, *Cockburn*, pp. 250-251.
13 E.H. Jenkins, *A History of the French Navy* (London: Macdonald & Janes, 1973), p. 290n.

for forcing the fires. She was 160 feet long and 30 ½ feet in the beam. Named *Princeton*, she was the first purpose-built screw propelled warship to go into service.[14]

The *Princeton* was armed with two 12 inch wrought iron guns. One of these, named the 'Oregon,' had been designed by Ericsson and brought from England; it was reinforced by two tiers of hoops each 3 ½ inches thick, shrunk onto the breech. The other, named the 'Peacemaker', had been forged under Stockton's direction in the United States, and then bored and finished under Ericsson's supervision. Unluckily, a trial trip on the Potomac River on February 28 1844 brought tragedy, when the 'Peacemaker' burst, killing Abel P. Upshur, the Secretary of State, Thomas W. Gilmer, Secretary of the Navy, and four others. Stockton was among the other individuals wounded in the explosion. He and Ericsson fell out when the latter declined to accept responsibility for the catastrophe.[15]

The *Princeton* had, before this disaster, been able to demonstrate the worth of Ericsson's design. She was tried against Brunel's paddle steamer, the *Great Western*, and beat her. The French government had, as has been seen, placed an order from Ericsson for a 200 hp engine for the *Pomone* in 1843, and in the following year the British Admiralty ordered a set of 300 hp machinery for the frigate *Amphion*. Both these vessels were built with their direct acting engines entirely below the waterline, and were the first European warships designed in this way. They each attained a speed of about 7 knots on their trials.

Meanwhile early in 1844 the *Rattler's* trials continued. Between February of that year and the following January there were twenty eight official trials testing various propellers, all of which took place on the Thames. This was not procrastination, but a thorough investigation of the *Rattler's* capabilities, which indicated when taken with the experiments carried out with the *Dwarf*, a careful assessment on the part of the Admiralty of the value of screw propulsion.[16]

All was not, however, entirely plain sailing. Early in 1845, in company with the steam yachts *Victoria and Albert*, and *Black Eagle*, the *Rattler* steamed from Portsmouth to Pembroke. Against a strong headwind the two paddle steamers performed significantly better than the *Rattler*. In 1850 Thomas Lloyd was to write of this experience: 'This comparative failure of the *Rattler* made an unfavourable impression on the public mind as to the efficiency of the screw against wind and sea in heavy weather, and this impression still remains.'[17]

While the Admiralty was exploring the potential of screw propulsion, the commercial sector had also been adopting the principle. In 1840, following the completion of the *Archimedes*, Henry Wimshurst built the 300 ton *Novelty*, the first screw propelled cargo ship. In the following year a small passenger ship, the *Princess Royal*, was built in the North of England, and in succeeding years these were followed by an increasing number of screw propelled merchant ships. When she was launched at Derry on July 23, 1842, the *Great Northern* was the largest screw steamer in the world. 217 feet long, of 1,111 tons, she was a fully rigged ship with her machinery in the after part of her hull, and with 360 hp was the most powerful screw ship so far built. Smith and his company were involved in her construction, in which the Admiralty took a great interest, commissioning a report on her during her construction. Symonds feared

14 Baxter, *Introduction*, pp. 13-14.
15 Baxter, *Introduction*, p. 14.
16 Brown, *Before the Ironclad*, p. 113.
17 Brown, *Introduction*, p. 114.

that 'some of the materials are of doubtful durability,' due to the extensive use of softwood.[18] Unfortunately, her machinery, assembled from parts made from different sources in the British Isles, appears to have been extremely unreliable. Nevertheless, when she came to London in December 1842 she was thoroughly examined by Parry and Lloyd, and again, when her engines had been refurbished, on a demonstration trip in October 1843. Her defects were, however, too great for Smith's hope of an Admiralty charter to be realised.

In March 1845 there began the celebrated series of trials in which the *Rattler* with her screw propeller was tried against the paddle steamer *Alecto*. A number of races took place between the two vessels, as well as towing trials. In the first race, from the Nore to Yarmouth, under steam alone, the *Rattler* won by some twenty minutes. Later that day, under sail and steam, she was again the faster, and on the following day, against a strong headwind and high sea, the same result was obtained, though *Rattler* was less effective when steaming directly into the wind. Towing trials, when each ship took the other in tow again showed the *Rattler* to best advantage, though it was the case that in all these trials her engines were developing greater power than those of the *Alecto*.

Finally, on April 3, there took place the famous trial when the two ships were fastened stern to stern in a tug-of-war. *Alecto* was given the chance to start her engines first, and was towing *Rattler* stern first at 2 knots before the screw steamer started her engines. When she did so, within five minutes the tables were turned, *Rattler* ultimately pulling *Alecto* backwards at full power at 2.8 knots. It had been a carefully staged and dramatically successful public relations exercise, which overcame most of the opposition to screw steamers.[19]

Not all opposition had been disposed of, however, Napier, who had been on shore on half pay since returning from the operations on the Syrian coast in which he had played such a successful part, was now occupying himself in the House of Commons. There, he frequently had much to say, especially on naval matters. At this time he was also much concerned with the paddle frigate *Sidon*, which had been built to his design. Napier was by no means convinced by the apparent success of the screw ship, and he made his views known with his characteristic force.

Cockburn, however, had seen and heard enough to write emphatically to Haddington, the First Lord, in June 1845:

> The proofs we have lately had of the efficiency of the screw as a propeller on board the *Rattler* convince me, that it will be in future generally adopted and we are now adapting those building for that description of propeller ... The French I believe have only one or two with screw propellers. We are therefore taking the lead in this important change of getting rid of the cumbersome paddle wheels, and with the advantage that a screw vessel may if required be converted into a paddle vessel but a paddle vessel cannot be converted to a screw vessel without much attention and expense.[20]

Cockburn also publicly expressed the hope that before long all new vessels would be fitted with screws instead of paddles, importantly taking advantage of being able to locate the machinery below the waterline.

18 Greenhill and Giffard, *Steam, Politics and Patronage*, pp 150-151.
19 Brown, *Before the Ironclad*, pp. 114-117.
20 Morriss, *Cockburn*, p. 252.

Even before the *Rattler-Alecto* trials had taken place, the Admiralty was sufficiently convinced of the prospects of screw ships that orders were being placed for operational warships. In May 1844 an enquiry was made about the possibility of fitting engines to an uncompleted 36 gun frigate, the *Ambuscade*. She had been laid down as long ago as 1830. It was resolved to fit machinery similar to that designed by Ericsson for the French *Pomone*, a two cylinder horizontal return piston rod engine directly driving the screw. She was to have a 15 foot propeller designed by Ericsson, and her machinery was below the waterline. She was finally launched in January 1846, having been renamed *Amphion*. She was seen very much as a potential pathfinder, Cockburn having reported to Haddington in June 1845 that they were now 'fitting the *Amphion*, a large frigate, with a screw and a small engine of 300 horses as an auxiliary to her sails. If we find this to answer, more of that class of ship and indeed our ships of the line may be so fitted at moderate expense without inconvenience to the interior arrangements.'[21]

The *Rattler*'s machinery had not been located below the waterline, but this defect was remedied by the invention by Smith of a new crankshaft which did away with the need for the cog wheels, straps, or other gearing. The Screw Propeller Company notified the Admiralty of this in a letter of June 11 1844. In reply a cross and longitudinal section of the *Ambuscade* was sent for Smith to work on. With this problem resolved, the way was clear for the wholesale introduction of the screw propeller, and the creation of a steam battle fleet.

21 Morriss, *Cockburn*, p. 252.

4

The Steam Battlefleet

Even as the *Rattler* was beginning her trials in 1844, a war scare had blown up which sharply concentrated the minds of those in government, and prompted an anxious reassessment of the state of Britain's defences. The first serious incident which contributed to this arose over the unauthorised annexation of the island of Tahiti in February 1844 by Dupetit-Thouars, the commander of the French fleet in the Pacific, in breach of his clear instructions. Guizot, the French Prime Minister, who had a good relationship with Lord Aberdeen, the British Foreign Secretary, was gravely embarrassed. The annexation caused disquiet in Britain; although Guizot disavowed it, the diplomatic retreat aroused anger in France, where it was seen as bowing the knee to Britain, and newspapers on both sides of the Channel worked themselves up into a considerable passion about it.[1]

Three months later the diplomatic situation took another turn for the worse, when in France the publication in May 1844 of a pamphlet written by the Prince de Joinville, the sailor son of King Louis Philippe, caused a sensation. His intention in producing this was to call attention to what he considered the weakness of the French navy, and to suggest ways in which what he saw as the wide gap in naval power between France and Britain might be reduced. It was in the development of steamers that he saw France's opportunity; they did not require the large pool of trained seamen that was necessary for a sailing battlefleet, which Britain possessed. The employment of steamers placed a greater emphasis on engineers and gunners.

Even more importantly, steamers, largely unaffected by changes in the wind, could go anywhere whenever they wished. Napoleon could, he thought, have put up to 20,000 men ashore in Britain in 1805 if he had had available a fleet of steamers.

To readers of the pamphlet in Britain, it struck an ominous note. Since it had been written by a member of the French royal family, it was seen as an authoritative statement of French policy. The fact that it was purely theoretical in nature was largely ignored, though Queen Victoria did recognise the real conclusion that could be drawn from it. Writing to her uncle King Leopold, she remarked that the pamphlet 'certainly is not written intentionally to offend England, and on the contrary frankly proves us to be immensely superior to the French navy in every way.'[2] Such

1 Hamilton, *Naval Rivalry*, p. 17.
2 Bartlett, *Sea Power*, p. 159n.

a calm and relaxed view was not generally taken in Britain, and there was a good deal of anxiety that an invasion could not be prevented.

In July, serious concerns arose in Whitehall about French intentions in Morocco, obliging Sir Robert Peel, the British Prime Minister, to insist that the British squadron at Gibraltar should be reinforced. Matters were not improved when it was learned that it was the Prince de Joinville who had been appointed to command a French punitive expedition to Tangier, which was at the very least seen as extremely provocative.

The next step downwards in the political relationship between the two countries came with the return to Britain in August of a Protestant missionary named Pritchard, who had also acted as the British consul in Tahiti, and who complained that he had been wrongly imprisoned and mistreated by Dupetit-Thouars. This prompted a huge public outcry in Britain, while in France national feelings were so much aroused that the government could not at first think of offering compensation to resolve the crisis. As a consequence, there was much talk of war on both sides of the Channel; the French ambassador in London observed that 'war is generally regarded as inevitable,' after news was received of the French bombardment of Tangier.[3]

In the British Cabinet, Aberdeen, who took a strongly pacific line, was opposed by Haddington, the First Lord of the Admiralty, and others who argued for the need to prepare for war. Peel was himself persuaded of the necessity to take preliminary steps, believing that the disclaimers of Guizot and King Louis Philippe could not be relied on, and that the French were ready to take advantage of British weakness in the Mediterranean. In the end Guizot was able to offer some compensation, and following a peace treaty between France and the Sultan of Morocco the crisis subsided. Ill feeling remained, though; Lord Shaftesbury was moved to comment on the response of the British government: 'What a disgusting and cowardly attitude for England thus to stand by and raise not a hand in defence of this merciful gift of Providence.'[4]

The fear of a sudden invasion which had been so widespread was more than just a knee-jerk reaction on the part of the popular Press. Haddington, for instance, had been pressing hard in Cabinet for the strengthening of the Navy, and the feelings of alarm about British vulnerability had led to the setting up in 1844 of the Commission on Coastal Defences. Its brief was to review the arrangements for safeguarding the Royal Dockyards in the event of war. Presided over by Captain Sir Thomas Hastings, the commission was dismayed by what it found: 'Sheerness was so defenceless that it could be captured by three steamers, and the Thames up to Tilbury was equally defenceless.' Other ports, such as Portsmouth, Plymouth, and Pembroke, were found to be in need of strengthening.[5] In addition to calling for the building of a number of forts at key locations, the commission also called for floating batteries to assist the defence. Here was the genesis of the 'blockship.'

Cockburn's increasing readiness to accept screw propulsion had led directly to the decision to convert the partly built frigate *Amphion*, although the fitting of steam machinery was seen as auxiliary to her sails. When her engines were fitted, she was the first steam warship to have these and her boilers below the waterline. The Admiralty now placed orders for the necessary engines which would be installed in screw ships. The programme was, as far as possible, carried

3 Bartlett, *Sea Power*, p. 161.
4 Bartlett, *Sea Power*, p. 162.
5 Brown, *Before the Ironclad*, p. 124.

out with the minimum of publicity, since the government was uneasy lest the weakness of the Navy's steam fleet in the Channel should thereby become apparent.

The concept of the blockship was to make use of a number of elderly ships of the line to be employed as floating batteries for the defence of Britain's key harbours. To be effective, they must be mobile; since they could not be converted to paddle steamers, the plan was to fit them with screw propellers. They would have engines capable of producing speeds of 5-6 knots, but would also retain a reduced sailing rig. The first ships selected for conversion were, on inspection, rejected due to their poor condition, and these were replaced by four 74s, the *Hogue*, *Blenheim*, *Ajax*, and *Edinburgh*. These vessels each displaced about 3,000 tons, and could carry some 212 tons of coal, provisions, and water, giving them an operating capacity of some five weeks. In practice, their speed was higher than planned; the *Edinburgh* attained 8.9 knots. Since their machinery when fitted took up a lot of space, their armament was reduced to 60 guns, albeit of larger calibre; on their gun deck they carried twenty eight 32 pounders, on the main deck twenty six 8 inch, and on the upper deck two 68 pounder pivot guns and four 10 inch.[6] The first of the group was ready for sea by September 1846. In due course they were to give good service during the Crimean War, and were not finally scrapped until the 1860s.

Four frigates (*Eurotas*, *Horatio*, *Seahorse*, and *Forte*) were identified for conversion to steam, but here the process was less successful; the only one of those selected that was actually converted was the *Horatio*. She was at first armed with eight 32 pounders, twelve 8 inch and four 10 inch guns, later altered to eighteen 8 inch and four 10 inch. The conversion of the other three frigates intended as blockships was not proceeded with.

Opinions at the Admiralty about the feasibility of screw driven warships were beginning to harden in its favour, and the commitment of the necessary resources to convert the blockships reflected this. Cockburn himself was convinced that enough was being done to strengthen the Navy, writing to Haddington in June 1845: 'With all these efforts and improvements in continual progress, in which we are decidedly taking the lead and therefore in advance, I feel very confident there is no just ground for … alarm.'[7] He felt much more assured about the utility of the blockships than the efforts to strengthen the landward side of the dockyard defences.

It was the blockships that were to pave the way for the steam battle fleet, though not immediately. Once the trials had shown that it was feasible to convert elderly ships of the line to screw propulsion, the way forward might have seemed obvious. In 1846, when the conversion of the *Ajax* and *Blenheim* had been completed, the navy had seventy one ships of the line, of which fifty nine were laid up in ordinary.[8] No immediate step was taken to continue the process of conversion, since understandably it was considered best to await the trials of *Ajax* and *Blenheim*. These were generally considered to have been successful, particularly in the case of *Blenheim*, which had been lengthened and upon which considerable work was done to her stern. However, these two vessels had been at sea since 1846, and no further move was made, which seems surprising, since although Cockburn left the Admiralty in July that year it might have been supposed that he left behind a strong commitment to screw propulsion, and an acceptance of the feasibility of converting ships of the line to steam. Cockburn was disappointed not to have been offered the post of First Lord when Haddington left at the beginning of 1846; but he agreed to stay on with

6 Brown, *Before the Ironclad*, p. 124.
7 Morriss, *Cockburn*, p. 256.
8 Bartlett, *Sea Power*, p. 342.

Ellenborough, the new First Lord, for a while. When the latter was replaced by Auckland in July, Cockburn stepped down as Senior Naval Lord. Sir William Parker succeeded him briefly before Sir Charles Adam returned to the post; of him, Professor Rodger wrote that he 'was a very poor man of business, and his handwriting was illegible even to himself.'[9] After a year, Adam was succeeded by Admiral James Deans Dundas, who served as Senior Naval Lord until 1852.

One reason for not immediately embarking on a large scale conversion programme for the fleet can be found in the establishment by Auckland in 1846 of the Committee of Reference on Shipbuilding under Captain Lord John Hay. Hay was not convinced of the effectiveness of blockships, writing: 'I am disposed to think, that on the coast of England a line of battle ship would be a better man-of-war without the screw than with it.'[10] Although he did propose converting as blockships two ships of the line, which had been waiting 10 years to be commissioned, he admitted that he only did so to make use of the engines which happened to be available. Hay thought that in combat the sailing battle fleet would be better assisted by the employment of steam tugs.

Meanwhile, following the placing of the order for the *Amphion* in 1844, a number of purpose-built screw frigates were ordered. The first of these was *Dauntless*, completed in 1848, followed by *Arrogant*. She was one of the first to receive the newly designed Penn trunk engine of 360 hp. When the *Arrogant* was sent to Lisbon in 1850 to join a squadron under Commodore William Fanshawe Martin, she underwent a series of trials which has been described as 'the last, and most significant, trial of the screw propeller for use in large ships.'[11] In all the trials against sailing frigates *Arrogant* surprised everyone by outperforming at least one of them. Martin's conclusion was that in the immediate future the auxiliary screw steamer was the proper solution. Full powered steamers, which were designed to achieve high speeds by the use of steam alone, were not efficient as cruisers, because their consumption of coal was so great. What the performance of the *Arrogant* had demonstrated was that a fully rigged ship with steam power 'could have all the virtues and broadside fighting power of the sailing vessel plus the greater mobility and safety of the steamer.'[12] This, Martin saw, was what was immediately required; in practical effect, the engines and the coal replaced the traditional ballast.

Although the Admiralty had made a brisk start, it had failed to maintain a sufficient building programme for screw frigates. This was apparently due in part to a hopeful belief that in time of war it would be possible to recruit a substantial number of commercial steamers as auxiliary warships. In 1849 a Select Committee enquired into this but found that in practice most commercial steamships were unsuitable for conversion into warships, since they did not carry enough canvas to keep up with the battle fleet under sail, nor enough coal to provide sufficient endurance under steam.[13]

With the viability of screw propulsion having been accepted, attention turned to the question of new construction. Symonds having departed in 1846, there was a short interregnum before his successor took office. Meanwhile during this period an order was placed by the Admiralty

9 Rodger, *Admiralty*, p. 100.
10 Lambert, *Battleships*, p. 27.
11 Lambert, *Battleships*, p. 32.
12 Greenhill and Giffard, *Steam, Politics and Patronage*, p. 161.
13 Brown, *Before the Ironclad*, p. 129.

for a screw battle ship designed by John Edye, the senior assistant surveyor, but in the event work on the ship was never started. The new Surveyor, Captain Baldwin Wake Walker, was appointed from February 1848. Born in 1802, he joined the navy at the age of ten, and reached the rank of lieutenant in 1820. He saw considerable service in the Mediterranean before being permitted to join the Ottoman navy, where he enjoyed considerable success. He returned to Britain in 1847; promoted to the rank of captain, he served at sea for a short while before taking up his appointment as Surveyor. He was chosen in large part because of his qualities as a seaman. The unhappy controversies that had marked Symonds' tenure as Surveyor had led the Admiralty to look, as his successor, for an officer with sound practical knowledge who would be able to take an objective look at the plans that were produced. Andrew Lambert has written of his term as Surveyor: 'Walker brought to the Surveyor's office a passion for order and certainty that filled the role set out for him by the Admiralty without preventing progress. He preferred to make certain of every step, and there were no rash experiments because every development was related to previous experience.'[14]

One of his first acts was to produce a five-year plan which outlined the fleet which should be built, taking account of the advance of steam, and this was adopted by the then First Lord, Lord Auckland. At the time of Walker's appointment there were still questions being raised about screw propulsion; in 1849 the new First Lord, Sir Francis Baring, was still suggesting that further trials were needed for the screw to be judged against the paddle. This was in spite of the successful introduction of the *Blenheim* as a screw driven block ship, which had so firmly strengthened the case for steam battleships.

In October 1848 it was decided to convert the unfinished *Sans Pareil*, which had been laid down in 1845 as an 80 gun sailing ship of the line, and had been designed on the lines of the French built ship of that name. She was lengthened by 18 feet, the intention being to create what would be the first seagoing steam battleship. She was fitted with 350 hp engines. After completion she displaced 3,800 tons, and was armed with 70 guns. She was, however, generally regarded as a failure, because the engines proved unreliable and she lacked stowage and stability. Later steam battleships, designed expressly for operation with screw propellers, were larger and with a quite different hull form: 'The bluff form of the sailing ship of the line was completely unsuited to screw propulsion; it quickly piled up a huge bow wave, while the propeller cavitated in the air pockets of the broken water created by the square stern.'[15]

This was not a good start. The news of the progress which the French were making with a new steam battleship laid down in February 1848 was becoming very disturbing. This was a vessel being built to the design of the outstanding French naval architect Henri Dupuy de Lôme. Born in 1816, he had after completing his professional education visited England to study iron shipbuilding and screw propulsion, and had paid particular attention to the building of the *Great Britain* at Bristol. On his return to France, he was employed at the Arsenal at Toulon. He was absolutely convinced of the necessity of steam power for warships, including ships of the line. In 1845 he had proposed the building of an iron hulled screw frigate, a concept which was much ahead of its time. Dupuy de Lôme enjoyed the full support and encouragement of the Prince de Joinville. In 1847 the French Ministry of Marine placed an order for what would be the first

14 Lambert, *Battleships*, p. 30.
15 Lambert, *Battleships*, p. 35.

purpose built steam powered screw driven battleship. Initially to be named *24 Février*, she was renamed *Napoleon* before her launch on May 16, 1850.

One feature of the *Napoleon's* design was only settled after a vigorous dispute as to the best way to deal with the screw when a vessel was under sail. In France a number of designers had opted for a system whereby the screw could then be disconnected from the shaft and allowed to revolve at will. This was known as the *helice affolée.* In Britain, on the other hand, the preference was to design warships with a screw well, and screws that could be raised into this when proceeding under sail. When the *Napoleon's* design was being considered, the *Conseil de Travaux* wished for her to be fitted with a screw well; Dupuy de Lôme was firmly opposed to this, preferring the *helice affolée*, and in the end he got his way.

The building of the *Napoleon* clearly called for a British response, and it came with an Admiralty order for the *Agamemnon*. Her designers were Walker's two assistants, John Edye and Isaac Watts, but she was based on the former's abortive design of 1847. Watts wrote of the new ship: 'She was a much larger ship, she was much longer, and with a much fuller midship section than it was the custom to build line-of-battleships at that time, with a view to her receiving the larger engines of 700 nhp, which were made for *Vulcan* and not put into her.'[16]

The *Agamemnon* was the first British ship expressly designed and built as a steam battleship. The new machinery that was installed, built by Penn, of 600 nhp was designed to produce a speed of 10 knots. She was 230 feet long, significantly longer than the typical sailing ship of the line of 190 feet, and she had a beam of 55 feet. She displaced 5,080 tons, compared to the typical ship of the line's 3,680 tons. Her initial armament was one 68 pounder, thirty four 8 inch, and fifty six 32 pounders. During her construction a careful watch was kept on the progress of the building of the *Napoleon*; in 1851 Thomas Lloyd and Isaac Watts visited France to inspect her, and the report which they made led to the acceleration of the building of the *Agamemnon*. She was launched on May 22, 1852, and completed that October; *Napoleon* had been completed and put to sea in July.

The *Agamemnon* was designed to perform well under both sail and steam, and this objective was largely achieved. As a result, her basic design was still being used ten years after it was first made. The *Napoleon*, essentially a steam ship with a sailing rig as an auxiliary, was fitted with engines of 900 nhp; although this capacity was much greater than her English counterpart, D.K. Brown has suggested that in fact *Agamemnon* put more power into her screw; he was sceptical about the claim that *Napoleon* was actually the faster ship.[17]

Construction of pure sailing ships had been finally halted by the Admiralty in 1849. At that time a class of four three deckers of 131 guns had been ordered, of which three had already been laid down, to the design of William Symonds. The first of these was the *Duke of Wellington*, originally named *Windsor Castle*. It was evident to Walker that the building of screw battleships must be accelerated, and he proposed the conversion of a number of sailing vessels already in course of construction. The *Duke of Wellington* was accordingly earmarked for conversion. Originally to have been 210 feet long, she was lengthened to 240 feet; she ultimately displaced 5,829 tons, and was fitted with machinery to produce 700 nhp. Her armament consisted of sixteen 8 inch, one hundred and thirteen 32 pounders, and one 68 pounder. She was launched in

16 Brown, *Before the Ironclad*, p. 131.
17 Brown, *Before the Ironclad*, p. 132.

September 1852. Her conversion as a steamer was generally regarded as having been a success, and the rest of her class (*Marlborough*, *Royal Sovereign*, and *Prince of Wales)* underwent a similar conversion. They were followed by eight more ships ordered already in course of construction, and then by some thirty three warships of the existing sailing fleet, of which five were emergency conversions as blockships.

The process of conversion was still going on as late as 1861; the programme had been fuelled by the revived mutual suspicions between France and Britain, which led to a further arms race. The British had a much larger pool of ships of the line available for conversion, as well as a greater shipbuilding capacity for new construction, and accordingly established a healthy advantage in the number of steam battleships. By the time the Crimean War broke out in 1854 she already had eighteen to France's nine. By 1857, however, France had almost closed the gap, the ratio then being 28:24, but thereafter Britain drew ahead again. The imminent arrival, though, of the armoured battleship would soon mean that these large fleets of wooden ships would become obsolete. A large number of them however, although laid up in the 1860s, would not be sold to the breakers for many years.

The reality of the crucial importance of steam had become increasingly evident to the Admiralty. Captain Alexander Milne, serving as Fourth Naval Lord between 1847 and 1853, was one of the most thoughtful members of the Board. He wrote in 1850 that 'ships of the line are useless for checking the rapid movements of a steam squadron. No officer will ever think of using them under such circumstances. They would be a drag on any operation… Steam power alone can be of service in such circumstances.' [18] This appeared in a paper which was written in contemplation of a possible war with France, and Milne was absolutely clear that three inshore squadrons of steamers would be essential for defence against an invasion. At that time, he was concerned that seven of the navy's steam frigates and twenty three steam sloops were serving overseas, and if the number of steamers was not increased, then those on foreign stations would have to be recalled.

18 John Beeler (ed.), *The Milne Papers* (Aldershot: Navy Records Society, 2004), vol. I, p. 286.

5

Ordnance

It appears that it was the Venetians who first armed warship with cannon. The earliest reliable record of this was in 1378 when a fleet of Venetian galleys attacked the Austrian ports of Zara and Cattaro, armed with 'bombards.' These weapons were short cannon firing a stone shot, and replaced the weapons previously mounted in the forecastle of the galleys such as catapults, ballistae, and slings.[1] During the fifteenth century the manufacture of guns had progressed, and in the sixteenth century in the Low Countries a thriving industry in gun making was widely exporting its products. Henry VIII enthusiastically took up the introduction of artillery to the ships of his navy, of which the *Mary Rose* and *Henry Grace á Dieu* were examples. Thereafter, cannon of various kinds were developed, warships carrying them in broadside batteries. Improvements in design were incremental. The work of Benjamin Robins in the middle of the eighteenth century marked a more reasoned scientific study of the effectiveness of naval cannon. Not much was done, however, to develop the basic design of naval guns at that time, but at the end of the century a private company, the Carron Ironworks, introduced the carronade, a short gun of lighter weight which could fire heavier shot.[2] Then, in the first quarter of the nineteenth century there began a revolution in naval ordnance, which was in its turn to trigger a requirement for the armoured protection of warships, and thus to a radical change in naval warfare. Professor Baxter described it as 'largely due to the efforts of one gifted French artillerist, Henri Joseph Paixhans.'[3] It was Paixhans who solved the problem which had hitherto confined naval gunnery to the use of solid shot, when he devised a means of achieving horizontal shellfire. Hitherto it had only been possible to fire explosive shells at a high angle, and at sea their use was confined to specially designed warships known as bomb vessels, armed with mortars that could throw shells at stationary targets with low velocities.

The concept of using explosive projectiles in warfare went back a long way. Instances of the use of some form of bomb or grenade are said to go back to a mortar employed at Jadia in 1376, at Rhodes in 1522, and Bordeaux in 1542.[4] A later example of their use was during the French

1 Ian Hogg and John Batchelor, *Naval Guns* (Poole: Blandford, 1978), p. 7.
2 Hogg and Batchelor, *Naval Guns*, p. 17.
3 Baxter, *Introduction*, p. 19.
4 Louis H. Bolander, 'The Introduction of Shells and Shell Guns in the United States Navy', *The Mariner's Mirror*, 17.2 (1931) p. 105.

bombardment of Algiers in 1682, an operation in which five bomb vessels took part. The lack of any sustained progress in the development of explosive projectiles appears to have been due not only to their limited success, but also to the fact that, as a shipborne weapon, they were seen as being as great a danger to their users as to their targets.

The ordinary mortar, such as was employed in siege operations on land, or aboard bomb vessels, was too heavy to use as a field piece, so in the course of the eighteenth century a light mortar had been devised, known as a howitzer. This provided the necessary mobility for use in open warfare, and was successfully employed by the armies of Frederick the Great. During the remainder of the century a number of experiments were made seeking to find a means whereby explosive shells could be fired horizontally by land-based cannon. The value of being able to do so at sea was obvious; only a flatter trajectory gave a reasonable prospect of hitting a target. If the difficulty of achieving this could be overcome, the effect of explosive shells hitting a wooden warship could be enormous. The risk of fire aboard such vessels firing shells from traditional cannon remained very great, however, and severely limited naval interest in pursuing the possibility. In 1701, for instance, a council of officers meeting at Spithead approved a proposal to provide a number of shells to ships of the line 'provided they can be well secured from taking fire and doing mischief in our own ships.'[5] The project does not appear to have been pursued.

Fresh impetus to explore the possibilities of horizontal shellfire as a weapon in the line of battle came in France in the eighteenth century, where it was seen as a possible means of overcoming British naval superiority. The first recorded experiment of horizontal shellfire at shipping appears to have been made in 1756. Then in 1795 a trial, using a timber target, was made at Toulon. This was followed by a further trial at Cherbourg in 1797, and in the following year Napoleon set up a special commission to test 24 and 36 pounder shells fired at a target representing a ship of the line. Napoleon was convinced of the value of horizontal shellfire, and ordered that 36 pounder shells be supplied to all warships carrying guns of that calibre. However, the shells and other incendiary projectiles issued to the French fleet soon confirmed the extent of the risks which they brought with them, as a result of their frequent premature explosion. Nevertheless, when war was resumed in 1803, Napoleon ordered that a shell firing gun be mounted in each pinnace of his invasion flotilla at Boulogne, while other experiments with shellfire continued to be made, not only in France but also in Britain, Russia and the United States.

General Bentham, who had previously risen high in the Russian service, had some valuable experience to bring to the British discussion of shell firing, having fitted out in 1788, for operations against a Turkish squadron a flotilla of longboats:

> These longboats he armed with brass cannon, and secured for them a great supply of shells and solid shot. At the mouth of the Liman River in the Sea of Azov he attacked a greatly superior Turkish force and gained a complete victory. The shells fired at close range tore great holes in the sides of the Turkish ships and started fires which spread rapidly and caused the destruction of the squadron. This event seems to have been almost completely ignored in European naval circles, and in the case of the British Admiralty designedly so.[6]

5 Baxter, *Introduction*, p. 19.
6 Bolander, 'Shells and Shell-Guns,' p. 107.

Bentham proposed in 1798 that 24 pounder carronades, fitted to throw shells and carcasses as well as solid shot, be mounted in small sloops, and various other suggestions were put forward. In July 1813 John Jacob Zornlin proposed a shell which he had designed to be fired aboard ship from a gun or carronade, which he claimed would rake the deck of a ship after passing through her side; but the British Admiralty rejected the proposal. Another project was taken much further:

> In July 1811 and again in January 1813, a committee of field officers of artillery, headed by Lieutenant General Vaughan Lloyd, approved proposals by Rear Admiral Sir Richard Keats and Lieutenant T.H. Stevens R.M.A. for the use of 68 pounder carronades as mortars in gun brigs and other small vessels. Experiments at Sutton showed that ranges of 3,500 yards could be thus obtained, which was much greater than the maximum range of under 2,000 yards attained by the ordinary 8 inch brass mortars, although inferior by nearly three quarters of a mile to the range of the heavy sea service mortars. The committee declined to pass on the proposal of Lieutenant Stevens to arm some gunboats with 68 pounder carronades for use as howitzers, on the ground that it was for naval officers to decide that question.[7]

In any case, what has been called 'calculated conservatism' characterised a good deal of British naval thought, as Simmons, a British naval writer, observed in 1837:

> So long as the maritime powers with which we are at war did not innovate by improving their guns, by extending the invention of carronades, or above all by projecting shells horizontally from shipping, so long was it the interest of Great Britain not to set the example of any improvement in naval ordnance, since such improvements must eventually be adopted by other nations, and not only would the value of our immense material be depreciated if not forced out of use, but a probability might arise that these innovations might tend to render less decisive our great advantages in nautical skill and experience.[8]

In the United States, one important development was the design by Colonel George Bomford, the Chief of Ordnance during the war of 1812, of a cast iron howitzer which he called a 'columbiad.' Designed principally for use in coast defence against shipping, it combined some of the qualities of the gun, the howitzer, and the mortar, and was capable of firing both solid shot and shells. It appears to have attained good results. Two of the weapons were mounted aboard Robert Fulton's *Demologos*.. Meanwhile in 1814 Colonel John Stevens and his two sons developed an elongated shell which tests showed was capable of hitting a target representing the side of a ship of the line with devastating effect.

Henri Joseph Paixhans was born in Metz in 1783. After graduating from the *École Polytechnique* he joined the French army, serving as an artillery officer during the Napoleonic Wars. In 1815 he published *Considérations sur l'état actuel de l'artillerie des places*, but it was in his next book that he opened the door to the future of naval gunnery. Published in 1822 under the title *Nouvelle force maritime,* he addressed the question of naval gunnery specifically, envisaging a fleet armed

7 Baxter, *Introduction*, p. 22n.
8 Bolander, 'Shells and Shell-Guns', pp. 106-107.

with guns capable of firing explosive shells, and itself protected by armour. In the following year he perfected his design for a delaying mechanism which allowed explosive shells to be fired safely with a flat trajectory at a high velocity. Paixhans was not, however, convinced of the effectiveness of the elongated shell as designed by John Stevens. He was, though, quite sure that shellfire spelt doom for the large warship. If constructed of wood, it would be vulnerable in the extreme; on the other hand, he believed that it could not be protected by armour of sufficient strength to resist shellfire, since the necessary weight of iron would be too great for a ship of the line to bear. In this, of course, he was to be proved wrong; but his conviction that his flat trajectory guns would not only be practicable for use aboard ship, but would be fatally destructive to wooden vessels, was soon proved correct.

In January 1824 tests were conducted at Brest, where an old 80 gun ship of the line, the *Pacificateur*, was used as a target for two guns built to Paixhans' design. The damage that the vessel suffered resulting from this demonstrated dramatically the effect of shellfire on a wooden ship. The shells used had a fuse which ignited automatically when the gun was fired and, lodged in the wooden hull of the target, exploded a moment later. The 16 member commission which conducted the experiments 'reported unanimously that Paixhans had solved the problem he had raised in a satisfactory manner; that the weapon he had created had terrible effects and would, after some improvements, be no more difficult to handle than the ordinary guns.'[9] A large majority also considered that Paixhans' shell gun would be suitable for use in coastal batteries, gunboats, floating and steam batteries, and might even be adapted for ships of the line, albeit in small numbers after taking the necessary precautions and conducting further research. Further successful tests took place later in the year, entirely confirming the initial results.

In 1825 Paixhans wrote a pamphlet with his own conclusions on the results of these experiments. He contended that armour plate at least seven or eight inches thick would be necessary to resist the heaviest shellfire, and the weight of this would be too great for the traditional wooden warship to bear. However, three deckers cut down to carry a single battery of six to eight shell guns could do so, and so could floating batteries and large steam frigates with a reduced sail area. Other French naval writers of the time took a similar view.

Paixhans' views were carefully studied in Britain. D. K. Brown noted that his hope that the building of a fleet of steamers to carry shell guns would reduce British naval supremacy was based upon assumptions which Paixhans made which were ahead of his time: 'The engines of the day were so heavy that few guns could be carried, fuses were highly unreliable, and the chance of a hit at long range was so remote that many guns were needed.' In particular, Britain's industrial superiority over France was even greater than its advantage in numbers of seamen, and Paixhans' plan would have had the effect of increasing rather than reducing Britain's advantage.[10]

Notwithstanding the continued prejudice against the use of shell guns at sea due to the risk of explosion, tests were carried out in Britain which led to the introduction of a few shell guns. Experience showed that the spherical shell with an asymmetrical fuse was less accurate than solid shot, and that the fuses themselves were unreliable, and it was hence not until the late 1830s that ships of the line were equipped with significant numbers of shell guns. Meanwhile

9 Baxter, *Introduction*, p. 25.
10 Brown, *Before the Ironclad*, p. 39.

paddle steamers were being equipped with larger guns capable of firing heavy shot. In 1835 trials were made using an old ship of the line, the *Prince George*, to test the new guns, including some shells. The results were not entirely satisfactory; nearly half the time fused shells failed to explode, while shells that ricocheted off the surface of the water generally failed. Nevertheless, the trials were regarded as important, and led to the steady introduction of the shell gun into the British navy.[11]

In one of the few early instances of their operating under actual combat conditions, shell guns proved their worth during the Greek War of Independence. Reference has already been made to the steamer *Karteria* commanded by Captain Frank Hastings used them to good effect. It was claimed that she had destroyed a large number of small Turkish vessels. A rather more dubious claim was made to the effect that in the course of her campaign in 1827-1828 she had fired no less than 18,000 rounds. Hastings was also a strong advocate for the use of heated shot, and appears to have trained his crew well, writing that they fired hot shot 'with as little apprehension as if using cold shot.'[12] The *Karteria*, originally built as the *Perseverance*, was intended to be the first of a planned squadron of six steamers which Lord Cochrane had ordered to support Greek independence. Douglas Dakin has written that if Cochrane had been able to achieve the flotilla which he intended, he would probably not only have been able to free Greece in a matter of weeks, but Codrington would have been denied the honour of fighting the battle of Navarino.[13]

Fought on October 20, 1827, the battle of Navarino was the last fleet action conducted entirely under sail, and the last in which shell guns played no part. The combined Anglo-French-Russian fleet under Sir Edward Codrington completely destroyed the Turkish-Egyptian fleet. It has been said of that battle that though it did not of itself bring about Greek independence, 'it had so revolutionised the situation that the Powers could no longer stand still. They had to go forward and find a solution, and Greek independence was the most obvious.'[14]

While European nations were feeling their way towards the introduction of shell guns, the US navy had been falling behind. It was the visit to America in 1838 of a French frigate entirely armed with guns capable of shell firing that awoke the Americans to the need to make improvements in their gunnery, and in the following year Captain Matthew Galbraith Perry was directed to carry out a series of experiments with hollow shot, and with shells and shell guns. He recommended that further trials be conducted with shell firing, and by 1841 a number of 8 inch Paixhans guns had been introduced.[15] John A. Dahlgren, then a lieutenant on board the *Cumberland*, described in his journal on December 8, 1843 his experience in firing shells:

> I had the opportunity of firing the first shot from the *Cumberland*. There are four Paixhans, or shell guns in the ship, and these have been assigned as my division. The captain sent me orders to fire a shell from each piece. Accordingly I had the heavy 68 pounder shot withdrawn and shells substituted. The guns were laid by myself, and the first grazes of these were point blank, the last much elevated … It was amusing, today, when about to fire to notice that the crew had left the gun, as if desirous of avoiding any accident from

11 Brown, *Before the Ironclad*, p. 136.
12 Douglas Dakin, 'Lord Cochrane's Greek Steam Fleet,' *The Mariner's Mirror* 39.3 (1953), p. 217.
13 Dakin, 'Greek Steam Fleet,'p. 216.
14 Bartlett, *Sea Power*, p. 80.
15 Bolander, 'Shells and Shell-Guns,'p. 111.

> the shell, which is new to them and seems alarming … Shot they do not mind, but shells they dread.[16]

Dahlgren went on to develop his own shell gun, with the object of overcoming the shortcomings of the Paixhans guns. He explained in 1849 the basis of his design:

> Paixhans had so far satisfied naval men of the power of shell guns as to obtain their admission on shipboard; but by unduly developing the explosive element, he had sacrificed accuracy and range … The difference between the system of Paixhans and my own was simply that Paixhans guns were strictly shell guns, and were not designed for shot, nor for great penetration or accuracy at long ranges. They were, therefore, auxiliary to, or associates of, the shot guns. This made a mixed armament, which was objectionable as such, and never was adopted to any extent in France… My idea was, to have a gun that should generally throw shells far and accurately, with the capacity to fire solid shot when needed. Also to compose the whole battery entirely of such guns.[17]

In France, the largest ships of the line (the policy of building only three deckers having been in force for some time) were from 1838 equipped with four 22cm shell guns on their main deck, in lieu of four 24 pounders; and with thirty eight 16cm shell guns on the upper deck, replacing an equal number of 18 pounders. 10 years later, the standard armament for three deckers was again changed by the replacement of twelve 30 pounders with 22cm shell guns. Thereafter, due to the rapid changes in ordnance technology, ships were equipped individually as new weapons became available.[18]

The British Admiralty had felt obliged to respond to the French introduction of shell guns, and by 1841 ships of the sailing battle fleet were carrying them alongside conventional cannon. It has to be said, however, that this step was taken without any marked enthusiasm. Cockburn, in particular, remained sceptical, admitting that he regarded 'with jealousy anddoubt all these explosive inventions.' He was particularly dubious about the designs produced by a Mr S.A. Warner, who made some very bold claims for their potential capabilities. Cockburn reluctantly accepted the probable power of what Warner called an 'exploding case,' but not the range which was claimed for it:

> If he could really send a shell with precision six miles, he would be able to effect what nobody else has hitherto attained and he would be entitled to a considerable reward from the government. It appears, however, he has hitherto invariably insisted on proving first the former (in my opinion) minor experiment which causes me to entertain the strongest doubt of his being able to execute the latter more important object.[19]

16 Bolander, Shells and Shell-Guns,'pp. 111-112.
17 Clarence S. Peterson, *Admiral John A Dahlgren: Father of United States Naval Ordnance* (New York: Publisher unknown, 1945), p. 26.
18 Rif Winfield and Stephen S. Roberts, *French Warships in the Age of Sail 1786-1861* (Barnsley: Seaforth Publishing, 2015), p. 49.
19 Morriss, *Cockburn*, p. 254.

By the 1840s, therefore, the steady introduction of shell guns was well advanced in the major navies of that time. This was based on the many experimental trials of shell guns, rather than more convincing evidence derived from actual combat. The success of shell guns during these trials proved not to be an entirely reliable indicator of their performance at sea. For this reason, therefore, Andrew Lambert has argued that 'the shell guns of the 1840s and 1850s did not revolutionise naval warfare.'[20] He rejected Baxter's view that the use of shell fire against wooden warships, as for instance at Hampton Roads in 1862, ended the era of the wooden warship, pointing out the experience of the Allied fleet before Sebastopol in 1854 and of the Austrian wooden battleship *Kaiser* at the battle of Lissa in 1866. Nevertheless, the capacity to inflict possibly terminal damage by the effect of shell fire on wooden hulls prompted greatly increased consideration of the possibility of producing armoured warships. The widespread equipment of warships with shell guns thus led inexorably to the development of armour plating, and was accordingly the immediate cause of the revolution in naval warfare. Although the earlier instances of the use of shell fire were not particularly impressive, due to inaccurate artillery and poor fuses, they had begun the revolution.

20 Lambert, *Battleships*, p. 92.

6

The Rise and Fall of the Iron Warship

At the start of the nineteenth century there were still perhaps some for whom the concept of a ship built of iron was entirely counter-intuitive – including the angry blacksmith who is said to have thrown a horseshoe into his water trough, crying 'Will that swim?' But it had become generally apparent that it did have considerable advantages over wood as a shipbuilding material. The steady advance of metalworking technology enabled the construction in 1787 of an iron canal barge some 70 feet in length which was capable of carrying four times its own weight.[1]

Over the next twenty years a large number of such barges were built, and then in 1821 came the first seagoing iron ship, a paddle steamer named *Aaron Manby* after its builder. This steamed from London up the River Seine to Paris, under the command of Captain Charles Napier, who had invested in Manby's company. Sadly, the business failed when Manby was obliged to abandon the shipbuilding industry, and as a result Napier lost most of the money which he had invested. This outcome left him bitterly opposed thereafter to the whole concept of iron ships, against which he frequently spoke with extremes of passion.

Before his company failed Manby had built a number of iron ships, and he was followed by other shipbuilders such as John Laird, of William Laird & Sons of Birkenhead, who quickly became one of the leaders in the field. An early success for ships built by Lairds came with the construction of two iron paddle steamers, the *Tigris* and *Euphrates*. These were built at Birkenhead, and then dismantled and shipped to the Middle East, where they were reassembled. The leader of the Euphrates expedition of 1833 wrote an extremely favourable report to Laird on their performance:

> The iron vessels constructed by you far exceeded my expectations, as well as those of the naval officers employed in the late expedition, who would one and all bear testimony anywhere to their extraordinary solidity; indeed, it was often repeated by Lieutenant Cleaveland, and the others, that any wooden vessel must have been destroyed before the service was one half completed – whereas the *Euphrates* was as perfect when they laid her up in Baghdad as the first day she was floated.[2]

1 Brown, *Before the Ironclad*, p. 79.
2 Greenhill and Giffard, *Steam, Politics and Patronage*, p. 126.

In 1836 Laird put forward a proposal for an iron frigate, which the Admiralty did not take up. The East India Company, on the other hand, showed more interest, and ordered two iron paddle steamers from Laird's, and two more from the rival firm of Fairbairn & Co. The last of the four on which construction was started was Laird's *Nemesis*, of 660 tons. She was 169 feet long and 29 feet in the beam, carrying two 32 pounders on swivel carriages, and was powered by engines delivering 120 hp. She was subsequently also equipped with five long brass 6 pounders and 10 small iron swivels.[3] Next came *Phlegethon*, slightly smaller at 510 tons, 161 feet long and 26 feet beam, with four guns, and engines of 90 hp. Fairbairn's, with a yard on the Thames, built *Pluto* and *Proserpina*. Laird's also constructed two other armed vessels for the East India Company, *Ariadne* and *Medusa*, of 432 tons; these were assembled in Bombay from parts which were sent out from Birkenhead in December 1839.[4]

The first of the Company's new iron ships to put to sea was the *Pluto* in 1839, but it appears that serious defects in her construction caused her to be brought back for repair and refitting. Thus it was the *Nemesis* that became the world's first active iron warship. She had an unfortunate start to her career, running aground in St Ives Bay in March 1840 when on her maiden voyage from Birkenhead to Southampton. But her construction stood the test of this incident; she was repaired in the Royal Navy's dockyard at Portsmouth, and before the end of the month she was able to set off for the Far East. She was commanded by Captain William Hall, who like many other senior officers of the East India Company's fleet came from the Royal Navy. Although the *Nemesis* suffered quite serious damage in huge storms soon after leaving the Cape, she was able to put into Delagoa Bay in Portuguese Mozambique for repairs, before resuming her journey to form part of the company's Bengal Marine.

An immediate problem which threatened the development of iron ships had been the discovery of the serious effect of iron on the magnetic compass. The extent of the deviation caused was so great that iron ships were obliged always to operate within sight of land. It was a problem with which the Admiralty became engaged. Captain B. J. Johnson was ordered to carry out a series of experiments to investigate ways in which the problem could be overcome. Following this, the Admiralty commissioned the Astronomer Royal, Sir George Airey, in 1837 to carry out further work on the problem. By 1838 he had been largely successful, and it was not long before the Admiralty ordered its first iron ship, the packet *Dover* of 224 tons, from Laird's yard.

Out east, the *Nemesis* was employed as a gunboat during the First Anglo-China War with considerable success. She took part in actions against Amoy, Ningpo, and Woosung, and in February 1841 participated in the bombardment of Whampoa, which Captain Hall later described:

> Was struck several times but fortunately only one man was wounded. One of the large shots passed completely through the outer casing of the steam chest and was very near to penetrating the steam chest itself. Besides receiving several shots in the hull she had her spars and rigging a good deal cut up.[5]

3 Baxter, *Introduction*, p. 34.

4 Adrian G. Marshall, *Nemesis: The First Iron Warship and her World* (Stroud: The History Press, 2016), p. 13.

5 Brown, *Before the Ironclad*, p. 83.

In 1845 she returned to India to refit at Bombay, where it was found that she needed much less maintenance than the wooden ships that had been similarly engaged, and that her riveting had been unaffected by her own gunfire. When Hall came back to the United Kingdom in November, he delivered an enthusiastic report of his ship's performance, which was highly influential in the formation of the Admiralty's policy at that time towards the construction of iron warships.

By then, a colossal step forward in the development of iron ships had been taken. Isambard Kingdom Brunel and his colleagues, who had built the successful wooden paddle steamship *Great Western*, were engaged in working on designs for her successor, when in 1838 the Channel packet *Rainbow*, an iron ship built by John Laird, visited Bristol. Brunel at once saw the possibilities of iron ship construction, and after two of his trusted colleagues had visited Antwerp aboard the *Rainbow*, they returned to Bristol absolutely converted to iron as a shipbuilding material. Brunel succeeded in persuading the directors of the Great Western Steamship Company that the new ship, to be named *Great Britain*, should be built of iron. In another departure from his original design, Brunel was considering the possibility of screw propulsion. After Francis Pettit Smith had lent him the *Archimedes* to test her propellers, Brunel became convinced that the new ship must be screw powered. This, he saw, would bring huge advantages; the engine was lighter and smaller, and could sit lower in the hull, and it was cheaper. Above all the bulky paddle wheels could be dispensed with. The SS *Great Britain* was finally launched on July 19, 1843, and made her maiden voyage to New York two years later. At that time she was the largest ship afloat; 322 feet long, and 50 feet in the beam, she displaced 3,400 tons.

John Laird was firmly convinced that iron warships were the future, and he began building at his company's own expense an iron hulled frigate which he hoped to sell to the Royal Navy. She was 187 feet long, and 30 feet in the beam, and displaced 878 tons fully loaded. Before the launch of ship No 42, as she was known, she was inspected on behalf of the Admiralty, and to Laird's dismay she was rejected as 'unfit for service.'[6] She was launched in April 1842, having been sold to the Mexican government and named *Guadelupe*. Her 180 hp engines were designed to achieve 9 knots. She was armed with a 68 pounder Paixhans pivot gun in the bow and stern; four 24 pounders were added later. During the course of her construction, she was visited by the young Henri Dupuy de Lôme who was touring Britain to study iron shipbuilding, on which he published a report in Paris in 1844. He considered the *Guadelupe* to be the strongest ship to have been built at that time. In his report Dupuy de Lôme drew a number of important conclusions about iron construction, which he was in no doubt had a number of very considerable advantages over that of wood. Apart from anything else, an iron ship did not require a complex system of diagonals, while the hull was more spacious, and not being vulnerable to hogging, could be longer. However, in spite of his enthusiastic report, the French government did not take up Laird's proposal for an iron frigate estimated to cost £36,000.[7]

The *Guadelupe* proved her worth in action during the Mexican war with Texas. The Mexican government had also acquired the wooden hulled *Montezuma*, of 1,110 tons. She was armed in a similar manner to the *Guadelupe*. Rebellion had broken out in the Yucatán, which was supported by the government of Texas, and the two steamers took part in the battle of Campeche on May

6 Brown, *Before the Ironclad*, p. 85.
7 Brown, *Before the Ironclad*, pp. 85-86.

16, 1843. In the course of this they became the first warships to fire their shell guns in action against an enemy squadron. The Texans had put together a force of sailing warships under the command of Commodore Edwin Moore, whose flagship was the sloop *Austin*. The battle ended with neither side having gained the upper hand, although considerable damage was inflicted on all the participants. The Mexican steamers were commanded by Tomas Marin, with whom apparently their British officers and crew did not work well. Each side claimed the engagement as a victory.[8] The British commander of the *Guadelupe*, Commander Charlwood, on leave from the Royal Navy, reported that during the action she was hit a number of times by solid shot. The holes made clean punctures and were easily plugged; overall he considered her a better gun platform than the wooden sloop *Salamander*, on which he had served, and he noted that 'the damage is considerably less than is usually suffered by a wood vessel, and I should also consider that there were nothing like the number of splinters which are generally forced out by shot sent through a wooden vessel's side.' His overall conclusion, which he repeated to a Parliamentary commission in 1847, was emphatic: 'for general purposes I am decidedly of the opinion that in several points iron is much preferable to wood for steam vessels.'[9]

Supporters of iron as a shipbuilding material were able to point to many of the advantages which had been apparent to Dupuy de Lôme. These included increased strength, solidity, durability, and salubrity, and reduced fire risk. Iron also effected a great saving in hull weight, increased the cargo space, saved money in construction and repairs, and facilitated watertight subdivision. With so many evident benefits on which to rely, the advocates of the iron ship might be thought to have decisively gained the upper hand. The Board of Admiralty, with Haddington as First Lord, in January 1844 ordered six small iron steamers for use as tenders to flagships. Then, taking into account the reports from Hall and Charlwood of the performance in action of the *Nemesis* and *Guadelupe* respectively, the Admiralty went on to order five iron frigates. One of these, the *Birkenhead*, was to be a paddle steamer; the other four, *Simoom, Vulcan, Greenock*, and *Megaera*, were to be screw ships.

However, the struggle to establish the suitability of iron over wood was not yet over. Both William Symonds, and John Edye, his principal assistant, remained extremely doubtful. There was an influential body of conservative professional opinion which pointed, among other things, to the rapidity with which the bottom of an iron ship became fouled with marine plants. It was also contended that iron ships would be more vulnerable to enemy fire; the holes made by solid shot in wooden hulls often closed almost completely by themselves.

During 1845 the strength of the opposition to the building of iron warships increased. Much of this was based on a widely held belief that they had not been sufficiently tested for the effect of gunfire. As a result, even Cockburn, who had himself become persuaded of the merits of iron ships, felt obliged to authorise a programme of secret tests at Woolwich Arsenal, which began in August 1845. The target which was constructed simulated the side of an iron ship, and in some tests also the deck. It was exposed to the fire of a 32 pounder firing solid shot at a range of 30 to 40 yards. In some tests, the iron plating was lined with wood or Kamptulicon, a rubber compound. These tests were in many ways inconclusive, but sufficient questions were raised to fuel anxieties about the building of iron warships. Among the leading opponents was General

8 Lawrence Sondhaus, *Naval Warfare 1815-1914* (London: Routledge, 2000), p. 44.
9 Brown, *Before the Ironclad*, p. 87.

Sir Howard Douglas, who saw in the tests confirmation of his strongly held opinion of iron built ships, observing that 'vessels entirely constructed of iron were utterly unfit for all the purposes of war, whether naval or is troopships.'

Admiral Sir Charles Napier, as he had now become, was another of the leaders of the opposition to iron ships, and he took full advantage of his position as a member of Parliament to argue his case. He based this not only on the alleged vulnerability of iron ships to enemy gunfire, but also to the problem of underwater fouling. The Woolwich tests had not provided the Admiralty with a very strong case to resist the campaign against iron ships, although Haddington and Cockburn had become strong supporters. When, in January 1846, Peel, at that time struggling with the issue of the repeal of the Corn Laws, wished to strengthen the Cabinet's representation in the House of Lords, he replaced Haddington with Ellenborough. The latter was a man of 'headstrong reforming zeal,' who was seen as a more effective politician. He brought to the position of First Lord a determination both to bring about administrative reform and to strengthen and expand the navy.

As previously noted, Ellenborough's appointment was a cause of considerable offence to Cockburn, who had expected to be invited to take up the post himself, as he explained: 'After having filled my present irksome and difficult station at the Admiralty seventeen years and being now nearly at the head of the list of officers of the navy, it is painful to me to add that I do not consider that attention has been shown to me which I think I had reason to look for on this occasion.'[10] He had agreed, however, to stay on as Senior Naval Lord for a while, due to the difficulty of finding a suitable successor, and he soon established an effective working relationship with Ellenborough. It was not long before the latter found, to his disappointment, that the Cabinet was not prepared to stand the cost of the proposals which he brought forward. He was also very dissatisfied with the way in which the navy was deployed. He was convinced that if war broke out with either France or the United States – in 1846 conflict with either was seen as not unlikely – it would soon become a war with both. During his term of office, therefore, he strongly argued for a great concentration of British naval resources in home waters.[11]

Ellenborough's term of office, however, was cut short. The fall of Peel's ministry in July 1846 brought into office a Liberal government. This produced a complete reversal of the official attitude towards iron ships. The new Board of Admiralty wasted little time in giving effect to a new policy towards the use of iron built vessels as warships. Although tests continued over the following years, a total of eight trials having been completed by 1851, the year 1846 saw the decision that the previous Board's new iron frigates should be converted to troopships. It was while serving in this capacity that the *Birkenhead* was to be lost in a celebrated shipwreck, breaking up after running aground on a reef in the Indian Ocean on February 26 1852, a disaster in which out of the total of 648 passengers and crew, 455 lives were lost. Iron ships did continue to be built for commercial purposes, and with considerable success; but the era of the iron warship had for the moment come to a premature end. It was to be in a very different set of circumstances that ship design in Britain got back onto a proper course at the end of the following decade.

10 Morriss, *Cockburn*, p. 275.
11 Bartlett, *Sea Power*, pp. 181-182.

The policy adopted by the British Admiralty following the experiments that were being conducted at Woolwich and elsewhere was naturally studied with great interest in France and the United States in particular. The French had embarked on a comprehensive series of experiments to test the resistance of iron plates to both solid shot and shell. These had begun not only to consider the suitability of iron as a shipbuilding material, but also to test the viability of the proposals put forward by Nicolas-Hippolyte Labrousse in 1840 for the construction of ironclad rams. This was an extremely radical concept, but the French were prepared to explore such ideas rather more vigorously than the British. Trials on the beach at Gavres, near Lorient between 1843 and 1845, though inconclusive, began to confirm the doubts in Britain about the building of iron warships. While these were going on, a striking proposal, certainly well ahead of its time, was put forward; of this, Baxter observed:

> Representing as it does the first phase in the evolution of the seagoing ironclad in the mind of its creator, Dupuy de Lôme's proposal dated Februaryy 20 1845 is of the highest interest. To render steam warships superior to sailors, he argued, we must reduce sails to the auxiliary role and instal machinery of great power. Since engines of this force cannot be placed far enough below water to be out of the way of plunging shot, protection is indispensable.[12]

This proposal will be considered further in the following chapter on the development of armour protection. For the moment the ideas put forward by Dupuy de Lôme went nowhere, because the tests which were conducted later in 1845 were taken as confirmation of the unsuitability of iron as a shipbuilding material, unless a satisfactory system of armour plating could be devised. Thus by the middle of the decade, which had begun with French opinion favourable to iron, official policy there was by now moving firmly in the opposite direction just as it was in Britain. Nevertheless, by 1853 the French had accumulated a total of eight iron corvettes of up to 950 tons, and 36 dispatch vessels of various sizes.

In the United States early in the 1840s Abel P. Upshur, at that time Secretary of the Navy, had become a supporter of iron ships. He reported on January 31, 1842:

> It seems now to be no longer doubtful, that iron ships will answer all the purposes of coast and harbour defence, and, probably, also of ocean cruising. It is the wish of this Department to construct as many vessels as possible of this material. This is desirable, not only on account of its superior durability and cheapness, but because, by extending the use of it, the government would afford a well-deserved encouragement to the industry of a large class of our people, and aid in developing and bringing into action, the most important part of our country's resources.[13]

This was a clear sighted statement of policy, and it was followed in December 1845 by a call from President Polk for the Congress to vote funds for the construction of iron warships, noting that they could be built in the interior of the country and that by reason of their light draft they could enter most harbours. However, in spite of the official approval at that time, the lack of

12 Baxter, *Introduction*, p. 60.
13 Baxter, *Introduction*, p. 41n.

enthusiasm of Britain and France led to a gradual shift of attitude. In the period leading up to the outbreak of the Civil War in 1861, only three iron warships were built in the United States, and it came to be accepted that unarmoured iron vessels were unsuitable for war purposes.

The current of professional opinion that ran so strongly against iron hulled ships of war was of course perverse; and for a long time it inhibited the development of the modern warship. The advantages possessed by iron hulled ships was not recognised, perhaps because at first it was the shot proof armour that was seen as the crucial advance in warship design. For many years, therefore, wooden hulled ships protected with armour plate continued to be the norm. Even after the launch of the iron hulled *Warrior*, Britain continued to build a large number of wooden hulled ships. The immediate consequence was that the development of larger ships was restricted, since there was an absolute upper limit to the size of a wooden hulled ship.

It was only gradually realised that an iron hulled ship was better able to bear the increasing weight of armour, and that building in iron permitted the division of the hull into watertight compartments. Once this essential truth had been grasped, the way would be clear for a progressive increase in the size of capital ships.

For Britain, the consequence would be of huge significance, as Bernard Brodie pointed out:

> Great Britain, fighting against steadily increasing odds to secure the sinews of maritime supremacy, found herself suddenly liberated from the difficulties of the three-centuries-old timber supply problem and placed gratuitously at the very pinnacle of advantage among nations for command of the raw materials upon which sea power depended. This place was to remain hers through the remainder of the century. Long after other states had surpassed Britain in the production of iron and steel, the specialisation of her resources in the shipbuilding industries enabled her to hold without disproportionate endeavour that rank of leader in naval power that was peculiarly essential to her security.[14]

14 Bernard Brodie, *Sea Power in the Machine Age* (New York: Greenwood Press, 1969), p. 129.

7

Armour

The concept of protecting a warship by covering it with armour goes back a long way. The potential benefits are immediately obvious; the technical difficulties of achieving a satisfactory solution, however, were considerable. Professor Baxter traced the history of plating ships with metal from the earliest times, noting that it was difficult to tell whether the object had been to protect them against fire and projectiles or simply the ravages of marine growths.[1] By 500 BC Greek trading ships appear to have been fitted with sheets of lead to protect their hulls against wood boring worms, and Roman vessels likewise. The Greek writer Athanasius of Naucratis, writing towards the end of the second century AD, described an enormous vessel built for the grain trade for the King of Syracuse in about 240 BC. This was plated with lead secured to a backing of tarred sailcloth and timber with bronze nails. Later some Roman warships were sheathed in lead. The long ships of the Norsemen, which were protected by their shields fixed along their sides, were in addition strengthened by a belt of iron or bronze.

In the early sixteenth century both Spanish and Portuguese began to sheath the underwater section of ships with lead. The Knights of St John provided the Emperor Charles V with the heavily armed carrack *Santa Anna* for his expedition against the Turks in Tunis in 1535, which was plated with lead, and which took part in the capture of the Goleta. At much the same time the Venetian flagship *Galleon of Venice* was armour plated, and she also operated successfully against the Turks. By the end of the century the Dutch had experimented with the use of iron plates to protect a warship during the siege of Antwerp.

In the eastern world the most famous use of armour to protect warships was in the Korean turtle ships, although it has been suggested that references to the use of iron in these vessels actually referred only to the fitting of iron spikes to deter boarders. At all events there were a considerable number of instances recorded where such vessels were employed as warships by Korea, China, and Japan.

In the eighteenth century the British navy began its extensive programme of coppering ships' bottoms to protect their wooden hulls from marine infestation, and it was followed by the navies of France and Spain. Difficulties were experienced with the fastening of the copper plates, but there was no doubt that coppered ships were able to sail faster. For protection against solid shot, however, shipbuilders relied merely on increasing the thickness of a warship's hull. However,

1 Baxter, *Introduction*, p. 4.

the Spanish navy in particular explored the possibility of plating a warship's sides with iron, one proposal being that put forward in 1727 by Don Juan de Ochoa for a 'baraza espin.' Later in the century the Spanish examined the possibility of using floating batteries in the siege of Gibraltar. A French officer, the Chevalier d'Arcon, designed ten of these; the inclined side of the ship which was to face the enemy was built of heavy timbers five feet thick. His idea was that these would be proof even against heated shot if water was pumped constantly between the timbers. There appears to be some doubt as to whether the wooden sides were further protected by the use of iron. The batteries mounted a total of 140 guns and were heavily manned with over 5,000 men. They went into action on September 13, 1782, but were not a success; d'Arcon ascribed this to a lack of cooperation on the part of other ships and the land forces:

> The floating batteries themselves, however, showed capital defects; too great draught to approach close enough for breaching; a field of fire much restricted by the great thickness of the bulwarks, and a defective circulation of water. Owing to imperfect caulking, the water leaked so rapidly into the interior that the circulating pumps had to be stopped. After several hours of fighting, hot shot set fire to some of the batteries, and the rest were abandoned and burned.[2]

This was not an encouraging precedent for naval designers; but during the war of 1812, the Americans began to explore a number of possible designs for floating batteries. Plated with iron, they mostly were to have sloping sides; as the war progressed one inventor, Uriah Brown, proposed a steamboat, with inclined sides and plated with sheet iron, which was estimated to have a speed of 5 miles an hour. The most significant development, however, came with the building of the *Demologos* by Robert Fulton for the defence of New York.

The *Demologos* was not the only project for an armoured ship that was under consideration in the United States during the war of 1812. Another was a plan for a shot proof floating battery which was submitted to Congress by Thomas Gregg in March 1814, while later that year Uriah Brown put forward his proposal, which he further developed with an idea for her to discharge liquid fire, which attracted favourable consideration. With the end of the war, however, work on this project was abandoned, and it was not until the 1840s, when war with Great Britain again seemed a possibility, that further ideas for armoured ships were put forward, including in particular a number based on the concept of vessels with inclined sides.

One of these was a revival by Uriah Brown of his 1814 project. He proposed an iron vessel 250 feet long and 60 feet wide which would be armed with a flamethrower. She was to present 'in no part of her surface an angle of more than 18 or 20° to the point-blank line of an enemy's fire,' so that she would have 'the appearance of a wedge, the acute angle of which is formed at or near the water's edge by the meeting of corresponding inclined planes, composing the sides and circular ends of the deck and lower parts of the vessel.'[3] Brown's project attracted sufficient official support for Congress to appropriate funds to test its viability, but these were exhausted after experiments with the proposed flamethrower had proved unsatisfactory.

2 Baxter, *Introduction*, pp. 7-8.
3 Baxter, *Introduction*, p. 53.

The most promising proposal, however, had been put forward by Robert L Stevens in January 1842, following a series of experiments by his brothers in the previous year which had led to the suggested construction of a fast iron screw steamer with iron armour 4-6 inches thick set at an angle of 45°. The new proposal was for a shot and shell proof steamer of at least 1,500 tons, which was to be faster than any warship then afloat, and armed with long guns adapted both to shot and to the Stevens elongated shells. The ship was to have boilers adapted to burn anthracite, and would have no rigging.

The proposal was favourably recommended by the Secretary of the Navy, and the report of the House Committee on Naval Affairs, which called for 'speedy and vigorous prosecution' of coastal defences, ensured the approval of Congress, which in April 14, 1842 authorised a contract for the building by Stevens of a steamer based on his plans. A quarter of a million dollars was appropriated for the project. However, it was not until the following February that a contract was signed for a vessel, principally of iron, that would be 'shot and shell proof against artillery now in use on board vessels of war, viz., from 18 pounders to 64 pounders; to be propelled by the submerged machinery called Stevens's circular sculls.' She was to be at least 250 feet long and 40 feet in the beam, powered by four or more condensing engines, and was to be armed with six or more large guns designed to fire shells. Stevens was given remarkable latitude over the dimensions of the vessel, with power reserved to him to vary 'the size of any and all the parts of the said war steamer or her machinery provided, however, that they shall not be made less than herein expressed.[4]'

On any view, this was much the most advanced project for an armoured warship that had been produced anywhere in the world. Progress, however, was slow, because Stevens reckoned that it was necessary first to excavate a dry dock for her construction and subsequent floating out. In November 1844 a new contract was signed, extending the date for completion of the vessel to November 1846, and fixing a price of almost $600,000. A year later, however, there was serious anxiety in the Navy Department about the progress of the project, and a suspension of work was ordered until Stevens provided a detailed plan. Work stopped, and Stevens went off to Europe for his health. In 1851 he claimed that he had in fact provided the detailed plan requested, but the project remained suspended, and in spite of the ingenuity of other inventors no further work was done for the time being on the development of armoured vessels in the United States. Admiral Ballard, in his review of Professor Baxter's book, pointed out that 'whenever iron came into the question Britain enjoyed great natural advantages; which fortunately came to the nation's aid just when the growing shortage in native oak supply was causing grave concern.'[5]

Ideas for the improvement of protection of warships exposed to enemy gunfire were never far away from the naval mind, and the advent of shellfire should certainly have concentrated that mind on the issue. With the advantage that Admiral Ballard pointed out that the use of iron might bring to Britain, it is perhaps surprising that the investigation of its potential for armouring warships was not instituted there sooner or with greater vigour. As it was, the prejudice that developed against iron warships inevitably influenced official attitudes to armour plating as a means of protection against shellfire. In December 1841 the Admiralty appointed a

4 Baxter, *Introduction*, p. 50.
5 Admiral George A Ballard, 'Some Observations on Professor Baxter's book on '*The Introduction of the Ironclad Warship*', *The Mariner's Mirror* 19.4(1933) 19.4, p. 405.

committee of master shipwrights 'to consider the best mode of strengthening ships of war and to recommend improvements, to give greater power of attack and defence, without interfering with the powers of sailing.' Symonds, after examining plans put forward, and after discussing some of these with their inventors, produced a report in January 1843, in which he was dismissive of their practicality: 'Whatever protection might be found, on experiment, to be given by any of these plans, the apparatus would occupy so much space and evolve so enormous an increase of weight, as to render the adoption of them entirely out of the question in HM's steam vessels.'[6]

Although Haddington's Board of Admiralty remained interested in iron ships as long as it remained in office, no further trials of armour plating for warships were undertaken, and after the new Board was appointed the only test firings against iron armour were designed to investigate its use in the construction of land-based fortifications. Even the shocking advice offered to Lord Auckland, the new First Lord, that a ship of the line of 84 guns, which would have cost £100,000 to build, could be destroyed by an enemy firing three broadsides of shells, failed to inspire further sustained research.[7] A few British naval officers continued to take an interest in the possibilities of armour plating, but there was for the moment no further official investigation.

On the other hand, as has been seen, France had been carrying out extensive experiments to test the resistance of iron plates to both solid shot and shell fire. These had been prompted not only to explore the suitability of iron as a shipbuilding material, but also to examine the proposals put forward in 1840 by Labrousse for the construction of a number of ironclad rams. The trials at Gavres that took place between 1843 and 1845, although inconclusive, were carefully considered by a high-powered commission, which found that sheet iron of 12 mm broke up all shells save those fired with reduced charges, and that nine sheets of 12 mm iron broke up solid 30 pounder shot. Further tests were also inconclusive, but did appear to confirm the growing doubts about the suitability of iron as a shipbuilding material.

It was in February 1845 that Dupuy de Lôme put forward his revolutionary proposal which, like that of Robert L. Stevens in America, was so far ahead of its time. Baxter justly described it as 'of the highest interest,' and went on to summarise the principal aspects of Dupuy de Lôme's proposals for armour:

> The minimum impenetrable thickness of oak, 1.8 metres, would render the whole far too heavy. In a steamer 68 metres long, and of 2,400 tons displacement, however, the weight saved by constructing the hull of iron instead of wood might be used for a belt of laminated iron armour 166 mm thick and 2.4 metres wide extending around the waterline. This reinforcement of the 11 mm skin of the ship would give far more than the necessary protection.[8]

Dupuy de Lôme claimed that fast steamers of this kind armed with a few heavy guns behind shot proof bulwarks could deal with any wooden ship and could defy land batteries.

In May 1845 he proposed a series of tests; this was refused, but later in the year a number of tests did take place, which led to a conclusion that the inclined targets tested provided no advantage in protection. The prevailing doubts about the suitability of iron as a shipbuilding material

6 Bartlett, *Sea Power*, pp. 217-218; Baxter, *Introduction*, p. 56.
7 Hamilton, *Naval Rivalry*, p. 74.
8 Baxter, *Introduction*, p. 60.

meant that his proposal was not taken further, and in 1847 the *Conseil des Travaux* decided to abandon ironclad construction altogether. None of the proposals for armoured ships received by the Ministry of Marine between 1846 and 1854 received official approval, which meant that worldwide only the Stevens design was still a current project. Revived in 1852, it still made only slow progress towards fruition. With the principal maritime nations thus dragging their heels over the introduction of armour plating for warships, it was to take a major European war to create the circumstances in which decisive progress came to be made.

8

Sinope

By the beginning of 1857 the diplomatic situation in the Near East was becoming extremely threatening. Tsar Nicholas I was pursuing a forward policy in the belief that the Ottoman Empire was on the point of final disintegration, and he intended to make sure that Russia gained the maximum advantage when this happened. He also felt certain that Britain, when it came to it, would not resort to armed force to prevent Russian expansion. Nicholas was wrong on both counts, as he was soon to learn; and it would not be with Britain alone with which he had to deal. In supporting the Turks, the newly proclaimed French emperor Napoleon III was also determined to take a strong line against Russian expansion.

For the moment, however, Napoleon was determined to confine this to diplomatic pressure. As late as November 11, 1853, Lord Cowley, the British ambassador in Paris, was still reporting confidentially to Lord Clarendon, the Foreign Secretary, that the Emperor had not become more warlike in his feelings, and that he was 'so anxious to preserve peace that he would not look very closely into any arrangement (that is, whether it would be acceptable to Turkey or not) provided he could induce the Four Powers to say to the Porte 'you shall accept it.'[1] As the situation deteriorated, Britain and France discussed cooperation, and on May 31, 1853 the British Cabinet gave Lord Stratford de Redcliffe, the ambassador in Constantinople, power to call up the Mediterranean Fleet to the Sea of Marmora if he judged it necessary. On June 2 both the British and French fleets were ordered to Besika Bay, some 190 miles from Constantinople. Vice Admiral Sir James Dundas, the commander of the Mediterranean fleet, and La Susse, his French counterpart, agreed that if it became necessary it would be the French fleet that would lead the combined force through the Dardanelles. Meanwhile the Russians took the decision to move into the Principalities of Moldavia and Wallachia; in response, the Western governments convened a conference of ambassadors in Vienna, which produced a note from the Four Powers outlining proposals to settle the crisis. Unfortunately, Turkey's acquiescence in what was put forward, which had been taken for granted, was not forthcoming. Stratford was suspected by the French of being responsible for this Turkish intransigence.

Besika Bay was not a healthy location for the fleets, and this tended to harden Anglo-French government opinion in favour of a move into the Dardanelles. Turkey, meanwhile, had declared

1 Sir Victor Wellesley and Robert Sencourt, *Conversations with Napoleon III* (London: Ernest Benn, 1934), p. 51.

war, and yet another Russo-Turkish war had begun. On October 22 the fleets began to make their way, not without difficulty due to adverse weather, up the Dardanelles, with the French steam battleship *Napoleon* leading, towing the French flagship *Ville de Paris*. On November 1 Dundas and Hamelin, the new French commander, met with Stratford and agreed to send a force of steamers into the Black Sea. The long-standing mutual suspicion that had characterised the relationship between the two nations had not disappeared; Clarendon wrote in December to Stratford remarking that 'the naval preparations of France are prodigious, there has been nothing like the present activity in their dockyards for a long time past. 80 gun screw steamers are the ships they are chiefly occupied with.'[2]

British Press and public opinion was entirely confident that the fleet was capable of asserting government policy effectively. *The Times* had smugly reported on what it saw as the overwhelming display of naval force that was presented by Queen Victoria's Spithead review of August 11, 1853. Looking back at the progress made since the ending of the Napoleonic wars, its editorial trumpeted its confidence in the power of the British navy:

> But, even in those days of effort and glory, the navy never presented a force comprising, in a comparatively small number of ships, such a union of strength and skill as may be seen in the squadron now assembled at Spithead. The structure of our vessels is largely expanded and improved; and, although many successive naval administrations have borne the not undeserved reproach of wasted expenditure and abortive experiments, we have now reached a point of excellence from which we look down on all that had been done before.[3]

The Times was distinctly overstating the case. In the autumn of 1853 Dundas was painfully aware of the limitations of his fleet, and the difficulties it faced. At the age of 68, he was still younger than many of the senior admirals of the British Navy, but he was coming to the end of his term as commander-in-chief of the Mediterranean Fleet. He was described by Captain Dewar as 'something of a martinet' but nevertheless 'an officer of sound judgment, anxious to do his utmost for the achievement of the common task.'[4] Andrew Lambert has argued that Dundas has been unfairly judged by inaccurate comparison with his second-in-command and successor, Rear Admiral Sir Edmund Lyons, noting that Dundas was able, reliable, and experienced. He had had a long and distinguished career, reaching the rank of captain as long ago as 1807 and had held various commands before entering Parliament in 1832, thereafter serving as flag captain to Admiral Sir Philip Durham as commander-in-chief at Portsmouth. In 1841 he became Fourth Naval Lord for a short spell, then later Second Naval Lord in 1846-1847 and finally Senior Naval Lord in July 1847. He went out to command the Mediterranean Fleet in 1852. He was popular and well known in the navy due to his time at the Admiralty. As a commander, he was cautious, but well understood the political implications of the tasks which he was set: 'His long experience of politics enabled him to appreciate the primacy of statecraft over strategy, a rare quality in the mid nineteenth century.'[5]

2 Andrew Lambert, *The Crimean War* (Manchester: Manchester University Press, 1990), p. 54.
3 Peter Duckers, *The Crimean War at Sea* (Barnsley: Pen and Sword, 2011), p. 158.
4 Captain A.C. Dewar and D. Bonner Smith, eds, *The Russian War, 1854, Baltic and Black Sea* (London: Navy Records Society, 1943), p. 210.
5 Lambert, *Crimean War*, p. 16.

Lyons, who was aged 63, had since 1835 been in the diplomatic service, but was recalled to the navy by Graham, and appointed as second-in-command to Dundas in late September. Lambert, while acknowledging that Lyons was popular and energetic, described him as 'a worthy if second-rate officer without the mental equipment for complex tasks,' who suffered from 'unbounded vanity.' He arrived at Constantinople aboard the steamer *Terrible,* and hoisted his flag as second-in-command aboard the *Sanspareil*, transferring to the *Agamemnon* when that ship arrived to join the fleet. Meanwhile Hamelin, who had replaced La Susse on July 11, was considered to be an abler officer than his predecessor; unlike him, he was outranked by Dundas, who was thereafter in overall command of the Allied fleet.

In the first instance, Dundas had with him the 90 gun *Britannia*, which served as his flagship, the 120 gun *Trafalgar*, the *Albion, Rodney*, *Vengeance*, and *Bellerophon* (all sailing battleships) and the 90 gun screw battleship *Sanspareil*, together with a number of steamers.

Hamelin flew his flag aboard the 120 gun sailing battleship *Ville de Paris*; the rest of his fleet comprised the screw battleships *Napoleon*, *Charlemagne* and *Bayard*, and the sailing battleships *Valmy, Montebello*, and *Jupiter*, with five steamers. The Turkish fleet consisted of three sailing three deckers, ten sailing frigates, thirty smaller sailing vessels, six new steam frigates, and twelve other steamers.[6] The total Russian fleet, divided between the Black Sea and the Baltic, consisted of sixty sailing battleships, one hundred frigates and smaller sailing vessels, and about forty paddle steamers.

In the Black Sea, once war had been declared, an immediate naval concern for Turkey was to establish a supply corridor to support her land forces in both the European and Asian theatres. Stratford de Redcliffe, with the powerful Russian naval presence at Sevastopol in mind, strongly advised against conducting any operations along the Turkish coasts.

The naval war in the Black Sea began in mid-November when the Russians despatched a squadron of two frigates, two corvettes, and four steamers to bombard the fortifications of the port of Batoum, crucial to the supply line to the Turkish army in the Caucasus. Subsequent to this, a squadron of Turkish steamers had been sent to Batoum. It was believed in Constantinople that it was safe to do this, and that notwithstanding the formal outbreak of war the Russians would make no significant aggressive moves in the Black Sea. All the same, the long coastline of Asia Minor was potentially extremely vulnerable to Russian forces operating out of Sevastopol, which were much superior to the Turkish fleet.

In spite of the views of the British ambassador, preparations to send a further squadron into the Black Sea were put in hand. Meanwhile the heavy frigate *Nasretieh* was sent to Sinope to reinforce the squadron returning from Batoum. Aboard her went Captain Adolphus Slade RN, serving in the Turkish navy with the title Mustafa Pasha; before leaving, he suggested that she should be accompanied by two sailing battleships, but this plan was not adopted. It was, however, agreed that future sorties of this kind should be composed of both battleships and frigates. Slade duly reached Sinope, where he joined the squadron from Batoum. There he found that the agreement to send battleships had been rescinded, and that Vice Admiral Osman Pasha had arrived at Sinope with a force consisting of six frigates, three corvettes, and two small steamers. Slade returned to Constantinople, leaving one ship to reinforce Osman; when he left Sinope, he was already aware that the Russians were at sea, as he reported when he got back.

6 Duckers, p. 2.

The senior Russian naval commander at Sevastopol, the popular and capable Admiral Pavel Nakhimov, had put to sea in order to interdict the Turkish supply line to the Caucasus, but in fierce storms his heavy ships were damaged and he sent them back to Sevastopol for repairs. He continued at sea with the vessels that remained to him, and when he reached Sinope on November 19 sighted Osman Pasha's squadron in harbour. Nakhimov remained off the port, sending to Sevastopol for reinforcements. His ships had been seen by the Turks, and Osman Pasha could, if he wished, have put to sea; with his much stronger force he would have been able to brush aside the small Russian squadron and safely to return to Constantinople. He chose, however, to remain anchored under the guns of the Sinope forts, which he strengthened by sending guns ashore.

Nakhimov was in due course reinforced by the bulk of the forces at Sevastopol, which arrived off Sinope under the command of Rear Admiral Novosilsky on November 27. This force consisted of six sailing battleships. Nakhimov hoisted his flag in the *Imperatritsa Maria*, 84; in addition he had the *Parizh*, 120, *Veliti Kniaz Konstantin*, 120, *Tre Sviatritelya*, 120, *Tchesma*, 84, and *Rostislav*, 84. There were two frigates, *Kulevtcha* and *Kagul*, and three steamers. The squadron was nowmassively superior to that of Osman Pasha; the Russian navy may not have matched the professional quality of Britain or France, but there could be no doubt of Nakhimov's ability to make short work of his Turkish opponents. His ships were well armed with shell guns.

Osman Pasha had with him his flagship, the *Avni Illah*, 44, and six other sailing frigates: *Nizamieh*, 62, *Nessun Zafer*, 60, *Navek Bahri*, 58, *Damiat*, 56, *Kaid Zafer*, 54 and *Fazl Illah*, 44. There were three corvettes, *Nejim Fishan*, 24, *Feyz Mabud*, 24 and *Kel Sefid*, 22, with two steamers, *Taif*, 12, and *Erkelye*, 10.

At about 12:30 pm on November 30 Nakhimov approached the Bay of Sinope in two columns before then deploying his battleships in line abreast. The Turks opened the firing, aiming high in the hope of damaging the masts and rigging of their adversaries. Nakhimov held his fire until, at close range, he opened a fierce bombardment of the Turkish line with his Paixhans shell guns, hitting these vulnerable targets repeatedly with explosive force. The Turks responded bravely, but there was little they could do against the overwhelming Russian firepower. Hit many times by the *Imperatritsa Maria*, the *Avni Illah* cut her cables and ran aground. The Russian flagship next turned her fire on the *Fazl Illah*, setting her ablaze, and she too ran ashore. In less than two hours the Turkish squadron was completely destroyed; the frigate *Navek Bahri* and the corvette *Kel Sefir* both blew up, and the remainder of the squadron was driven ashore, there subsequently to be burnt by the Russians. Only the little steamer *Taif* escaped; although pursued by the three Russian steamers, she was able to make her way to bring the catastrophic news to Constantinople, which was received with near panic. Mortally wounded, Osman Pasha had been taken prisoner, with three of his captains and 150 of his men; overall, Turkish casualties amounted to at least 3,000, some three quarters of the total number of men engaged. The Russians lost 32 men killed and 229 wounded.[7]

Sinope provided a crucial impetus to the development of the modern warship. Here was sudden and brutal confirmation of what had been predicted as the fate of a squadron of wooden warships assailed by shell guns on a large scale. The tangible proof of what this meant was all the more shocking having been delayed for so many years since Paixhans had first invented his

7 Mitchell, *Russian Sea Power*, p. 158.

shell gun, and the fiery obliteration of the Turkish squadron left little doubt where the future of warship design must lie.

The massacre of Sinope, as it soon came to be called, gave rise to immediate consideration on the part of the Western Powers as to how to respond. It was still their wish to bring about a peaceful resolution of the conflict. In Constantinople, the British and French ambassadors raised with their admirals the question of whether their fleets should navigate the Black Sea in winter. In a letter to the Secretary of the Admiralty giving his opinion, Lyons wrote: 'I said that if we should be called upon by the ambassadors to put to sea for any determinate object, whether for the purpose of defending the Ottoman Empire from attack, or for the purpose of producing a moral effect in aid of the policy of our government, I thought we should go.'[8]

Public opinion had been greatly stirred by the battle of Sinope. The First Lord wrote on December 24 to Dundas with instructions that reflected this, to the effect that the Black Sea should be immediately occupied by the Allied fleets 'to the exclusion of Russian ships of war.' It was a move which took Britain and France a long stride towards war, which Graham justified in emphatic terms: 'The attack on Sinope has produced an immense effect on the public mind both in France and England. It is difficult to put any restraint on the national desire to avenge what is regarded as a contempt and defiance of our flag.'[9]

What was certain was that Sinope had so changed the political situation that Palmerston, whose brief resignation from the Cabinet as Home Secretary ostensibly over franchise reform had taken effect just after news of the battle had been received, returned to it in a position of great moral advantage on Christmas Eve, swept back into office by the strength of public opinion. In Constantinople, however, the rift between Dundas and Stratford de Redcliffe was deepening. It was far from clear to the commander-in-chief that he should intervene with his fleet if the Russians launched an attack. As it was, the Allied fleet sailed to Sinope in January, returning after a fortnight.

Napoleon III, who had consistently resisted the suggestion of sending troops to the Near East, and who up to now had shaped all his policy towards a peaceful solution, was, significantly, beginning to change his mind. He told Cowley that, with the fleet in the Black Sea 'we might say to Russia that, as a last chance of peace, we offered to quit the Black Sea if she would evacuate the Principalities.' Otherwise, he thought, France and Britain should declare war.[10] And, after considerable further diplomatic efforts, the two countries declared war on March 27, Tsar Nicholas having made no response to an ultimatum that he evacuate the Principalities.

Meanwhile Napoleon had been the first to react to the news of Sinope and its implications for the future of naval warfare, giving instructions for the development of a design of steam powered armoured batteries. It was his conviction that the Russian fleet would not challenge the Allied command of the sea, but would remain under the protection of their shore batteries. In the first instance it was for the campaign in the Baltic that these armoured batteries were envisaged. It was apparently originally proposed that the protection of the armoured batteries might consist of boxes of cannonballs; but Thomas Lloyd, on a visit to Paris, urged the use of armour

8 Captain S Eardley-Wilmot, *Life of Vice Admiral Edmund, Lord Lyons* (London: Sampson Low Marston, 1898), pp. 133-134.
9 Eardley-Wilmot, *Lyons*, p. 135.
10 Wellesley and Sencourt, *Conversations*, p. 52.

plate, and this was adopted.[11] By May 5, Garnier, the Inspector General of Naval Construction, was able to report to the Emperor the outline proposals that had been worked out. At this stage it was thought that each of these vessels would displace about 950 tons. Tests were carried out at Vincennes to determine how best to armour them with the least weight; the Emperor made a point of attending these experiments. They appeared to demonstrate that a target faced with iron plates 10 cm thick could satisfactorily resist a number of hits, and the decision was taken to proceed with the detailed design and construction of the proposed armoured batteries.

In July 1854 the Minister of Marine placed a preliminary order for the construction of ten of these vessels. At the same time, Lord Cowley was notified of the project, and was promised copies of the detailed plans. Contracts were duly signed with iron founders for the necessary armour plate, but it soon became clear that the facilities available in France for this work were not adequate for the completion of as many as ten vessels. Accordingly, a proposal was made to the British Admiralty that five of them should be built in Britain for the Royal Navy, and on September 16 Graham agreed to this, subject to the carrying out of further tests to verify the conclusions of those tests previously undertaken. This stipulation arose from Graham's recollection of the problems that had been experienced with the iron hulled unarmoured frigates of the previous decade, and he insisted on the further tests notwithstanding the Surveyor's assurance. None of the first ten armoured batteries were iron hulled, all being wooden vessels with armour plate. The British tests were conducted at Portsmouth on September 26 and 27 and were attended by French representatives. Of ten 32 pounder solid shot that struck the four and a half inch thick armour plates at a range of 360 yards, the greatest indentation by any single round was 2 inches. At a range of 1,250 yards, two 68 pounder solid shot each cracked a plate.[12] These results were sufficiently satisfactory for orders to be placed on October 4 for five armoured batteries. In exchange, the British Admiralty supplied the French with plans for mortar vessels to be constructed in France.

The first of the French armoured batteries, the *Tonnante,* was launched at Brest on March 17, 1855, followed by the *Dévastation* at Cherbourg on April 17, the *Lave* at Lorient on May 27, the *Congreve* at Rochefort on June 1, and finally on the following day the *Foudroyant* at Lorient. Since it was anticipated that the lives of these vessels would be short, they were built of green rather than seasoned timber. Their British counterparts were launched at much the same time; the *Meteor* and *Thunder* at Blackwall on April 17, and the *Glatton* and *Trusty* at Blackwall on April 18 and May 3. The fifth ship, the *Aetna,* was destroyed by a fire in the yard at Millwall during the night of May 3/4. When completed, the batteries could not be described as beautiful. G.A. Osbon wrote:

> Never before, nor since for that matter, had vessels quite resembling their design been built for the Royal Navy. The hulls had flat bottoms, straight flat sides, sloping inboard rather like a gigantic boot box with its sides pressed in at the top, and tapered off to a point at both ends, both the stem and the stern above the waterline being vertical. Originally it was intended that they should have an armoured 'lid' over the battery, but when it was found

11 Brown, *Before the Ironclad*, p. 162.
12 Baxter, *Introduction*, p. 75; Brown, *Before the Ironclad*, pp. 162-163.

> that they would be floating too deeply, this was altered to a substantial oak deck instead. As it was they were already down to their marks before taking a gun on board.[13]

Unfortunately, a number of the defects that had been foreseen proved to be even more serious than had been supposed. The French found their batteries to be 'excessively hot and ill ventilated, hard to steer and inferior in speed to the similar British ironclads.'[14] In addition the engines were regarded as unsatisfactory, and Guieysse, one of the French naval constructors, went over to England to inspect the batteries under construction there. Following this, the French vessels were fitted with three rudders and two leeboards.

There were slight variations in the actual dimensions of each armoured battery, but they were generally about 174 feet in length and 42 feet in the beam, and displaced about 1,500 tons. The French batteries were armed with sixteen 50 pounders, and carried a crew of 280 men; the British vessels carried fourteen 68 pounders. They could barely reach a speed of 5 knots, and their minimal sailing rig was not of much use. Of the British ships, only the *Glatton* and the *Meteor* made it to the Black Sea, arriving at the end of 1855, but too late to see any action before the war came to an end.

While the process of designing and constructing the armoured batteries was under way, naval architects were provided with a further reminder of the vulnerability of wooden warships. Following the landing of the Allied army in the Crimea in September 1854, and the ensuing battle of the Alma, it was resolved to move on to Sevastopol. An assault on the city was planned, commencing with the bombardment of its fortifications. The Allied fleet was asked by Lord Raglan and General Canrobert to contribute to this by bombarding from the sea the forts protecting the harbour. It was a plan about which Dundas had the gravest reservations, but since Hamelin was disposed to agree to it, he felt it was his duty to fall in with the proposal. Lyons, on the other hand, was enthusiastically in favour of the bombardment; he was in close touch with Raglan and was influential in the commander-in-chief's thinking. An early historian of the war, Sir Edward Hamley, was sharply critical of Lyons:

> In these earlier stages of the war his rash desire to do something effective rendered him Lord Raglan's evil genius, and how rash his impulses could be was shown a little later, when he succeeded Dundas in command of the fleet, for he who now so hotly urged a naval attack, never made the slightest attempt on Sevastopol when he became responsible for such an action, and had found by experience how fruitless it would be.[15]

The plan was for the French fleet to form a line on the south side of the harbour extending to the centre of the entrance, and for the British fleet to prolong the line northwards. The sailing battleships would be towed into position by steamers. As planned, most of the British ships would be some 1,800 yards from the forts which were to be their target; the northern end of the line, though, under the command of Lyons, would take up a position only 800 yards offshore. Lyons had asked Dundas for permission to take his squadron closer in, along a channel recently

13 G.A. Osbon, 'The First of the Ironclads: The Armoured Batteries of the 1850s', *The Mariner's Mirror*, 50:3 (1964), pp. 189-190.
14 Baxter, Introduction, p. 79.
15 Eardley-Wilmot, *Lyons*, pp. 238-239.

surveyed by Captain Spratt, the Fleet Surveying Officer, and this was agreed. His squadron consisted of the screw battleships *Agamemnon* and *Sanspareil* and the sailing battleships *Albion* and *London*, with the frigate *Arethusa*. The doubts felt by Dundas had not waned, and his orders for the operation were cautious in the extreme. Even on the morning of October 17, when the bombardment was to take place, he complained to Captain Spratt, showing him the chart: 'But look at my position. I shall be exposed to the fire of the batteries which can reach me and my guns will be all out of range but the lower deck guns.'[16] Nevertheless, he allowed the action to proceed, although in little doubt as to what the harvest would be.

Apart from Lyons' squadron, therefore, the Allied fleet took up a position across the entrance to the harbour at ranges of 1,600 to 2,000 yards. The ships were unable to manoeuvre, and thus presented a stationary target for the Russian gunners in the forts. After some time, however, the volume of smoke greatly reduced the visibility. It had been intended that the naval bombardment should coincide with the artillery attack on shore, but this did not happen, because the French ships were late getting into position. As the fleets moved forward, the guns in the forts opened fire at 12:55 p.m. It was 1:20 p.m. before Hamelin, with the French and Turkish ships, opened fire, but they achieved little, at the cost of some 200 casualties of which about a quarter were killed. In this sector, the Russian gunners lost 11 men killed and 39 wounded; only six of their guns were dismounted.

Lyons, in the *Agamemnon*, opened fire at 1:55 p.m., and was at once joined by the rest of his squadron. The rest of the British ships took up their station between 2.25 p.m. and 3.20 p.m. All of Lyons' ships were heavily engaged, and soon began to suffer serious damage and casualties. The *Albion*, *London*, and *Arethusa* were obliged to haul out of line, and only the *London* was able to return to action. The *Agamemnon* and *Sanspareil*, at the head of the line, were particularly hard hit, the former being struck some 200 times and the latter 50 times. Dundas ordered the recall at 5.30 p.m. By then all of his ships had suffered damage, some of them seriously, while his fleet had lost a total of 44 men killed and 266 wounded. Only minor damage had been inflicted on the fortifications. The long held belief that, in a contest between stone fortifications and wooden warships, the former would usually prevail, had been emphatically confirmed.

16 Eardley-Wilmot, *Lyons*, p. 241.

9

Kinburn

Napoleon III was always particularly interested in artillery, and had been reflecting on the reverses suffered by the Allied fleet in the Baltic and, more particularly, before Sebastopol on October 17. The problem of attacking fortresses from the sea was one which he considered should be looked at entirely afresh. On November 16, 1854 he sent to his Minister of Marine an important letter containing a number of detailed proposals, forwarding a copy to Lord Cowley, asking that it be passed to the British Admiralty. In this letter the Emperor set out a number of observations, which he wished should be considered by a commission of experts:

> It is an acknowledged fact that ships are intended to fight against enemy ships and not against fortresses ... But when a fleet attacks fortifications, the conditions change completely. Not only is a ship inferior to a land battery, because the vessel offers a large target whereas the battery occupies a small space and is protected by battlements, but the stake is altogether different. In the case of a ship like the *Napoleon* I am risking 5 millions in money, 1,200 men, and 100 guns against an earthwork or a stone fortress, which have cost little money, and which are supplied with at most a score of guns, served by a handful of men. The chances are not equal.[1]

Napoleon went on to consider the huge costs involved in bombarding a fortress by, for example ten ships of 100 guns each and ten steam frigates each of 40 guns, comparing this to the potential damage to the enemy. It would, he thought, expose the state to huge sacrifices, for which the possible gain would be hopelessly inadequate. Instead, his idea was to 'create a besieging fleet capable of producing decisive results, and reduce for the state the possible loss of men and money.' He went on to put forward his suggested solutions, which went well beyond the concept of the armoured batteries with which he had previously been concerned:

> In accordance with my suggestions, floating batteries have already been constructed which, though they do not supply a complete protection against live munitions, are certainly a protection against spent balls, a most dangerous projectile for the navy. But that is not sufficient. I would select some ten old vessels no longer seaworthy. I would supply them

1 Wellesley and Sencourt, *Conversations*, pp. 64-65.

> with small engines of minor capacity. I would fit them with a very light mast which could be unshipped on the day of action, and cover their sides with iron plating after the manner of floating batteries. The armament of the lower battery would consist of 25 cannon of 60, that of the upper of 25 cannon of 30; 10 cannon would be held in reserve on the other deck. The weight can be balanced when moving. I would place no guns on the bridge. The armoured sides should be pierced with loopholes, behind which would be placed a score of men armed with carbines *a tige.*[2]

Instead of risking modern, expensive battleships, he would in this way 'risk much less and obtain vastly more.'

Cowley, forwarding a copy of the letter to Clarendon, found particularly gratifying 'the readiness with which his Majesty imparts plans for rendering more efficient a branch of our service, of which France might, almost without causing surprise, retain feelings of jealousy and caution.' Bearing in mind the age-old naval rivalry between France and Britain, the Emperor was certainly showing a remarkably generous spirit towards his ally. With this letter, Napoleon may be said to have emphatically established himself as one of the godfathers of the ironclad warship, and he was to go on to confirm this during the years which followed the Crimean War.

By now he was taking a continuous interest in the development of his navy, so much so that he was described by one historian as an active lobbyist in policy matters, 'even taking the part of a superior Minister of Marine by sending his own proposals for action.'[3] He was also very supportive of his actual ministers: Hamelin, when appointed later during the Crimean War after the death of Ducos, served five years in the post, as did his two successors. This enabled them to become fully conversant with the issues of their department, establishing their authority as they learned from experience. In Britain, on the other hand, governments had tended to have short periods in office, resulting in frequent changes at the head of the Admiralty.

While the armouring of warships was at the top of the list of Napoleon's priorities, his support for the extremely expensive ship building programme and the creation of an effective infrastructure to sustain the development of the navy was crucially important at a time of great technological change. It has been pointed out that the drive to create an ironclad fleet was not only especially costly, increasing the vote for construction and provisioning by over 50% between 1857 and 1860; it also drew heavily on scarce industrial and scientific resources.[4]

The most important and far-reaching of the decisions which the Emperor made was the appointment with effect from January 1 1857 of Henri Dupuy de Lôme as *Directeur de Matériel.* With Napoleon's consistent support, the results of the appointment would soon become apparent; it has been described as 'one of the outstanding dates in the history of naval architecture:'

> The man whose rules on shipbuilding had for more than a decade been the standard for French shipyards, who had submitted his first plan for a seagoing ironclad as early as 1845, now at the age of forty took the key position in the French Ministry of Marine and set his hand to the great revolution. As an English master of the craft well said: 'In boldness of

2 Wellesley and Sencourt, *Conversations*, p. 66.
3 Hamilton, *Naval Rivalry*, pp. 268-269.
4 Hamilton, *Naval Rivalry*, p. 269.

> conception and in executive skill he takes the first place among the naval constructors of our time.' [5]

Dupuy de Lôme's greatest achievements still lay ahead, however; the immediate question was whether the armoured batteries being built could justify the Emperor's hopes.

Following the taking of Sevastopol on September 8, 1855, the Allies reviewed the possibility of undertaking further operations in and around the Black Sea. A list of options was compiled; Napoleon, who had previously been of the view that the fall of Sevastopol would mark the end of the war, had been obliged to alter his opinion. Earlier in the year he had identified the fortifications of Kinburn, at the mouth of the river Dnieper, as being a suitable target. These fortifications, built on a narrow spit of land, were open to a bombardment from the sea, while they could be cut off by landing a force to the east. It would clearly have to be a combined operation with a substantial military component; this was placed under the command of General Francois Achille Bazaine. The Anglo-French fleet was led by Admirals Bruat and Lyons, the latter having now succeeded to the command of the British fleet.

An important element of the force to attack Kinburn was provided by the three French ironclad floating batteries *Dévastation*, *Lave*, and *Tonnante*. The first of these had been intended for the Baltic, but she was rerouted to the Black Sea in the wake of the other two, which in spite of their undoubted deficiencies survived a heavy storm in the Bay of Biscay before making their way across the Mediterranean to join the fleet in the Black Sea in September. A substantial force was assembled for the assault of Kinburn; six British screw battleships (*Royal Albert, Algiers, Agamemnon, Princess Royal, Hannibal*, and *St Jean d'Acre*) were joined by Bruat's four (*Montebello, Wagram, Ulm*, and *Jean Bart*). They were accompanied by seventeen frigates and sloops, the three armoured batteries, three corvettes, four dispatch boats, twenty two gunboats and eleven mortar vessels. The fleet escorted a convoy of ten transports carrying 8,000 troops. As they made their ungainly way towards their destination, the performance of the batteries has been described as 'wallowing, obstinate tows... behaving more like tea trays being dragged over a beach.'[6] The launching of the attack was delayed for several days by fog, but on October 14 the whole force sailed for Kinburn.

The principal fortification on Kinburn's long sandy spit was a quadrangular stone fort with bastions at the four angles, mounting 50 guns, some in casemates and some in barbettes. There were also two sand batteries, mounting 10 and 11 guns, towards the tip of the promontory. The total garrison was 1,500 men, commanded by General Kokonovitch. The Allies resolved to launch an attack on both sides of the spit, and on the night of October 14/15 five English and four French gunboats entered the Dnieper and took up a position on the landward side of the fortifications. Next day, Bazaine led his troops ashore some three miles to the east of the fortress, cutting Kokonovitch's line of retreat.

Due to bad weather, it was not until the morning of October 17 that the fleet was able to move into position. During the night three buoys had been placed to guide the armoured batteries into the position which they were to take up; it was intended that they should move to within 600 metres of the shore, though in the event they anchored, at between 8.45 a.m. and 9:30

5 Baxter, *Introduction*, p. 97. Baxter is quoting Nathaniel Barnaby.
6 Osbon, 'First of the Ironclads', p. 190.

a.m., at a range of between 850 and 1,150 metres. The *Dévastation* was the first to open fire, at 9:06 a.m., and was soon joined by the others. They were supported by the mortar vessels and gunboats. As they moved into position, one observer described them as 'great square looking iron boxes … crawling up slowly against the largest fort.'[7]

At 12.30 p.m. *Princess Royal* took up a position some 650 yards from the centre battery and opened fire. She was followed by the remaining battleships which steadily increased the intensity of the bombardment; *Agamemnon*, for instance, fired some 500 rounds in three quarters of an hour. By 2:10 p.m. it was clear that the fort had been reduced to silence and a ceasefire was ordered. A flag of truce was sent in, and Kokonovitch, left with no alternative, agreed to capitulate.[8]

During the course of their bombardment, the ironclad batteries had fired 3,177 shot and shell. They had hit their target with remarkable accuracy, setting the fort on fire, silencing most of its guns, and smashing down its walls in several places. By the time the battleships opened fire, the engagement was already as good as over. It was, though, the extent to which they had stood up to the enemy fire that was the crucial test by which the armoured batteries would be judged:

> It was on the *Dévastation* that the Russian 24 pounders concentrated their heaviest fire. Twenty nine shot rattled off her four-inch armour and thirty five ploughed furrows in her deck of heavy oak. One shell, however, entered the battery through the imperfectly protected main hatch, and two more through the ports, killing two men and wounding thirteen others. The *Lave* suffered no casualties and no injuries to her plates; but fragments of two shot which entered the ports of the *Tonnante* wounded nine men. Of sixty six shot which struck the latter, fifty five slightly dented the plates, ten swept the deck, and one cut the main piece of the starboard rudder.[9]

Admiral Bruat was warm in his praise of the performance of the floating batteries, reporting to the Emperor: 'On peut tout attendre de l'emploi de ces formidables machines de guerre.' While they had only been exposed to 24 pounders, and it was a matter of presumption as to how they would stand up to heavier shot, it seemed evident that they could not be seriously harmed by 30 pounder shot at a range of up to 1,200 metres.

Lyons reported on the performance of the ironclads to the Senior Naval Lord at the Admiralty, Sir Maurice Berkely. Having been initially sceptical about their usefulness, he wrote in October 20:

> The French floating batteries have gained golden opinions here by the effect produced by their fire on the ramparts as well as by the little or no effect made upon them by the fire from the fort. They may not have contributed so much to the fall of the place as the mortar vessels and the gun vessels, nor can it be denied that the *coup de grâce* was given by the ships of the line, but it is nevertheless certain that in two or three hours more firing they would have brought the walls down by the lump and the whole sea face would have been

7 Duckers, *Crimean War at Sea*, p. 139.
8 Lambert, *Crimean War*, p. 259.
9 Baxter, *Introduction*, p. 84.

> accessible, whilst the only effect upon them was the appearance of a few rust like marks where the shot struck and bounced off.

He was amused at the way in which Admiral Bruat talked up their performance in an effort to please the Emperor, whose brain children they were, but he was clear that ironclads had come to stay, observing: 'Still you may take it for granted that floating batteries have become elements in amphibious warfare, so the sooner you set about having as many good ones as the French the better it will be for you.'[10]

Another observer, the young Lieutenant George Tryon, wrote that 'the palm and honour of this late attack belongs to the French floating batteries.' Lyons' flag captain, Meads, was particularly impressed with their success, writing in his diary on the day after the battle that they had been 'perfect;' shells, he observed, 'broke against them like glass.' Rear Admiral Sir Houston Stewart, who was Lyons' second-in-command, and who had observed the batteries at close quarters, was equally enthusiastic, and saw another possible use for them after Kinburn: 'they will be admirable for assisting the ascent of the Bug to Nikolaev – and in every conceivable case of assault and battery they must be formidable and valuable.'[11]

On the other hand, Andrew Lambert reckoned that later historians had failed to recognise that much of the favourable comment made was intended to please Napoleon III. However, while a desire to promote the success of the batteries for the Emperor's benefit might have contributed to Bruat's enthusiasm, this was hardly true of the reactions of Lyons and other British officers who had been able to see for themselves their considerable potential. The introduction of the armoured batteries had been an undoubted success and their place in naval history is assured, since the performance at Kinburn confirmed Napoleon in his intention of taking the next crucial steps in the development of the armoured warship. Symbolically it was indeed the start of a new era.

News of the success achieved by the armoured batteries at Kinburn prompted immediate action on the part of the British Admiralty. In November, a wooden hulled replacement for the *Aetna* was ordered from Chatham Dockyard. She was to displace 1,580 tons, to carry sixteen 68 pounders, and to be powered by machinery delivering 200 hp. She was launched on April 5, 1856, but with the war having ended was never completed for sea, and was passed straight into reserve. Meanwhile, in December 1855 the Admiralty took a further step forward, ordering three more armoured batteries from private contractors. These were *Erebus*, *Terror* and *Thunderbolt*. Iron hulled vessels, they were 186 feet long and 48 ½ feet in the beam. Their machinery was to deliver 200 hp, and their armament was also to consist of sixteen 68 pounders:

> While their measurements closely resembled the previous *Aetna*, the marked tumble home was an important difference in their appearance, the total width of the upper deck being only 35feet three inches … After arrival from their builders no attempt was made to fit them out for service, in fact only the *Terror* was to feel blue water beneath her keel on a one-way voyage to Bermuda.[12]

10 Eardley-Wilmot, *Lyons*, pp. 368-369.
11 Lambert, *Crimean War*, p. 260.
12 Osbon, 'First of the Ironclads', p. 196.

The *Terror* was launched on April 18, 1856, and was the only one of her class to be commissioned. Her posting to Bermuda was to serve as a base and receiving ship there. Originally painted black like her sisters, a white strake was subsequently added. Although all of them were condemned for their ugliness, a photograph of the *Terror* later in her career while serving at Bermuda suggests that in this respect she has been unfairly criticised; she presents a perfectly satisfactory appearance. Even if she was never required to do anything much, she was the first iron hulled armoured ship to be launched; she survived until going to the breakers in 1901, and she does, therefore, have a place in naval history.

The speed with which the Admiralty placed these orders following Kinburn seems an adequate answer to the criticism made by Captain Eardley-Wilmot in his biography of Lyons, in which he wrote of the battle:

> As is well known our naval authorities failed to discern the important bearing of this incident, that if ships so constructed could withstand heavy shellfire from a fort, they would equally be protected if these projectiles were fired from another ship, and that the day of unprotected wooden ships was past from that hour. They continued placidly to go on building the latter.[13]

He went on to compare this with the policy of the French in seeking to develop a seagoing ironclad.

The French naval constructor sent to examine the *Erebus* was unimpressed with the fact that her four inch wrought iron armour was backed by only five or six inches of oak, compared to the backing for the wooden hulled vessels, four times as thick: 'This type of backing was so little suited to withstand hammering by solid shot that, before an action had long continued, the plates would be damaged, the rivets started, and the battery leaking.'[14]

There was now no shortage of ideas for the future development of the ironclad. During the course of the Crimean War the British Admiralty received seventy three proposals for armoured vessels of all kinds, and the French Ministry of Marine received twenty three. None of them were adopted. Baxter suggested that among them all only two were to have any influence on the future design of the ironclad. These were the concept put forward by Captain Cowper Coles, working on his ideas for a battleship turret; and J. Scott Russell, whose proposal was to have some effect in due course on the design of the *Warrior*.[15]

Admiral Ballard made the point that the ironclad warship, as developed in the form of the French floating battery, was introduced not to fight for command of the sea, but only for coastal operation. As such, she lacked many of the vital attributes of either a true battleship or true cruiser: 'Her shape was merely that of an exaggerated armed lighter or gun brig; incapable of self movement except at a crawl for very short distances.'[16] He felt that Professor Baxter had failed to emphasise this and had not sufficiently explained that for some time the responsible authorities focused their attention on coastal operations rather than fleet actions.

13 Eardley-Wilmot, *Lyons*, p. 369.
14 Baxter, *Introduction*, p. 90.
15 Baxter, *Introductions*, pp. 87-88.
16 Ballard, *Observations*, p. 409.

Nevertheless, the concept of larger, seagoing ironclads had come to stay; this was the principal lesson to be learned from the events of the Crimean War, and it was inevitable that warship designers should move on to the development of armoured vessels whose objective would be to win command of the sea. The Italian artillerist Giovanni Cavalli was one of the first to apply this lesson, proposing an iron hulled ironclad of 1,600 tons, carrying 24 guns, with inclined sides, 'a sort of corrugated iron armour, and sufficient strength to permit use as a ram.' He argued that the creation of larger ironclads had become inevitable by reason of technological improvements. It was to be in France that this prophecy became a reality, when Napoleon III and Henri Dupuy de Lôme would make the crucial breakthrough in warship design.

10

Gloire

The movement of naval opinion towards the concept of the seagoing ironclad had begun even before the action at Kinburn. On his way to the Black Sea, Captain de Montaignac, the captain of the *Dévastation*, had written a report predicting the feasibility of armoured seagoing frigates. After Kinburn, and following the end of the war, the French Ministry of Marine received a large number of proposals for the construction of seagoing ironclads. In its consideration of these, however, the *Conseil des Travaux* showed in its first reaction that its collective mind was entirely focused on the operations in the Black Sea and the immediate lessons to be learned from them. It concluded that 'the new ships must be considered from three points of view: coastal defence, cruising warfare, and attack on the enemy's coast.'[1] In making this response it had lost sight of the primary purpose of a battle fleet, which as Admiral Ballard pointed out was to obtain command of the sea:

> It never occurred to them that fleets which are powerful enough to force the enemy to retire to his own harbours and remain there are already defending their own coasts in the surest way possible, though that was precisely the great lesson of the war. The shores of Britain and France never heard the sound of a Russian gun, just because the shores of Russia heard the Franco-British gunfire night and day.[2]

The *Conseil des Travaux* did not approve any of the suggestions for ironclad construction which they received before the end of 1856, insisting that further studies must be made of the best means of fitting the armour to a ship's hull, but it did consider some general principles on which designs should be based. These included a requirement that the minimum speed for the vessel should be 13 knots, a provision that she should have armour at least 10 cm thick, extending 1.5 m below the waterline, have gun ports at least 2 m above the surface of the sea, be rigged as a corvette for cruising, and have the screw protected. These requirements indicated a substantial increase in size from many of the earliest designs. The largest plan considered in 1856 was that of naval constructor de Ferranty, who proposed a frigate of 4,000 tons, and even this was considered to be too small.

1 Baxter, *Introduction*, p. 93.
2 Ballard, *Observations*, p. 410.

The discussions of the *Conseil des Travaux* took place against the background of a huge planned expansion of the French steam navy, put forward by the *Commission Supreme Centrale* under the presidency of Vice Admiral Parseval-Deschênes, who had been the French commander in the Baltic. As early as August 1855 it had been proposed that there should be a fleet of forty fast wooden steam battleships, with twenty frigates, thirty corvettes, sixty despatch vessels, and a steam ram, as well as transports capable of carrying an expeditionary force of up to 40,000 men. The proposition that wood was no longer to be considered as the most suitable shipbuilding material had not then taken hold; but eighteen months later there was a total reversal in French naval thinking, when the *Conseil des Travaux* proposed that all work on wooden ships should cease immediately. The revolution in design was almost complete, and derived from the practical experiences of the Allied fleets in the Black Sea and the Baltic in 1854 and 1855, as Admiral Hamelin observed in 1857: 'If war had not broken out in 1854, one would perhaps still be discussing today the utility of the sailing Navy compared to a steam Navy … The hostilities were hardly declared when already the opinion of a few became the opinion of the majority.'[3]

By then the programme of August 1855 was already under comprehensive review by a new commission appointed in November 1856. The Emperor was coming to the conclusion that the previous plan was altogether too conservative. One of the members of the new commission was Dupuy de Lôme, and his influence on the thinking of his colleagues was of crucial significance. He saw more clearly than anyone else that this must be the way forward; he set out the vision which inspired him in a paper which he wrote 10 years later:

> He wrote that iron armour was a means to equal the Royal Navy: invulnerability, coupled with great speed, meant that one did not need to fear inferior numbers. And since armoured raiders could not be destroyed, the nation with the most to fear from naval war, he added pointedly, was the one with the greatest seaborne trade. Armour, in short, further satisfied the tactical and strategical principles that lay behind the *vaisseau à vapeur.*[4]

Dupuy de Lôme took up his post as *Directeur de Matériel* on January 1, 1857; Napoleon III further reinforced his position and his influence by appointing him also as *Directeur des Constructions Navales*, which meant that he was now directly responsible to Hamelin, as Minister, for the design, construction and repair of France's battle fleet. The Emperor was taking a close interest in the development of the fleet and the plans for seagoing ironclads, and he put forward his own proposals for reducing the weight of the necessary armour plates, suggesting several variations of corrugated and grooved plates of his own design, which were tested at Vincennes in the autumn of 1857; however, their stopping power proved to be less than ordinary armour plate. Other designs of armour were also tested, and the Vincennes commission arrived at the conclusion that plates manufactured by the La Chaussade works for Fourchambaultt were the best that had yet been evolved.

The accelerating process of change in ship design was reinforced by a programme of tests of rifled guns at Lorient. This demonstrated the vulnerability of wooden targets, and indicated that such weapons would prove a serious threat to the unarmoured wooden battleship. The coming of

3 Hamilton, *Naval Rivalry*, p. 85.
4 Hamilton, *Naval Rivalry*, p. 87.

rifled guns now finally validated the original prediction of Henri Paixhans, and this was a major component in the thinking of the *Conseil des Travaux* when it made its recommendation that all work on wooden warships should be halted.

Although the first reaction of those in authority may have been to concentrate on the priority of coastal operations, Dupuy de Lôme saw clearly beyond this. In the account which he wrote in 1866 of his thinking, as he prepared to take up his new post, and had joined the new commission, he explained that he had by then concluded that the real lesson to be drawn from Kinburn was the need to create a seagoing fleet of ironclads:

> He had already conceived the plan of a fast seagoing frigate sufficiently armoured to withstand at close range the heaviest guns afloat. Arguing that the substitution of these ironclad frigates in place of the fast wooden ships of the line in the program proposed by the commission of 1855 would constitute an advance of the French navy in the direction of a balance of power at sea, he persuaded his colleagues to leave room, in their report on the transformation of the fleet, for the possible substitution of these ironclads as units equivalent to the ships provided by the 1855 program.[5]

Now that he had assumed a position in the hierarchy of the French navy that enabled him to put into effect his beliefs, Dupuy de Lôme began work on his design for the vessel that became the *Gloire*. Contrary to the widespread belief in England at that time that she was 'merely a wooden warship that had been razeed, armoured and renamed,' this was an entirely original and ground-breaking design. The *Gloire* was to be a frigate of 5,620 tons, which was 500 tons more than the displacement of the *Napoleon*. Of the same beam and draft as her successful predecessor, she was 20 feet longer; with her machinery designed to produce the same horsepower, her greater length and finer lines enabled her, notwithstanding the weight of her armour, to achieve a similar speed. She was intended to carry thirty six 6.4 inch rifled muzzle loaders. Admiral Ballard, when considering the design of the *Gloire*, concluded that it marked what he saw as 'the great dividing line between French and British naval architects. The former thought of warfare in sight of land, the latter of the open oceans; and what a profundity of difference lay there!'[6] This, though, was being scarcely fair to Dupuy de Lôme; he was building a battle fleet that would be capable of meeting the British navy in battle, and in the *Gloire* he created a vessel that was a better sea boat than her unarmoured predecessors. He recognised, though, that such a conflict would probably take place in European waters.

Designating the *Gloire* as a frigate was intended to distinguish her from the steam battleships that had preceded her; and the same term would be used by the British to describe the *Warrior*. It represented a further variant of the meaning of the word. By the time of the Napoleonic Wars, the British navy possessed about 150 frigates, which had gradually increased in size to a point where they carried 44 guns. They were, however, frequently the subject of experimentation, since there was a reluctance to tinker with the basic design of the ship of the line which had served the navy so well. It was not only the *Gloire* and the *Warrior* that would be so described;

5 Baxter, *Introduction*, p. 98.
6 Ballard, *Observations*, p. 411.

the same term would be used, for instance, to designate the *Erzherzog Ferdinand Max*, which would carry Tegetthoff's flag at the battle of Lissa.

The *Gloire* was to have a wooden hull. It was originally intended that her armour should consist of plates in three layers, but the continuing series of tests at Vincennes led to the adoption of single plates 11 cm thick for the eight upper strakes and 12 cm thick for the five lower strakes. Her overall design raised a number of problems of transverse strength, which Dupuy de Lôme dealt with by inserting a layer of sheet iron under the wooden upper deck, securely fastened to the vessel's sides; her increased weight, and lower height, meant that he also had to address her lower centre of gravity compared with that of unarmoured ships. The design received the approval of the Ministry of Marine, and on March 4, 1858 Hamelin signed an order, which had been drafted by Dupuy de Lôme, for the laying down of three ironclads, two at Toulon and one at Lorient. Dupuy de Lôme followed this up with a report to Hamelin on April 16 which demonstrated his open-mindedness; looking beyond the first three ironclads, he recommended that consideration should be given to more than one type:

> Any project that met the three tests of sufficient impenetrability, sufficient strength for use as a ram, and speed and radius of action equal to the *Napoleon*, deserved serious consideration. He proposed that his plan for wooden hulled ironclads, already adopted for the *Gloire* and *Invincible*, which were to be built at Toulon, should not serve for all of the armoured vessels to be laid down in 1858, but the ideas of other constructors be tested. He therefore suggested that Audenet's plans for an iron hulled armoured vessel should, if approved by the Conseil des Travaux, serve for the ironclad to be laid down at Lorient.[7]

On September 1 the plan put forward by Camille Audenet for the *Couronne*, as she was to be called, was adopted; she was to be of 6,114 tons with machinery producing 900 hp, with armour of 10 cm plates, backed by 10 cm of teak; her stem was to be strengthened for ramming.

The French ironclad programme was gathering speed; on September 3 Hamelin signed an order for a fourth ironclad, to be named *Normandie*, to be laid down at Cherbourg, intended to be a sister ship of the *Gloire*. In the following month Dupuy de Lôme put forward a proposal for four more ironclads to be laid down in 1859, which replaced the wooden screw battleships that had originally been planned. Now, at last, the recommendation of the *Conseil des Travaux* was put into practice; no wooden warships larger than a traditional frigate were ordered. Dupuy de Lôme continued his policy of seeking ideas from the widest possible spectrum, and called for proposals for ironclads from all French naval constructors; he required only that their designs should provide for a minimum speed of 12.25 knots, and should allow for generous supplies of coal, food, and water. The Emperor remained in close touch with the Ministry of Marine, continuing to put forward his own suggestions for the form of armour plating to be adopted.

Andrew Lambert has suggested that the impetus behind the French decision to build the *Gloire* was more complex than merely a recognition of the new power of rifled artillery, arguing that it derived from the failure to build a wooden steam battle fleet to match that of Britain. In continuing the naval race by developing the ironclad, the French did so, he wrote, 'mainly to preserve the brilliant position secured at the Peace of Paris in 1856. French naval opinion

7 Baxter, *Introduction*, p. 100.

now favoured the ironclad, and it was the development of this novel weapon that was chosen as a means of obtaining parity with Britain.'[8] In his view, though, the policy was ultimately disastrous because of Britain's massive advantage in iron shipbuilding experience and industrial resources. For the moment, however, the boldness of Francis ironclad construction programme put ahead of her British rival.

In creating the *Gloire*, Dupuy de Lôme had produced a vessel that certainly justified Admiral Ballard's comment that 'she was beyond the slightest doubt immensely more formidable as a war machine than anything afloat when launched; and realising this Napoleon III made a determined bid for the trident by ordering more of her kind forthwith in such numbers to make England gasp.'[9]

The *Gloire* was launched on November 24, 1859; she was commissioned a month later while still incomplete. In the following year she ran preliminary trials in June and her official trials in August. She was criticised for rolling more than would have been the case of a wooden battleship in calm seas, and also for the low height of her battery above sea level, but apart from these faults she was hailed as a masterpiece. She escorted the Imperial yacht when Napoleon III visited Algiers in September 1860, and on the return trip behaved admirably during a severe storm. On the basis of this performance Dupuy de Lôme estimated that the 675 tons of coal which she carried would enable her to steam for 27 days at 8 knots, 14 days at 11 knots, or 7 days at full speed. He declared 'that in steaming and nautical qualities she equalled or surpassed the best steamships of the line afloat.' She was originally given a barquentine rig, but this was changed to a full ship rig during the following winter. Later, together with all the other French ironclads she was rerigged as a barque. In 1863, after a series of comparative trials, she was re-equipped with 34 breech loading rifles. During her trials, the *Gloire* attained a speed of 12.3 knots. She carried a crew of 570 men. All in all, Dupuy de Lôme had every reason to feel extremely proud of her.[10]

The *Gloire's* sister *Invincible*, also built at Toulon, spent much longer on the building slip; her keel had been laid at the same time as that of the *Gloire*, on May 5, 1858, but it was not until April 1861 that she was finally launched. She was provisionally commissioned two days later, but it was only in March 1862 that she officially joined the fleet. The third ship of the class, *Normandie*, was launched at Cherbourg in March 1860, was provisionally commissioned in July, and officially entered service in May 1862. When she finally joined the fleet she brought the total of French ironclads to four, the iron hulled *Couronne*, built at Lorient, having been launched on March 20 1861, provisionally commissioned in October and finally commissioned in February 1862. On her trials the *Couronne* reached a speed of 12.6 knots. She was initially equipped with ten 50 pounder and thirty 6.4 inch muzzleloaders, later changed for rifled shell guns. She was slightly larger than the ships of the *Gloire* class.

Hamelin's original programme had envisaged the laying down of four ironclads during 1859. This led to lengthy consideration of a plan put forward by Picot de Moras, which Dupuy de Lôme suggested should be adopted for one of the four, while the remainder were built to a plan of his own. Picot proposed a two decker carrying 56 guns, with engines of 1,200 hp to produce

8 Lambert, *Battleships*, p. 101.
9 Ballard, *Observations*, p. 411.
10 Raf Winfield and Stephen S Roberts, *French Warships in the Age of Sail 1786–1861* (Barnsley: Seaforth Publishing, 2015), p. 420.

a speed of 13.5 knots. She was to have a removable ram. Dupuy de Lôme thought that this design was very good, but the *Conseil des Travaux* was dubious on account of the vessel's size (just under 300 feet long and 58 feet in the beam) and also the removable ram. There followed a series of negotiations with the designer, but these ultimately led to Picot's design being rejected. Following this, Hamelin decided that ironclad construction to be commenced during 1859 should be limited to two vessels, to be built to Dupuy de Lôme's new design.

This was based on his firm conviction that the French ironclads must be designed to ensure that they were able to attain the highest speed possible. For the new ships, he proposed that they should carry more guns, have a higher speed and a greater range than their predecessors. They were to be of 6,724 tons, with a length of 282 feet and a breadth of 57 feet, and were designed to carry an armament of fifty two rifled 30 pounders. Their machinery, of 1,000 hp, was intended to produce a speed of 14 knots. The armour, at 12 cm thick on wooden backing of 67 cm, would extend from end to end at the waterline and orlop deck, but above this was limited to a midships section. The guns were concentrated behind the armour on the main and upper decks, and were also protected by shockproof transverse bulkheads. This design put half the guns at an increased elevation, and kept down the weight at bow and stern. A conical ram was fitted; many of the designs which had been received from French naval constructors since 1856 had included the provision of a ram, and although rejected, these may have influenced Dupuy de Lôme in his latest design.[11]

The two ships of the 1859 programme, named *Magenta* and *Solferino*, were laid down in June, and launched two years later. They were both commissioned in 1862. As with all the French ironclads, their armament underwent a series of changes. Due to the rapid technological advances in naval artillery, which greatly increased the effectiveness of the latest guns, the extensive armament of this class was, by the end of the 1860s reduced to ten 9.6 inch muzzle loading rifles, and ten 6.2 inch, all in the upper battery, the lower battery being left vacant.

The voyage to Algiers and back in 1860, which had given Napoleon III the chance to observe the *Gloire* at first hand, had left him extremely impressed with her performance, and on his return he gave instructions for a major acceleration in the building of ironclads. It was in response to this that Dupuy de Lôme produced a report which Professor Baxter described as being 'of capital importance in naval history:'

> In view of the great success of the *Gloire*, and of the obvious superiority of armoured frigates to the largest wooden warships, he remarked that France might congratulate herself on having laid down no ship of the line since 1855. Now the way was clear for a great ironclad program. To her six seagoing and nine coast defence ironclads built or building, France must add twenty seagoing ironclads for the active fleet, ten for the reserve, and eleven armoured floating batteries. Since the national finances and the capacity of the shipyards did not permit undertaking all these ships simultaneously, he proposed that ten seagoing ironclads, nine with wooden hulls and one of iron, should be laid down at once and pushed on to completion within 18 months, and that eleven armoured floating batteries should be undertaken simultaneously.[12]

11 Winfield and Roberts, *French Warships*, pp 421-422
12 Baxter, *Introduction*, pp. 111-112.

Italian Ironclad *Varese*, the sister ship of *Palestro*, the latter of which blew up during the battle of Lissa.

Italian Captain Augosto Riboty, commander of the *Re di Portogallo.*

Italian Captain Simone Pacoret di Saint-Bon, commander of the *Formidabile*.

Admiral Carlo
Pellion di Persano.

Italian Ironclad *Formidabile.*

Austrian Ironclad *Erzherzog Ferdinand Maximilian*, flagship of Admiral Tegetthoff.

Italian Ironclad *Re d'Italia*, original flagship of Admiral Persano.

Italian Ironclad *Ancona.*

Austrian wooden ship of the line *Kaiser*, following the battle.

Italian turret Ironclad *Affondatore*, subsequently flagship of Admiral Persano.

Italian Ironclad *Castelfidardo.*

Italian despatch vessel *Messaggiere.*

Warrior, Britain's first Ironclad.

The Italian fleet anchored in the harbour at Ancona.

The Austrian Armoured Corvette, or Frigate, *Drache*.

Austrian Casemate Ironclad *Habsburg*.

Austrian Commodore Anton von Petz.

Austrian Captain Maximilian von Sterneck, commander of the *Erzherzog Ferdinand Maximilian.*

Rear-Admiral Wilhelm von Tegetthoff.

With the enthusiastic support of the Emperor behind him, Hamelin at once approved Dupuy de Lôme's proposals. With so many ironclads to be built simultaneously, there was a vigorous debate among naval constructors as to a number of important design aspects of the new vessels; there was a determination to avoid making mistakes that would be repeated tenfold. The height of the gun battery above water level, the best type of armoured conning tower, the size of the gun ports and the most appropriate sailing rig were among the issues discussed. The Emperor himself took a hand in the debate; after having received a good deal of advice, he fixed the height of the battery above water at 2 metres. The question of the armoured conning tower was gone into with particular care. Aboard the *Gloire*, it took the form of an unroofed two-storey construction about twelve feet high, located just forward of the mizzen mast, protected by four-inch armour plate. Subsequently, the conning tower as fitted was roofed, and relocated just abaft the funnel. Since none of the ironclads ever saw action, the efficacy of these conning towers was never tested in battle, though it is worth remarking that half a century later many commanders declined to make use of them in action.

Dupuy de Lôme wasted no time in drawing up plans for the ten new ironclads. Though based generally on the design of the *Gloire*, they were in effect an entirely new class. They were to be of 5,800 tons, and have machinery producing 1,000 hp. His design was adopted for all the new vessels, for which orders were placed on November 16, 1860. Three ships, *Gauloise*, *Magnanime*, and *Valeureuse* were to be built at Brest; three more. *Provence*, *Savoie*, and *Revanche*, were assigned to Toulon. *Flandre* was to be built at Cherbourg, *Guyenne* at Rochefort, and *Surveillante* and *Heroine* at Lorient. It was the last of these that was to be the only iron hulled vessel of her class; Dupuy de Lôme was realistic about the fact that the French iron industry had neither the facilities nor the skilled workforce to build more, which the *Conseil des Travaux* would greatly have preferred. However, it was found possible for the armoured floating batteries to be iron hulled, although in the event only seven of these were laid down. In an effort to raise the level of expertise among French shipbuilders in the construction of iron hulled warships, no less than eight naval constructors were sent to Britain between 1857 and 1861 to study British methods.

The *Heroine* was laid down at Lorient on the slip vacated by the *Couronne* on June 10, 1861, and was launched on December 10, 1863. Provisionally commissioned in April 1864, she formally joined the fleet on June 7, 1865. She was of 5,969 tons, was 262 feet long and 56 feet in the beam. On her trials, she attained a speed of just over 13 knots. Her armour at the waterline was 15 cm thick on 38 cm wood backing on 2cm hull plating. The battery was protected by 11 cm armour plate. Her armament consisted of four 9.6 inch seven 6.4 inch and six 6.2 inch muzzle loading rifles[13].

With the large number of wooden steam battleships which the French navy possessed, and which were being reduced to immediate obsolescence by the *Gloire* and her successors, consideration was given to the possibility of doing something with them. One interesting project involved the largest sailing warship in the navy, the 120 gun *Valmy*. In 1856 a plan for converting her to steam was considered, and three years later an ambitious plan for converting her to an ironclad was put forward at Brest. This involved removing two of her decks, and arming her with twenty

13 Winfield and Roberts, *French Warships*, p. 424.

50 pounders, sixteen 6.2 inch rifles and eight 30 pounder carronades. Planned armour plating would be 12 cm thick. In the event, however, the scheme was abandoned.

Napoleon III had, in the programme of ironclad development which he sponsored, played an enormously significant role in the introduction of the armoured warship. He was fortunate in finding, in Dupuy de Lôme, a man with the vision and determination to carry his programme into effect, and he supported him all the way. Dupuy de Lôme was justly rewarded for his endeavours, becoming a grand officer of the Legion d'Honneur, and a councillor of state, and in 1866 was elected a member of the Academy of Sciences. He served as a deputy from 1869 to 1875, and in 1877 was elected a senator for life. He died in 1885; it is pleasant to record that his achievements have been recognised by the French navy, which has named a number of warships after him.

11

Warrior

Towards the end of the 1850s, a number of factors combined to intensify the naval rivalry between Britain and France. C.I. Hamilton has described how at this time it had become an almost permanent feature of the relationship between the two countries: 'It appears that the navies of Britain and France were woven into a bipolar relationship of a particular concentration and simplicity, involving a rivalry – and a concomitant naval race – that can well be described as self-sustaining.'[1] Of course there were plenty of other aspects of the Franco-British relationship that tended towards mutual suspicion, not least the centuries-old history of actual conflict. By the middle of the nineteenth century a much larger part of each population was aware of and interested in international politics, due to a far more developed popular Press which easily aroused national feeling: this could and did lead to a rapidly developing concern about potential threats. And for Britain and France, and especially their navies, it was only the other that consistently represented a serious source of danger.

Thus it was that when at the end of February 1858 a new Tory administration took office, it almost immediately encountered a rising wave of public concern about the increasing strength of the French navy and the feeling that something needed to be done about it. This was largely due to the French programme of converting their wooden sailing battle fleet to steam as quickly as possible. This had been, for those at the head of the French navy, the answer to the lessons to be learned from the Crimean War, albeit one that was to have, as it turned out, only a short-term relevance to naval planning. Although with the benefit of hindsight the anxiety felt in Britain may be seen to have been overdone, the speed at which French sailing battleships were being converted to steam certainly narrowed the gap between the two navies to a point at which professional concern had some basis in reality. And, in the early stages of their ironclad programme, the French had a decided advantage.

Newly in office as First Lord, Sir John Pakington, with the evident encouragement of Queen Victoria, was soon addressing what he saw as a potentially serious crisis in the relative strength of the British and French navies. In March, he produced a memorandum on the state of the navy, in which he arrived at an unfavourable conclusion:

1 Hamilton, *Naval Rivalry*, p. 273.

> The general result of the comparison, excluding altogether our old and comparatively useless blockships is that, either afloat or building: England has 42 [line of battle] ships with 4,005 guns and 23,750 hp. France has 37 ships with 3,412 guns and 26,150 hp … Considering the immense importance to England of maintaining her naval superiority this comparison, especially of the ships immediately available, cannot be considered entirely satisfactory[2].

He first circulated a copy of this report to the Cabinet, and then sent a copy to the Queen. She and the Prince Consort were profoundly disturbed by the report, and she called for more information. She emphasised the form that such information should take:

> This investigation and thorough consideration the Queen expects from her Board of Admiralty, chosen with great care and composed of the most complete naval authorities. She does not wish for the opinion of this or that person, given without any responsibility attaching to it, nor for yet more returns prepared in the office for the First Lord, but for the collective opinion of Sir John Pakington and his Board with the responsibility attaching to such opinion, given to the Sovereign upon a subject upon which the safety of the empire depends.[3]

Among the junior naval members of the Board, it was Rear Admiral Alexander Milne who responded first, and most comprehensively, to the memorandum which the First Lord circulated. It appears that he wrote his paper as soon as the Queen's request for more information had been received, and that his paper was then circulated to the rest of the Board with a request that each member produce his own paper on the subjects covered. Milne has been described by Professor John Beeler, the editor of his papers, as 'the pre-eminent naval administrator in the Victorian period,' and he exerted considerable influence both as a member of the Board and later as commander-in-chief of the North America and West Indies Station during the crucial years of the American Civil War. He had entered the Navy in 1817, passing for lieutenant in 1823 and being promoted to commander in 1828. He was made post captain in 1839, and thereafter served as flag captain, first to his father Admiral Sir David Milne and later to Admiral Sir Charles Ogle. In December 1847 he became a junior naval Lord of the Admiralty, and served there during five successive political administrations.

In his 'Memorandum on the State of the Navy' which was dated April-May 1858, he dealt with each of the specific questions raised by the Queen. He remarked that 'the change of system in the Naval Service caused by the introduction of screw propulsion, has no doubt been detrimental to the interests of Great Britain, as it has enabled France to commence a new steam fleet, nearly on equal terms with this country.' He concluded by calling for 'a considerably superior force in ships to that of France, and thus maintain the superiority afloat which has heretofore enabled England to maintain the command of the sea.'[4] When the remaining members of the

2 Andrew Harris, *Sir John Pakington: His Ministerial Career 1852-1868* (Leominster: Harris, 2013), pp. 205-206.
3 Harris, *Pakington*, p. 207.
4 John F. Beeler, ed *The Milne Papers 1820-1859* (Aldershot: Navy Records Society, 2004), I, pp. 690-691.

Board came to submit their individual responses to the Queen's request, they were united in the extremely alarmist conclusions which they reached.

It is no great surprise that the leaders of the navy, invited to comment on its needs, should uniformly express the necessity for expansion. Mindful of the annual difficulty of extracting approval for the Naval Estimates from a sceptical Treasury and a suspicious House of Commons, this was only to be expected. They had no doubt had much to say to each other as to where to lay the emphasis in their individual papers most effectively. What is a little surprising, though, is their failure, with one exception, to tackle the issue of ironclads. However, what they were concerned with was the here and now, and what was exercising their minds above all was the growth in the number of French steam battleships which had brought, on paper at any rate, the French navy dangerously close to parity.

The Surveyor of the Navy had already sounded the alarm. In an often quoted passage in a submission to the Board of June 22, 1858 Walker set out again the basic policy of the Admiralty and its application to the current situation. The construction of ironclads had, he contended, become of the highest importance to maintain British naval supremacy:

> Although I have frequently stated that it is not to the interest of Great Britain – possessing as she does so large a navy – to adopt any important change in the construction of ships of war which might have the effect of rendering necessary the introduction of a new class of very costly vessels, until such a course is forced upon her by the adoption by foreign powers of formidable ships of a novel character requiring similar ships to cope with them, yet it then becomes a matter not only of expediency, but of absolute necessity ... This time has arrived. France has now commenced to build frigates of great speed with their sides protected by thick metal plates, and this renders it imperative for this country to do the same without a moment's delay.[5]

The only member of the Board who did allude to the potential threat of French ironclads was Henry Corry, MP, recently reappointed as Secretary to the Admiralty. Outspoken in his views, he would in later years himself become First Lord of the Admiralty. Now, in a memorandum which he wrote on July 29, he first drew attention to the steady decline in the actual number of effective line of battleships, and to the fact that it would be too late to remedy this if it was deferred until the outbreak or near approach of war. By the end of 1859, and at the present rate of building, he calculated that France would have 40 screw ships of the line and England only 36. He reminded his colleagues that Sir George Cockburn had argued that the British navy should be double that of any other navy, and pointed out that, with the advent of steam, French fleets could have a much greater ability to concentrate swiftly than was the case in the days of sail.[6]

But it was in his references to the reports of Colonel Claremont, the British military attaché in Paris, that Corry looked beyond the immediate situation. Claremont had been investigating the French ironclad programme, and had reported:

5 Oscar Parkes, *British Battleships* (London: Seeley Service, 1970), p. 11.
6 *Milne Papers*, I, p, 748.

> They were laying down (at Toulon) the first timbers of an iron sided frigate (*Fregate blindée*) to be called *La Gloire*, and these timbers appear to me quite as large and heavy as those of a three decker. There are to be two of these frigates built here, and four others in other ports. They are to have thirty six heavy guns, most of them rifled 50 pounders, which will throw an 80 pound hollow shot; the engines will be of 800 or 900 hp, and they will be cased with wrought iron.[7]

Corry reckoned that if the experiment proved successful, these vessels would be as formidable, at least, as any ship of the line – which was undoubtedly an understatement.

He wrote his memorandum two days after the Surveyor had put forward his own submission, in which he had pointed out the effect of postponing the proposed conversion of six two decker sailing battleships, and 'the certain superiority which France will in a few months have obtained.' Taking account of this, the Board had minuted that they considered no time should be lost in giving the necessary authority for this work, and a letter went to the Treasury accordingly. It was not until late autumn that a fresh round of individual memoranda from the members of the Board again addressed the perceived need for urgent action. On November 22 Corry wrote that 'the necessity for a great and immediate effort for the maintenance of the superiority of our naval forces over those of France can no longer be a matter of opinion;' and Milne firmly agreed with him.[8]

In his submission of July 27 the Surveyor had addressed directly the mounting threat posed by the French ironclads, writing that if they were not met by similar ships, the French 'would still further increase their superiority as regards the most formidable class of ships of war.' In November, he renewed his plea for increased naval strength, arguing that if the result of the armour plate tests at Portsmouth led to the construction of ironclads, 'they must be regarded as an addition to our force as a balance to those of France, and not as calculated to supersede any existing class of ships, – indeed, no prudent man would at present consider it safe to risk, upon the performance of ships of this novel character, the naval supremacy of Great Britain.[9]

Corry agreed with this, but also argued that if these tests did prove the ability of the latest wrought iron satisfactorily to resist shot and shell, it would not be prudent 'to shut our eyes to the enormous advantage ships thus defended would have over wooden ships which might be sunk by a single broadside from guns of the description now in ordinary use.'[10] It was Corry's view that the ironclad problem was no longer one for future discussion; it demanded immediate action and was, 'in some degree at least, already ripe for decision.'

Thus the Board, cautiously at first, was beginning to move. The visit of the Queen and Prince Consort to Cherbourg in August 1858 had lent further impetus to the mounting sense of urgency at the Admiralty. What he saw there had strongly reinforced the Prince Consort's concern about the French navy in general, and in particular about the French ironclads that were on order. He had previously written to Pakington in June to enquire: 'What have we got to meet this new engine of war?' The First Lord's reply referred to the round of experiments being conducted at Portsmouth into the resistance of iron plating; acknowledging this, Prince Albert

7 *Milne Papers*, I, p. 744.
8 *Milne Papers*, I, pp. 763-764.
9 Baxter, *Introduction*, p. 127.
10 *Milne Papers*, I, p. 766.

replied: 'I trust they are being carried out to the fullest extent possible and not with foregone conclusions.'[11]

The question of ironclads continued to be explored during the winter of 1858-1859, and the first practical step towards the building of a British ironclad was taken on November 27 when the Surveyor was instructed to prepare a project for a 'wooden steam man-of-war to be cased with wrought iron four and a half inches thick.' Walker wasted no time. Within four days he put forward a proposal for a ship capable of 14 knots, to be armed with thirty four guns on her main deck and two on her upper deck, with iron armour backed by substantial woodwork 'so as to afford about the same resistance to the passage of shot, independently of the iron plates, as would obtain in a wood built vessel.' He put the cost at about £250,000.[12]

Designs were sought both from shipwrights in the Royal Dockyards and the private sector. By now the Surveyor's Department had concluded that an iron hulled ship would be preferable, but was prepared to look at plans for a wooden ship. If an iron hulled ship was decided upon, the armour need not extend from stem to stern, but only for about 200 feet of the mid-ships section, the unarmoured ends being subdivided by as many bulkheads as possible. In the event, fifteen designs were received for ships ranging from 340 to 450 feet in length, and with displacements ranging from 6,507 to 11,180 tons. Four of the six designs from the Royal Dockyards proposed a wooden hull; the other two, and all the private shipbuilders put forward plans for an iron hulled vessel. However, none of the proposals were accepted and the Surveyor's Department now worked on its own plans. The experience of the structural problems of the large wooden frigates *Mersey* and *Orlando*, 336 feet long, convinced Isaac Watts and Joseph Large, principally responsible for the design, that an iron hull must be adopted; the vessel was to be 418 feet long, with an ironclad midships section of four a half inch armour plating backed by eighteen inches of teak.

The task of designing such a novel vessel was extremely demanding. Isaac Watts had, as he rose to his position as the senior naval architect in the Surveyor's Department, become increasingly autocratic, and might have been expected to be conservative in approach; as it was, he was now obliged to innovate to a considerable extent. In 1861 he described his methods to a Parliamentary commission:

> When a drawing is being prepared I have frequent communications with the Controller (Surveyor). I consult him many times during the course of construction and also... with my fellow constructor (Large) and... with the chief engineer (Lloyd). In building *Warrior*... it was a novel character, and very frequent communications took place between the Controller of the Navy, the Chief Engineer and myself with regard to carrying it into practical execution.[13]

It was, however, Walker, as Surveyor of the Navy, who must take most of the credit for the inception of the vessel that, it was announced on October 5, would be named *Warrior*. The extent of his contribution to the development of the navy at a time of continuous change had

11 Harris, *Pakington*, p. 215.
12 Baxter, *Introduction*, p. 128.
13 Captain John Wells, *The Immortal Warrior: Britain's First and Last Battleship* (Emsworth: Kenneth Mason, 1987), p. 31.

been huge. Serving seven successive Boards of Admiralty, it was he who oversaw the creation of the steam battle fleet, drew conclusions from the experiences of the Crimean War and, above all, during the ironclad discussions of 1858-1859, argued for an evolutionary approach to the design of the new ships. Ironically, when the design for the *Warrior* was finalised, it could be said that it was in fact by no means evolutionary. In many respects she represented a far more revolutionary approach than the *Gloire.* Walker enjoyed the firm support of Pakington as First Lord. However, by the end of his career, he ran into opposition from hostile opinion, such as that of Lord Clarence Paget, who succeeded Corry as Secretary, and in 1861 Walker resigned his post, which had in the meantime been renamed as Controller of the Navy.

In preparing the Naval Estimates to be presented to Parliament in February 1859, Pakington had obtained Cabinet approval for the inclusion of ironclad vessels in the building programme, and when he addressed the House of Commons he insisted that during the coming year at least two such vessels would be constructed, 'which would be the most expensive ships ever built.' Due to pressure of work in the Royal Dockyards, they would be built by private contractors. He ended his speech: 'It is our duty to take care that our naval force is not only adequate to preserve our position in Europe, but sufficient to answer the demands made upon us in all parts of the world. Let me add, above all, that we make these proposals in the interests of peace.'[14] In the existing climate of public opinion, it is no surprise that in this year at any rate the Naval Estimates were greeted with general approval.

Public concern about the relative naval strength of Britain and France had reached a new height during the crisis which followed the attempt on Napoleon's life by Orsini in February. During the spring of 1859 there was born the Volunteer Rifle movement, prompted by rising fears of a possible French invasion; it received the official approval of the War Office on May 12, and at its peak reached a total strength of 170,000 men. There were even fears of a possible alliance being formed between France and Russia, directed in the first instance against Austria. The mounting panic led to the collapse of the stock market. It was against this background that with the estimates duly approved, the Admiralty placed an order with the Thames Iron Shipbuilding Company of Blackwall to construct an ironclad frigate, to be launched within 11 months and completed for sea except for masting three months later. She was categorised as a frigate, having only one gun deck, though she was one and a half times longer than the largest wooden battleship ever built, and very much more expensive.

Having placed the order for the *Warrior*, the Board of Admiralty then had a momentary, though complete, loss of nerve. Reviewing the size of the ship and the cost of building her, the members of the Board professed themselves as 'startled and astonished' at what they were about to do. They looked at the possibility of reducing the armour of her intended sister from 4.5inches to 2.5 inches, building a smaller vessel that would have a speed of 12 knots and an armament of 22 guns. Walker, however, pointed out that such a vessel would be unable to choose its range and would suffer 'serious consequences from the effect of concentrated broadsides from screw battleships from which it was unable to withdraw.'[15] In the face of this, the Board regained its nerve, and agreed to build the second ironclad on plans similar to those of the *Warrior.* After calling for tenders from four private yards, the contract was awarded to Robert Napier and

14 Harris, *Pakington*, p. 236.
15 Wells, *Warrior*, p. 37.

Sons, on the Clyde, the ship to be built within twelve months at £37.50 per ton. At this stage, however, it was decided to complete only two ironclads before the success of the *Warrior* could be fully tested.[16]

The First Lord did not long remain in office after the contract for the *Warrior* had been placed. On June 10, 1859 the government was defeated on a motion of confidence in the House of Commons, and Lord Derby resigned. The new government was headed by Lord Palmerston; the incoming First Lord was the Duke of Somerset, who had served as chairman of several important military and naval Parliamentary committees, and who came with the strong recommendation of Sir James Graham. This change of government came at a critical point in the development of Britain's response to naval expansion on the other side of the Channel. Appropriately, it was Pakington who was invited to launch the *Warrior*, and he did so on December 29 before a huge crowd at Blackwall on the Thames.

The fine lines of the *Warrior* (and her sister *Black Prince*, who would have been named *Invincible* if the French had not got there first by choosing that name for the sister of the *Gloire*) made her one of the handsomest warships hitherto designed, and enabled her to attain her planned high speed. Admiral Ballard, in his detailed studies of the first ironclads, remarked that it could be said of the *Warrior* 'that at the date of her launch she was in herself a match for all her existing line of battle consorts put together.' He described the revolutionary nature of her design:

> Thus the *Warrior* introduced four great departures simultaneously from all traditions and customs in British Admiralty shipbuilding; that is to say, an armour protection, a length of 6½ beams, an iron structure in frame and shell, and a new safeguard of flotation. Such a wholesale abandonment of long established practice, in a service previously ruled by uncompromising veneration and adherence to precedent, was something quite unheard of, and deserves proportionate recognition. But even in giving credit where it was officially due, it must in truth be admitted that the general public apprehension awakened by the launching of the *Gloire* had a good deal to do with Admiralty activity. The British Parliament and press were in vociferous mood.[17]

16 Baxter, *Introduction*, p. 156.
17 Admiral George A Ballard, *The Black Battlefleet* (Annapolis Maryland: Naval Institute Press 1980), p. 51.

12

The Black Battlefleet

The British Admiralty, as part of its cautious approach to ironclad design, went step by step in selecting designs that varied considerably. The French Ministry of Marine in embarking on a programme to build a class of ten ships basically to the one design, created an essentially homogenous fleet. The first British fleet of ironclads, on the other hand, consisted of a number of warships that would, if it had come to war, have found it more difficult to operate together as a whole.

Palmerston brought to the new administration firm support for a powerful navy, but he was far from convinced that ironclads represented the most important element in a strengthened fleet. As a result, the Somerset Board of Admiralty was obliged to continue the building of wooden steam battleships, a decision which may have accorded with public opinion but which contrasted markedly with the policy across the Channel, where the French had not laid down a wooden ship of the line since 1855. Sir William White, writing in 1873, was scathing:

> The conduct of our naval affairs from 1858 to 1860 appears almost inexplicable; and the Admiralty Boards holding office during that period cannot be freed from censure for their sins both of omission and commission. They simply yielded to a *vis inertia* which carried them on smoothly in a well worn track long after it should have been left; and instead of initiating a policy, or relying, as the French did, upon the skill of their naval architects, they waited for the pressure of public opinion before venturing on anything like extensive changes.[1]

Meanwhile Lord Clarence Paget was obliged to appear in the House of Commons to announce the building of more wooden screw battleships. For him, this was a mortifying experience; in August he had pressed the Board of Admiralty to agree to the building of three new ironclads rather than new wooden ships, and when overruled endeavoured to resign as Secretary, though the Prime Minister talked him out of it.

Palmerston and Somerset were certainly influenced by public concern about the strength of the French fleet in wooden screw battleships resulting from the extensive conversion programme. The First Lord, however, also still had serious reservations about ironclads:

1 Quoted Parkes, *British Battleships*, p. 14.

> The Duke of Somerset's own attitude towards the ironclad was based on several considerations; in the first place, the Admiralty had no practical experience with a seagoing ironclad since the *Warrior* was still under construction; secondly, her great size and cost required that the Admiralty proceed cautiously; and most importantly, there was the question of whether armour actually could keep out shells.[2]

The Prime Minister was himself unready to accept that the era of the wooden battleship was over, remarking 'whether iron plated ships will stand such shot as improved science will bring to bear against them remains to be seen, but even then it will be some time before they can be completed in sufficient numbers by any Power to constitute the main arm of naval warfare.'[3] He was, however, prepared to go along with the construction of the first two ships of a class of smaller ironclads which the Surveyor had proposed on November 24, 1859. Walker's original suggestion had been for the construction of six ironclads of 3,668 tons, which would be designed for Channel and home service. His intention was to try to close the gap in numbers with the French ironclads as quickly as possible. His design was for the ships to be 280 feet long and 54 feet beam, to carry 16 guns. Their engines of 600 hp would give them a speed of 10.75 knots. Designed by Isaac Watts, they, like the *Warrior* and *Black Prince*, were protected amidships, their unarmoured ends being subdivided with watertight bulkheads. The hope had been that they would be considerably cheaper than their immediate predecessors; the two ships that were authorised, named *Defence* and *Resistance*, actually cost between £250,000 and £260,000 each, earning them the description of being 'the most uneconomical ever built for the British navy.' Gladstone, the Chancellor of the Exchequer, had urged the building of a larger number of ironclads in preference to the wooden ships on the stocks, but Palmerston would have none of this, and the Admiralty settled for only two. It was a foolish decision:

> As a result, the navy was saddled with a couple of ships which would reduce the speed of the *Warrior* in squadron to 10 ¾ knots, and as fighting units rank inferior to their French opposite numbers both in protection to their batteries and steering gear as well as in armament, speed and sea keeping qualities. In fact, Sir Nathanial Barnaby thought so little of them that he estimated that total efficiency compared to the *Warrior* as 1 to 4.[4]

These two ships were commissioned in December 1861 and July 1862 respectively. Designed with armoured rams shaped in the rounded outline of a ploughshare, they were referred to as 'steam rams,' until ram bows became generally fitted to new battleships. They were initially armed, as with all the early British ironclads, with a combination of smoothbore and rifled guns, though later receiving two 8 inch and fourteen 7 inch rifled muzzle loaders. The midships armour was designed on the same basis as that of the *Warrior*, and was 4.5 inches thick. The

2 Colin F. Baxter, 'The Duke of Somerset and the Creation of the British Ironclad Navy', *The Mariner's Mirror* 63.3 (1977) p. 280.
3 Baxter, *Introduction*, p. 157.
4 Parkes, *British Battleships*, p. 25.

Defence was built by Palmer at Jarrow, and the *Resistance* on the Thames at Poplar by Westwood and Baillie.[5]

Palmerston continued to take a close interest in the question of ironclad construction, and characteristically expressed strong views on their design. He wrote, for instance, to Somerset in June 1862 to offer his opinion on the armour of the *Warrior*, commenting that 'it would be impossible to strengthen the stem and stern of the *Warrior* and her companions without materially impairing her seagoing qualities. She is at present, there is no denying it, a fine yacht, but not an efficient ship of war.'[6]

While the *Warrior* was still completing, reservations about the concept of the seagoing ironclad still remained, but news of the successful trials of the *Gloire*, and of the huge building programme to which France was now committed, compelled the Admiralty to do something more, and to do it quickly. This led Walker to propose that three more ironclads of the *Warrior* type should be built. The Board agreed, though flagging up the possibility that when it came to it iron hulled ships would not be a success by directing him to report on their fitness for use as transports if it became necessary to remove their armour. This attitude has been described as one of 'almost pusillanimous uncertainty.'[7] Instead of three *Warriors*, however, the Board finally opted for one only, together with two modified *Defences*, which of course would be cheaper. Known *as Hector* and *Valiant*, these two ships were of 6,710 tons; intended at first to carry twenty four guns, they had the standard 4.5 inch armour, in their case tapering to 2.5 inches fore and aft. They attained over 12 knots speed on their trials, but overall they were not a success.

On the other hand, the third *Warrior* class ironclad, named *Achilles*, the first iron hulled ship built in the Royal Dockyards, was extremely successful. Built originally as a four masted ship, her foremast was subsequently removed. The *Achilles* was laid down in August 1861, and was completed in 1864. 380 feet long, and 50 a half feet in the beam, she was of 9,820 tons. Initially, her armament was sixteen 100 pounders and four 7 inch breech loaders; six 68 pounders were later added. Her speed was 14.3 knots. She was the first ship to be designed for a four bladed non-hoisting screw. Admiral Ballard wrote: 'She was a very taking vessel to the eye. She sat the water on a remarkably even keel, and it was said of her that the placing and proportions of her spars and funnels were symmetrically perfect in their relation to the general outline and shape of her hull.' And Oscar Parkes considered that she ranked as Watts' most successful creation.

At the same time as the ongoing discussion about ironclad design continued, the Admiralty's technical department had been subjected to considerable pressure from Captain Cowper Coles, who advocated the design of a ship equipped with armoured revolving turrets. He argued that such a vessel would be very much more powerful than the traditional broadside battleship. He won the support of the Prince Consort, who wrote on December 10, 1860 to Somerset to urge the construction of a turret ship to Coles' design 'at once, with such modifications as may be suggested to him.' He did, however, accept that 'it would not be prudent to restrict ourselves to vessels of this novel construction, but we should certainly give the country the benefit of some such … Should Captain Coles' plan succeed, his ships will be vastly superior to those we are

5 Admiral George A Ballard, *The Black Battlefleet* (Annapolis, Md: Naval Institute Press,1980), pp. 165-168.
6 Howard J. Fuller, *Clad in Iron* (Annapolis, Md: Naval Institute Press 2008), p. 5.
7 Parkes, *British Battleships*, p. 30.

now building.'[8] In the early stages of their development, Coles' turrets were in the shape of truncated cones, and were known as cupolas, but were called turrets after their design was altered to that of a cylinder.

Early in 1861 the Admiralty ordered that the experimental turret being built to test Coles' design should be completed at Woolwich, and the Board approved the proposal by Robinson, the new Controller, that it should be tested 'in as perfect and thorough a manner as possible.' The trials that took place later that year went extremely well. Captain Ashmore Powell, who supervised these, wrote an extremely favourable report, describing the turret as 'one of the most formidable inventions adapted to naval warfare, as well as coast defences, that has ever come to my notice.' Perhaps because it might be possible to mount turrets on smaller, less expensive ships, Somerset was delighted, as Palmerston told Lord John Russell, the Foreign Secretary, on September 24:

> I saw Somerset today who is in great glee at the success of Capt. Coles' cupola covers for cannon on a ship's deck. These iron domes from under which heavy guns are to fire have been pounded at from short distance by all the heaviest guns we have and nothing has made any impression on them. Somerset thinks that comparatively small iron cased ships armed in this way with all their guns, perhaps 16 on deck, without any portholes and therefore low in the water, will prove formidable ships of war.[9]

Coles had originally proposed that a ship built to his design should carry only two turrets. When the Admiralty decided to proceed, he suggested a much larger vessel carrying eight turrets. This was a step too far; but Robinson did favour more than two, 'which might prove a match in mere fighting for the *Warrior*.' A decision was taken in January 1862 to include a provision for a mastless vessel in the 1862-1863 estimates. She would be of 2,529 tons, and carry six of Coles' turrets. Appropriately, she would be given the name *Prince Albert*.

The Admiralty's choice was Rear Admiral Robert Spencer Robinson to succeed Walker as Controller following the latter's retirement in February 1861 was inspired. Robinson, who joined the navy in 1821, reached the rank of captain in 1840. He was the author of a book on steam navigation published in 1839, and of a further book, *Observations on the Steam Ships of the Royal Navy*, in 1847. During the Crimean War he served in the Baltic, and was subsequently appointed as Superintendent of the Steam Reserve. He was promoted to rear admiral in June 1860. Robinson was in the forefront of those calling for the building of ironclads; on the day before his appointment as Controller he wrote a memorandum addressed to the Dockyard Commission deploring the delay in their construction. He rejected the doctrine 'that it was not for England… to take the lead in adopting inventions, which would go far to render the expenditure already incurred in a great measure useless… Superiority on the sea is vital to our national existence, and five years ago an invention for resisting to an immense extent the destroying power of projectiles, was applied to ships with a large measure of success.'[10]

In this opinion Robinson was by no means alone among the First Lord's professional advisers. On the day after he took up his new position, the Senior Naval Lord, Vice Admiral Sir

8 Parkes, *British Battleships*, p. 45; Baxter, *Introduction*, p. 190.
9 Baxter, pp. 191-192.
10 Baxter, *Introduction*, p. 169.

Richard Dundas, called for the substitution of ironclads for the new fortifications that had been authorised for Spithead, proposing instead the conversion of sailing or steam battleships into coast defence ironclads. In the House of Commons, Lord Clarence Paget promised that if the Admiralty 'found much more progress over the water or among any other nations in building these ships,' they would take steps to match them. That was on February 28; by then news had already reached the Admiralty of Napoleon III's plan for ten new ironclads in addition to those already launched or under construction.

The naval members of the Board grasped more clearly than either Somerset or Palmerston that the French plan fundamentally altered the situation, and demanded that immediate action be taken to meet the threat. They minuted that 'otherwise, the Spring of 1862 might see the French in possession of such a fleet of iron cased ships as would give them the command of the Channel.' Somerset was not at one with his professional advisers. He would have preferred to await the conclusions that might be drawn from the trials of the *Warrior* and *Black Prince* before placing further orders for ironclads. He maintained this view in the face of explicit advice to the contrary, such as that from Robinson, who had reminded the Board 'that every maritime power in Europe is advancing in this direction, and that unprotected wooden ships cannot contend with success against their iron coated rivals.' The Controller kept up the pressure with a submission to the Board on May 22, 1861 spelling out the position with the utmost clarity:

> Without adverting in a spirit of jealousy to the progress which every Naval Power in Europe is making in the direction of protecting their military navy by iron plating, it is evident that a complete revolution has taken place in the requirements of naval architecture, and that an ordinary ship of war unprotected by iron plates, is certain to be destroyed in action even by any wooden ship of the same force as herself.[11]

The Board was in no doubt that this was right, urging the Cabinet next day to recognise the need to build more ironclads of the first class, being 'convinced that none but the most vigorous and energetic measures will prevent the command of the Channel at an early date falling into the hands of the French Emperor.'

Not surprisingly, the Treasury was decidedly unenthusiastic about a building programme on the scale called for by the naval members of the Board of Admiralty. With the belated suspension of work on the wooden battleships on the stocks, Robinson now proposed that the frames of six of them should be adapted to receive 4.5 inch armour plate. He suggested that a start should be made with the *Royal Oak*, which had been laid down in 1860. This was agreed, and she was completed in April 1863 at a cost of just over a quarter of a million pounds. She was the first British wooden hulled ironclad, and the first to have end-to-end protection. She was armed with eleven 7 inch breech loaders and twenty four 68 pounders. On her trials she attained a speed of 12.5 knots.

Overcoming the First Lord's unconcealed reluctance, the Board next insisted that more ironclads should be ordered, and this resulted in the conversion of four more wooden battleships that were on the stocks. These were the *Caledonia, Ocean, Prince Consort*, and *Royal Alfred.* The first three of these followed the general design of the *Royal Oak*, though with two funnels,

11 Baxter, *Introduction*, pp. 173-174.

which Parkes considered made them 'rather sullen looking.' Completion of the *Royal Alfred* was delayed until the others had undergone trials. Robinson was under no illusion about the quality of the conversions, which he admitted were inferior to ships such as the *Achilles*. Nevertheless, he insisted that it was

> so important … to have some ships constructed to meet the navies of other powers at least on equal terms, that, rather than be without such ships … not as the wisest, nor as the most economical, nor as the safest way to meeting the exigencies of the case, but because other considerations make this plan the only practicable one at the present moment.[12]

Later in 1861 the three iron hulled ironclads of the *Minotaur* class were ordered. Of 6,621 tons, with engines producing 1350 hp, they were originally designed to carry forty 100 pounder Armstrong guns on the main deck, and ten on pivots on the upper deck. Admiral Ballard wrote of them that they were 'the longest and largest single screw fighting ships ever built, as well as the longest and largest to carry their heaviest guns mounted between decks.

They were also the only fighting ships ever rigged with five masts.'[13] In spite of their imposing row of masts, they were the dullest performers under canvas of the whole masted fleet of their day; Ballard remarked that 'no ships ever carried so much dress to so little purpose.'

The competition between guns and armour plating had been in full swing for some time. Early in the century, the arrival of the Paixhans gun had conferred on ordnance a crucial advantage; but after a hesitant start the adoption of armour had reversed the balance in favour of the defence. This, though, was not to be the case for very long. Armour plating 4.5 inches thick, with timber backing, had for a while become the standard, and provided satisfactory protection against the current weaponry, but the development of rifled ordnance began quickly to shift the pendulum once more in favour of the offence. First trials of rifled guns had shown mixed results; but experiments carried out in 1861 prompted Somerset to tell the House of Lords that he had insisted that the *Achilles* should have sufficient displacement to carry 6 inch plates, but that he was no longer sure that this would be invulnerable. In France, the early trials of rifled guns had not been effective, but continued development led the Ministry of Marine to call for increased thickness of armour plates for the ironclads under construction. In response, the gunmakers rapidly developed new products, as a result of which the earlier ironclads repeatedly underwent a process of rearmament as the latest weapons became available.

In the continuous struggle for advantage between armour and ordnance, the naval gun would ultimately always have the edge, for reasons which Bernard Brodie explained:

> From the very beginning of serious efforts to construct shot-proof warships, the naval gun showed itself capable of expanding almost at once to a power sufficient to perforate the latest armour developed. Whatever invulnerability was achieved was evanescent in the extreme. This was no historical accident, for the same metallurgical advances that made possible the forging of thicker and more resistant armour plates likewise made possible the

12 Fuller, *Clad in Iron*, p. 7.
13 Ballard, *Black Battlefleet*, p. 24.

> construction of stronger ordnance, capable of withstanding heavier propelling charges and hurling greater projectiles.[14]

The Duke of Somerset remained at the Admiralty until 1866. His tenure of office was a time of rapid technological advance. It was also a period of great tension in international politics, and the responsibilities of a First Lord during this period were very considerable. Colin Baxter boldly claimed for Somerset's performance there that 'his achievement must surely rank him as one of the most effective First Lords in the history of the Admiralty.'[15] Bearing in mind that he oversaw the futile and wasteful laying down of unarmoured wooden battleships (albeit at Palmerston's urging), and that his Board's haphazard introduction of ironclads left the Channel Fleet as a heterogenous collection of individual ships barely compatible for its operations together, the claim is scarcely justified. It must be acknowledged, though, that Somerset was responsible for making two crucially important appointments, first in choosing Robinson as Controller and then, more controversially, the 33-year-old Edward Reed as Chief Constructor.

In retrospect, the threat from French naval expansion can be seen to have been less serious than appeared to an anxious British public at the time. France's industrial base was insufficient to support any sustained competition with Britain in the matter of shipbuilding, and particularly in building iron hulled ships. In addition the other materials supplied to French shipbuilders were both costly, and constantly unsatisfactory in terms of quality. The enormous cost of building an ironclad fleet from scratch was too great for French finances, the Navy's budget rising from 158 million francs in 1858 to 219 million francs in 1864.[16]

Nevertheless, beginning with the *Gloire*, and then followed by the ambitious programme of ironclad construction, it had been France that had taken the first decisive steps towards a shipbuilding revolution. The need to obtain ironclads was quickly apparent to other European navies, and they reacted accordingly. In the meantime, however, a conflict had begun on the other side of the Atlantic that was about to provide the first practical experience of the performance of ironclads in actual battle conditions.

14 Brodie, *Machine Age*, p. 178.
15 Colin F. Baxter, 'Somerset', p. 284.
16 Theodore Ropp, *The Development of a Modern Navy* (Annapolis, Maryland: Naval Institute Press 1987), pp. 9-10.

13

The American Civil War

A great deal of ingenuity in the development of ironclads would be displayed by both sides during the course of the American Civil War. However, their extensive employment throughout the war was largely confined to inland waters and coastal operations, and the experience gained was not therefore directly relevant to the design of seagoing ironclads. Nevertheless, as the war proceeded, the American experience pointed to a number of lessons that could be learned.

When the war broke out, the United States possessed no ironclads. The only significant initiative taken in the previous decade had been the work done on the much delayed Stevens ironclad. Funds had been provided from time to time, while technological advances led to frequent modifications to the initial design, but by the time war broke out the project was still incomplete. The lack of any wholehearted ironclad development in the United States prompted *The Times* on January 11, 1861 to express surprise at the failure there to respond to 'the one question which has absorbed for months past the thoughts of the maritime powers of Europe … the invention of iron cased ships.' Commenting on this, the Philadelphia *Press* remarked:

> It is a curious fact that the United States … should be charged with being behind the age. Yet there is a good prima facie case … It is more than probable that, and without much further delay, if we intend to have a national and naval force worthy of our power and pretensions, we shall have to follow suit, and build iron-cased vessels, as France and England have done, and are doing. Before the end of this year France will have *eight* and England *six* such vessels. How many are we to have?[1]

Professor Baxter effectively demolished the suggestion that the American lack of ironclads in 1861 was due to a fundamental scepticism on the part of the Navy Department. In January 1861 the Senate called for an estimate of the cost of building 'a steel or iron cased gunboat.' The Naval Appropriations Act of February 21 made no financial provision for ironclads, however, and it was in the South that activity first began in that direction. As well as constructing a battery on Morris Island in South Carolina early in 1861, a primitive floating battery was constructed, with a sloping armoured side facing the enemy. Both this vessel and the land battery contributed with considerable effect to the bombardment of Fort Sumter with little damage to themselves.

1 Baxter, *Introduction*, p. 220.

President Jefferson Davis appointed Stephen Russell Mallory, previously a senator for Florida, as Secretary of the Confederate Navy. He was not, instinctively, a great innovator; and he took the view that armoured ships were only suitable for harbour and coast defence. He was, however, able to see the importance of ironclads to the Confederacy, and in May 1861 he wrote that he considered 'the possession of an iron-armoured ship as a matter of the first necessity. Such a vessel at this time could traverse the entire coast of the United States, prevent all blockades, and encounter, with a fair prospect of success, their entire navy.' While in office, Mallory was much criticised; but a historian of the Confederate Navy was able to write of him:

> He was a gentleman of excellent sense, unpretending manners, and probably conducted his department as successfully as was possible with the limited naval resources of the South … He could not command success, but he deserved it by faithful and diligent labour, and by intelligent and discreet effort.[2]

Thwarted in an entirely unrealistic effort to purchase the *Gloire* or one of her class, Mallory authorised his representative Lieutenant James H. North to attempt to arrange the building of two ironclads in Europe, one in France and one in Great Britain. This was a long-term project; meanwhile there had arisen an immediate opportunity for the construction of an ironclad in the Norfolk Navy Yard, recently seized by Confederate forces. The Union army had pulled out from there on April 20, after Virginia's secession, and all the officers at the yard had resigned their commissions. Lying in the yard, her guns unshipped and her engines dismantled, was the large steam frigate *Merrimac.* Efforts had been made to get her ready for sea so that she might safely reach northern waters, but at the last the timid and vacillating Union commander of the yard held her back and then, as the Confederate forces approached, ordered her to be scuttled. She sank to the bottom of the harbour, and was then burned to the waterline. When the Confederates arrived, inspection of the wreck led to the conclusion that she could be salvaged, and her hull was raised and towed into the yard's massive dry dock.[3]

It was also decided that her engines could be utilised, and since it represented the only opportunity of getting an ironclad in a short time, it was resolved that she be rebuilt, at an estimated cost of $110,000. The hull was cut down to the gun deck, and an armoured casemate was built, originally intended to house ten guns, including two Brooke 6.4 inch rifled guns. Work began in July, and it was estimated that as many as 1,500 men were engaged in her reconstruction. She was to bear the name *Virginia.* Since it was impossible to access accurate data from the European experiments, it was deemed necessary to carry out a series of tests to determine the inclination of the plates and their thickness by actual experiment. This led to the conclusion that her armour should consist of two layers of 2 inch plates backed by 24 inches of wood.

Some efforts were made to keep details of the vessel's construction confidential; disinformation about the effectiveness of her armour plating was released to the local press. Generally, though, the Federals kept themselves very well informed of her progress. She was launched on February 17 1862. She was 262 feet long; her armoured casemate sloped at about 36°, and was just over 78 feet long at its base. Behind ports in the casemate she carried two 6.4 inch rifles

2 J. Thomas Scharf, *History of the Confederate States Navy* (New York: Roger & Sherwood, 1894), p. 30.
3 Jay W. Simson, *Naval Strategies of the Civil War* (Nashville, Tennessee: Cumberland House Publishing, 2001), p. 46.

and six 9 inch smoothbores, together with four 7 inch pivot guns. She was fitted with a cast iron ram. On February 24 Captain Franklin Buchanan was assigned to command the James River squadron, and hoisted his flag in the *Virginia*.

In the North, even before the fall of Fort Sumter, proposals for ironclad ships had begun to arrive at the Navy Department. The problem for the US Navy was that the 'Anaconda' plan designed to suppress the rebellion required it to blockade the whole of the coastline of the Confederacy, some 3500 miles in length. Priority had to be given to the building of a large number of vessels to supplement the United States fleet that already existed. The development of an ironclad fleet would take a considerable time, which meant that it would be unable to make any contribution to the task, which was immediate. John Lenthall, the Chief of the Bureau of Construction and Repair, wrote on May 11, 1861:

> The necessarily large size, the cost and the time required for building an iron cased steam vessel is such that it is not recommended to adopt any plan at present ... The subject of ironclad vessels with inclined sides has been freely discussed in the European mechanical journals, but their draught of water, cost, and the time required in the introduction of a new system render it inexpedient at this time to commence such vessels which will require very careful consideration.[4]

In fact, the first steps taken to build ironclads for the Union were taken by the army. The War Department was responsible for the conduct of operations on the rivers in the West, and soon after the surrender of Fort Sumter there began to come into existence a fleet of gunboats on the Mississippi. Seven small wooden steamers, driven by a single large paddlewheel at the stern, were ordered in August 1861. They were designed to carry thirteen guns in a central armoured casemate with sloping ends and sides.

In Washington the Navy Secretary Gideon Welles wondered, in July 1861, whether 'the period is perhaps not one best adapted to heavy expenditure by way of experiment and the time and attention of some of those who are most competent to investigate and form correct conclusions are otherwise employed.'[5] Congress had on June 24 authorised the appointment of a board to examine the unfinished Stevens ironclad and advise whether it would be worth completing her. In her current development she was intended to be a vessel of 5,000 tons, 420 feet long and 53 feet in the beam, with a central casemate with inclined sides protected by 6.75 inch armour plating; she was to carry seven huge guns on rotating platforms. The naval members of the board were unimpressed, and on December 24 recommended that the vessel be not completed. This was not, as it turned out, the end; the proposal to complete her was later again revived.

Meanwhile, though not without difficulty, the Congress was finally persuaded to pass a bill directing the Secretary of the Navy to appoint a board to investigate the construction of an ironclad from scratch, setting aside the sum of $1.5 million if a favourable conclusion was reached. This board was led by Commodore Joseph Smith, a close friend of Welles. On August 7 the Secretary published an advertisement calling for offers 'for the construction of one or more ironclad steam vessels of war.' The Ironclad Board, reviewing the proposals before it, wasted no

4 Baxter, *Introduction*, p. 242.
5 Fuller, *Clad in Iron*, p. 50.

time, on September 5 recommending the construction of the three very different ironclads that would in due course be known as the *Monitor*, *Galena*, and *New Ironsides*.

The stream of proposals for ironclad ships naturally increased once the appointment of the Ironclad Board was mooted. Among those interested was Cornelius Bushnell, who prepared plans for an ironclad which he submitted for review to John Ericsson, who approved them. This was the vessel which in due course would be completed as the *Galena*. Ericsson then showed Bushnell his own plans for a 'perfect ironclad,' together with a cardboard model, and was persuaded by the latter to put his design forward. On August 29 Ericsson wrote to President Abraham Lincoln with his proposal, pointing out the 'now well established fact that steel clad vessels cannot be arrested in their course by land batteries,' which he said meant that New York would be at the mercy of such ships.[6]

Although Ericsson was officially informed on September 7 that his design was approved, he still faced a good deal of healthy scepticism, particularly about the turret, its armour, and the probable effect on the guns' crew if it was hit by enemy shot. Ericsson brushed aside such doubts, supremely confident in his design. Commodore Smith was one who remained uneasy, though, writing to Ericsson on October 11: 'I understand computations have been made by expert Naval Architects of the displacement of your vessel and ... she will not float with the load you propose to put upon her, nor attain a speed of 4 knots.'[7] Mastering his impatience, Ericsson satisfied Smith with a full response. His assurance was so great that he willingly accepted a condition imposed by the Ironclad Board that his battery must prove itself in combat before the full contract price of $275,000 was paid, a term which his partners considered unreasonable. The contractual date for completion was January 12, 1862, but the vessel was not launched until January 30; she was finally commissioned on February 25. The *Monitor* consisted effectively of two vessels, the lower hull of iron and a raft like vessel of wood and iron above, overhanging the other. As finally completed, the lower hull was 124 feet long and 18 feet in the beam. Her turret was protected by eight inches of armour; her deck armour was one inch thick, and she had an armoured belt of five inches, tapering to three inches below the waterline. She was armed with two 11 inch Dahlgren guns.

As the *Monitor* neared completion, information continued to reach the Navy Department of the progress of work on the *Virginia*; surprisingly comprehensive, this caused the most profound concern, and completion of Ericsson's vessel was anxiously awaited. Unfortunately her first trials were unsuccessful, with defects found in both engines and steering gear, and it was not until March 6 that, escorted by two gunboats and a tug she finally left the New York Navy Yard en route for Hampton Roads.

It was only just in time. On March 8 the *Virginia* finally emerged to attack the Union fleet of wooden warships in Hampton Roads. Professor Baxter remarked of what followed that 'few naval actions in history have made so profound an impression on the popular imagination:'

> The combats of March 8 and 9 symbolised the passing of the old fleets and the coming of the new. Symbol they were, and not the cause, for they did not initiate the great revolution in naval architecture, they crowned it. They taught the man in the street what the naval

6 Fuller, *Clad in Iron*, p. 52.
7 Fuller, *Clad in Iron*, p. 60.

> constructors already knew: that shell guns had sounded the doom of the wooden navies of the world. On the chief problem confronting the naval constructors of Europe – the best design for seagoing ironclads – these battles threw little light. Nevertheless fate had provided for the first fight of ironclads so incomparable a setting that the *Merrimac* and the *Monitor* have monopolised public attention in the United States, to the exclusion of the scores of ironclads then already built or building in Europe.[8]

It had been Buchanan's intention to take the *Virginia* downriver during the night of March 6/7 and occupy a position from which to surprise the principal ships of the blockading squadron at dawn. His plan was confounded, however, by a storm which blew up, causing a postponement until the following night. It was then concluded that it would be too risky to take her downriver during the hours of darkness, so it was not until the morning of March 8, with much improved weather conditions, that she began her sortie. Casting off at 11:00 a.m., the *Virginia* steamed away from the Gosport Navy Yard, accompanied by two small steamers. Buchanan kept his plans to himself, telling only Lieutenant Catesby ap Jones, his executive officer, of his intention to ram the frigate *Cumberland*, anchored with the frigate *Congress* off Newport News. The Union vessels first sighted the *Virginia* at about 12:40 p.m.; the *Cumberland* swung round on her anchor so that her broadside was towards the Confederate ironclad's direct line of approach.

Both the Union frigates opened fire on the *Virginia*, as did the shore batteries, but the ironclad made no reply until 2:00 p.m.; it was one of her accompanying steamers that fired the first shot from the Confederate squadron. The *Virginia* fired her forward pivot gun at the *Cumberland*, hitting her on her starboard quarter. Her second shot also hit the frigate, disabling one of her forward guns. As the ironclad steamed on, she was quite untroubled by the shots that struck her from the *Congress*. Coming abreast of that vessel, the *Virginia's* starboard battery fired hot shot at her, setting her on fire, and she then steamed on towards the *Cumberland*. Her iron ram smashed into the frigate's side, opening a hole some 7 feet wide, and it was almost at once apparent that she was mortally damaged. Momentarily, the *Virginia's* ram was trapped in the *Cumberland's* side, and as she reversed it was broken loose. The *Virginia's* engineer later wrote: 'Like the wasp, we could sting but once, leaving the sting in the wound.'[9] As the *Virginia* pulled away, she and the *Cumberland* exchanged fire, the shells of the ironclad smashing the wooden sides of the frigate 'as if they had been made of paper.' The *Cumberland's* reply had no effect at all on her adversary. This went on for about half an hour, before the *Cumberland* began slowly to go down.

Buchanan next turned on the *Congress*. He was now supported by the rest of the ships of the James River squadron which had come up. Meanwhile the Union frigates *Roanoke* and *Minnesota*, and behind them the *St Lawrence*, were steaming up to aid the *Congress*, but first the *Roanoke* and then the *Minnesota* went aground. The *Congress*, towed by the tug *Zouave*, made for the shore, hoping to go to ground in a position where the water would be too shallow for the *Virginia* to follow. She came under intensive fire from the ironclad; her stern was demolished, and several fires were blazing as she ran aground well within her opponent's range. There was nothing to do but to strike her colours. Buchanan ordered that she be burned, though an

8 Baxter, *Introduction*, p. 285.

9 William C Davis, *Duel Between the First Ironclads* (Baton Rouge, Louisiana: Louisiana State University Press, 1975), p. 92.

attempt to board her for this purpose was thwarted by fire from Union troops onshore. At about this time Buchanan was wounded, and Jones took command of the ironclad. After continuing to rake the burning *Congress* for several minutes, the *Virginia* turned towards the *Minnesota*, but although damaging the grounded frigate, could not get close enough to finish her off, and at 6:30 p.m. the ironclad retired to anchor under the Confederate batteries on Sewell's Point. She had entirely fulfilled Dupuy de Lôme's prophecy that an ironclad amid a wooden fleet would be like a lion in a flock of sheep.

The *Virginia* had lost her anchors, and her flag staffs, and her funnel was riddled with holes, but her armoured casemate, hit 98 times, had not been breached. There was a small leak in the bow where the ram had been torn off, but she was perfectly fit for further action on the following day. She had, however, proved very difficult to handle, and in Buchanan's opinion, if she encountered a gale or very heavy swell, it was very likely that she would founder. In addition to this difficulty of manoeuvre, her engines were exceedingly unreliable.

That night, at about midnight, the *Congress* blew up. By now the *Monitor* had arrived at Hampton Roads, and was anchored alongside the *Minnesota*. It remained to be seen what she could do against the apparently unstoppable *Virginia*. News of the disastrous outcome of the action on March 8 only reached Washington on the following morning, and caused an immediate panic among the members of the Cabinet meeting at the White House. Secretary of War Edwin Stanton was particularly dismayed, predicting that the *Virginia* would steam up the Potomac and shell the White House; he was unpersuaded by Welles' assurance that her draught was too great for this. Nor did the information that the *Monitor* should by now have arrived at Hampton Roads calm the Cabinet's anxiety, which was sharpened by the knowledge that the Confederacy was already engaged in building other ironclads. Welles wrote in his diary: 'There was throughout the whole day something inexpressibly ludicrous in the wild, frantic talk, action and rage of Stanton as he ran from room to room, sat down and jumped up after writing a few words, swung his arms, scolded, and raved.'[10] When news reached the Press, there was a similar reaction; but the events of March 9 were to restore a sense of proportion.

At 6:30 a.m. that morning the *Virginia* got up steam, and accompanied again by a number of small steamers of the James River squadron headed for the *Minnesota*. As they neared the grounded frigate, those aboard the *Virginia* could see a strange vessel alongside her, looking like an immense raft with a cheese box rising from its centre. And to many among the Union onlookers onshore, and aboard the *Minnesota*, the *Monitor* seemed altogether much too small to be any sort of match for the *Virginia*.

As the Confederate ironclad approached, she opened fire on the frigate, but was unable to get closer than a mile, and Jones turned to engage the *Monitor*. It was now about 8:45 a.m., and for the next two hours the two ironclads engaged each other at close range. The *Monitor* was much handier than the *Virginia*, able to change course at will; the Confederate ironclad could turn only slowly as the two vessels manoeuvred. Each ship took many hits, but suffered little damage. Oscar Parkes summarised some of the key elements of the battle:

> This, the first engagement between ironclads, was a drawn battle, as neither ship succeeded in putting the other out of action, and the fight had to be called off when it became apparent

10 Davis, *Duel*, p. 114.

> that both ships were more or less immune to the opposing gunfire. Had the *Virginia* used solid shot instead of shells, or the *Monitor* full 30-50 lb charges instead of only 15 lb behind her 170 lb shot, the result might have been different. As it was, there was a long drawn out and resultless cannonade with the *Monitor* firing once in seven minutes, and the *Virginia* discharging a broadside about once in fifteen minutes. Attempts to ram by both ships were frustrated by the use of the helm.[11]

Gustavus Fox, the Assistant Secretary of the Navy, had hurried to Hampton Roads, and sent a telegram to Welles to report on the events of the day:

> The *Monitor* arrived at 10.00 pm last night and went immediately to the protection of the *Minnesota*, lying aground just below Newport News. 7.00 am today the *Merrimac*, accompanied by two wooden steamers and several tugs, stood out towards the *Minnesota* and opened fire. The *Monitor* met them at once and opened her fire, when all the enemy's vessels retired, excepting the *Merrimac*. These two ironclad vessels fought part of the time touching each other, from 8.00 am to noon, when the *Merrimac* retired. Whether she is injured or not it is impossible to say.[12]

The battle had demonstrated that each of the ironclads was effectively 'shotproof.' It seemed evident to Fox that only the Union guns of the largest calibre would have any chance of overcoming the *Virginia's* armoured protection, and that concentrated broadsides of smaller guns were of no effect. The *Minnesota*, for instance, fired 247 rounds of 9 inch and 10 inch shot at the *Virginia* with no effect at all. For those designing ironclads, there were a number of important conclusions to be drawn immediately from the events of the battle.

Painfully aware that the *Monitor* was all that stood between the *Virginia* and their vulnerable fleet of wooden steamers, the Federals displayed great caution in committing her to further action. The *Virginia*, on returning to Norfolk, underwent extensive refitting; her underwater armoured belt, improved ram and set of port shutters made her a much more formidable craft than when she appeared on March 8 and 9. And Captain Paulding, one of Welles' most influential advisers, was pessimistic about the outcome of a further engagement between the two ironclads, writing to the Navy Secretary on April 12:

> If now there shall be a want of resolution and skill, our naval force may be destroyed and even the great army at the mercy of the enemy for the gunboats cannot contend with the ironclad rebels. As for the *Monitor*, she is formidable but is not equal to the *Merrimac*. The *Merrimac* under full steam may in my belief run over her and this to my mind is a very simple problem.[13]

On April 11 the *Virginia* had come out again, accompanied as before by a number of small steamers. Captain Hewitt, the commander of the British sloop *Rinaldo*, observed her closely, and in his report expressed an improbably favourable view of the ironclad's mobility, reckoning

11 Parkes, *British Battleships*, p. 46.
12 Fuller, *Clad in Iron*, p. 88.
13 Baxter, *Introduction*, p. 298n.

that she steamed at 7 knots and was able to turn with surprising ease. The *Virginia* was now commanded by Flag Officer Josiah Tattnall, and he was determined to do all he could to destroy the *Monitor.* In Hewitt's opinion, the *Monitor* might easily be taken by boarding, while a concentrated fire against the perpendicular sides of her turret would damage the machinery by which it was turned. He reported that on April 11 the Confederate squadron 'cruised about the Roads without opposition, the *Virginia* occasionally going within range of the Federal guns on the Rip Raps, and Fortress Monroe, as well as those of the large squadron under the guns of the fortress.'[14] On the orders of Flag Officer Goldsborough, the *Monitor* did not take up the *Virginia's* challenge on that day or the next.

However, the *Virginia's* short lived dominance of the waters of Hampton Roads was soon to come to an end. On May 3 General Joseph E. Johnston abandoned the Confederate lines at Yorktown, and the evacuation of Norfolk was ordered. The *Monitor* emerged on May 8 and attacked the Confederate batteries on Sewell's Point, but retreated when the *Virginia* appeared. However, with Union troops approaching Norfolk, the *Virginia's* days were numbered; her draught was too great to get up the James River, and on the morning of May 11, with a heavy heart, Tattnall ordered that she be blown up.

Inconclusive though the battle of Hampton Roads had been, it was to have enormous consequences. In the United States, Ericsson was naturally at the centre of the discussions with the Navy Department, much of the time in close association with Fox. He met the Assistant Secretary on March 15 to consider future ironclad designs. As always, Ericsson was hugely optimistic, telling Fox that 'the building of a dozen monitors is a mere trifle with the enormous engineering capabilities of the United States at this moment.'[15]

Meanwhile Welles was finding himself under considerable pressure; he complained that instead of being given credit for his labour and care in getting the *Monitor* built, he was abused for not having built more. Although she had been seen by most as having proved a success, there were other opinions which held that what was required was a fleet of seagoing ironclads. Moving in this direction, Lenthall, with Engineer in Chief Isherwood, now advocated the armour plating of the navy's larger wooden vessels; their plan was to cut down the *Roanoke,* arming her with eight 12 inch or 15 inch guns in 'Cole' (sic) turrets, and giving her the protection of 4.5 inch iron plates.

The British Admiralty was naturally taking a keen interest in events on the other side of the Atlantic, and Milne, as commander-in-chief of the North America and West Indies Station was required to find out all he could about the *Monitor,* and he sent back reports based on the information he received from those of his officers who had visited the Union fleet blockading the Confederate coastline. The ease with which they were able to collect information was remarkable, as Lord Lyons, the British Minister in Washington, explained to Lord John Russell on November 3, 1862: 'Indeed in military and naval affairs as well as in matters in general, the national tendency here is towards publicity, and men with competent professional knowledge, knowing how to observe, have little difficulty in acquiring whatever information they may seek.[16]

14 Baxter, *Introduction*, p. 299.
15 Fuller, *Clad in Iron*, p. 95.
16 Regis A Courtemanche, *No Need of Glory* (Annapolis, Md: Naval Institute Press,1977), p. 159.

The reports which Milne received indicated that monitors were unpopular due to their cramped quarters and poor ventilation. He himself was not yet persuaded about their general effectiveness, due to their slowness of fire, the risk of the turret jamming and the damaging effect on the crew of the concussion of their own gunfire. He did, though, acknowledge that changes were constantly being made, and recognised that the development of the Union ironclads was very much a matter of trial and error.

Immediately, the Federals possessed the other two ironclads which had been authorised, the *Galena* and *New Ironsides*. The former did not prove very successful. Designed with a considerable tumblehome, the original intention was for her to have armour 2.7 inches thick, formed of a combination of plates and rails, backed by 1.5 inches of rubber. On further consideration, the rubber was dispensed with, and the plating increased to 3.2 inches at and near the waterline, rising amidships to the port sills. She mounted four 9 inch Dahlgren guns and two Parrott rifled guns. Launched on February 14, 1862, she was commissioned on April 21. Goldsborough described her as 'a most miserable contrivance ...entirely beneath naval criticism ... She is a pretty good ram, and that, in general terms, is about the amount of her, unless she is kept bows on in fighting her guns. At best, however, she is a poor stick for an ironclad. Her moral is better than her physical effect.[17] She took part in an action at Drewery's Bluff on May 15, losing 13 men killed and 11 wounded; as her commander remarked, she had plainly demonstrated that she was not shot proof.

The *New Ironsides*, on the other hand, was very much more successful. A wooden hulled broadside ironclad of 4,120 tons, she was 230 feet long and 57 ½ feet in the beam. Her four water tube boilers produced 1,800 hp, giving a speed of 7 knots. Her armoured sides had a tumblehome of 17°. She had a complete waterline belt of armour plate four and a half inches thick; below the waterline it was reduced to three inches. Her broadside battery, 170 feet long, was protected by the four and a half inch armour, but bow and stern were left unprotected. The deck was of one inch wrought iron backed by three inches of pine. She was fitted with a rectangular ram projecting six feet from her bow. Originally intended to carry sixteen smoothbore muzzle loading 9 inch Dahlgren guns, it was decided during the course of her construction, on the basis of the experience of such guns at Hampton Roads, to equip her with fourteen 11 inch Dahlgren guns, two muzzle loading 8 inch Parrott rifled guns, and two 5.1 inch Dahlgren rifles as chase guns. She was barque rigged with three masts, which were used only for long voyages, and which were struck down when she was on station. She was launched on May 10 and commissioned on August 21, when she joined the blockade. Later, she participated in a large number of operations on the Confederate coast; she was said to have taken part in more days of actual fighting than any other Civil War ironclad, and though hit many times in action suffered little damage.

In addition to his proposal to armour plate a number of wooden warships, Lenthall had during the autumn of 1861 been exploring the possibility of ordering a fleet of double turreted ironclads of the Bureau's own design, preferring turrets based on the system advocated by Captain Coles to those designed by Ericsson. In his annual report he asked for a sum of over $16.5 million, of which $12 million was for the construction of twenty ironclads. The necessary bill passed the House of Representatives on December 19, but was held up in the Senate, possibly due to the

17 Baxter, *Introduction*, p. 268.

influence of supporters of Ericsson's design. Certainly Ericsson and his partner were actively lobbying the Navy Department hard to block the Bureau's proposals at least until the *Monitor's* performance had been tested. In these efforts they were ultimately very successful. The Senate finally passed the bill for twenty new ironclads on February 7, and the Navy Department's call for bids for the new vessels appeared on February 20. By March 9, however, the *Monitor* had made her debut. Her evident success ensured that thereafter Ericsson's prestige soared. Hampton Roads had effectively foreclosed further experimentation, and shipbuilders outside Ericsson's group were able to produce little meaningful counter pressure, though Charles Cramp, whose shipyard had built the *New Ironsides*, scornfully dismissed the navy's 'monitor craze.'[18]

That Spring, the Navy Department set about the task of placing contracts for the twenty new ironclads. Ten of these were 'improved *Monitors*' of the *Passaic* class. There were also five twin turreted *Monitor* types, while the *Roanoke* was converted to what in appearance looked very much like a triple turreted monitor with a higher freeboard. Six of the *Passaic* class were awarded to Ericsson and his partners, who subcontracted the building of all of them to various yards, predominantly machinery manufacturers or ironworks rather than traditional shipyards. The Navy Department, in allocating the remaining four ships of the class, pursued a similar policy.[19]

Elsewhere in the Confederacy, the first of a number of ironclads built for operations on the Mississippi was the *Manassas*, converted from a tugboat named *Enoch Train*. When completed, she was 143 feet long and 33 feet in the beam, with a turtle back covered with one inch armour plating. She was armed with a single gun, and was by no means a formidable warship. However, on October 10, 1861 she took part in a successful operation against the Union squadron blockading the mouth of the Mississippi. In the following year she was engaged in the defence of New Orleans against the advancing fleet of David Farragut and put up a gallant struggle against overwhelming odds before her destruction.

Two further ironclads had been under construction at New Orleans. The first of these was the *Mississippi*, 4,000 tons, 260 feet long, and 58 feet in the beam, armed with sixteen guns. She was the prototype for almost all the ironclads built by the Confederacy; her designer Nelson Tift 'devised a system of construction that was both novel and, in an agricultural nation nearly destitute of shipwrights and skilled labourers, quite practical; his ship would be built with all surfaces flat. Where a curve or bend was needed, he straightened it out and compensated with a sharp angle.[20] The *Mississippi* was followed by the *Louisiana*, which was slightly larger. Neither vessel had been fully completed when Farragut launched his attack on New Orleans, and both were destroyed.

Upriver, at Memphis, work had begun in October 1861 on two ironclads, the *Arkansas* and *Tennessee*. The latter was still only in frame when Union troops approached the city, and she was burned to prevent her capture. The *Arkansas*, however, was in a more advanced state of construction and her hull and casemate backing were complete, and she was towed downriver to Greenwood, some 160 miles from Yazoo City. In May 1862 Lieutenant Isaac Brown came to take command of the incomplete vessel, and he floated her downriver to Yazoo City, where he set about completing her. She was 165 feet in length and 35 feet in the beam. Her armour plating

18 William H. Roberts, *Civil War Ironclads* (Baltimore, Md: Johns Hopkins University Press, 2002), p. 23.
19 Roberts, *Civil War Ironclads*, p. 35.
20 Maurice Melton, *The Confederate Ironclads* (Cranbury, New Jersey: Thomas Yoseloff, 1968), p. 61.

was scarcely adequate; a double layer of one-inch bar iron covered the pilothouse and the casemate top and this was overlaid with a half inch layer of iron plating. She carried two guns facing forward and two astern, and three guns in each broadside. She was fitted with an iron ram.[21] In July 1862 the *Arkansas* was engaged in a series of spectacular battles with the Union fleets threatening Vicksburg. She emerged from her confinement in the Yazoo River on July 15, and headed for the Mississippi, where she intended to break through the Federals. Her appearance came as a complete surprise. As she closed on the enemy; she was struck many times without serious damage, while wrecking first one and then another of the Union ships before coming on Farragut's fleet anchored along the east side of the river. As she passed, each ship delivered a broadside, but although by now heavily damaged she reached Vicksburg successfully. Next day the Federals steamed down on the city, pouring broadsides into the anchored *Arkansas*, but failed to destroy her. On July 22 they made a further attack, in the course of which she inflicted serious damage on several of her adversaries, before her always unreliable engines broke down, and she ran aground. There was nothing more she could do, and she suffered the same fate as so many of the Confederate ironclads, and was blown up by her crew to avoid capture.

The Confederacy launched a considerable number of ironclads throughout the course of the war, but their design did not take the development of ironclads very far, built as they were for river and coastal operations. One of the most successful was the shallow draught *Albemarle,* built and operated in North Carolina. In the spring of 1862 she engaged a number of ships of the North Atlantic Blockading Squadron, sinking one and damaging another before playing a crucial part in the capture of Fort Williams, the key to the defences of Plymouth, under siege by Confederate forces. Thereafter the Federals made a number of attempts to destroy her, and ultimately succeeded when a spar torpedo launch broke through the cordon of logs that had been laid to defend her, and exploded against the ironclad's side.[22]

Given the limitations of its industrial base, the Confederacy was remarkably successful in building ironclads, albeit with the special needs in mind of operating in confined waters. Stephen Mallory looked also to Europe for the building of warships, both with a view to breaking the blockade, and to act as raiders to prey on Federal commerce. Of these, the most spectacularly successful was the *Alabama,* commanded by Raphael Semmes. Her escape from Liverpool, where she was built, caused a major diplomatic incident. It also prejudiced the chances of the Confederacy obtaining two other vessels in particular, which had been ordered by Captain James T. Bulloch, the Confederacy's principal agent in Great Britain. These were to be built by John Laird. They represented the most ambitious attempt by the South to challenge the Federal navy.

They were double turreted rams, laid down by Lairds in April 1862, and were launched in July and August respectively in the following year. By then they were the subject of fierce protests from the Federal government. In July 1863, when they were half finished, the British Foreign Secretary Lord John Russell made it clear that the government was aware of their intended destination, and told Bulloch that they would not be allowed to leave otherwise than as the property of a nation not at war. In an effort to get round this, Bulloch arranged through a French bank for their purchase on behalf of the Egyptian government, and they were named *El Toussan* and *El Mounassir.* Bulloch's intention was that after delivery they would be

21 Melton, *Confederate Ironclads*, p. 117.
22 Melton, *Confederate Ironclads*, pp. 189-198.

transferred to the Confederacy while at sea. It was not difficult to see through this deception, and the British Cabinet was becoming deeply concerned at the developing crisis. Palmerston put forward a solution to Somerset on September 13, 1863, which seemed to him to kill several birds with one stone:

> Now what I wish you to consider is whether it would not be a good thing to buy these Ironclad Rams for our Navy; we are short of Ironclads, and it takes time to build them, we want a good many more to put us on a proper level with France; here are Two nearly finished, no doubt well built, fast sailors, and fitted as rams; if you want Two such either in our dockyards or in a private yard you would not get them until the end of next year, and these will be available before the End of this year. If the Federals get them they will strengthen the Yankees against us if they should be disposed and able next year to execute their threatened vengeance for all the forbearance we have shown them; if we get these ships they will tend to give us moral as well as maritime strength.[23]

Ericsson, when shown a plan of one of the Laird rams, dismissed it as a 'gingerbread affair,' but in fact the two ships would, if they had been able to join the Confederate navy, have been a serious threat; Parkes observed that 'as units of the Confederate Navy having seagoing qualities possessed by none of the US ironclads, they would probably have been exceedingly troublesome to the Federals … For their size they were good enough little ships, very well armed and sufficiently protected to stand up to anything flying the Federal colours on the high seas.'[24]

Displacing 2,750 tons, they were 224 ½ feet long and 42 ½ feet in the beam. They were to carry a crew of 153. As designed, the two turrets would each contain two 9 inch muzzle loading rifles. Their machinery, producing 1,450 hp was designed for a maximum speed of 11½ knots. Their armour was 4 ½ inches thick, reducing to 3 inches at the bow; the turrets were armoured with 5 inch plate. Importantly, for the Confederates expected them to operate at sea for long periods, they could carry 336 tons of coal, which gave them a radius of 1,210 miles at 10 knots.

In October 1863 the two ships were seized by the British government, a step that had very questionable legal validity, since the Court of Exchequer had ruled in a previous case that the subjects of a neutral power had as much right to sell ships to a belligerent as they had to sell munitions. Ultimately, in order to avoid a successful challenge over the legality of the seizure, the government in 1864 adopted Palmerston's suggestion, and purchased the two ironclads for a sum of £30,000 over their contract price, and they joined the Royal Navy as the *Scorpion* and *Wivern*. They were reported to be satisfactory sea boats, though rolling deeply. Amidships their freeboard was only 6 feet, but hinged bulwarks raised this another five feet.

By the end of the war the United States had built a huge number of ironclads based on the original design of the *Monitor*, and did so very rapidly. By the time Britain had, built or building, 24 ironclads, the United States during the same period had commenced more than 50. Ten of the British ships were converted from partially built wooden hulls; the remainder averaged about 3 ½ years to build, but the American ships were on average completed in just under two years.[25] The American ironclad fleet was not, however, designed for seagoing operations.

23 Fuller, *Clad in Iron*, p. 232.
24 Parkes, *British Battleships*, pp. 78-79.
25 Roberts, *Civil War Ironclads*, p. 5

The *Monitor* herself went down in a storm in December 1862, and the ships of the *Passaic* class which followed her were equally unseaworthy.

Ericsson himself devoted particular attention to his design for a very large monitor; the Navy Department placed orders for two of these, which were in due course named *Dictator* and *Puritan*. They were designed to attain 17 knots, which would make them the fastest warships in the world. They were to be protected with side armour of six layers of one inch iron plate backed by four and a half inch iron stringers and three feet nine inches of wood. The turret would have a total thickness of 24 inches, composed of 10 inch iron bars between layers of one inch plates. These vessels were designed to carry a ram, which at the high speed they could attain would make them far more formidable than anything that Europe had yet produced.[26] Ericsson had more than Confederate opposition in his mind when he produced this design. The armoured protection of the *Warrior* was considered to be very weak, and his conception was that the *Passaic* class monitors would be able to harry her and the *Dictator* could then hunt her down. In Ericsson's opinion, since her armour protection was so much greater than that of any British ironclad, there were 'substantial reasons for believing the *Dictator* will prove a dictator.'[27]

Although monitors generally were not to be regarded as oceangoing warships, one of them, the *Miantonomoh*, was chosen by Fox to carry him to Europe to deliver personally the deep sympathy of the United States to Tsar Alexander II following an assassination attempt on April 16, 1866. There was a particular motive in sending her:

> It was for no mere display of national pride or power that the Navy Department ordered the *Miantonomoh* to Europe. The purpose was to show to the people of Europe the power of free institutions. It was to give them visible and tangible proof that the thinking force of a free republic is greater than that of a monarchy when the masses are forced and held down.[28]

Not everyone in government thought this gesture a good idea; Welles wrote in his diary that Fox was reflecting a 'shambling statesmanship.'

Nevertheless, the *Miantonomoh*, and her sister the *Monadnock*, which also undertook a lengthy sea voyage, performed remarkably well. They were large monitors, of 3,400 tons, carrying four 11 inch smoothbore guns in two turrets. They reached their respective destinations unscathed, although Parkes pointed out that they did so 'under conditions which would have precluded their going into action as well as being productive of extreme discomfort and unhealthiness to their personnel.'

The monitors were an ingenious solution to the short term problem which the Union faced in conducting coastal operations, and played a very substantial part in the success of these. But their lack of a seagoing capability meant that in terms of the development of the ironclad as a fighting warship they represented more or less a dead end. Although monitors remained in the U.S. Navy, and took part in operations during the Spanish-American war of 1898, their limitations were cruelly exposed.

26 Fuller, *Clad in Iron*, pp. 118-119.
27 Fuller, *Clad in Iron*, p. 216.
28 Fuller, *Clad in Iron*, p. 271, quoting Charles B Boynton, *The History of the Navy During the Rebellion* (New York: Publisher unknown, 1867-1868), pp 66-67.

14

The Ironclad in 1866

By 1866 the number of ironclads built or building for European navies was rising rapidly. Including coast defence ships the total had reached, by the spring of that year, 116, of which the largest part was of course made up of the British and French ironclad fleets. Most other European nations with any pretension to possessing a navy had begun to acquire ironclads, which were distributed as follows:

Britain 29
France 27
Russia 18
Italy 16
Austria 7
Spain 6
Denmark 4
Turkey 4
Prussia 2
Netherlands 2

Their number would continue to increase, while at the same time the US navy, which ended the American Civil War with some 71 ironclads, began the process of decay and decline which was to continue for the best part of three decades. The European vessels included both broadside ironclads, such as the *Gloire* and the *Warrior*, and a growing number of turret ships inspired by the success of the monitors during the Civil War. It was already a matter of historical dispute as to who could justly claim to have first invented the concept of the armoured turret. Oscar Parkes, describing the genesis of the turret ship, wrote:

> At the time when the plans of the *Warrior* were still under consideration a far more novel and epoch making type of fighting was being evolved in the brain of Captain Cowper Coles R.N., who was destined to become the most outstanding influence in the history of battleship development. Gifted by imagination and ability to make practical application of his theories, with a dogged persistence which won recognition after years of official opposition to his inventions, during which he was a sick man, Coles' name will ever be associated with turret ships and the loss of the *Captain*. There has been much controversy as to who

> invented the turret ship – John Ericsson, the Swedish engineer, or Cowper Coles. Actually the idea of the revolving gun tower dates back long before either of them started working out their own ideas on the subject – Ericsson himself stated that 'this obvious device of installing guns on a revolving platform, open or covered, dates back to the first introduction of artillery.'[1]

Although the concept of a revolving turret was not original, the respective systems designed by Coles and Ericsson were very different. The armoured part of Coles' turret rose 4.5 feet above the main deck, which sloped upwards towards it. The lower section revolved on a central cylinder resting on bevelled wheels on a metal ring like a turntable on the lower deck. The turret was trained by hand, by rack and pinion and a system of hand spikes. Ericsson's turret was supported by and revolved on a central spindle turned by steam training gear; it normally rested on the deck and before turning had to be keyed up by rack and pinion. The conning tower was mounted on the turret's roof. Solid iron port stoppers hung from the roof to close the ports when the guns were run in.[2]

In 1864 Coles published a pamphlet comparing his design with that of Ericsson in the light of the setback which the Ericsson monitors had experienced in the unsuccessful attacks on Charleston in January and February 1863:

> He attributed the injuries of the Ericsson turrets to the use of laminated armour instead of thick plates with heavy wooden backing, and to the fact that the entire surface of the turret, 9 feet in height, and of the superposed pilot house, was exposed to the enemy fire, while his turret had only four feet ten inches exposed, or less than half its height, since the base and working portion were protected on the lower deck.[3]

Ericsson, on the other hand, objected to wooden backing to the turret armour, because 'there the impact of the shot not only depresses the wood in a radial direction but causes an enormous tangential strain on the wooden block nearly in the ratio of the chord to the versed sine.'

Coles had not confined himself to vigorous public advocacy of his design for turret ships; he also gave evidence to the National Defences Commission on the subject of the forts which it was proposed to build on the shoals between Portsea Island and the Isle of Wight:

> In giving evidence he had taken the bit between his teeth in characteristically vehement fashion and strayed widely from the questions put to him, haranguing the members on the danger of enemy steamships running past the projected forts into Spithead and on the merits of his turret ships (despite his opening declaration that the less he had to say about his invention the more gratified he would be), handing round copies of his pamphlet, and complaining of the chairman's attempts to bring him back to the points under discussion as interruptions.[4]

1 Parkes, *British Battleships*, p. 44.
2 Parkes, *British Battleships*, p. 47.
3 Baxter, *Introduction*, p. 328.
4 A. Temple Patterson, 'Captain Cowper Coles and Palmerston's Folly', *The Mariner;s Mirror* 51:1 (1955), pp. 24-25.

Coles was never short of self-confidence; he claimed in the Press that a seagoing turret ship built to his design could 'disable and capture the *Warrior* within an hour.'

As has been seen, Coles designed his vessels as multi-turreted. Essentially, Coles was endeavouring to create a seagoing warship, while Ericsson was content that his vessels should be effective only in coastal waters. The lack of seagoing capability of the monitors was vigorously denied by Ericsson's adherents; John Bourne, an English civilian engineer representing Ericsson in London wrote:

> There has been a great misstatement as to the seagoing properties of the monitors, and I think two parties have been interested in running them down; first, Coles' party, who hope thus to conceal their piracies, and second, the Admiralty people who have been against Coles, and who, to resist him, have been willing to deal a thrust at the turret system.[5]

Ericsson was doubtful when Bourne reported that his first interviews with Edward Reed, the new Admiralty Chief Constructor, had been favourable, observing: 'I have been amazed that one so intelligent should fail to see that he has much to fear from the monitor system. Mr Reed probably understands that a raking 15 inch shot put through the stern of the *Royal Sovereign* would crush the gingerbread work comprising the lower part of Captain Coles' four turrets and thus by a single blow cripple the whole concern.'[6]

The debate about Coles and Ericsson and their respective systems for a turret ship had by then been going on for a considerable time. In the House of Commons in 1862, soon after the battle of Hampton Roads, George Bentinck, an opposition spokesman, attacked the government's failure to grasp the nettle, saying that 'while we have been thinking, the Americans have been acting:'

> They have been satisfied by the experiment, which is doubted upon the Treasury bench here, in the same way as the efficiency of the matchlock was doubted when it superseded the crossbow; of 'Brown Bess' when it superseded the matchlock; and of the Enfield rifle, when it superseded Brown Bess. Our great men are very slow to be convinced; and unless the House of Commons urges them on – unless a lesson is taught us on our own shores by the burning of some of our own ships – they will be as slow as the men of former times were.[7]

It was Bentinck's contention that it would be 'perfectly easy' to build ships as invulnerable as the *Monitor* that possessed all the requisite seagoing qualities.

Reference has already been made to the decision to order the *Prince Albert*, laid down in April 1862 and completed in February 1866. She was a coast defence ship which after some design changes, was of 3,880 tons, 240 feet long, and 40 feet abeam, mounting four 9 inch guns in two turrets, based on Coles' system. Her side armour was four a half inches, and that on the turrets from five inches to ten inches thick. Her designed speed was 11.25 knots. At the same time the Admiralty also decided to adopt the suggestion put forward by Coles of cutting down a wooden ship of the line, armouring her and equipping her with turrets. This was the *Royal Sovereign*,

5 Fuller, *Clad in Iron*, p. 270.
6 Fuller, *Clad in Iron*, p. 270.
7 Fuller, *Clad in Iron*, p. 138.

of 5,080 tons, 240 feet long, and 62 feet abeam, which carried five 10.5 inch guns, three in single turrets and two in a double turret. She had side armour of 5.5 inches, and the turrets were armoured with 5.5-10 inch plate. She was designed to attain 11 knots. Though both ships could be regarded as successful, the Admiralty position on arming ships with turrets was that they should continue to be mastless coast defence vessels, so that for some time their role was destined to be limited. Nevertheless, if history had shown that the best form of coast defence was the seeking out and destruction of an enemy fleet, the building of ships only for coastal operation was the negation of naval strategy.[8] Edward Reed, when appointed Chief Constructor in 1863, was not hostile to the concept of the turret ship, but rejected the possibility of such a vessel being a fully rigged masted ship where arcs of fire were limited to the broadside. For such ships he favoured the 'box battery' in which the broadside guns were concentrated in a heavily armoured battery amidships.

Reed held to this view notwithstanding his design of the *Monarch*, which after lengthy debate was laid down in June 1866. The Board had decided that she was to have a forecastle and be fully rigged, which meant depriving the two turrets of axial fire and locating them amidships in what was a variant of the box battery concept. The *Monarch*, of 8,300 tons, was 330 feet long and 57.5 feet in the beam; her four turret guns were 12 inch, and she had three 7 inch pivot guns. Her side armour was 7 inches thick amidships, and 4.5 inches forward and aft of the central battery. She was designed for a speed of almost 15 knots. Reed was dissatisfied with her; he wrote in 1869 of his conviction that thus far no satisfactorily designed turret ship with rigging had yet been built or even laid down.

The decision to build the *Monarch* was taken before the arrival of the *Miantonomoh* in Europe, where she made a considerable impression on both professional and public opinion. *The Times* regarded the vessel as 'a very extraordinary and – we wish we could not feel it – a portentous spectacle.'[9] Pakington, now again at the head of the Board of Admiralty as First Lord in the minority administration of Lord Derby that had just taken office, accepted that turret ships were the answer: 'We have, I think, already seen enough from what has taken place in foreign nations, as well as from the experiments made by ourselves, to lead us to the conclusion that the time has arrived when experiments should cease and action commence.'[10]

Pakington, who was entirely persuaded of the need to lay down more turret ships, nevertheless ran into considerable opposition within the Cabinet, where there was concern about his proposals for increased naval expenditure. Lord Stanley, Lord Derby's son, who was a member of the Cabinet, wrote in his diary of 'the necessity of checking Pakington's plans of expenditure, which are extravagant. He is honest and hard working but vain, and anxious to distinguish himself personally by another reconstruction of the navy.'[11]

Meanwhile Ericsson had been persuaded by Bourne to offer his services to the British Admiralty in January 1866. However, Bourne unwittingly published a letter from Ericsson describing how a monitor of the same displacement as a double turreted, high freeboard ship such as the *Monarch* would probably settle the contest by smashing the mechanism of the turrets and the ship's side at the waterline, due to her insufficient side armour. Ericsson was in little

8 Parkes, *British Battleships*, p. 68.
9 Fuller, *Clad in Iron*, p. 277.
10 Fuller, *Clad in Iron*, p. 277.
11 Harris, *Pakington*, p. 354.

doubt of the effect of the letter, observing that 'it will bring out the whole strength of the Admiralty against yourself and the monitor system.' He was quite right; shortly after this the Admiralty told Bourne that Ericsson's services would not be required.[12]

The problem with the design of a turret ship was that if the deck was low, there was the risk that she would be swamped in a seaway. If it was high, it would have to be much larger to carry the weight of armour required. If she was fully rigged, which the Admiralty required in cruising ships, the wide arc of fire afforded by the turrets was limited. These considerations accounted for the hesitation of the Admiralty in adopting the concept.

Prior to 1866 only one of the European ironclads had gone into action. This was the Danish *Rolf Krake*, a well designed three masted turret ship built by Robert Napier on Clydebank. Laid down in October 1862, she was completed in July of the following year, which was a remarkably short period for construction. She was of 3,382 tons, measuring 183.75 feet in length, and was armed with four Swedish 6.4 inch smoothbores in two turrets designed by Coles. Both hull and turrets were protected by 4.5 inches of wrought iron plate. Operating against the Prussian forces besieging Dybbol in the Second Schleswig-Holstein War in 1864, she was struck no less than 150 times by the Prussian batteries equipped with 24 pounder Krupp rifles, but suffered little or no damage, as for instance on February 18, as described in a Dutch study published in 1913/1914:

> According to one navy officer the Prussians had fired more than 2,500 pounds of iron. The iron plates were hit in 66 points but did not show much damage, some hit the turrets, 16 went through this smoke stack, one through the steam pipe, five in the masts and 60-70 pierced the superstructure, the boats and bulwarks. The deck was opened in some points by flying splinters which passed through the deck's iron grate. According to eyewitnesses there was not a single safe place on the deck. The ship left pumping water out (though this was in part due to her ability to lower herself).[13]

The *Dannebrog* and *Peder Skram* were two Danish wooden hulled vessels cut down and armoured with 4.5 inch wrought iron. The *Dannebrog* had been a 74 gun ship of the line; when converted she was of 3,330 tons, 228 feet long, and initially equipped with sixteen 6 inch muzzle loading rifles. Although completed in March 1864 she took no part in the war. *Peder Skram*, a steam frigate, was similarly converted; she was of 3,057 tons, 185 feet long, and carried twelve 6 inch muzzle loading rifles; she did not enter service until 1866. The fourth Danish ironclad was the *Danmark,* another spin-off from the Confederacy, purchased while she was on the stocks on Clydebank. She only joined the Danish fleet in 1869. Of 4,670 tons, she was 270 feet long, and was armoured with 4.5 inch iron plate. She carried twelve 8 inch and twelve 6 inch muzzle loading rifles. She was said to be 'an ungainly, uncomfortable ship.'[14]

After Britain and France, the European navy with the greatest number of ironclads built or building in 1866 was Russia, where the possibilities of turret ships were held in particularly high regard. The Russians began, however, with the conversion of two wooden hulled steam frigates,

12 Fuller, *Clad in Iron*, p. 279.
13 Jack Greene and Alessandro Massignani, *Ironclads at War* (Consohocken, Pennsylvania: Combined Publishing, 1998), p. 200.
14 Angus Konstam, *European Ironclads 1860-75* (Oxford: Osprey, 2019) p. 17.

the *Sevastopol* and *Petropavlovsk*. They were of 6,210 tons, 295 feet long, and 52 feet in the beam. They had a trial speed of 11 knots. They were protected with 4.5 inch iron plates; *Petropavlovsk* was armed with twenty four 8 inch muzzle loading rifles, and two 6 inch smoothbores, and *Sevastopol* with twenty eight 8 inch muzzle loading rifles.[15]

In 1861 Russia ordered from Thames Ironworks the 3,279 ton *Pervenets*, 220 feet long and 52.5 feet abeam. Although dismissed by Fred T Jane as practically a floating battery, he still considered her a formidable ship. She was protected by 4.5 inch iron plate. She was initially armed with twenty six 7.7 inch smoothbore muzzle loaders. Her speed was low, at 9 knots. Two sister ships, the *Kreml* and *Ne Trou Menia*, were built in St Petersburg, completed in 1866 and 1865 respectively.

The casemate ironclad *Kniaz Pojarski*, of 5,000 tons, laid down in St Petersburg in 1864, was based on the British ironclad *Penelope*. She was 272 feet long and 49 feet in the beam, armoured with 4.5 inch plate on her belt and over her battery of eight 8 inch and two six-inch muzzle loading rifles. Her trial speed was said to be 12.5 knots, but Jane recorded her sea speed as only 9 knots; none of the Russian ironclads were very fast. Russia had begun to lay down a large number of single turreted monitors as coast defence ships, based on Ericsson's original design; there were 10 of these in the *Ouragan* class. Russia also ordered a double turreted monitor from Robert Napier, the *Smertch* of 1,460 tons, which had one 9 inch gun in each of her turrets, which were armoured with 6 inch plate. She also laid down the *Minin*, a vessel based on the British *Monarch*, but her construction was long delayed.[16]

Apart from those of the navies of Italy and Austria, dealt with in succeeding chapters, the remaining European ironclads built or building in 1866 can be briefly summarised. Spain had six; the first of these was built at Toulon. Admiral Ballard considered her to be 'the most formidable capital ship begun in the whole world in 1861.' This was the 'magnificent Spanish iron hulled *Numancia*; larger than any French rival and better in material than nine tenths; more powerfully armed and strongly protected than any French or British, unless perhaps the *Minotaur* or *Agincourt*. A splendid sea boat and good steamer.' [17] 315 feet long, she was protected by a 5.5 inch belt. She was initially armed with forty 8 inch muzzle loading smooth bores. She was not, however, particularly fast, with a speed of 10 knots. The wooden hulled *Arapiles*, building on the Thames, was redesigned as a 5,700 ton ironclad. Another Thames built ironclad was the 7,135 ton *Vitoria*; she was similar to British ironclads of the period. The first Spanish built ironclad was the *Tetuan*, laid down in the Royal Dockyard at Ferrol in 1861; like the *Arapiles*, she resembled the *Gloire*. The somewhat smaller *Zaragoza*, of 5,530 tons, with an armoured belt of 5 inch plate, carried twenty one 8 inch guns. Finally, the *Sagunto*, a converted ship of the line of 7,352 tons, with 6 inch armour, carried a mixed armament of six 9 inch and two 8 inch smoothbore muzzle loaders and three 7.9 inch breech loaders.[18]

Turkey commissioned the building of the four broadside ironclads of the *Ommanieh* class. In addition to the name ship there were the *Abdul Aziz*, *Mahmudieh*, and *Orkanieh*; all were completed by July 1866. They were of 6,400 tons, 293 feet long and had an armoured belt of 5.5 inches. Their speed was 12 knots. They were armed with fourteen 8 inch muzzle loading rifles

15 Fred T Jane, *The Imperial Russian Navy* (London: Conway Maritime Press, 1983) p. 156.
16 Jane, *Imperial Russian Navy*, pp. 159-160.
17 Ballard, *Black Battlefleet*, p. 414.
18 Konstam, *European Ironclads*, pp. 38-40.

with a 9 inch pivot gun on the forecastle. The unfinished *Fatikh*, laid down on the Thames in 1865 and designed by Edward Reed, was subsequently sold to Prussia and completed as the *König Wilhelm*. She was a powerful casemate ironclad of 10,761 tons, with a relatively high speed of 14.5 knots. She was particularly heavily armoured with a belt of 12 inches covering the casemate, tapering to 6 inches at bow and stern, and was armed with eighteen 9.4 inch muzzle loading rifles and five 8.2 inch muzzle loading rifles. She was said to be the most powerful ship in the world when newly built. Prussia also had under construction two more casemate ironclads, the *Friedrich Karl* and *Kronprinz* of 6,200 tons; 297 feet long, they had a 4.5 inch armoured belt. They carried sixteen 8.2 inch muzzle loading rifles and had a speed of 13.5 knots. Finally, Prussia possessed the two small coast defence ironclads, *Arminius* built in Britain and *Prince Adalbert* built in France, the latter originally having been built for the Confederacy.[19]

The Netherlands had two small ironclads under construction. The first of these was the *De Ruyter*, a not very satisfactory conversion based on the *Virginia*. She was followed by the turret ship *Prins Hendrik*, described by Angus Konstam as 'a scaled-down version of the British turret ship *Monarch*;' she was armed with four 9 inch muzzle loading rifles in two turrets.[20]

The large scale coastal operations of the American Civil War, and the European experience of the *Rolf Krake* in 1864 did not offer much guidance for the development of a coherent system of fleet tactics for steam powered ironclads. One difficulty, which affected the British fleet in particular, was the wide variation between ships of differing speed, size, manoeuvrability, and armament. To be able to operate effectively, a heterogenous fleet of this kind would require a great deal of training in tactical evolutions.

Since most of the European ships were broadside ironclads, it might well be that to maximise its fire power a fleet would deploy in line. On the other hand, with higher speeds possible than had been the case under sail, breaking the line might be more readily achieved, though this would increase the possibility of ships being rammed. The American experience during the Civil War, particularly at Mobile Bay, had demonstrated that ramming was not easy to achieve, and was not necessarily effective. It was a battle technique that called for great skill, and as a means of attack was not only extremely difficult to execute but which exposed the assailant to at least as much danger as to its target.

Another key consideration was getting into effective range – that is, close enough for the fleet's guns seriously to damage the enemy ships in spite of their armour plate. As new and improved ordnance came into use, it was not an easy matter to determine exactly what would be the effective range of the guns in operational conditions. A fleet must, however, shorten the range to that at which the enemy armour could be penetrated. In the opinion of Admiral Custance, writing in 1912 and looking back at the early ironclads, 'no one, except the late Lord Armstrong, and a few other far-seeing men, seemed to realise that more powerful guns in greater numbers might have been an effective reply to armour.'[21]

The offensive capability of his monitors in the attacks launched on Charleston in 1863 was a matter of real concern to Ericsson, who wrote to Fox before the first attack took place:

19 Erich Groener, *German Warships 1815-1945* (London: Conway Maritime Press, 1990), vol. I, pp. 1-3.
20 Konstam, *European Ironclads*, p. 33.
21 Admiral Sir Reginald Custance, *The Ship of the Line in Battle* (Edinburgh: William Blackwood & Sons, 1912), p. 42.

> I cannot share in your confidence relative to the capture of Charleston. I am so much in the habit of estimating force and resistance that I cannot feel sanguine of success. If you do succeed, it will not be a mechanical consequence of your 'marvellous' vessels, but because you are marvellously fortunate. The most I dare hope is that the contest will end without the loss of that prestige which your ironclads have conferred on the nation abroad … A single shot will sink a ship while a hundred rounds cannot silence a fort.[22]

Admiral Custance was struck by the way in which the outcome of the Charleston assaults was recorded:

> In the official records of the war nothing is more striking than the stress laid on the defensive qualities of the monitors, as measured by the number of hits received, compared with the little attention paid to those officers who pointed out their deficient offensive power. That they were not scored by the enemy's hits struck people much more than that they failed to score hits against the enemy. The military value of the monitor class was as limited as was that of the uncertain ram.[23]

Reviewing the design of the early ironclads, Custance addressed the question of their ability to get into effective range. He considered that they had 'little power of defeating an enemy because the small number of their guns limited the chance of hitting.' Since the effective range of the muzzle loading guns with which ironclads were at this time equipped was so short, it was, or should have been, evident that whatever tactical formation was chosen by a commander, a battle would speedily disintegrate into a melée, in which his control of his fleet would be almost completely lost.

What was certainly necessary was that the commander should be able to count on the ability of his fleet to come into action when and how he wanted, and that all the units of the fleet should be capable of performing the tactical evolutions necessary. There were, though, real difficulties in achieving this, even if there had been sufficient training, as Sir John Knox Laughton pointed out:

> Theoretically, an evolution is laid down on paper; the circles, the distances, and the times calculated; and the fleet, the squadrons and the ships are in exact position, in exact time. Practically, the result of the evolution is not so exact; neither position nor time can be strictly accurate; that they may be approximately so, is the most we can hope, under favourable circumstances.[24]

22 Fuller, *Clad in Iron*, p. 254.
23 Custance, *Ship of the Line*, p. 29.
24 Sir John Knox Laughton, 'Essay on Global Tactics' in *The Gun, Ram and Torpedo* (London: J Griffin & Co 1874) pp 86-87

15

The Italian Navy

The Royal Italian Navy, the *Regia Marina*, came into existence as a result of the unification of Italy in 1861. It represented the merger of the navies of the Kingdom of Sardinia, and the Kingdom of Naples and the Two Sicilies. Sardinia, which prior to unification comprised Sardinia and the state of Piedmont, had its capital at Turin. On its throne had sat a series of ambitious if not altogether effective monarchs who were ultimately to succeed in making their country the focus of the Risorgimento. This movement united the patchwork of individual states in the Italian peninsula, and with the assistance of the French alliance in 1859 drove the Austrians out of northern Italy, with the exception of Venetia. Two years later, largely thanks to Garibaldi, the Bourbon monarchy in the Kingdom of Naples and Sicily fell, which then became part of the united Italy.

Both nations had an extensive maritime trade; indeed, the Neapolitan merchant fleet was said to account for 80% of merchant shipping in the Mediterranean. Both, therefore, had found it necessary to maintain a fleet to protect that trade, and in the first half of the nineteenth century had been strengthening their navies.

The Sardinian navy had been founded originally in 1713 by King Victor Amadeus II, who in conjunction with his Neapolitan counterpart, acquired a number of galleys and sailing warships abandoned by the Spanish in the ports of Sicily. The Sardinians maintained a small fleet during the rest of the century, but following their defeat by Napoleon it was disbanded. The navy was re-established by King Victor Emmanuel I after the end of the Napoleonic wars and a programme of expansion began. Several new warships were ordered, some from British shipyards. The fleet undertook a successful expedition against the Vilayet of Tripoli in 1825. Further warships were ordered; King Charles Felix was an enthusiast for the navy, and in 1834 it acquired its first steamer, the sloop *Gulnara*. Four additional steamers were also acquired.[1] This expansion culminated in the arrival of the 64 gun frigate *San Michele*, which was the first Sardinian warship to carry Paixhans shell firing guns. In 1848 a squadron under Vice Admiral Giuseppe Albini was sent to the Adriatic in support of the Venetian revolt against Austrian rule, where it conducted a blockade. Neapolitan warships under Admiral Rafaele de Cosa also arrived to join the blockade, although their cooperation proved only temporary; de Cosa had

1 Lawrence Sondhaus, *Naval Warfare 1815-1914* (London: Routledge, 2001), p. 31.

arrived with very equivocal orders, due to the political situation in Naples. When a counter revolution restored the absolute monarchy, he was ordered to return with his squadron.

In due course the Austrian military successes at Custozza and Novara led to the conclusion of an armistice, and in August 1848 Albini was ordered home. His squadron had not particularly distinguished itself; there was a marked lack of discipline, and morale was low, and in the following year there was a mutiny in the fleet. There was also resistance among senior officers to the transition to a steam powered navy.

In October 1850, however, Count Camillo Cavour, recently appointed to the Sardinian Cabinet as Minister for Economic Affairs, took over the Navy Ministry as well. His first task was to oversee the preparation of the navy estimates which he would have to present early in the new year. Characteristically, he embarked on a close study of the navy in its present situation and of its future requirements, and he prepared a scheme of reorganisation of the service which, unfortunately, was not put into effect. He immediately recognised that one of the navy's most serious shortcomings was a lack of discipline and a rigid caste system among officers, who were frequently insubordinate. He made known to the commander in chief of the navy that he would crack down on indiscipline in future no matter how senior an offender might be.[2]

Normally, the navy estimates received only perfunctory attention from the Chamber, and were discussed as part of the army estimates; on this occasion, however, ten days were spent reviewing them in a series of debates in which Cavour spoke several times a day:

> In the course of the debate every aspect of the navy was brought under review; pay and pensions, administration, naval construction and coast defence, training and equipment, gunnery and navigation, all alike were subjected to discussion. Among Cavour's suggestions was the transfer of the naval arsenal from Genoa to La Spezia, and the creation of a great naval base at this latter place. The reasons were partly strategic and partly commercial. He had great schemes for the development of Genoa, by linking it to the continental railway system, building docks, opening a transatlantic steamship service, and thus making Genoa the first commercial port in the Mediterranean. Hitherto, the fact that Genoa was a naval as well as a commercial port had prevented expansion and cramped both sides of marine activity.[3]

One of Cavour's reforms which failed to receive acceptance from the Chamber was his proposal to disband the existing regiment of marines; this was supposed to provide part of the crew of each warship, but in practice this was not the case. It had been Cavour's intention to reduce their numbers, and divide them into separate corps; one would be responsible for coast defence and one would consist of specialists in naval gunnery. The Chamber, however, would have none of it, and all Cavour could achieve was the appointment of a commission on naval gunnery. He was more successful with his efforts to improve navigation, by ensuring that all officers were sufficiently proficient, and he successfully proposed that the subject should be thoroughly studied. He also proposed the establishment of a naval school linked to the university, which would

2 A.J. Whyte, *The Political Life and Letters of Cavour 1848-1861* (Oxford: Oxford University Press, 1930), p. 63.

3 Whyte, *Life and Letters of Cavour*, pp. 63-64.

provide courses in the theoretical side of navigation. Cavour's wide-ranging proposals lifted the profile of the navy, and his estimates were duly passed.

It was the policy of the government that the navy should become at least as strong as any other fleet in Italy, which meant that it must catch up with the fleet of the Kingdom of Naples and the Two Sicilies. Cavour recognised the need to accelerate the switch to steam propulsion, a development which was unpopular with many of the more conservative members of the officer corps, and he encouraged the introduction of screw propellers. He ordered a new frigate from England, which served as a model for three further steam frigates; these became the *Carlo Alberto*, *Vittorio Emanuele*, *Maria Adelaide*, and *Duca di Genova*.

However, unfortunately for the navy, Cavour did not long remain in his post. In April 1851 he accepted office as Minister of Finance and stepped down as Navy Minister, later to become Minister President. In the short time in which he had held office, he had achieved a great deal to improve the efficiency of the navy, and had set it on a path which, if it had been continued, would greatly have enhanced its effectiveness:

> His outline of reorganisation was scarcely more than sketched in before it had to be abandoned. His handling of the root problem of discipline is instructive. He was too wise to believe that, however necessary, a series of reprimands and court martials would effect a radical cure. His first step was to increase the funds allotted for the education of the seamen, and to recommend a special course of study for the officers ... His idea of a theoretical course in navigation at the university, to be attended by relays of officers, was not only as modern in conception as it would have been valuable in practice, but was aimed at breaking down that exclusive spirit that made the naval officer a man apart. Equally sound was his idea of a gunnery school ashore, in which to train officers and men.[4]

The indiscipline with which Cavour had to deal involved senior officers, usually of an aristocratic background. One captain, the Marquis Incisa, took his ship *Aurora* into Cagliari, and stayed there contrary to orders; he was tried by a Council of Discipline. So was Captain Paroldo, of the *Eridano*, who was charged with conduct unbecoming of an officer, having been involved in an amorous escapade; this offence was compounded by his having connived at smuggling. Cavour was, however, dismayed to find that they enjoyed considerable protection from the throne. The founder of the Sardinian navy, Admiral de Geneys, who had been in command for a quarter of a century, had a very relaxed attitude to indiscipline, remarking that 'rules and regulations were made for imbeciles,' with the result that commanding officers felt able to do much as they wanted once safely out of sight of land. Another instance of the endemic problem of insubordination was the case of Captain Persano, described in Chapter 17.

The navy of the Kingdom of Naples and the Two Sicilies had for many years been much the largest in Italy. It had the benefit of a substantial shipyard in Castellamare at Naples, which had built a large number of warships for the Neapolitan navy. It had constructed the first steamship to be built in Italy. King Ferdinand II was another monarch who was extremely supportive of his navy, and recognised its important role in protecting the kingdom's very large maritime trade. The navy had, however, been slow in making the transition from sail to steam and as late as

4 Whyte, *Life and Letters of Cavour*, p. 72.

1859 this process was far from complete. At that date the fleet included a considerable number of sailing warships, including the two ships of the line *Monarca* and *Vesuvio*, of 86 and 80 guns respectively. There were also four sailing frigates and a number of smaller vessels. There were 11 steam frigates in commission, one of which, the *Borbone*, mounted 64 guns. The remainder were much smaller, carrying ten or twelve guns. Some of these had been built in British shipyards, and others at Naples. There was also a large number of smaller steamers.[5] The Neapolitan navy clung to the concept of paddle steamers, launching its last in 1856; its first screw frigate was laid down in the following year.

The defeat of the Austrians at Magenta and Solferino in 1859 led to the Treaty of Zürich, which gave only Lombardy to Sardinia, leaving the question of the central Italian duchies and the possibility of an Italian confederation to be resolved later. In the late summer, however, constituent assemblies in Modena, Parma and the Romagna voted to join Sardinia, and in March 1860 their annexation and that of Tuscany was confirmed. Cavour, who had resigned as Minister President following the armistice with Austria, returned to power in January 1860 and now also became Navy Minister again, and in April he incorporated the navy of Tuscany into the Sardinian navy. He also began to plan for what would become the future navy of Italy and ordered two ironclads from a French shipyard in Toulon. The first of these, the *Terribile*, was laid down in June 1860 and her sister, the *Formidabile*, in December.

The political situation in 1860 continued to be extremely complex. Matters came to a head when Giuseppe Garibaldi, with whom Cavour enjoyed an extremely equivocal relationship, landed with his 'Thousand' in Sicily with a view to overthrowing Bourbon rule. He captured Palermo on May 30, and on August 18 crossed the Straits of Messina to land in Calabria. The Neapolitan army was soon in full retreat, and on September 5 the King abandoned Naples and took refuge in the fortress of Gaeta, where he was kept under observation by the Sardinian fleet under Rear Admiral Persano. The fleet could take no action against Gaeta, however, since on the orders of the Emperor Napoleon III a French Squadron blocked the roadstead. Persano wrote to Cavour on September 6 to say that he hoped that he had won over the Neapolitan Navy 'with a few thousand ducats.'[6] There was much confusion as to the exact stance of the Neapolitan navy; Villamarina, Cavour's ambassador in Naples, told him at that time that it was impossible for it to fly the Sardinian flag because it was afraid of Garibaldi. It need not have been; one of Garibaldi's first acts on establishing control of Naples was to put the Neapolitan Navy under Persano's orders.

Later in September Cavour ordered Persano to take the fleet into the Adriatic to assist in the siege of Ancona, where the Papal garrison was holding out against the Sardinian forces; the city surrendered on September 29. Meanwhile events were moving fast elsewhere in the Papal States, into which Sardinian troops had marched on September 11, defeating the Papal army at Castelfidardo a week later. On October 1 Garibaldi defeated the Neapolitan army at the battle of the Volturno. His original invasion of Sicily had set in motion the final step towards the unification of Italy, but when, having decided to retire again to Caprera, his steamer passed Persano's fleet on November 9, the admiral was forbidden to fire a salute in Garibaldi's honour.

5 Sondhaus, *Naval Warfare*, p. 31.
6 Denis Mack Smith, *Cavour and Garibaldi 1860* (Cambridge: Weidenfeld & Nicolson, 1985), p. 205.

On October 21 a plebiscite was held in Naples and Sicily, both of which voted to join the Kingdom of Italy and the rule of the Sardinian dynasty. In mid-January 1861, recognising the inevitable, Napoleon III withdrew his fleet from off Gaeta, and in February the fortress surrendered. With the virtual completion of Italian unification, the government had one particular problem, and that was what to do with Garibaldi. There were various suggestions; Palmerston proposed that he be put in charge of the Italian navy, while another idea was that he be sent as ambassador to South America, where his reputation was extremely high. Persano suggested that he be made nominal governor of Naples, since he was very popular among the peoples of the south. Cavour though, preferred to see him safely out of the way, pensioned off with money, titles, and gifts.

Victor Emmanuel was formally declared King of Italy on March 17, 1861, and the *Regia Marina* was officially founded two weeks later. Cavour made a powerful appeal to the Chamber of Deputies for an extraordinary grant of 20 million lire for naval construction and for the creation of a naval base at Ancona, crucial to the future deployment of an Italian fleet in any war against Austria. No less important was the task of rapidly building an ironclad fleet, and this Cavour now proceeded to do. He was not, however, to have much time to devote to the task; in May 1861 he became ill and he died on June 6, with many of the new kingdom's problems unresolved.

Menabrea, his successor as Navy Minister, did not share Cavour's belief in an ironclad fleet, and was supported in this by Nino Bixio, a hugely influential member of the Chamber of Deputies. On the other hand he was opposed by Persano, who strongly argued for the building of ironclads. In the autumn of 1861 Menabrea convened a special commission, which at once determined that Italy must possess a fleet that was equal to the combined strength of Austria and Spain, taking account of the fact that Spain had strongly opposed the unification of Italy.[7]

However, although the commission called for a strong fleet, its composition reflected Menabrea's view of the necessity for ironclads. As a result, its recommendations called for unarmoured screw ships of the line rather than ironclads. Menabrea accordingly based his construction programme on the building of four such vessels in the period 1862-1865. Beyond this, his programme attempted to please everyone. It provided for two ironclads to be built in Britain, a dozen screw gunboats for coast defence and 'a number of transports to appease the hotheads who called for immediate invasions of Venetia, Istria and Dalmatia.'[8] The programme was not well received; but before it could be taken further the ministry fell in February 1862, and Menabrea was replaced by Persano in the new cabinet formed by Urbano Rattazzi.

Those in favour of ironclads now pressed Persano to abandon Menabrea's programme; as luck would have it, news was soon received of the battle of Hampton Roads, which materially strengthened their argument. In June 1862, addressing the Chamber of Deputies, Persano said that 'the recent events in the American War have shown that wooden warships can be taken into little account, given the incontestable superiority of the ironclad ships, only one of which could with her ram sink an entire wooden fleet.' Following this, he cancelled the proposal for the four ships of the line, replacing them with four ironclads to be built in France, with three more to be built in Italy. In June Persano put before the Chamber a plan based on this, which included in

7 Lawrence Sondhaus, *The Habsburg Empire and the Sea: Austrian Naval Policy 1797-1866* (West Lafayette, Indiana: Purdue University Press, 1989), p. 220.

8 Sondhaus, *Habsburg Empire*, p. 220.

addition the two ironclads which Menabrea's plan had called for to be built in Britain. Persano pressed on with his programme, in the face of continued protests from Menabrea. When he left office, on the fall of the Rattazzi government, Italy had fourteen ironclads on order, building or built. The most striking of these was the Italian navy's first turret ship, the *Affondatore*, which was built on the Thames to the design of Simone Antonio de Saint Bon. She was described as an ironclad ram, and in her earliest design was intended to be just that, with no offensive armament other than her very large iron ram.

It has been pointed out that at this time there was considerable discussion as to the type of guns with which the fleet should be equipped. The *Studio per la compilazione di un piano organico per la Marina Italiana,* published in 1863, was intended to establish the navy's policy towards its artillery:

> Tests carried out in recent times, and especially in England, to establish the penetration power and the effectiveness of shots on the armour plates, seem to incline towards the solution of spherical shots and smoothbore guns. The friction in the rifled guns is much more than in the smooth ones, and consequently the muscle velocity is lower in rifled guns; and the effective short range is lower.[9]

Notwithstanding this the navy continued to purchase many wrought iron rifled guns from Sweden. Armour plating was ordered in Sweden, Great Britain, and France, but also from the Ansaldo company. A recognition that weapons must continue to be purchased abroad led at the end of 1865 to the decision to order the new Armstrong guns. Many of these had still not been delivered by the time hostilities commenced.

In the new ministry of Marco Minghetti, the Navy Ministry was headed by General Efusio Cugia, who took office on a wave of public support for a greatly enlarged navy. Nino Bixio now reversed his opinion of ironclads and vigorously supported the navy's construction programme. This included two further ironclads which were, however, not laid down until August 1865. Cugia was not to remain long in office; the Minghetti government fell in 1864. The new ministry was headed by General Alfonso La Marmora, who sought to reduce the naval budget. Cugia's successor, General Diego Angioletti succeeded in doing so by turning away from new construction, a policy which attracted bitter protests from Nino Bixio and others of like mind. The government, confident that with the ships already with the fleet and those under construction the navy was strong enough to dominate the Adriatic, turned its attention to the development of land installations.[10]

By the time war broke out with Austria in 1866, the Italian navy possessed 12 ironclads. The first of these to join the fleet had been the *Formidabile* and *Terribile*. They were originally intended to be built as armoured floating batteries on the lines of the French vessels that had been employed at Kinburn, and were ordered from La Seyne at Toulon; after work began they were redesigned as seagoing broadside ironclads mounting four 8 inch and sixteen 6 inch muzzleloading rifles. They were not large, of 2,807 tons, and just under 207 feet long.

9 Greene and Massignani, *Ironclads at War*, p. 389.
10 Sondhaus, *Habsburg Empire*, p. 222.

Their armour plating was 4.3 inches thick. They were designed to attain a speed of 10 knots. Essentially, they were smaller versions of the *Gloire*.[11]

They were followed by the *Principe di Carignano* class, which were also converted to broadside ironclads after having been laid down as unarmoured steam frigates. The three ships of the class were built in Italy the *Principe di Carignano* at Genoa, the *Messina* at Naples and the *Conte Verde* at Livorno. Somewhat larger than the *Formidabiles,* they were of 3,912 tons and 241 feet long. They mounted twenty two muzzleloading rifles; *Principe di Carignano* carried ten 8 inch and twelve 6 inch, while the other two carried four 8 inch and eighteen 6 inch. The first two ships had a complete armoured belt of 4.75 inches; the *Conte Verde's* armour protection was incomplete. Only the name ship of the class was completed in time to join the fleet in 1866. As with their predecessors, they were not fast ships, attaining 10.4 knots.[12]

In 1861 two larger ironclads were ordered from the United States; the *Re d'Italia* and *Re di Portogallo* were laid down at William H. Webb's shipyard in New York in November and December respectively. Of 5,700 tons, they were just under 327 feet long and 55 feet in the beam. They were the most powerful ironclads Italy had so far acquired, designed to carry 36 muzzleloading rifles; *Re d'Italia* had six 8 inch and thirty 6 inch, and her sister was equipped with two 10 inch and the remainder 6 inch. They were somewhat faster than the earlier classes, at 12 knots. Their armoured belt was 4.75 inches, but did not extend to cover their stern. They, like their predecessors, were wooden hulled vessels; it is said that their American builders used unseasoned timber in their construction. They were both completed in the summer of 1864. Their general design was not dissimilar from the *Gloire*.[13]

The limited capacity of Italian shipyards led to the next order, of the four ships of the *Regina Maria Pia* class, being placed with French shipyards. They were laid down in July and August 1862; the *Regina Maria Pia* was completed in April 1864, the *Castelfidardo* in May, the *San Martino* in November and the *Ancona* in 1866. Their design varied slightly but they were of the order of 4,527 tons, and were just over 268 feet long. Their armour plate was 4.75 inches. They carried most of their battery of twenty six guns in a broadside arrangement save for three located fore and aft as chase guns. Each carried four 8 inch muzzleloading rifles and twenty 6 inch; *Ancona* and *Castelfidardodo* each carried an additional 6 inch gun. Speed was again increased, up to 13.5 knots.[14]

The last ironclad to join the Italian fleet before the outbreak of war was the *Affondatore*, of 4,307 tons. She was still fitting out on the Thames as war became imminent, and her crew were sent to bring the ship to Cherbourg, to complete the work before heading to Italy. In the event she was still not finally complete when she arrived. Just under 310 feet long and 40 feet in the beam, she was protected by 5 inch armour plate on her turrets and hull. She was designed with an extremely low freeboard and minimal superstructure, with only a small conning tower. When her design was altered to incorporate her two single turrets, these were each fitted with a 9 inch Armstrong muzzleloading rifle. She was fitted with a two masted schooner rig to

11 Konstam, *European Ironclads*, p. 28.
12 Konstam, *European Ironclads*, p. 29.
13 Konstam, *European Ironclads*, p. 28.
14 Konstam, *European Ironclads*, p. 29.

supplement her engine on longer voyages; her single expansion steam engine gave her a top speed of 12 knots.[15]

Finally, there were two coast defence ironclads, the *Palestro* and *Varese*, each of about 2,000 tons, and carrying five guns. In addition to the ironclads, Italy possessed a large number of wooden steam powered warships, of which the largest was the ship of the line *Re Galantuomo,* carrying 43 guns. There were eight steam frigates, each armed with between fifty and fifty four guns, and four corvettes carrying between ten and twenty guns. In addition there were three gunboats and about twenty four seagoing and auxiliary steamers.[16]

15 Konstam, *European Iron Ironclads*, pp. 29-30.
16 Sondhaus, *Habsburg Empire*, pp. 279-280.

16

The Austrian Navy

Austria, by the terms of the Treaty of Campoformio of 1797, received the territory, navy, and merchant marine of the former Venetian Republic. It had previously begun to acquire a navy of sorts in 1786, but this was confined to a small squadron established in Trieste to protect trade against pirates. Now, however, the inheritance which Austria received 'was a tremendous windfall that added a new dimension to her strategic horizons.'[1]

However, it was a windfall that Austria at first did little to exploit; the government in Vienna cut back on naval expenditure, and Austria's fleet was much reduced. In its early days, of course, a majority of the personnel was Italian, which was the language of command and of legal education. Austria had scarcely had time to accustom itself to the possession of Venice and its navy, however, before defeat at Austerlitz meant that the Habsburg Empire lost them again, and the fleet that remained was pitifully small. Worse was to follow. When Austria was beaten again at Wagram its navy disappeared altogether when for a while she became landlocked as a result of losing her possessions on the Adriatic. In 1814, though, the Habsburg Empire became a maritime power again, recovering the territorial gains which had originally been made at Campoformio, and re-acquiring the fleet that had temporarily been Napoleon I's Royal Italian Navy. It was a substantial force, consisting of ten ships of the line, eight frigates, and a large number of smaller vessels, but it was not kept up to this strength. It was extensively cut back again, and energetic efforts were made to sell off the bulk of the ships that had been acquired. In 1817 Emperor Francis II fixed the active strength of the navy at two frigates and eight brigs, with a third frigate in reserve. Venice remained the principal base, from where the navy patrolled the Adriatic.

In 1821 Major General Marquis Amilcare Paulucci became commander-in-chief. At that time the navy's principal role was to support the operations of the Austrian army as it endeavoured to execute Metternich's policy of restoring order in the Italian peninsula. In this task the navy did not distinguish itself. Its ships steadily deteriorated in condition as the government continued to limit spending. An attempt to increase the navy's strength by proposing that it be fixed at eight frigates was rejected. However, in 1824 it entered a new era when Paulucci was appointed as *Marineoberkommandant*. He successfully resisted any further reduction in the strength of the navy; but although he also succeeded in expanding the officer corps, the lack

1 Sondhaus, *Habsburg Empire*, p. ix.

of sufficient funds to pay adequate salaries led to officers resorting to smuggling to supplement their incomes, creating a regrettable culture of misconduct.

In 1828 Captain Antonio Bandiera, one of the navy's more promising officers, successfully led a mission against the Sultan of Morocco to obtain the release of an Austrian merchant brig, and by so doing he effectively put paid to the raiding of Austrian ships by North African pirates. Generally, however, the navy's profile in these years was low, though Paulucci did succeed in quietly strengthening it by the expedient of replacing old worn out warships with new vessels. By 1832 the navy consisted of four active frigates, with a fifth in reserve, with five corvettes, four brigs and a large number of smaller vessels, which has been described as 'the greatest collection of Habsburg warships since the days of Charles VI.'[2] It was not, however much of a navy for a Great Power, and it was not strong enough to avoid humiliation at the hands of the French when King Louis Philippe sent a squadron to occupy Ancona.

Although the financial situation of the Austrian Empire continued to limit spending on the navy, funds were grudgingly made available for the construction of additional ships and the purchase of new equipment. In 1836 the trials began of the navy's first steamship, the paddle steamer *Maria Anna*. In the following year the third son of the Archduke Charles, Archduke Frederick Leopold, joined the navy, a move which considerably enhanced its prestige. In 1840, when in command of the frigate *Guerriera*, part of an Austrian squadron under Rear Admiral Bandiera, Frederick distinguished himself in operations against the Egyptian forces of Mohammad Ali at Sidon and Acre. The success of the Austrian squadron there added enormously to the navy's national and international reputation. The British commander-in-chief wrote subsequently to Metternich that he had been 'satisfied with the zeal, tact, and bravery displayed on all occasions by the Rear Admiral, his Royal Imperial Highness the Archduke Frederick, and every officer and man' of the Austrian squadron.[3]

In 1844, though, the burgeoning reputation of the Austrian navy was shaken by the desertion of the two sons of Rear Admiral Bandiera, Attilio and Emilio. They had taken up the cause of Italian independence, and were followed by the desertion of another officer, Domenico Moro, the leader of the movement. This dismayed Metternich and convinced him of the fundamental unreliability of the fleet. The Bandiera brothers and Moro made an abortive attempt to launch a revolution in Italy, landing in Calabria on June 16. The Neapolitan authorities, warned of the attempt, reacted quickly; after a shootout in which two of the party were killed, the rest were taken prisoner. Nine of them were executed, including the Bandieras and Moro. It left the Austrian navy in disarray; but the government seized the opportunity to retire Paulucci and to appoint Archduke Frederick, promoted to vice admiral, to head the navy as *Marineoberkommandant.* Antonio Bandiera was obliged to retire. Steps were taken to introduce a number of urgent reforms, and to increase the recruitment of officers of German origin. Frederick was less successful in his efforts to increase the strength of the fleet with the acquisition of more steam warships; on the other hand, he made good progress with the development of the naval base at Pola.

With the situation in Italy continuing to deteriorate, Frederick took steps to station his largest vessels away from Venice. In this, as in the general management of the fleet, he was displaying

2 Sondhaus, *Habsburg Empire*, p. 77.
3 Sondhaus, *Habsburg Empire*, p. 105.

sound common sense, notwithstanding the niggardly resources made available to him by the government. It was, therefore, a serious blow when he was taken ill suddenly in October 1847, and died after a few days. After his death the aged Vice Admiral Count Silvestro Dandolo, who had briefly headed the navy more than 40 years previously, was provisionally appointed as *Marineoberkommandant,* only himself to die in office within a few weeks. To succeed him an army general, Anton von Martini, was brought in. Meanwhile the situation in Italy became further inflamed, and in March 1848 a disordered uprising began in Venice. When Martini visited the city in an attempt to restore calm, he went to the Arsenal; there, amid scenes of fearful brutality, the deeply unpopular Captain Johann Marinovich, the governor, was dragged out by the mob and lynched, and Martini was taken prisoner. The Venetian Republic was proclaimed by Daniel Manin, and the Austrian garrison was withdrawn. The Austrian authorities, with more than half of the navy's personnel of Italian descent, relieved them from their duty and allowed them to return home. Out of the total complement of the navy of 5,000 men before the revolutions of March 1848 began, only 72 officers and 605 sailors remained, with the result that the Austrian ships at Pola lacked a large part of their crews. At this time the fleet consisted of three frigates, two corvettes, eight brigs, thirty four small gunboats, and two steamers.

Austria was now at war with Sardinia-Piedmont, which had now occupied Milan. Radetzky was regrouping in Verona; the Papal states and the Kingdom of Naples and the Two Sicilies had joined in the war. The Sardinian and Neapolitan navies sent squadrons into the Adriatic to help defend Venice; the attenuated Austrian navy was not strong enough to resist this force, and General Gyulai, who had taken command of the navy in Martini's absence, withdrew the fleet first to Pola and then to Trieste. The Italian commander, Rear Admiral Giuseppe Albini, had orders not to attack Trieste, and a stalemate ensued, until the Papal States, and then the Kingdom of Naples and the Two Sicilies pulled out of the war. In July 1848 Radetzky's victory at Custozza turned the tide, and an armistice concluded on August 9 led to Martini's release. The Sardinian squadron withdrew; Austrian forces continued to besiege Venice, and the Austrian fleet emerged from Trieste to blockade the city. In March 1849 the armistice ended; when the campaign resumed in northern Italy, Radetzky won a decisive battle at Novara, and the First War of Italian Independence came to an end. One casualty was the throne of King Charles Albert of Sardinia, who abdicated in favour of his son, King Victor Emmanuel II. Venice finally fell to the Austrians on August 27. In the Arsenal the almost complete frigate *Italia* was taken over, and was renamed *Novara.*

In February 1849 the Emperor Franz Joseph looked abroad for a new commander for the navy, with the object of diminishing Italian influence, and found him in the Danish Commodore Hans Birch von Dahlerup. He arrived in March, two days after Sardinia had resumed hostilities, but the victory at Novara meant that operationally he did not have to deal with the Sardinian navy, but only the blockade of Venice. Dahlerup did not think much of the ships that constituted the Austrian fleet, a large number of which he dismissed as worthless. He produced a new plan for the fleet based on an establishment of six ships of the line, ten frigates, six corvettes, six brigs, and six schooners, together with twelve large and six small paddle steamers. In the context of the straitened resources of the Austrian government, this was an enormous request; but in a response quite contrary to previous decisions, Franz Joseph approved the plan.

Efforts were now put in hand to increase the use of the German language in the fleet, and Dahlerup introduced a number of important reforms, including a reorganisation of the command structure, new service regulations and the establishment of a school for naval officers. However, the decision taken by the Emperor that his younger brother Archduke Ferdinand Max, aged 19, should enter the navy convinced Dahlerup that he would thereafter be merely keeping the seat warm until Franz Joseph was satisfied that the young man was ready to take command. In the spring of 1851 he resigned, and a temporary successor Count Franz von Wimpffen, the army commander in Trieste, took over.

The Austrian navy was not technologically advanced. Both Naples and Sardinia possessed more steamships, and although Austria had in Josef Ressel an early pioneer of screw propeller technology, an unfortunate accident during the trial of his design led to further development being banned and the Imperial government resisted the introduction of the screw propeller on financial grounds. In 1852 Wimpffen proposed the conversion of a number of sailing warships to screw propulsion, but the existing capability of the domestic shipyards was insufficient for them to carry out the work.

Wimpffen was, though, more successful in completing some of Dahlerup's reforms, and in particular was able to accelerate the use of the German language. He remained in office for three years. During this time Ferdinand Max was learning his trade. He was soon promoted to the rank of captain and placed in command of the corvette *Minerva*, in which post he was such a success that one officer, Maximilian von Sterneck, observed two years after he had entered the service that 'it is inconceivable to all of us, how he has acquired so much maritime knowledge … in such a short time.[4]

In September 1854 Franz Joseph duly promoted Ferdinand Max to the rank of rear admiral and appointed him as *Marineoberkommandant.* It was a decision that was of enormous benefit to the Austrian navy. Sir John Knox Laughton wrote:

> He was then only twenty two: but his zeal compensated, to some extent, for his want of experience; and for the next ten years he devoted himself to the good of the service over which he really presided. Under his fostering care an excellent dockyard and arsenal were constructed and fortified at Pola. Many ships were built, amongst them a line of battleship and three large frigates. One of these, the *Novara*, was sent on a combined scientific and training expedition, a voyage round the world.[5]

The appointment of Ferdinand Max was welcomed by many in the navy, including one of the most promising officers of Austria's fleet, Wilhelm von Tegetthoff, who wrote of his appointment: 'The Archduke is displaying the greatest activity and altogether he arouses the most encouraging expectations. He goes into every detail, and through his love of business and determined zeal I feel that he will at last bring about a thorough reorganisation of our service, which Dahlerup and Wimpffen merely bungled through their superficial policy.'[6]

Ferdinand Max brought to his command an enthusiastic personality, together with a determination to develop the navy and assert its independence. He was greatly assisted by the fact that for the time being Franz Joseph was disposed to give him a free hand, not least by allowing him to exceed by far the official navy budget. The Archduke proceeded with the construction of a ship of the line, to be built at Pola, together with two screw frigates at Trieste and two screw

4 Sondhaus, *Habsburg Empire*, p. 180.
5 Sir John Knox Laughton, *Studies in Naval History* (London: Longmans Green, 1887), p. 154.
6 H. Montgomery Hyde, *Mexican Empire* (London: Macmillan 1946), pp. 46-47.

corvettes at Venice. It was still necessary, though, for their engines to be imported from Britain. Meanwhile his decision to send the *Novara* on the world cruise was an important step in raising the Navy's profile.

In March 1857 Ferdinand Max acquired an additional responsibility when Franz Joseph appointed him as governor general of Lombardy and Venetia; he continued as head of the navy, but with his headquarters at Milan. A second-in-command was based in Trieste. The new post put the Archduke at odds with Vienna due to the liberal reforms which he wished to introduce in Lombardy and Venetia as a means of reducing tensions. He continued to discharge his responsibilities as head of the navy with his customary enthusiasm, but the war of 1859, when it came, brought with it a huge challenge. He felt sure that the navy could beat the Sardinian navy, if it came to it; but there was no way that it could stand up against the powerful French fleet that entered the Adriatic. The Austrian fleet was obliged to remain in port, incapable of hampering the French blockade of Venice. Admiral Jurien de la Gravière, the commander of the French fleet, later wrote:

> The officers of the Austrian squadron were full of ardour; they were, even then, the same brave officers who afterwards triumphed at Lissa. They asked to be led out. They felt humiliated by the blockade; they would endeavour to raise it. But the Archduke would not venture his fleet. If it should be lost, Austria would never sanction its being replaced.[7]

After the peace, Ferdinand Max appointed Tegetthoff as his aide-de-camp, and in the winter of 1859-1860 they journeyed together to Brazil. The relationship soon became one of personal friendship, and the Archduke, recognising Tegetthoff's outstanding merit, ensured his rapid promotion. The period immediately following the end of the war was a bad time both for Ferdinand Max and for the navy. The Archduke's influence with his brother had greatly declined, and the government in Vienna was extremely resistant to his requests for additional funding. In the winter of 1860-1861, however, the new finance minister Ignaz von Plener relented, and the Archduke was able to order two ironclads, to be built at Trieste. An ironclad arms race with Italy was, in the ongoing political situation, an almost inevitable development.

The easily perceived threat from Italy, therefore, gave considerable impetus to the navy's campaign for additional warships, and the Archduke took as much advantage as he could from this. He sought funds for the construction of three additional ironclads and for the conversion to screw propulsion of the sailing frigates *Schwartzenberg* and *Novara*. In spite of objections from his government, Franz Joseph approved the plans. There were problems in sourcing part of the armour plating required, but French foundries were contracted to supply this together with the iron rams for the new ships.

In March 1862 a high-powered commission was established to consider the future role and consequent size of the fleet. There was a violent disagreement among its members between those who wanted a powerful seagoing fleet and those who considered that all that was required was a coast defence force. Before the commission finished its work, though, there came news of the battle of Hampton Roads, and the government authorised the continuation of the ironclad construction programme. Looking back at the state of the Austrian navy at this time,

7 Laughton, *Studies*, p. 156.

the naval officer Maximilian Rottauscher, then a midshipman, described the situation as he saw it, perhaps with a degree of overstatement: 'Ship after ship was decommissioned and lay as wretched sad things behind barricades; of the entire fleet, but one frigate, one corvette and seven gunboats were manned. Work in the Arsenal halted, and the midshipmen, out of work, travelled through Pola's filthy streets.'[8]

Stuart Sutherland, the editor of Rottauscher's memoirs, noted that recent work on the history of the Austrian navy during this period suggested that the policy of Ferdinand Max was to sacrifice much other activity that would have contributed to the Navy's readiness for war in order to free funds for ship construction. As a result the fleet put to sea rarely, educational standards dropped and seamanship declined, with a consequent loss of morale.[9]

During the Greek Revolution of 1862-1863 an Austrian squadron commanded by Tegetthoff was sent to the Piraeus. At this time, however, events were taking place which would lead to a change in the leadership of the Austrian navy. Tentative negotiations had been going on since 1861 which were intended to lead to an offer to Ferdinand Max of the throne of Mexico, which was in a turbulent state. In 1863 these discussions resulted in a formal offer being made to him, and in March 1864, with his wife Carlotta, he set off to France where he discussed the project with its sponsor Napoleon III. There was a brief setback when the Emperor Franz Joseph made his agreement to what was proposed conditional on Ferdinand Max renouncing for himself and his heirs any claim to the Austrian throne. In the end, the Archduke put up with this, and formally accepted the offer of the Mexican throne. On April 14, 1864 he sailed in the *Novara* to Mexico to become Emperor. His influence on the navy had been immense; he has been described as 'a talented man with a dynamic personality, desperate for a challenging occupation and, by the end of 1863, without options at home.'[10] It is easy to understand how his ambition led the Archduke to accept the challenge; but it was a profoundly tragic decision. On his departure, no attempt was made to replace him as *Marineoberkommandant*. The establishment of a Navy Ministry appeared to have firmly secured its future independence from the army, and Ferdinand Max could leave his post in the knowledge that the ironclad programme which he had initiated would be completed.

Within a very short time of his departure, the Austrian navy was to be subjected to its severest test since its foundation. In 1864, the Second Schleswig War pitted the alliance of Austria and Prussia against Denmark. The Prussian navy was tiny; it would be Austria that must shoulder the burden of naval operations in the North Sea. While the rest of the fleet was preparing, a small squadron under Tegetthoff was sent to cruise against the Danish fleet, which was blockading Hamburg. On May 9, Tegetthoff, with the *Schwartzenberg*, *Radetzky*, and *Seehund*, and three small Prussian gunboats, encountered a Danish squadron off Heligoland. The engagement is described in chapter 18; it ended inconclusively, with the Austrian squadron taking refuge in the territorial waters of Heligoland, but Tegetthoff had succeeded in raising the blockade. When news of this reached Vienna, he was hailed as a national hero and promoted to rear admiral. Due to his lack of seniority, it was a promotion that led to a good deal of envy among Tegetthoff's peers.

8 Maximilian Rottauscher, *With Tegetthoff at Lissa* (Solihull: Helion, 2010) p. 15.
9 Rottauscher, *With Tegetthoff*, p. 15n.
10 Sondhaus, *Habsburg Empire*, p. 227.

The navy's hope of independence from the army was short lived. In January 1865 it was once again placed under the War Ministry, and administered by a *Marinesektion* headed by Vice Admiral Fautz. Franz Joseph refused to fill the vacant post of *Marineoberkommandant;* instead, he created the post of *Marine Truppen und Flotten Inspektor* for his cousin Archduke Leopold, who was a soldier by training and had no knowledge of the navy. He responded to Tegetthoff's promotion by promoting Captain Pöck to the rank of rear admiral, backdating this to restore his seniority over Tegetthoff.[11] In the following year, as war clouds once again gathered, it would be necessary to appoint a commander for the fleet, and in early May 1866, notwithstanding his lack of seniority, Tegetthoff was given the post. He took command of a fleet that was ill-prepared for war as a result of the concentration of resources on shipbuilding.

Well though Ferdinand Max had done in providing the Austrian fleet with ironclads, the arms race in the Adriatic had been decisively won by Italy. Against her twelve ironclads, Austria could deploy only seven. The first two of these to join the fleet were the small broadside ironclads *Drache* and *Salamander*, both laid down in Trieste in February 1861. Of 2,750 tons, and 206 feet in length, they mounted eighteen 6 inch muzzleloading rifles and ten 7 inch smoothbores. They were protected by an armoured belt of 4.5 inches and had a speed of 11 knots. They were followed by the *Kaiser Max* class of three broadside ironclads, also built at Trieste, where they were laid down in October 1861. The class consisted of the *Kaiser Max, Prinz Eugen* and *Don Juan d'Austria*; the armour plating of the last of these was incomplete. They were of 3,588 tons, and were 232 feet long. They were armed with fifteen 6 inch muzzleloading rifles, one 4.7 inch muzzleloading rifle and sixteen 7 inch smoothbores. They had an armoured belt of 4.5 inches. Their speed was also 11 knots. They joined the fleet in 1863.[12]

The last two ironclads to be completed in time for the war of 1866 were the *Erzherzog Ferdinand Max* and *Habsburg*. Laid down at Trieste in 1863, they were both completed in July 1866. They were somewhat larger than their predecessors, being of 5,130 tons and just under 275 feet long, and they had a slightly thicker armoured belt of 4.8 inches. They carried sixteen 7 inch muzzleloading rifles, and had a top speed of 12.5 knots. Like all the Austrian ironclads they were wooden hulled.[13]

Austria also possessed a number of unarmoured steam warships, led by the ship of the line *Kaiser*, which mounted 92 guns, and five frigates, the 51 gun *Novara*, 46 gun *Schwartzenberg*, and the 31 gun *Radetzky*, *Adria* and *Donau*. There were four 22 gun corvettes and a number of smaller vessels. The *Novara* had been severely damaged by fire while in dock, and was undergoing hasty repairs.[14]

11 Sondhaus, *Habsburg Empire*, pp. 245-246.
12 Konstam, *European Ironclads*, p. 14.
13 Konstam, *European Ironclads*, p. 15.
14 Sondhaus, *Habsburg Empire*, pp. 277-278.

17

Persano

Count Carlo Pellion di Persano was born on March 11, 1806 at Vercelli in Piedmont. He joined the navy at a young age, and in 1825 served in the Sardinian fleet at the battle of Tripoli, in which he distinguished himself when in command of an assault boat. He rose quickly in the navy, though one historian doubted whether that was entirely due to his professional ability:

> Count Persano had had a distinguished career, more perhaps owing to his connections and friendships and the use he made of them, than from any superlative merit. He was a close friend of Massimo d'Azeglio, and was in close touch with very influential circles. He was not popular in the service and he had a lasting feud with Admiral d'Auvare, of whom he was jealous.[1]

Regrettably, Persano was one of those captains guilty of extreme indiscipline with whom Cavour, when he became Navy Minister in 1850. had to deal. Persano was captain of the corvette *Governolo*, which had been chosen as the ship aboard which students of the Naval School were to have their annual cruise of instruction. To save expense, Cavour ordered that the vessel should sail to London to deliver the national exhibits for the Great Exhibition, and that it should thereafter visit a number of ports in Britain and France before returning home. Unfortunately, on leaving Genoa harbour, Persano ran the *Governolo* aground, and it was two days before she could be refloated. As soon as she was able to do so, Persano set off in her again without making any report, and headed directly for London. Back in Italy there was a good deal of public criticism of Persano over the Genoa incident. Officers of the Italian merchant marine were generally contemptuous of the navy's navigational skills, and the Press had much to say about the mishap of the *Governolo*. Cavour was furious, and ordered Persano to transfer his command to another officer, and return home to be court martialled. Persano's reaction to this was symptomatic of the attitude of the Sardinian navy's officer class:

> Count Persano's idea of discipline was elastic. It did not include returning for a court martial nominated by his enemy Admiral d'Auvare, until he had played all his cards. He wrote at once to Massimo d' Azeglio for help, and then, in a sudden fit of anger, resigned his commission in the service. But he did not escape. D'Azeglio appealed to the

1 Whyte, *Life and Letters of Cavour*, p. 70.

> King and tried to soften Cavour, but the latter was adamant. He refused either to accept Persano's resignation or to counter order the court martial. But the influence of d'Azeglio and Persano's other highly placed friends was not without effect, and when he learnt from his correspondents that the court martial would let him off, he returned to await his trial.[2]

At his court-martial Persano was indeed treated lightly, being acquitted of insubordination and negligence, though he was not restored to his command of the *Governolo*. Cavour was satisfied; he did not bear a grudge against Persano, and soon after offered him a post normally reserved for an officer holding the rank of rear admiral. According to Dennis Mack Smith, Persano's error when running aground at Genoa was not the only instance of lapses of this kind. Apparently on another occasion he ran his ship aground when she was carrying the King and the whole Royal family; but he escaped without punishment.[3]

Whether, as Mack Smith suggests, such incidents led to Persano's incompetence becoming 'legendary' in the Sardinian navy is uncertain; at all events, when Sardinia joined the alliance fighting against Russia during the Crimean War of 1854-1856, Persano went with the squadron that was sent to the Black Sea, and there apparently performed well, earning from French Admiral Bruat praise for his conduct during the bombardment of Odessa.[4]

There was little opportunity for the Sardinian navy to distinguish itself during the brief war of 1859, but in the complex and confused situation that followed the ending of the war, the role of the navy assumed considerable importance. Persano's reputation with Cavour, following the latter's return to power in January 1860, was sufficiently high for him to be placed in command of the squadron with which Cavour intended to monitor the developing situation in southern Italy. Cavour had to pick his way carefully through a diplomatic minefield throughout that year, much of the time obliged to conceal his true intentions. When Garibaldi, in May, sailed with the 'Thousand' for Sicily, Cavour's orders to Persano were that he should proceed from Livorno to Cagliari in Sardinia without using his engines. The effect of this limitation necessarily meant that Persano would find it difficult to overtake Garibaldi's steamers once they were en route for Sicily. It also meant that Persano would be able to conserve fuel against any emergency that might require his squadron to move quickly. Off Sardinia, he would be in a position to meet all eventualities.

In effectively allowing Garibaldi's expedition to reach Sicily in this way, Cavour understood that it could only be justified by success, and accordingly did what he could to facilitate it while being careful to avoid compromising his government. Having failed to prevent the sailing of the expedition, he sent ambiguous orders to Persano to arrest it if it stopped in Sardinia, but to leave it alone if he encountered it at sea. Persano responded by sending a message to Cavour asking him, if the expedition was really to be stopped, to telegraph to him the word 'Cagliari,' but if not, 'Malta.' Cavour's reply was to the effect that the Cabinet had decided for 'Cagliari;' Persano correctly judged that this was not Cavour's own view, and Garibaldi, unimpeded, landed with his small force at Quarto in Sicily on May 6.

When Garibaldi, against all the odds, succeeded in expelling the substantial Bourbon army from Sicily, Cavour had to face the possibility that he would go on to cross to the mainland, something that for the time being he wished to postpone for as long as he could. For this,

2 Whyte, *Life and Letters of Cavour*, p. 71.
3 Denis Mack Smith, *Cavour* (London: Weidenfeld & Nicolson, 1985), p. 54
4 H.W. Wilson, *Ironclads in Action* (London: Sampson Low & Co, 1897), vol. I, p. 211.

Cavour needed to send someone to make contact with Garibaldi. Persano might have been a candidate for this extremely delicate task:

> The question was whom to send. Admiral Persano was still in Garibaldi's good books, but he was a serving officer who might be required elsewhere, and his past history did not suggest that he was above average as a politician any more than he was above average as a naval officer.[5]

Whether this judgment is fair, Cavour gave the mission to Agostini Depretis, who would later play a key role in Italian politics and in due course become prime minister of Italy. To Persano, Cavour wrote on August 1: 'Do not assist Garibaldi's passage to the continent but instead, try to delay it by indirect means as long as possible.' Persano was, perhaps, sufficiently devious to make him an ideal instrument to execute Cavour's circumspect policies at this time.

Certainly Persano and his squadron remained central to the development of Cavour's policy. The minister president was endeavouring to convince Garibaldi of the possibility that he might in due course gain the support of Sardinia's government; Mack Smith suggests that he had succeeded in doing so, and that Persano may have been crucial in this:

> Garibaldi seems to have been genuinely convinced at this point that Cavour as well as the King might come in with him, and one may guess that Persano's playacting was chiefly responsible for this. The admiral's most notable qualities in a long and inglorious career seem to have been a skill in flattery, and a penchant for taking imaginative liberties with the truth; and at Palermo he used both assiduously to allay Garibaldi's suspicions.[6]

Following Garibaldi's capture of Messina, which took him a step closer to an invasion of the mainland, Cavour wrote to Persano in terms which belied his true feelings at this time:

> Please convey my warm and sincere thanks to General Garibaldi ... After so splendid a victory I do not see how he can be stopped from crossing to the continent ... Garibaldi must do it. The work cannot stop half done. The national flag raised in Sicily must be unfurled on the mainland and carried along the Adriatic coast until it reaches the Queen of the Sea.[7]

In fact, Cavour was still hoping to be able to engineer a coup d'etat by liberal elements in Naples; if this was successful, it would be followed by a request to Victor Emmanuel for protection, which would give Cavour greater control over the situation than would be possible if it was Garibaldi who succeeded in expelling Francis II and his government from Naples.

However, once Garibaldi had done just that, he displayed rather more loyalty to Victor Emmanuel and the concept of unification than he was receiving from Cavour. His first act on taking the city of Naples was, as has been seen, to transfer the Neapolitan fleet to Persano. In doing so, he may have had in mind that he might be able to look for support from the admiral for his next move, to Rome. Just at this time however, and before he had an opportunity to meet

5 Mack Smith, *1860*, p. 105.
6 Mack Smith, *1860*, p. 122.
7 George Martin, *The Red Shirt and the Cross of Savoy* (London: Eyre & Spottiswood, 1969), p. 372.

personally with Garibaldi at Naples, Persano set the cat among the pigeons with an alarmist telegram which suggested that Garibaldi was highly critical of Cavour, and was bent on challenging Napoleon III at Rome, a move which might scupper Cavour's plans for getting international acceptance of Italian unification. It led Cavour to fear that his own position with the King might be in jeopardy, and he used Persano's telegram to prejudice Victor Emmanuel against Garibaldi. Persano, having next day had an interview with Garibaldi, corrected his earlier telegram, but the damage was done. Persano continued to reflect Cavour's two-faced attitude to Garibaldi: 'Admiral Persano had given many private words of sympathy to the volunteers, but his practical insincerity was exposed when the Piedmontese ships had stood aloof and unhelpful during Garibaldi's perilous crossing of the Straits.'[8]

Once it was clear that there was nothing further that Persano could achieve at Naples, Cavour sent him off to Ancona, which Piedmontese troops had reached on September 28. Nevertheless, with the political situation that would bring unification still not resolved, Cavour had not ruled out bringing Persano's squadron back to Sicily to make an armed demonstration at Palermo if the situation there was not resolved satisfactorily. By early October, though, progress had been made in the course of extremely complex negotiations involving Cavour, Garibaldi, their various representatives and those in authority in Naples and Sicily. On October 21 the plebiscite to determine the question of the unification of Italy with Victor Emmanuel as King was held in both Naples and Sicily, and passed with an overwhelming majority.

With unification at last achieved, Persano was by now the most notable officer in the kingdom's navy. When Menabrea left office as Navy Minister in February 1862, it was no surprise that Persano should be appointed to succeed him. He held office for only a short time, but as has been seen the decisions which he took reversing Menabrea's policy on warship construction were of great importance in strengthening the fleet by the acquisition of a large number of ironclads.

Persano's public character was, notwithstanding the vicissitudes of his earlier career, perceived as being perfectly satisfactory. Laughton wrote of him:

> He was generally esteemed as a man of good family and of amiable temper; he had married an English lady, and being thus connected with English society, was looked on as partly an Englishman, or at least was supposed to have caught, as if by infection, the good qualities of the typical English naval officer. When the war broke out in 1866, he was considered the man of the day, and great things were expected of him.[9]

Not everyone, though, was of that opinion. In 1866 General Alfonso La Marmora was at the head of the government, though soon to leave office to take command of the Italian army in the field. Considering the question of the leadership of the Italian fleet, La Marmora had little personal confidence in Persano. In nevertheless appointing him, it has been suggested that he was heavily influenced by the Prince of Carignano, a cousin of Victor Emmanuel, who was described by one historian as being the Admiral's 'compagnon de plaisirs.' [10] Admiral Iachino considered, though, that there was no evidence that Persano was appointed as a result of Royal or political influence:

8 Mack Smith, *1860*, p. 217.
9 Laughton, *Studies*, p. 168.
10 W.J. Stillman, *The Union of Italy 1815-1895* (Cambridge: Cambridge University Press, 1900), p. 334.

> Some historians believed that court intrigue or pressure from politicians had influenced Persano's appointment, but this does not seem to be correct. Although Persano had an excellent relationship with the King, and particularly also with his cousin the Prince of Carignano, it does not appear from any document that the Royal family suggested his name for the command.[11]

Iachino observed that in former days Persano had enjoyed both an appreciation of his professional merit as well as the friendship of both d'Azeglio and Cavour; and the former, he thought, would certainly have favoured his appointment, and probably Cavour as well, since he had highly praised the admiral's leadership during the siege of Ancona in 1860.

Historians have in general been extremely harsh in appraising Persano's competence. He did, though, possess some abilities that had served his country well. Half a century later, in conversation with the journalist Alfonso Mongiardini, Admiral Felice Canevaro reflected on Persano's qualities, and why he might have appeared at the time to be the right choice as commander-in-chief. Canevaro had been a young lieutenant aboard the *Re di Portogallo* during the battle of Lissa, and looked back at Persano's qualifications to lead the fleet:

> He was a great friend of mine, and wanted me with him at Lissa and later in the time preceding his trial. I can say dispassionately of him that his virtues and his defects served very well, under the direction of Cavour, for our purposes at the time of Garibaldi's campaigns in Sicily and southern Italy. Indeed, I affirm that at one time he rendered great and real services to the Fatherland. However, precisely for those qualities that made him so valuable in those special circumstances I have always judged him unable to command the fleet in a real war.[12]

It has also been suggested, however, that Persano was extremely reluctant to take command of the fleet, and did what he could to avoid doing so:

> When invited to assume command of the Italian fleet, Admiral Persano twice refused; it was only when the King pressed on him the third invitation that he weakly accepted a charge to which he felt himself unequal. He had been living in retirement for some years and neither knew nor was known by most of the officers and men whom he was to command.[13]

His lack of knowledge of the senior officers of the Italian Navy may perhaps have been exaggerated. It was only a very few years since he had been Navy Minister and, before that, he was active during the operations which culminated in the unification of Italy. At the same time, it remained to be seen whether his personality, and his abilities, really fitted him to lead the fleet against the Austrians.

11 Admiral Angelo Iachino, *La Campagna di Lissa 1866* (Milan: Il Saggiatore, 1966), p. 37.
12 Iachino, *Lissa*, p. 37.
13 Countess E. Martinengo Cesaresco, *The Liberation of Italy* (London: Seeley & Co1895), pp. 372-373.

18

Tegetthoff

Many distinguished admirals in other nations came from a well-established naval background, but Austria had no maritime tradition, and Wilhelm von Tegetthoff was descended from a military family. Originally from Westphalia, his great-grandfather fought for Austria in the Seven Years War as a captain of cavalry, and was raised to the hereditary nobility by Maria Theresa. One of Tegetthoff's great uncles won the Empire's highest military decoration in the war against France in 1799. His father Karl also served in the Imperial army, which he joined in 1805; he fought in the War of Liberation, and when peace came was posted to the garrison of Marburg an der Drau in Styria (now Maribor, Slovenia). Tegetthoff's mother was the daughter of a civil servant in Prague. She bore five sons, of whom Wilhelm, born on December 23, 1827 at Marburg, was the second. Helmut Pemsel described his upbringing:

> When the boy was three years old, his father was temporarily detailed to the garrison at Piacenza in northern Italy, then under Austrian rule. Wilhelm therefore spent his early, most impressionable years under his mother's loving care. Throughout his life, he never again experienced love and affection in like measure. During his long shipboard service he scarcely had the opportunity to find someone else prepared to give him such devotion, and the love and warmheartedness of which he was capable would be expressed solely in letters to his mother. On each of his rare leaves, he endeavoured to spend most of his time with her.[1]

It was Tegetthoff's own choice to make the navy his career, and in November 1840 he went to the Naval Academy at Venice. In 1845 he became a *Seekadett*, and in July of that year he went to sea in the *Montecuccoli* brig, and later in the frigate *Adria*, where he learned the practical side of his profession. In 1848 he became an ensign. During the Venetian uprising he served in a number of different vessels; first the *Montecuccoli* again, then the *Triest* brig, then the frigate *Bellona* and finally in the *Adria*, which was taking part in the blockade of Venice. After the war ended, he served in the steamer *Maria Anna* in the Levant, and was promoted to lieutenant in 1851. After two more postings, he received in 1850 his first command, the schooner *Elisabeth*

1 Helmut Pemsel, 'Wilhelm von Tegetthoff: Admiral of the Unexpected' in Jack Sweetman (ed.), *The Great Admirals* (Annapolis, Md: Naval Institute Press, 1997), p. 279.

and then, soon after, took command of the steamer *Taurus*, in which he served for some time. He was employed, at the time of the Crimean War, 'in a sort of police duty in the Sulina mouth of the Danube. This duty was neither pleasant nor easy, and Tegetthoff not only gained credit by the way in which he performed it, but was brought to the favourable notice of the Archduke Maximilian.'[2]

In 1857 Tegetthoff was selected to accompany a distinguished ornithologist, a Doctor Heuglin, in a semi-official expedition to Egypt and Arabia. One of its objects was to collect information relevant to the projected canal through the Suez Isthmus, in order that the Austrian Empire should be well placed to take advantage of it if it was built. He was also instructed to select a location for a coaling station. He and Doctor Heuglin travelled up the Nile, but when they reached Somaliland they were seized by bandits and held prisoner until a ransom was paid. Doctor Heuglin, who had been injured, returned to Cairo, while Tegetthoff made his way to the coast and sailed in an open boat down the Red Sea to the island of Socotra, before returning first to Aden and then back to Europe. By the time he returned to Austria he had been promoted to *Korvettenkapitan*.

After serving in a position on the staff for several months, Tegetthoff was posted to the command of the screw corvette *Erzherzog Friedrich*, in which he was sent to Morocco in 1859 to investigate the fate of the crew of an Austrian merchant vessel that had been wrecked on the coast, and who had apparently been carried into slavery. The whole of that area was in a confused state of disorder. The corvette worked her way along the coast as far as the Straits of Gibraltar without finding any trace of the castaways. Tegetthoff put into Gibraltar for letters, and found orders awaiting him to return home, in view of the threatening international situation.

The imminent war with France and Sardinia, when it came, would find the Austrian navy in no state to stand up against the enemy, as has already been described, and when the French squadron entered the Adriatic it was obliged to remain, frustrated, in port. There was nothing that the fleet could do to contest the French command of the sea, or to prevent the French squadron from preparing to attack Venice. Tegetthoff was one of the officers who chafed at the navy's enforced inactivity:

> We are told that amongst those anxious to make a dash against the French squadron Tegetthoff was conspicuous; and it seems not improbable that a man of courage and resource, such as he afterwards proved himself to be, might have cut off some of the small cruisers or store ships in the Adriatic, and have made an unexpected diversion by an attack on the coast of France. But the attempt was not permitted; and till the close of the war the *Erzherzog Friedrich* remained as inactive as the other ships.[3]

His appointment as aide-de-camp to Ferdinand Max, and their visit together to Brazil cemented the Archduke's high regard for Tegetthoff. Laughton wrote of their relationship:

> Of the two, Tegetthoff was five years the senior; he was altogether the stronger intellect, and there seems reason to believe that the relation between them was of friend to friend

2 Laughton, *Studies*, p. 153.
3 Laughton, *Studies*, pp. 156-157.

> rather than of commander to admiral, or of lordling to prince. It is certain that there was a close intimacy, and the Archduke was able to advance his friend's interests at the same time that he advanced those of the service.[4]

On their return from Brazil in 1860, Tegetthoff was promoted to *Fregattenkapitan* and assigned to the command of the 31 gun frigate *Radetzky*. He served in her in the Levant until the autumn of 1861. In November he reached the rank of *Linienschiffkapitan*, and was appointed to the *Novara*. In her, in the following year, he was sent to Greece with orders to monitor the situation there following the deposition of King Otto and the accession of King George. There is a glimpse of Tegetthoff's reputation in Austria at this time from the pen of Maximilian Rottauscher, then a young midshipman who was hoping for a transfer to the *Novara*:

> To serve with Tegetthoff was deemed a high honour. He had had a legendary career, and as the most junior captain he had commanded the vessels in Greece for a long time. The great respect in which he was held was based not only on the firmness with which he acted on behalf of Austria's interests in the Greek disorders with his weak force (a frigate and two gunboats), it was also because his name already had a good reputation in other navies and that his opinion was greatly valued by many senior officers in the international councils in Piraeus.[5]

The *Novara* was now found to be in need of extensive repair, and he was next appointed to command the frigate *Schwartzenberg* of 48 guns. Accompanied by the *Radetzky*, he sailed to the Middle East, where there had been further anti-Western disturbances. At the end of 1863 he visited Port Said to inspect the work of digging the Suez Canal. While there, he was again compelled to break off his mission due to international complications. This time it was the imminent Second Schleswig War, between Denmark and Austria and Prussia.

Tegetthoff was ordered to sail at once with the *Schwartzenberg* and *Radetzky*, together with the small gun vessel *Seehund*, to northern waters without waiting for the larger squadron that was being prepared under Rear Admiral von Wüllerstorff. In February 1864 Tegetthoff reached Brest, where he was joined by three small Prussian gunboats, the *Blitz, Basilisk*, and *Adler*. With this modest squadron Tegetthoff made his way to the North Sea. The Danes were now blockading Hamburg, and his orders were to do what he could to lift the blockade. An attempted been made to do so by a small Prussian squadron, facing a much superior Danish force off Jasmund on March 17, but without success.

Tegetthoff arrived at Cuxhaven, but without the *Seehund*, which had been damaged in a storm and further damaged in an incident in Ramsgate harbour. The Danish squadron blockading Hamburg, under the command of Commodore Eduard Suenson, consisted of the steam frigates *Niels Juel* (42 guns) and *Jylland* (44 guns) and the steam corvette *Heimdall* (16 guns). On May 6 Suenson steamed south towards Heligoland. On the same day Tegetthoff left Cuxhaven, heading north. He first encountered the British frigate *Aurora*, on patrol near Heligoland, which was at that time a British possession. After this contact he made for Sylt, where he dropped

4 Laughton, *Studies*, p. 157.
5 Rottauscher, *With Tegetthoff*, p. 26.

anchor, returning next day to Cuxhaven. Suenson, meanwhile, had himself met the *Aurora*, from which he learned that Tegetthoff had been at sea.

On May 9, receiving news that the Danish squadron was again off Heligoland, Tegetthoff raised steam and headed northwards. The two squadrons came in sight of one another at about 1:00 p.m., to the east of the island. At 1:30 p.m. Tegetthoff signalled to his squadron: 'Our armies have been victorious; we will do the same.'[6] The encounter was one of considerable historical significance:

> The action which followed was the first, and with the exception of that, a few months later, between the *Kearsarge* and *Alabama*, remains the only one fought between wooden ships under steam and armed with heavy shell guns; but on neither side does any exceptional use seem to have been made of the steam power; and the damage and loss inflicted by the shells were no greater than were in many cases, during the old French war, inflicted by much smaller cold shot.[7]

At a range of 3,750 yards, the *Schwartzenberg* opened fire with her bow pivot guns; soon her whole starboard battery was in action, as the range rapidly closed. The two Austrian frigates and the Danish squadron passed in opposite directions at a range of 2,000 yards. Suenson now manoeuvred in an attempt to cut off the Prussian gunboats, which were well in rear of the Austrian vessels. To counter this, Tegetthoff turned to starboard, shortening the range to as little as 400 yards, and both the *Schwartzenberg* and *Radetzky* came under heavy fire. During these exchanges the *Niels Juel* was hit by an Austrian shell which wiped out an entire gun crew.

At about 3:30 p.m. a shell exploded on the furled foretopsail of the *Schwartzenberg*, setting it afire; this quickly spread, and the whole foretopmast was ablaze. The *Niels Juel* maintained her attack, preventing the crew from extinguishing the fire. To carry the flames away from the rest of the ship, Tegetthoff was obliged to turn north-west and steam in the direction of Heligoland. He ordered the *Radetzky* to come on a parallel course, so that both frigates could continue to fire their stern pivot guns; but Captain Jeremiasch remained astern of the *Schwartzenberg* to cover her as she withdrew. It was only when Tegetthoff repeated his signal that he obeyed the order to disengage.[8]

Suenson now ordered his squadron to turn eight points to starboard to follow the retreating Austrians, but at this point *Jylland* was hit by a shell which damaged her steering gear, and she could no longer answer her helm. She hove to, to make repairs; by now Tegetthoff had entered British territorial waters, and Suenson, unable to continue his pursuit without violating British neutrality, was obliged to cease fire, and he steamed to the north east.

Tegetthoff was now engaged in fighting the fires aboard his flagship, but it was as late as 10:00 p.m. before the foremast was finally cut away and went over the side. Next morning Tegetthoff sailed with his whole squadron to Cuxhaven. Meanwhile Suenson, although none of his ships had been as badly damaged as the *Schwarzenberg*, found that they had been sufficiently injured to oblige him to lift the blockade of Hamburg, and he sailed to the North Frisian island

6 Michael Embree, *Bismarck's First War* (Solihull: Helion, 2006), p. 283.
7 Laughton, *Studies*, p. 159.
8 Embree, *Bismarck's First War*, p. 285.

of Föhr to land his casualties, and make repairs. His ships had lost a total of 17 killed and 49 wounded; the Austrian casualties amounted to 37 killed and 93 wounded.

Years later, the Austrian Rear Admiral Geza dell Adani looked back at the engagement:

> Public opinion was in the dark for a long time about the meaning of the battle of Heligoland. Some considered the outcome as a defeat of the Allied fleet, which was due to the superiority of the enemy. Others were of the opinion that the result was a draw and strongly praised the crews. Only in northern Germany did public opinion, after a few days, conclude that the battle should be considered a glorious success over the enemy navy because the purpose had been served to lift the Danish blockade of the German North Sea ports.[9]

Although the Danes with their superior force might be said to have had rather the better of the engagement, in strategic terms Tegetthoff could justly claim success in having lifted the blockade. When his telegram arrived in Vienna reporting the outcome of the engagement, the Emperor Franz Joseph was in no doubt how it should be regarded, at once promoting Tegetthoff to the rank of rear admiral. Tegetthoff subsequently joined the rest of the Austrian squadron which had reached the Texel. Neither Wüllerstorff nor his flag captain Friedrich von Pöck were unequivocally pleased to hear of Tegetthoff's success, as Rottauscher commented: 'As we heard, the victor had been received with no special amiability by these two. The thorn of Heligoland sat in the hearts of these ambitious men; moreover, by Tegetthoff's appointment as rear admiral he had been put over the head of Pöck, who was senior in rank as captain.'[10]

Following the end of the war with Denmark, Tegetthoff was posted for a time to the War Office in Vienna. Then, in 1865, he was appointed to the command of a small squadron cruising in the eastern Mediterranean. He had time to make a thorough examination of all aspects of the action of Heligoland, and the lessons that might be learned from it, though it was plain that in the event of war with Italy, an engagement between ironclad fleets would be a very different affair.

Helmut Pemsel has written that 'Tegetthoff was not an agreeable subordinate. He defended his opinions vigorously and tenaciously even against his superiors and was not disposed to deviate from his conclusions once he was convinced that they were correct.' Pemsel went on to discuss the effect of his character on those around him:

> The higher Tegetthoff advanced in rank, the more isolated he became. His self-discipline and dedication made him a constant critic of the navy's many deficiencies. Few of his superiors had any love for this troublesome fault finder, although they could hardly overlook him for difficult missions. Most of his comrades of the same rank were jealous of his advancement; only the junior officers and enlisted men were enthusiastic about him. Despite his stern and often stormy manner, he was fair and won the support of subordinates by taking an interest in their problems, a quite unusual practice at the time.[11]

9 Embree, *Bismarck's First War*, p. 286.
10 Rottauscher, *With Tegetthoff*, p. 46.
11 Pemsel, 'Wilhelm von Tegetthoff,' p. 285.

For a while Tegetthoff was president of the commission which examined potential officers. Rottauscher found the experience of appearing before him distinctly uncomfortable:

> The admiral was bored by having been removed from his exercises, and apart from that he had, to his great misfortune, different opinions from those of the other commissioners. While the latter only asked about the most minute details of rigging, tacking, bracing yards and the confusion of towing the battleship or the frigates, Tegetthoff lay sunk in his easy chair, interrupting by firing short questions about armour or engines, causing the members of the commission to lose their composure, as no less the candidates.[12]

As the political situation again began to deteriorate it was becoming plain that war with Italy might not be avoidable. In that situation, an appointment must be made, sooner rather than later, of a commander-in-chief of the fleet. For its officers, it was a matter of real concern that Tegetthoff's youth put his appointment in question. Rottauscher, returning to Pola, was overjoyed to be greeted by the news that Tegetthoff had indeed been appointed. He described the general response:

> Suddenly, however, Tegetthoff was summoned to Vienna and returned as commander-in-chief of the fleet. Depression vanished in the boundless joy with which he was greeted. A storm of high spirits rushed through Pola; the ships tore themselves free from the land, the funnels smoked, people ran about the decks like industrious ants and countless coal carriers and steamers filled with workmen came over from the Venice Arsenal.[13]

12 Rottauscher, *With Tegetthoff*, p. 52.
13 Rottauscher, *With Tegetthoff*, p. 56.

19

Ancona

When Bismarck had settled with Austria the temporary future of the Duchies of Schleswig-Holstein, he did so in terms which meant that conflict between Prussia and Austria might be triggered at almost any time. Franz Joseph, in spite of the many indications that Bismarck did indeed intend to provoke a war, preferred not to meet trouble halfway. On February 21 1866, at a meeting with his ministers, he concluded 'that he should leave warlike preparations for the time being aside and should continue to seek the maintenance of the honour and dignity, as well as of the interests, of the country by diplomatic means.'[1] This was a very high-minded position to take, but in all the circumstances it was unwise. There was plenty of evidence that Bismarck meant business, and it was imprudent to postpone military preparations. This attitude could not long prevail, and at the beginning of March partial mobilisation of some Austrian units began. In Prussia, where Moltke was urgently pressing for mobilisation to begin, Bismarck still wanted to order events so that Austria appeared the aggressor. He also wanted to achieve the participation of Italy, which Moltke required as necessary to ensure victory.

In the middle of March the Italian General Giuseppe Govone arrived in Berlin to negotiate a treaty between the two countries, which was finally signed on April 8. The movement towards war was accelerating. On April 21 the Austrian Army of the South was mobilised, and the rest of the army followed suit; the process was completed by May 9. On May 10 Italian naval preparations began, and Persano was appointed as commander-in-chief of the fleet. Austria, meanwhile, had begun preparing her navy on April 30. When the question of a commander-in-chief arose, Archduke Leopold, now in command of an army corps in Bohemia, did not press for Pöck to be appointed; had he done so, he would probably been overruled in any case, since Tegetthoff alone had recent battle experience. Tegetthoff was duly appointed on May 9.

As soon as he took charge, the admiral ordered the concentration of all Austrian warships in the Adriatic, recalling all those on overseas stations with the exception of the 22 gun corvette *Dandolo*, which was in Mexican waters in support of the Emperor Maximilian. Tegetthoff was conscious of the fact that whatever he might do, his fleet would be substantially outnumbered, both in ironclads and in wooden ships. He arranged to lease five steamers from the steamship line Austrian Lloyd, which were hastily armed. Many of his wooden warships were given

1 H. Böhme, (ed.), *The Foundation of the German Empire* (Oxford: Oxford University Press, 1971), pp. 156-160.

protection for their boilers and guns by being draped in chains and scrap iron. Tegetthoff refused to be downcast about the limited value of his wooden ships, writing that 'behind wooden walls beat hearts of iron.'[2]

While, towards the end of June, the Prussian armies were advancing through the mountains of northern Bohemia, the Italian army was preparing to cross the Mincio. Its first objective was to occupy the Quadrilateral, the four fortresses that guarded Venetia. The army was commanded by La Marmora, who surrendered the office of Prime Minister on June 18. Facing him, the Army of the South was led by Archduke Albert. The two armies met on June 24 at Custozza, and the ensuing battle resulted in a convincing victory for the Austrian army. However, the battle that would determine the outcome of the war was not fought until July 3, when Moltke's three armies united on the battlefield of Königgrätz, and inflicted a crushing defeat on the Austrian army commanded by General Ludwig von Benedek.

Naval preparations on both sides of the Adriatic proceeded apace, for neither fleet was, in the spring of 1866, ready to undertake operations. Laughton described the condition of the Austrian fleet:

> The ships which were unfinished when the Archduke Maximilian went to Mexico, were unfinished still; and what ships there were had been permitted to lie by, waiting till it was convenient to repair them. But though Maximilian was no longer there to direct the work or to push it forward, when the necessity occurred the navy still enjoyed the benefit of his rule. He had insisted that the navy should be a national force, that the ships and their engines, as well as their men, should be Austrian. The Arsenal at Pola was a reality; and the ships, though unfinished, were in their own hands, to be got ready as soon as possible.[3]

Tegetthoff's approach to his situation was entirely positive; he was determined to make the best of what he had got, writing: 'Only send them, send them as they are, I'll find some use for them.'

It had been the practice for the Austrian navy in peacetime to keep only a small squadron in commission in home waters, consisting of three frigates and three gunboats. As a result, the mobilisation of crews to bring the fleet to a state of battle readiness meant that a large number of the sailors lacked even basic training. As soon as he took command Tegetthoff began a programme of seagoing exercises. His reputation, and the energy which he displayed, was an inspiration to his fleet. His task was considerable, but his vigour contrasted with that of his opponent:

> While Persano was spending week after week in depressing inactivity, Tegetthoff, face to face with difficulties far greater, with unready ships and an imperfectly equipped arsenal, was yet building up a fleet. His crews were strange to ironclads and to rifled guns; he wanted engineers, for of the Austrian ships in regular commission some had hitherto been sailing vessels, which could consequently train no engineers; his guns were feeble in power. But everything which could be done, he did.[4]

2 Sondhaus, *Habsburg Empire*, p. 252.
3 Laughton, *Studies*, p. 169.
4 Wilson, *Ironclads in Action*. vol.I, p. 228.

As well as training his crews by the constant exercises to which they were subjected, Tegetthoff spent a great deal of time with his officers, discussing the tactical considerations that would determine the outcome of a battle. In particular, very conscious of the fact that the overall power of his broadsides would be inferior to that of the enemy, he emphasised the need for these to be concentrated, so that all the guns which could bear should be aimed at a particular point of an enemy ship, and fired simultaneously. Above all, it was central to his tactical thinking that wherever possible his ships should endeavour to ram the enemy. 'Rush on the enemy and sink him' was said to be his oft repeated watchword.

The fitting out of the two largest Austrian ironclads, the *Erzherzog Ferdinand Max* and *Habsburg* proceeded swiftly, but they were not finally completed until June 21 and 27 respectively. Tegetthoff hoisted his flag in the former. They lacked, however, the guns that had been ordered for them from Krupp; naturally, with hostilities being imminent, the Prussian government suspended their delivery, and it was necessary for the ships to be armed with makeshift batteries of older smoothbore 48 pounders. By now, practically the whole of the Austrian fleet was in hand; the ship of the line *Kaiser* was ready for action by June 25.

Even the *Novara*, patched up and armoured with railway ties for want of anything better, was able to join the fleet by July 4. Much of the credit for the speedy fitting out of the fleet belonged to the commandant of the arsenal at Pola, Captain Eberan von Eberhorst. Highly praised by Tegetthoff for his work in preparing the ships for action, his contribution to the fighting efficiency of the fleet was considerable.[5]

Tegetthoff's captains had adopted his offensive spirit, and he was able to feel confident that they understood his intentions. His personal position, though, was not without some possible difficulty:

> Promoted as he had been, for actual service without reference to seniority, Tegetthoff was probably junior to many of those under his command. Possibly he felt this might be a difficulty in his way. It does not appear to have been so; the hopes, and fears, and plans, and strategy, and tactics of the campaign before them seem to have been discussed in friendly conclave, of which Tegetthoff was the president and the soul. He imbued them with his fiery spirit.[6]

Fasana Roads, at Pola, provided the Austrian fleet with a large stretch of open water in which it could securely carry out the evolutions by which Tegetthoff was training his fleet. Rottauscher described the roadstead in the last weeks of peace:

> A heavy summer storm passed over the squadron, rain lashing the dripping planks of the deck and the watch. From hanging cloud banks bursting away sharply, our shots flashed from the gun ports, and the balls skipped twice, three times with fountains of spray over the dark sea. All day long the echoes of gunfire boomed through the marshy woods of the Brioni Islands. Mines were laid in front of Pola, and two ships were constantly on duty as

5 Rottauscher, *With Tegetthoff*, p. 56n.
6 Laughton, *Studies*, p. 164.

> pickets, one to the north, the other to the south, and the fleet kept banked fires in all of its boilers. We may still have been at peace, but no one trusted the enemy.[7]

The general instructions which Tegetthoff had received were that he was to act in conjunction with the Archduke Albert, but that he was not to undertake any operation which would jeopardise his fleet, or to take risks which outweighed the advantages to be gained. Cautious though these directions were, he was in no doubt where his duty lay. Reviewing his situation, he had reached a number of conclusions. First, that his overriding aim should be to fight and beat the Italian fleet. Next, he must ensure that the weapons which he had were used properly; this was more important than to have and to misuse weapons of the latest pattern.

He was firmly convinced that the ram would prove to be a more effective weapon than the gun, which meant that he must seek to fight at close quarters. Finally, he must ensure that every ship, armoured or not, every man and every gun should be brought into action once battle had been joined.[8]

Evidently, in considering the tactics to be employed, Tegetthoff had in mind the experiences of Farragut and others during the American Civil War. Writing after his own campaign had ended, he referred specifically to the battle of Mobile Bay in 1864: 'In the American Civil War, wooden ships were already successfully employed among ironclads, for they were employed against ironclads at Mobile, and in the battle of Lissa the Austrian fleet offered again the proof that this can always be done without danger.'[9] As has been observed, Tegetthoff intended to make the best of what he had; but to describe the employment of wooden ships against ironclads as a practice that was 'without danger' was certainly overstating the case.

During the period before the campaign began, the situation of the Italian fleet was very different. To begin with, Persano was not a universally popular figure with some of his officers, and he by no means commanded the level of general respect which Tegetthoff enjoyed. His appointment as commander-in-chief had run from May 16, and he proceeded at once to Taranto, where the Italian fleet was assembled. He was extremely disappointed by its condition:

> He found that a great deal was still wanting to make the fleet fit for active service; the equipment was imperfect, the men were newly raised, the senior and commissioned officers were inefficient, and of petty officers there was a great scarcity. Such defects were, of course, very real, but Tegetthoff, at Fasana, was struggling manfully against the same; at Taranto or Ancona Persano does not seem to have realised that it was his duty to do this.[10]

Persano was so dispirited by what he saw of his fleet that within a week of taking command he was writing: 'I fear we shall go down.' To be of such a defeatist turn of mind so soon after he joined his fleet boded ill for the coming campaign. It is no great surprise that instead of tackling his problems effectively, he failed to do the things that needed doing. He was, undoubtedly, faced with incapacity and mismanagement, but he brought to his task such an extreme pessimism that he seemed hardly to know where to begin. Manifestly he lacked the ability

7 Rottauscher, *With Tegetthoff*, pp. 58-59.
8 Custance, *Ship of the Line*, p. 49.
9 Greene and Massignani, *Ironclads at War*, p. 221.
10 Laughton, *Studies*, p. 168.

to organise an efficient fleet. He wrote to General Diego Angioletti, the Navy Minister, in despairing terms:

> It is my duty to submit to your Excellency that the ships which join the fleet from day to day are incompletely manned, especially in regard to their petty officers; and – which is of more consequence – are without trained gunners, who are now more than ever necessary, on account of the greater number of rifled guns, which require long and careful drill. And this when hostilities every moment are expected to begin! This awakens very serious thoughts. The fleet is not ready for war. It will take at least a month to bring it to a tolerable pitch. Help me, I earnestly entreat you.

History has been extremely severe in its assessment of Persano; and yet perhaps he does deserve some sympathy as he confronted the task of creating an efficient fleet from the resources which he was given. He was, though, not the right man to raise the morale of a fleet that was badly in need of inspiration. There were, moreover, already those in the Italian government who doubted whether a vigorous offensive at sea was the wisest policy to pursue. Bismarck had urged La Marmora to undertake the strongest possible naval activity, with a landing on the Dalmatian coast to coincide with a hoped for revolution in Hungary, but the Italian prime minister was not at all tempted by the prospect of such a stroke. Angioletti, for his part, advised against an active war at sea, and was especially opposed to the idea of a landing in Dalmatia. He must have been aware, even before he received Persano's *cri de coeur*, of the shortcomings of the Italian fleet, despite its numerical superiority over its adversary. Nor did the navy's officer corps, composed of members of the mutually mistrustful Sardinian and Neapolitan navies, and of Venetian emigrés, who despised both the other groups, represent a united and cohesive body of men.

These divisions went to the top of the navy's command structure. Persano's immediate subordinates, Vice-Admiral Giovanni Battista Albini and Rear Admiral Giovanni Vacca were united in little but their contempt for the admiral. Vacca, in particular, was especially hostile. On May 19, soon after Persano had arrived at Taranto, he wrote to Captain Enrico Brocchetti, the director-general of the Navy Ministry, who had replaced Captain d'Amico when the latter was appointed as Persano's chief of staff. He did so in terms which gave a clear idea of his feelings towards Persano: 'I hope that d'Amico will arrive today to rectify several matters about which I have the gravest doubts, and will have to be smoothed over by the Ministry.' He went on to quote several passages from Persano's order of the day; he was particularly irritated with the way in which his position and that of Albini had been dealt with, appearing to give them a lower status than had been assigned by the decree issued by the ministry.[11]

Ten days later Vacca was to be found protesting bitterly to Brocchetti that Persano was acting as a despot in everything. He went on to remark in extravagant terms that it was singular that those who had stood out against a king's despotism should now have to tolerate that of a *coglione* (asshole). As for d'Amico, he thought that the chief of staff was not very effective in moderating Persano's arbitrary conduct.[12]

11 Iachino, *Lissa*, p. 151.
12 Iachino, *Lissa*, p. 151.

Vice-Admiral Albini, the brother of another admiral and the son of Rear Admiral Giuseppe Albini, who had commanded the Sardinian fleet in 1848, would have perhaps been considered as an alternative to Persano. Of him, Admiral Iachino wrote: 'It would have been possible to appoint Albini as commander-in-chief. He was, however, generally judged to be old-fashioned, of limited intelligence and culture, and tenaciously attached to the sailing tradition of his family.' [13]In the circumstances, it is not surprising that Albini would have been seen as an unsuitable appointment. He was, however, well regarded as a brave fighter, having displayed particular courage during the siege of Ancona in 1860.

Angioletti had designated the force to be commanded by Persano as a 'fleet of operations,' and divided it into three squadrons. The *squadra di battaglia*, consisting of the six larger ironclads, was to be commanded by Persano. The *squadra subsidiaria*, composed of the wooden ships, was to be commanded by Albini, while the *squadra d'assedio*, composed of the six small ironclads, was to be under the orders of Vacca.

The way in which the fleet was organised was a matter of considerable importance, not least bearing in mind the personalities of its principal commanders and their lack of mutual sympathy, and Angioletti's decision to divide the fleet into the three squadrons was, according to the Italian staff history, made in order to form squadrons equal in strength and composed of ships of similar types, rather than with combat in mind. In a minute which Persano circulated on the subject on June 15 he made clear that this organisation was for administrative rather than tactical purposes. Admiral Custance summarised its terms:

> That minute proceeds to direct that when the armada acts together it will be divided into an armoured fleet and unarmoured fleet, each of which will be divided into groups. Also that when the armoured fleet cruises either in line ahead or in line abreast, the unarmoured fleet will form a second line to starboard, to port, or astern, at a distance which will be signalled. The minute sets forth two organisations, one for cruising and the other for fighting. In the former the armoured ships are arranged in three groups of four ships each, while the unarmoured ships are simply told that they are to be in line ahead. In the latter the armoured ships are entirely rearranged into groups of four ships each, with a reserve of three ships, and the *Affondatore* not in the line.[14]

This meant that effectively three different organisations had been created, for administration, cruising and fighting respectively. To switch from the cruising to the fighting organisation would have required time, and would inevitably have led to a great deal of confusion in such an untrained fleet. The triple organisation was quite unnecessary, and shows Persano's confusion of mind.

Having regard to the way in which the fleet was to manoeuvre when it did come face to face with the enemy, it is instructive to see what Persano expected of Albini's squadron:

> The unarmoured fleet will take station 3,000 metres from the armoured fleet on the bearing signalled. In the case in which the unarmoured fleet is called upon to take part

13 Iachino, *Lissa*, p. 36.
14 Custance, *Ship of the Line*, p. 51.

> in the attack, it will, in default of special orders, form a second column indented with the armoured fleet. The *Esploratore* and *Messagiere* will take station between the two fleets to transmit orders, but will avoid entering the zone of the enemy's fire.[15]

In this minute Persano reveals the limited value which he placed on his unarmoured ships as a battle asset, even though they were manned by 5,000 men and were armed with a total of 382 guns. In this way he deliberately placed a large portion of his force in a passive and demoralising position. He also included in the minute some revealing instructions as to the ranges at which the enemy was to be engaged: 'Outside 500 metres range 10 inch guns only will be used against ironclads. An armoured ship will always engage an unarmoured ship at a distance of 1,000 metres unless it is intended to use the ram.' This, Custance thought, demonstrated that there was in Persano's mind 'no ardent desire or intention' to bring all the guns of his fleet into action at decisive ranges. There does not appear to have been any assessment of the likely effect of employing the fleet's guns in the manner directed.

In considering the tactics to be adopted by fleets of ironclads, particular attention had been paid by the navies of Europe to the principles evolved by the French Vice-Admiral Louis Bouet-Willaumez, published in 1865. These were based on a set of tactical rules originally published in France in 1857 under the title *Naval Tactics*. Bouet-Willaumez had for two years been in command of a squadron consisting entirely of ironclads, before he published his treatise entitled *Tactiques Supplementaire à l'usage d'une flotte cuirassée*, which was based on the experimentation he had been able to carry out. In the introduction to his work he summarised the main concepts on which it was based:

> a) An unarmoured vessel whose strength lies in guns distributed along its sides and not in its ramming ability is at the same time stronger and less vulnerable on the side than at the bow, by reason of the fact that enemy projectiles penetrating the hull at the bow cause much more serious effects over the entire length of the ship than do projectiles which come in at right angles.
>
> b) An armoured vessel whose greatest strength lies in ramming with its bow and its greatest weakness in the portholes and openings in its sides finds its best employment in bringing its bow to the enemy rather than in turning broadside to the enemy.
>
> c) It follows that while the line abreast should be considered only as a formation preparatory to attack for an unarmoured fleet, on the other hand this may become the effective attacking formation for an armoured fleet.
>
> d) It also follows that in evolutions executed by a fleet of armourclads in the presence of the enemy it is appropriate to execute movements whereby they bring their bows to the enemy or face him obliquely, rather than movements whereby they turn broadside to him. By manoeuvring in this way armourclads not only present the smallest profile to shells and ramming instead of their more vulnerable sides, but they will constantly be in position to use their own rams even in the course of the evolution.[16]

15 Custance, *Ship of the Line*, pp. 51-52.

16 Giuseppe Fioranzo, *A History of Naval Tactical Thought* (Annapolis, Md: Naval Institute Press, 1979), pp. 137-138.

List of Maps

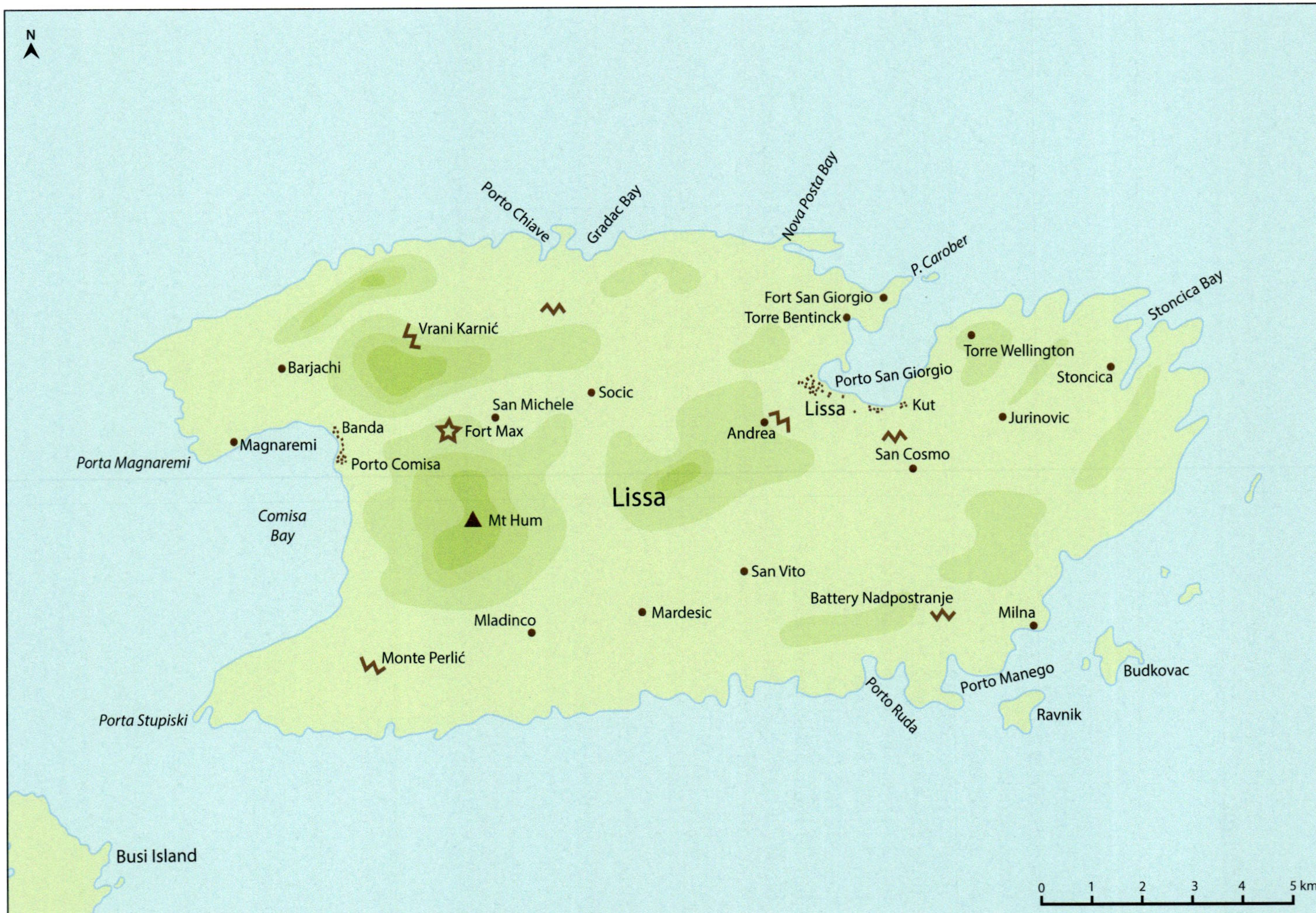

1 The Island of Lissa.

2 The Adriatic Sea.

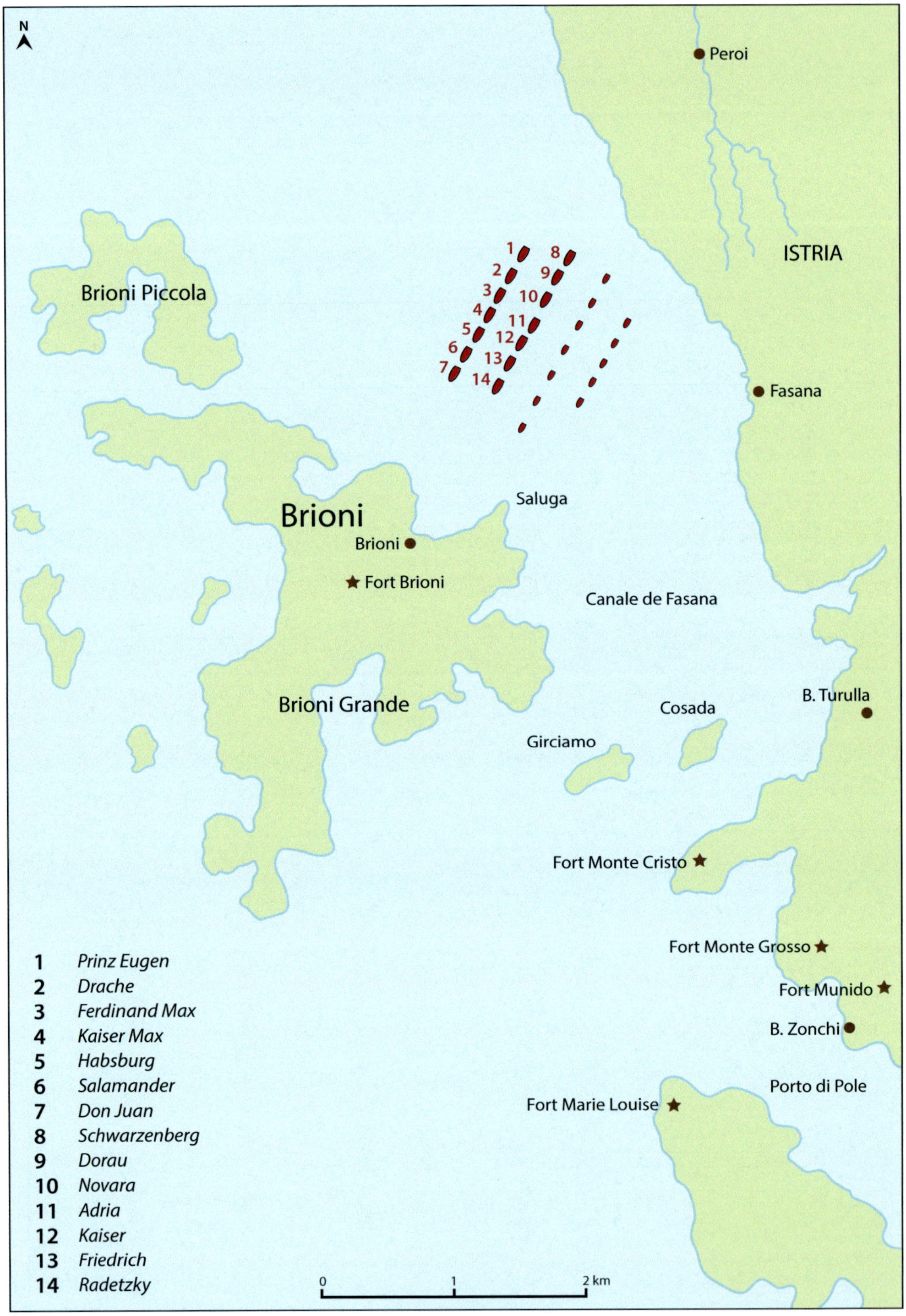

3 Fasana Roads.

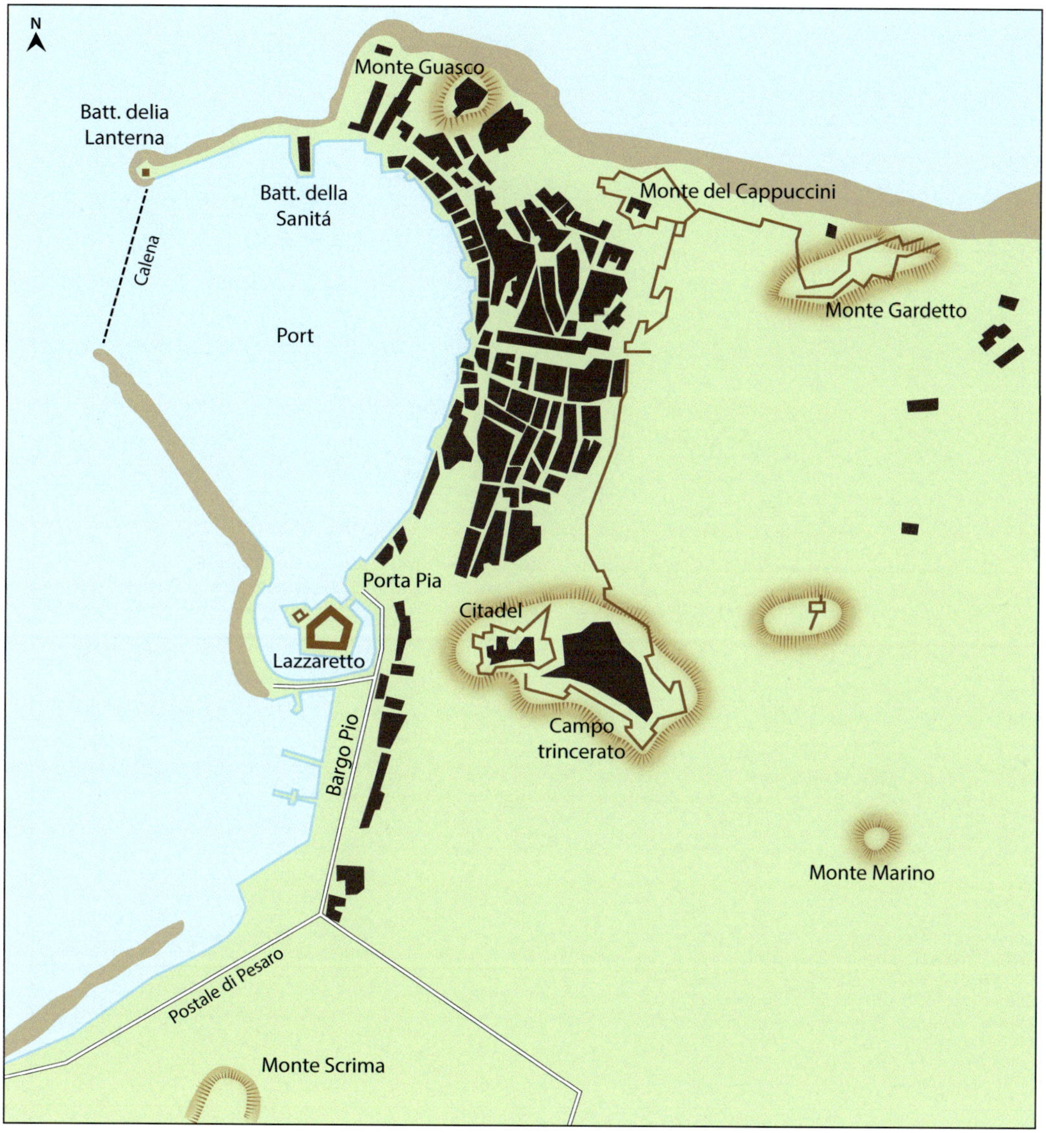

4 Ancona Harbour.

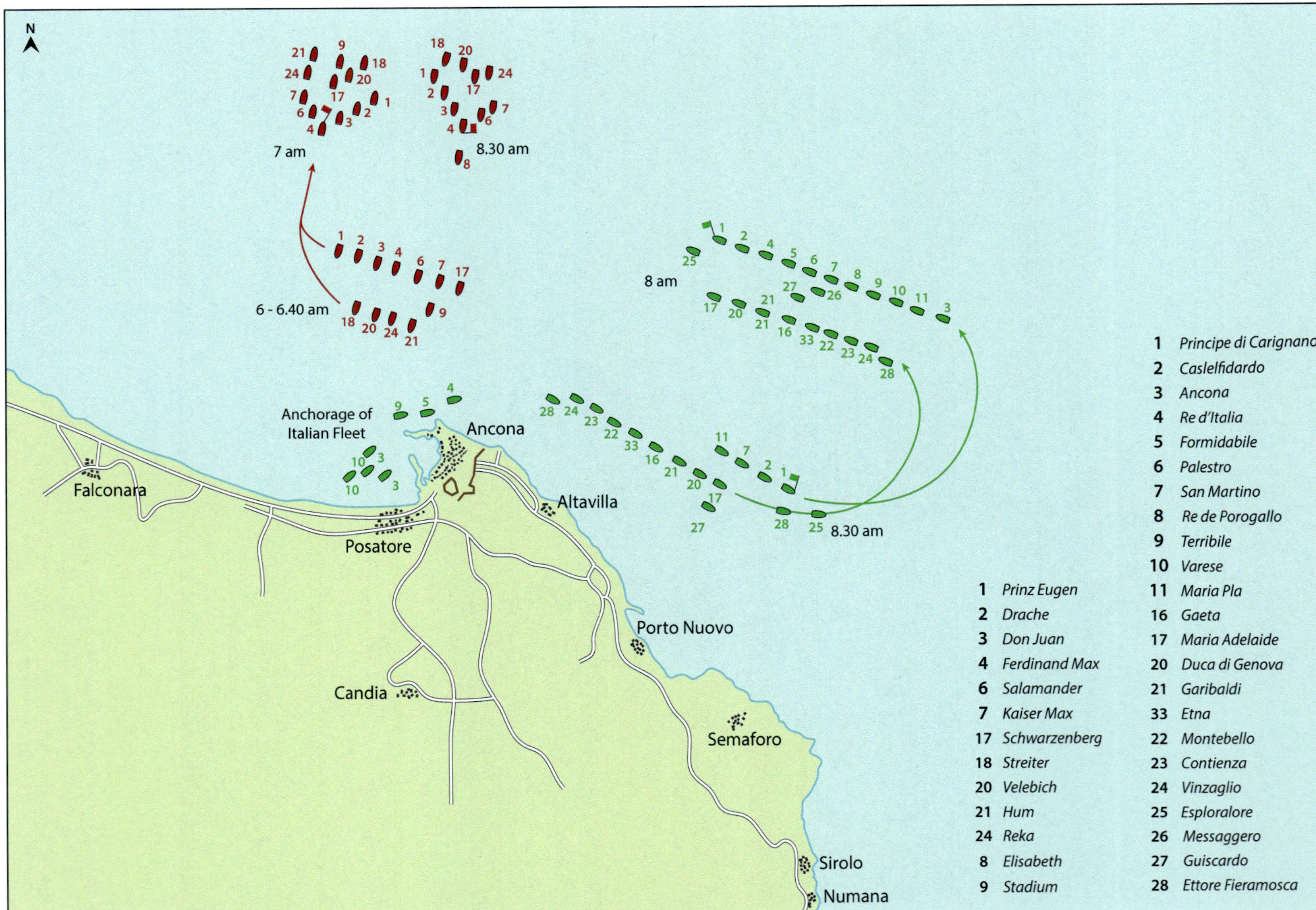

5 The fleets off Ancona, June 27 1866.

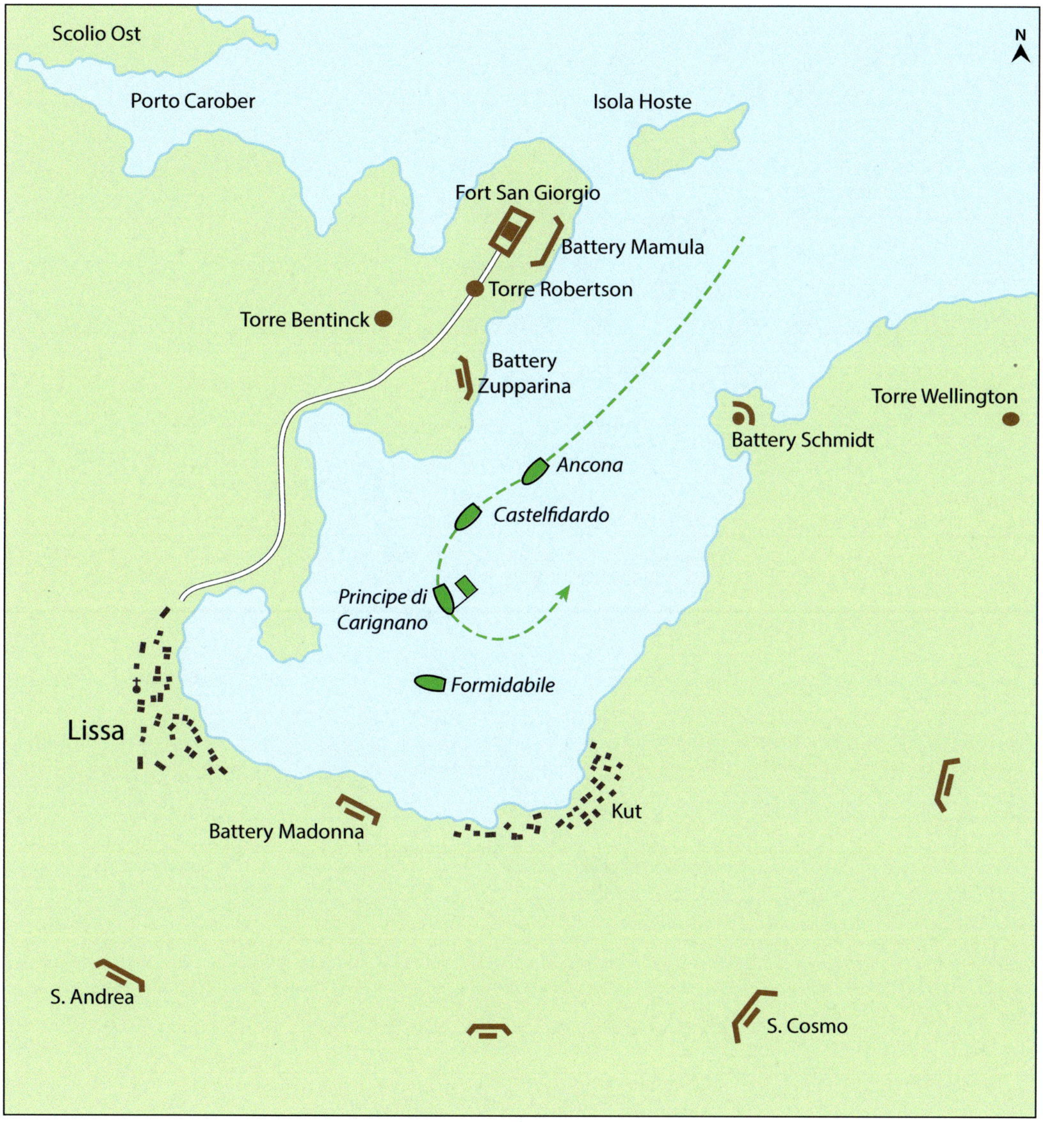

6 Porto San Giorgio, July 19 1866.

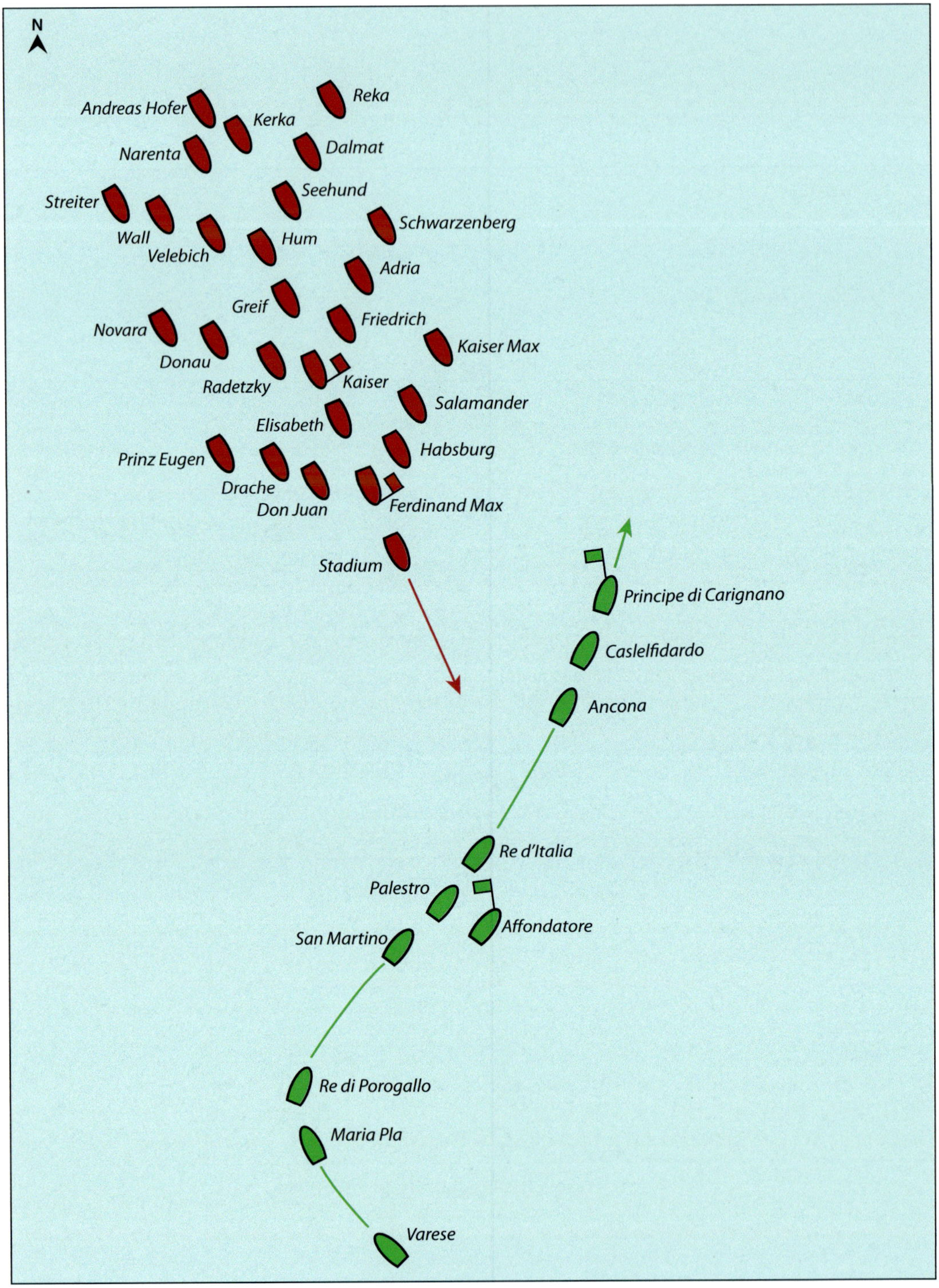

7 July 20 1866: The Austrian approach.

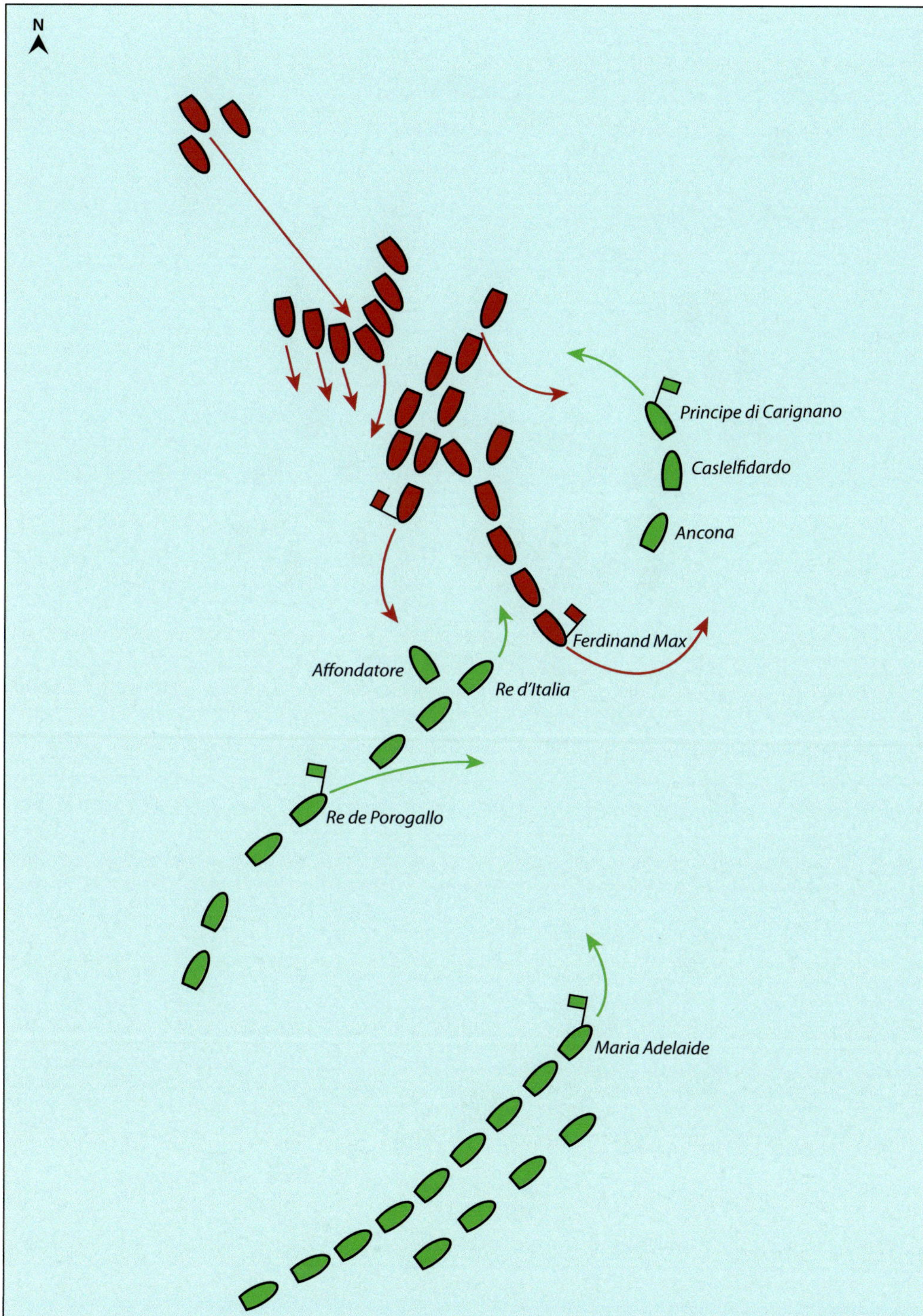

8 July 20 1866: Situation at 1100hrs.

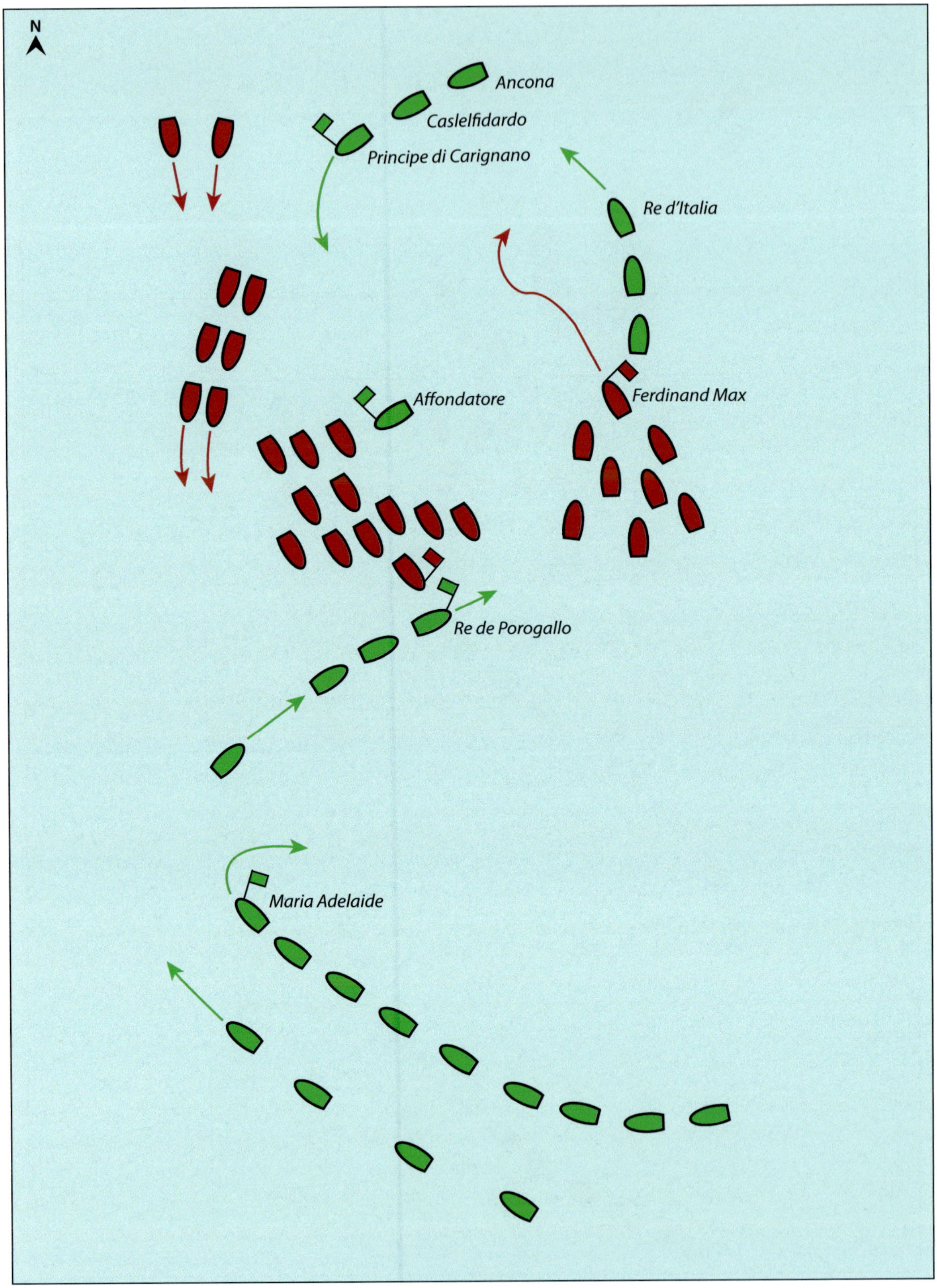

9 July 20 1866: Situation at 1115hrs.

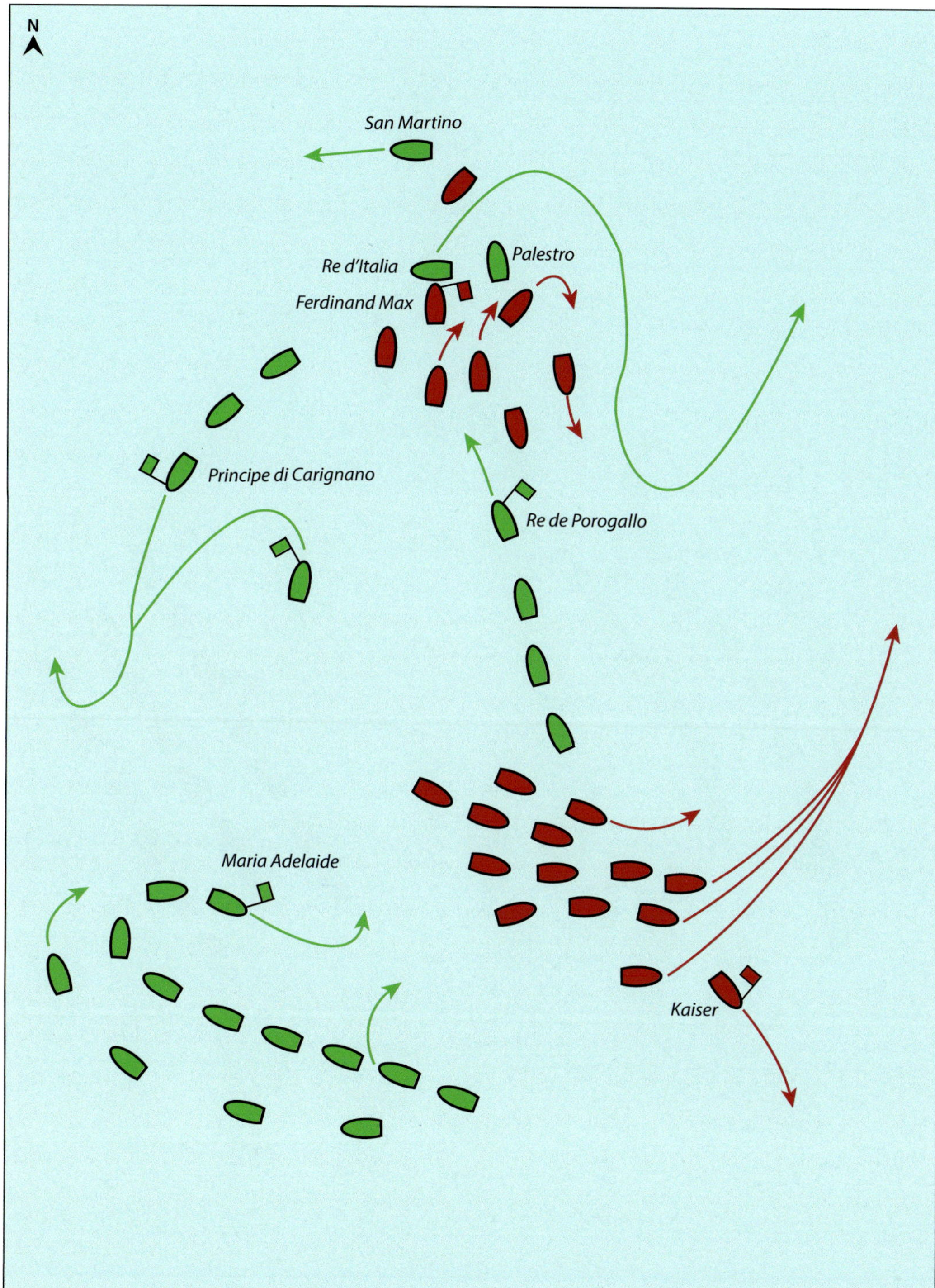

10 July 20 1866: Situation at 1130hrs.

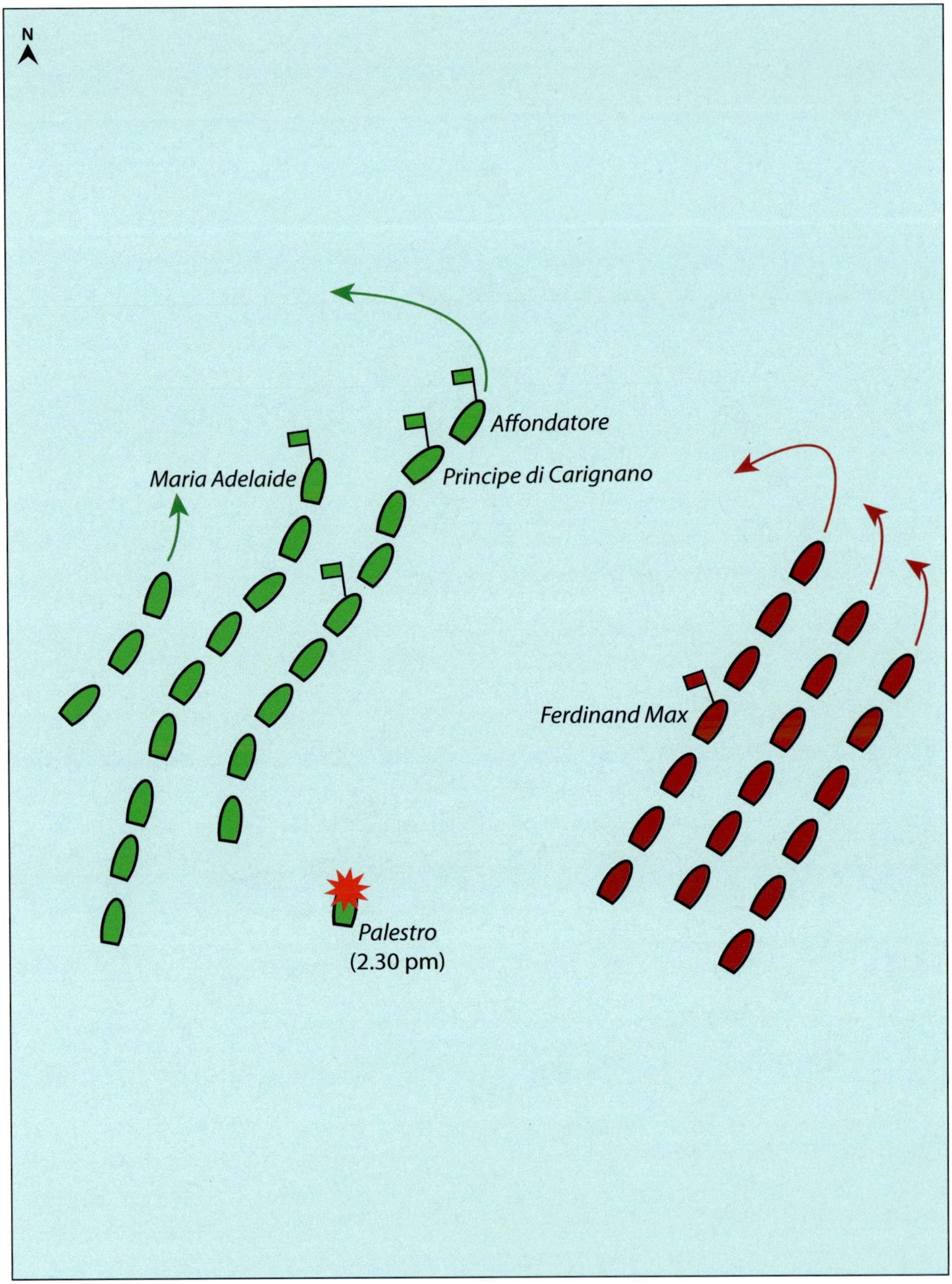

11 Situation between 1300hrs and 1500hrs. The two fleets sailed parallel to each other, frequently altering course to match. At 1430hrs the *Palestro* blew up.

All this may seem, with the hindsight of a century and a half, a series of statements of the obvious; but at the time naval theorists were feeling their way only gradually as they assessed the new weapons that had been created.

The Italian navy had adopted Bouet-Willaumez's tactical considerations, and Persano expressly embodied these principles in his minute of June 15, remarking: 'The armoured fleet, in addition to the official tactical regulations, will apply the additional tactics of Vice Admiral Bouet-Willaumez. The unarmoured fleet will apply only the official tactical regulations.' Admiral Iachino observes, having regard to the criticisms made of these tactical instructions by many writers, that it should be noted that although these were signed by Persano, and accordingly reflected his tactical thinking, they were probably drafted by his chief of staff, Captain d'Amico, whose reputation was that of one of the most educated officers of the Italian navy at that time.[17]

On June 20, the date of Italy's declaration of war, not only did Italy receive a new Prime minister when La Marmora handed over to Bettino Ricasoli, but also a new Navy Minister. Angioletti went off to command an infantry division, and he was succeeded by Agostino Depretis, who was far more bullish than his predecessor. He was soon making very clear to Persano just what he expected of his fleet. Mindful of its numerical superiority, he insisted that an early offensive be launched.

Persano sailed from Taranto on the evening of June 21. He issued instructions for the cruising order to be adopted during the voyage; the ironclads were to steam in groups disposed astern 1,200 metres apart, and the unarmoured vessels in one group on the port beam of the ironclads. The ships were to be 400 metres apart. The group formation was for there to be a ship on each quarter of the leader. Lookouts would be posted ahead, astern, and on either beam. When he set off, Persano had no news of the Austrian fleet, but a message brought to him by the *Terribile* and *Formidabile* when they joined the fleet, to the effect that an Austrian scout had been reconnoitring the Italian coast, made him uneasy, and he sent into Bari a message for the ministry asking for news of the Austrians. The prompt response did nothing to allay his fears: 'Latest information: at Fasana five armoured ships and as many screw frigates: Admiral Tegetthoff anxious for a bold stroke and to board: would like to surprise the fleet by night: his flagship would use the ram.'[18] In response to this Persano issued instructions to his fleet as to how to meet a night attack which, if they had been acted upon, would have caused great confusion.

As it was, Persano finally arrived at Ancona on June 25, after what had been a slow passage, and anchored outside the port. A number of his ships went into the harbour to continue the process of refitting their guns, and the fleet took on coal and provisions. His instructions from Depretis were succinct and entirely clear: 'The Adriatic is an Italian sea, and the Austrian flag must disappear from it. Do as you think best, but this end must be attained.' Persano had arrived at Ancona without the *Affondatore*, which he regarded as the most powerful unit of his fleet, and he was soon making it evident that until she joined him he could do nothing.

H.W. Wilson pondered the reason why the personnel of the Italian navy fell so far short of what was required:

17 Iachino, *Lissa*, p. 183.
18 Custance, *Ship of the Line*, p. 54.

> The Italians have always been a seafaring people. Their coastline is long; they have considerable fisheries; and the history of Venice and Genoa is the history of naval states. Their past was not ignoble, and they were fired by a great idea. The freedom of Italy appealed strongly to every Italian; they had fought and suffered in 1848 and 1859 for that worthy cause, but in 1866 it was to be won by them ignobly and ingloriously, through the aid of their ally. History teaches that men fight best when they have a good cause behind them; here there was a good cause, which did not bring its devotees success.[19]

Wilson found the reason for this lack of success in 'incapable generals, irresolute admirals, under trained officers and undisciplined sailors.' He compared the relationship between officers unfavourably with Nelson's 'band of brothers,' noting that there was 'none of that prompt and unquestioning obedience, which is the preliminary of successful war.'

Persano, as soon as he arrived at Ancona, urgently pressed Depretis to send him the *Affondatore*, as well as the other vessels of his fleet that were to follow him there. He called for the delivery of telescopes, despatch boats that were faster than those which he possessed, as many of the new Armstrong guns as possible and, oddly, for more ironclads. He was perfectly aware of the total establishment of the Italian navy in terms of ironclads, and it was only the *Affondatore* that was lacking. The fleet had left Taranto before the rearming of the *Re d'Italia*, *Palestro*, and *Varese* could be carried out, but on arrival at Ancona each was supplied with two 150 pounder (8 inch) Armstrong guns.[20] It was while Persano, with his fleet at Ancona, was impatiently waiting for the *Affondatore* (which passed Gibraltar on June 28), that there was a sudden and unexpected development, when Tegetthoff appeared off the port.

What had happened was that the scouting vessel *Stadion*, which the Austrian admiral had sent to look into Ancona immediately after the declaration of war, had returned on June 23 to report that there was no evidence of any Italian naval concentration there. Accordingly, Tegetthoff next day telegraphed Archduke Albert to seek permission to take the offensive, or at least to reconnoitre the Italian coast in force. At this time it was his understanding that the Italian fleet was still at Taranto. He hoped that it might make its way to Ancona piecemeal, and that by putting to sea he might encounter some of its units in circumstances that would enable him to destroy them. This was the day of the battle of Custozza, and the Archduke was understandably preoccupied; but he responded on June 26 to say that, within limits, nothing stood in the way of Tegetthoff's freedom of action. He was, though, warned not to go south of the island of Lissa, and must ensure that the mouth of the Po and the Venetian coast remained covered. While he was waiting for the Archduke's reply, Tegetthoff convened a meeting of his captains, and discussed preliminary arrangements to sail to Ancona to see for himself. On the evening of June 26 he sailed with six ironclads (the *Habsburg* alone was left behind, her fitting out still incomplete) and seven of his wooden steamers. He arrived off Ancona at daybreak on June 27.

At about 3:00 a.m. the steamer *Elisabeth*, scouting ahead of the fleet, sighted the Italian *Esploratore*, which was cruising outside the port. With the support of the *Velebich* and *Reka*, the *Elisabeth* closed with the Italian vessel, opening fire and chasing her inshore. Tegetthoff signalled the rest of his fleet to clear for action, and from 5:30 a.m. to 7:30 a.m. steamed slowly

19 Wilson, *Ironclads in Action*, I pp. 213-214.
20 Sir William L Clowes, *Four Modern Campaigns* (London: Unit Library, 1902), p. 16.

back and forward off Ancona, at a distance of about two and a half miles. It was immediately obvious to him that the bulk of the Italian fleet had arrived there, and he remained off the port waiting to see if it would emerge.[21]

It was in no immediate state to do so. The *Re d'Italia* had the coal in her bunkers on fire; the *Re di Portogallo* was unable to get her engines started; the *Terribile* still lacked half her guns, and the *Ancona* was also entirely unprepared for battle. The engineers aboard the *Varese* and *Palestro* were also having difficulty managing their engines, while most of the remainder were haphazardly engaged in coaling. However, after Persano had toured the harbour in the *Esploratore* visiting each of his warships, four ironclads, the *San Martino, Maria Pia, Castelfidardo* and *Principe di Carignano* (which also lacked her heavy guns) were able to get up steam and formed into line. Persano's grandiloquent boast had previously been that it was his intention 'to entice the hostile fleet to offer battle, and to annihilate it if it makes the attempt.' Now, given that opportunity, he did nothing of the kind. Instead, after making a signal that was generally not understood, he steamed out of harbour at the head of his line. He did not, however, steer for the Austrian fleet, which was already preparing to retire, but instead led his ships to a position under the protection of the guns of Monte Conero, a fort at the entrance to the harbour, where they were one by one joined by other ships as they emerged. By the time most of the fleet was assembled, Tegetthoff had departed. It had appeared to him that there was no percentage in launching an attack on a superior force that lay under the protection of shore batteries. He had not won a battle, but as he steamed away he could certainly regard the operation as a moral victory, as he wrote to his friend Emma Lutteroth, remarking that to achieve a success, albeit 'not material, but moral' was not to be undervalued.[22]

Persano was evidently uncomfortable about the way matters had gone that morning, and after the Austrians had gone he held a conference aboard the *Principe di Carignano*, attended by Rear Admiral Vacca, Captains Jauch and Bucchia, and his chief of staff d'Amico. In the course of this meeting, he explained that the reason why he had not taken action to attack the Austrians was because three of his ironclads, the *Re d'Italia, Re di Portogallo* and *Ancona* would not have been able to take part. Persano added another explanation:

> He is also understood to have intimated that his instructions assigned to him more important operations – that he had orders not to risk the fleet – and that he looked for no advantage in following the foe. It is evident, not only that Persano misrepresented his instructions, but also that he was so strategically blind, and so morally timid, if nothing worse, that he was practically paralysed. It is known, too, that the reverses which had been suffered already by the Italians onshore had taken the heart out of him.[23]

At the council of war, Vacca is reported to have said: 'I am happy to return to Ancona, but having received a challenge from Admiral Tegetthoff, I believe that as soon as the fleet has been refuelled and is ready to put to sea, we must go to Pola and accept the challenge that was

21 Clowes, *Four Modern Campaigns*, p. 7.
22 Greene and Massignani, *Ironclads at War*, p. 218.
23 Clowes, *Four Modern Campaigns*, p. 17.

thrown down to us.' To this, Persano replied that this was what he intended: 'We are going to fight Tegetthoff.'[24]

After the war, when he was put on trial, Persano defended his actions on June 27:

> I cannot understand how I am charged with failing to meet the call of duty against the enemy fleet that had appeared almost before it was signalled. We were severely hampered because ships that had arrived were not fully equipped; aboard the *Re d'Italia* the coal was burning in the bunkers and it was necessary to throw water on the coal dust to prevent greater damage.[25]

Persano went on to list a number of the defects affecting various ships of his fleet:

> So that of the eleven ironclads there were not more than four fit for a long chase. The other seven were, at best, only fit to take part in a battle, but could not be relied on for a chase; and the more so as most of them wanted the guns and ammunition necessary for fighting with ironclads. If Tegetthoff had come really with a wish to fight, he would not have withdrawn as soon as we were ready to meet and attack him. I could not, of course, suppose that he had come merely to go away again; and it was therefore my duty, in the first place, to form the fleet so as not to expose it to needless risk; and then to oppose and attack the enemy. But instead of that he went off after a short time, two or three hours perhaps, much to our regret, and notwithstanding the dashing conduct of our ships' companies.[26]

Laughton rejected this defence almost entirely, observing that a great part of it was untrue, a great part was irrelevant, a great part was self condemnatory, and all of it was extremely silly.

On the other hand, Admiral Iachino acknowledged that Persano's justification was not entirely without merit: 'In his defence, Persano did make two good points; the first, with regard to the length of time which the fleet took to leave the harbour on the morning of June 27, and the second with regard to Tegetthoff's withdrawal and his implicit refusal to stand and fight.'[27]

24 Iachino, *Lissa*, p. 238.
25 Iachino, *Lissa*, p. 234.
26 Laughton, *Studies*, p. 190.
27 Iachino, *Lissa*, pp. 234-235.

20

Target Lissa

On any view the Italian fleet had not made a good start. On July 2 Persano telegraphed Depretis to tell him that he was indeed anxious to fight, but repeating his entreaties for the *Affondatore* to be sent to him before he did so. He also called for more gunners. He was continuing to receive additions to his fleet, the screw frigate *Vittorio Emanuele*, the screw corvette *San Giovanni* and the paddle steamer *Sirena* having now arrived at Ancona. For the ensuing ten days he took no action other than to complete the equipment of his fleet, and put them, as far as he could, into fighting order, particularly with regard to the fitting of their guns.

In that respect at least Persano's critics have not given him credit that he perhaps deserved. Greene and Massignani made a careful study of the armament with which the Italian fleet was equipped, and the changes that were made during the period of preparation. There is conflicting information about exactly what was done during the process of rearmament of Persano's ships, first at Taranto and then at Ancona. The commission of enquiry established by the Italian government after the war did make a particular effort to determine the reason for the apparent lack of effect of the Italian gunfire, but reached no final conclusions.

As early as May 29 Persano was writing to Angioletti to seek permission to make changes additional to those that the ministry had already ordered. One request he made was that 'the ironclad gunboats be supplied with a 12 inch rifled gun of wrought iron.' This was a reference to the *Palestro* and *Varese*, which were equipped with a pivot in their bow with a gun port, which enabled them to fire both forward and broadside. It is unclear what calibre of gun was ultimately fitted to these ships, since Persano wrote that 'it is only a pity that it cannot be used with a gun of more powerful calibre, but the requested gun will be always effective against wooden ships.'[1]

What Persano was endeavouring to do was to concentrate as far as he could the rifled guns actually available aboard those of his ironclads where they would be most effective. On June 7 he wrote for permission to transfer out of the *Formidabile* and *Terribile* their rifled guns, since it was anticipated that they would be operating in particular against shore based fortifications, and to install them in other ironclads. Permission for this was granted on June 12, and the *Principe di Carignano* received eight rifled or banded guns from each of the *Formidabile* and *Terribile*. The *San Martino* received the 6.4 inch rifles transferred from the wooden frigate *Duca degli Abruzzi*. In making these changes, Persano was certainly acting sensibly, and it is not unreasonable to

1 Greene and Massignani, *Ironclads at War*, p. 251.

assume that a desire to complete the process was an important factor in his procrastination. By the time that he came to fight the Austrians, he had succeeded in changing the guns on his ironclads so that he had the highest number available of rifled and banded guns aboard them, although apparently unable to receive all the ordered Armstrong guns in time.[2]

It appears that Persano had managed to exchange between ships of various types as many as eighty 6.4 inch rifled guns, which certainly strengthened the hitting power of his ironclads. Although there is apparently no precise record of the changes made, it has been calculated that seven of the ironclads received them as follows:

Re di Portogallo 12 guns
San Martino 8 guns
Maria Pia 16 guns
Principe di Carignano 8 guns
Re d'Italia 12 guns
Castelfidardo 20 guns
Varese 4 guns

Only four such guns were supplied by the Naples artillery depot, and all the remainder were transferred out of wooden warships. Unhappily, when the battle came to be fought, the fire of the Italian gunners was to prove less effective than that of their Austrian counterparts, for a number of reasons to be considered further.

The political leaders of the Italian government who had taken office immediately prior to the battle of Custozza were now confronted with an entirely different situation. Ricasoli and Depretis, in the aftermath of the battle, were looking to the navy to counterbalance the defeat, and were increasingly agitated about Persano's lack of effective action. Given the superiority of the Italian fleet, it seemed to them that a stroke across the Adriatic at the Dalmatian coastline had an excellent chance of success. La Marmora, however, had not changed his view about this. The news of the battle of Königgrätz on July 3, which on the face of it confirmed the prospect of the cession of Venetia to Italy, led him strongly to urge Ricasoli to do nothing to jeopardise this.

At this time, the proposal, sensibly enough, that Depretis was putting forward, was for Persano to move at once to blockade Tegetthoff's fleet, and this was also what the admiral, if he proposed to do anything, had in mind. His own idea was thereafter to operate against the coast of Istria and Dalmatia, particularly the ships and docks of the Austrian Lloyd. Depretis suggested that once Persano had dealt with Tegetthoff's fleet he should land troops at Nabresina, on the coast north of Trieste, to cut off the city's rail and telegraph links; and then occupy a number of Dalmatian islands.

Ricasoli, meanwhile, was working on a plan to take advantage of the Prussian victory at Königgrätz, involving an invasion of the Croatian coast by Garibaldi with a force of 40,000 volunteers, together with the occupation of the Tyrol, and 'the destruction of the enemy fleet and the occupation of Istria.' What was clear to Ricasoli, and everybody else, was that there was not much time left to achieve this sort of success before an armistice brought fighting to a halt.

2 Greene and Massignani, *Ironclads at War*, p. 251.

Depretis, accordingly, continued to apply pressure for some effective action. On July 5 he telegraphed Persano:

> The most serious considerations call for the hastening of the complete equipment of the fleet. I have dispatched the *Carlo Alberto*, *Principe Umberto* (screw frigate), and *Governolo* (paddle corvette) from Naples, and ordered the immediate completion of the *Affondatore*. Inform me as to when the fleet will be ready to go to sea, and of what vessels it will consist.[3]

In reply, Persano was still making belligerent noises, expressing the hope that peace would not be made until the fleet had fought the enemy. To this, Depretis was quick to respond: 'The proposals of the Emperor of the French do not hinder the prosecution of hostilities; on the contrary, an action with definite results would be useful. The hastening of the equipment is pressing.' Persano's reply could not have failed to irritate the minister: 'If the matter be pressing, the fleet is completely ready to put to sea; but two days are yet needed, if the guns are to be embarked and the carriages fitted. The other needs are secondary. But I desire instructions, for I have none of any value except those of June 8.' Depretis was curt in his response: 'Let the fleet put to sea tonight, and do you await at sea those ships which are still engaged in getting their guns on board. Despatch is essential.'

Persano had still not run out of excuses, telegraphing to Depretis:

> I beg you to state definitely whether I am to attack the enemy should he be protected by fortresses. It would be better if the *Affondatore* were here; yet I will proceed without her. You know the situation, and will therefore be able to say whether an action will be sufficient, or whether a definite result is required.[4]

Depretis was annoyed by this, and sent a stinging despatch:

> Would you tell the people who in their mad vanity believe their sailors the best in the world – that in spite of the twelve millions we have added to their debt, the squadron that we have collected is one incapable of facing the enemy? We should be stoned. And who has ever heard the Austrian fleet mentioned except with contempt?[5]

The time which Persano's procrastination was wasting so prodigally was valuable in political rather than military terms. If the navy did not make its contribution to Italy's bargaining position soon, by winning a victory at sea, it would not be able to make it at all. Of this, Depretis was painfully aware, and the admiral perfectly understood it as well. The minister had done all he could to spell out his instructions, which were unmistakable. They were that Persano should seek out and attack the enemy, with a view to fighting a decisive battle, and do so at once. If the Austrian fleet remained in port at Pola, he was to blockade it, while keeping out of range of the forts. His overall objective, of which he had been frequently reminded, was to obtain command of the Adriatic, denying the Austrian fleet any access to it. The final and peremptory

3 Clowes, *Four Modern Campaigns*, p. 18.
4 Clowes, *Four Modern Campaigns*, p. 19.
5 Wilson, *Ironclads in Action*, vol. I, p. 212.

instruction from Depretis was that Persano should proceed to sea immediately, leaving behind any ships that had not yet been fully armed. On July 8, at 4:30 p.m., the admiral finally yielded to the minister's urging, and issued an order that the fleet should put to sea, although he was still without the *Affondatore*.[6] The ships that were not yet ready were left behind under Rear Admiral Provano, with orders to join the fleet at a prearranged rendezvous.

The fleet finally left harbour at 6:00 p.m., and by the following morning had reached a point towards the entrance to the Gulf of Quarnero, though careful to remain out of sight of land. Persano then reversed his course, and headed back in the general direction of Ancona, proceeding to a point some 40 miles south-east of Monte Conero which was the rendezvous agreed with Provano. He then, on July 10, took the fleet towards the Dalmatian coast, approaching first to within about twenty five miles of Isola Grosso and then sailing south eastwards towards the island of Lissa, before turning back into the middle of the Adriatic. There, undisturbed by the enemy or by importunate messages from the Navy Minister, Persano exercised his fleet in steam tactics, signalling and gun drill. He did not, however, fire the guns which had been newly installed aboard his ships; some concentrated target practice would have been much the most useful exercise through which he could put his inexperienced undertrained crews:

> It had been rumoured that the fleet was to range the Istrian coast, and confront Tegetthoff at Fasana. It did nothing of the kind; it stood to the south east, and in mid-channel sailed backwards and forwards in open order, the ships keeping 1000 yards apart from each other, and exercising none of the manoeuvres of battle. They were better hidden, it was said, in the middle of the Adriatic than were the Austrians at Pola[7].

Certainly throughout his cruise Persano had no intention of confronting the Austrian fleet, and he made no attempt to ascertain its whereabouts. His intention was solely to engage in fleet exercise, which was all very well as far as it went, but what was abundantly clear was that it was certainly not far enough. He does not appear to have held any discussion with his subordinate commanders or the captains as to the tactics to be employed if and when the Austrian fleet was actually encountered. Tegetthoff, meanwhile, had been made aware of the fact that Persano had put to sea, having received two messages reporting the sighting of the Italian fleet as it approached first is Isola Grosso and then Lissa. For the moment he was prepared to wait for a more favourable opportunity to strike.

One witness of the fleet's proceedings was a member of the Italian Chamber of Deputies. Pier Carlo Boggio, who was also a journalist, had gone to sea with the fleet as a guest of Persano. He was not, however, a dispassionate observer. He remarked to Albini's flag captain, Marquis Paulucci: 'How cowardly are these Austrians! They will not give us a chance; they fly before us.' Paulucci was unimpressed, pointing out the truth of the matter by replying to Boggio that it was not the Austrians who could be called cowardly, but the Italians who had been humiliated. His opinion was shared by Albini, who had said: 'This is not the way to make war! We have lost an opportunity which may never return.'[8] And d'Amico, in his capacity as Persano's chief of staff, had candidly questioned the Admiral's strategy, which can scarcely have improved their relationship.

6 Wilson, *Ironclads in Action*, vol. I, p. 218.
7 Laughton, *Studies*, p. 172.
8 Laughton, *Studies*, p. 172.

Persano took the fleet back to Ancona early on the morning of July 13, having expended a large part of the fleet's supply of coal, which could not be replenished at sea. When he returned he found waiting for him two messages from Depretis dated July 10 and 11, ordering him to coal his fleet in the shortest possible time, before again putting to sea to carry out the orders which he had been given. His cruise had not, however, encouraged him to think that he could do so successfully:

> Admiral Persano evidently considered himself to be still too weak to attempt decisive action against the imperial fleet, and his three days' experimental cruise in the Adriatic seems to have convinced him that, before risking an engagement, further exercises were very necessary; nor can it be pretended that the Italian fleet, even at that period, was in the condition of perfection which, at the beginning of mobilisation, the Marine Ministry had considered it should attain ere it could successfully engage the Austrians. Persano was not the man to correct the shortcomings in indiscipline and training. On the other hand, the dockyard authorities, it must be admitted, were much to blame.[9]

Persano's relationship with Depretis had not been improved by the minister's arbitrary conduct in relation to a number of appointments in the fleet. With what Iachino calls 'very questionable motives,' he transferred a number of commanding officers without even consulting Persano to seek his opinion. Thus Captain Martin-Franklin was moved from the *Formidabile* to the *Re d'Italia,* being replaced by Captain Saint Bon of the frigate *Principessa Clothilde.* In his turn he was succeeded by Captain Acton, who came from the *Etna*, whose new commander was Captain Pepi from the *Guiscardo.* Persano, when he heard of them, protested about these changes, but in vain.[10]

Depretis followed up his messages to Persano by himself going to Ancona to meet with the admiral face to face, since it seemed that this might be the only way to compel him to carry out the government's instructions. Arriving on July 15, he also met with the subordinate commanders Albini and Vacca, who with d'Amico told him that they did not support Persano's strategy. These conversations demonstrated to the minister that Persano no longer enjoyed the confidence of the fleet, but it left him with the serious problem of how, if he was to relieve him from command, he was to be replaced. It was apparently the case that neither Albini nor Vacca would be prepared to serve under the other.

Persano's immediate response to the further pressure now being applied by Depretis was to say that he would move against Pola as soon as the *Affondatore* joined his fleet. To this, Depretis assented; but he went on to tell the admiral that as soon as the ironclad arrived 'you must take to the sea and begin against the fortresses and against the enemy fleet those operations you think most convenient in order to obtain an important success.' He was emphatic that this instruction was to be strictly observed; otherwise, Depretis told him, he would be forced to relieve him of command.[11]

During the day, in the course of a discussion with d'Amico, Depretis explored the possibility of making an attack on the island of Lissa. It appears that the idea may have originated with Vacca. The minister asked the chief of staff whether a sudden assault on the island could

9 Clowes, *Four Modern Campaigns*, p. 21.
10 Iachino, *Lissa*, p. 339-340.
11 Greene and Massignani, *Ironclads*, p. 222.

succeed. D'Amico told him that since it seemed likely that a truce would be concluded soon, neither Venice nor Pola could be attacked, but that if it were required to deal some swift blow, there was no place more suitable than Lissa as a target. Vacca was present at this meeting, and endorsed D'Amico's opinion.[12]

Vacca, evidently wishing to keep on the right side of Depretis, wrote an oily letter to the Minister during the course of the day: 'I have received your letter and I thank you for the trust placed in me, and even more for your concern to show that the navy is acting vigorously without further delay. I will confer immediately with the admiral and will write to you with the outcome of our discussion.'[13] While Vacca was firmly in favour of an assault on Lissa, it appears that Albini was opposed to this.

After this, Depretis himself put the proposal to Persano, who raised no objections, stipulating only that he should have at his disposal a landing force of four or five thousand men. The consideration of the planned attack on Lissa apparently took place without any clear thought being given as to what Tegetthoff might be expected to do while the assault was taking place (although Captain Fincati, of the *Varese*, is said to have pointed out that the Austrians might attack Ancona while Persano was at Lissa):

> It seems to have been concluded that, because the Austrians had not attacked the Italians under the batteries of Ancona, they would not attack them anywhere. Indeed, Persano's feeble mind swung over readily from the extreme of moral timidity to the extreme of insensate rashness; and he finally went out on his mad expedition without an ounce of coal save what his ships had in their bunkers – coal, that is, sufficient only for four or five days' steaming – though he realised clearly enough that he was not in the least likely to capture Lissa in a day or to find any fuel there.[14]

This was perhaps to overstate the position; his fleet had been in port three days before sailing to Lissa, and there was no reason why the coaling ordered by Depretis should not have been at least partially completed. Nor was the expedition entirely 'mad;' this was a tempting strategic target if a quick victory was required, and it was evident to all that there could be no further delay. A message had been received from the Royal headquarters at Ferrara insisting that the fleet should sail at once. Laughton caustically summarised Persano's reaction:

> Lissa had been suggested, and Persano had not sufficient force of character or originality of judgement to disapprove of it, or to suggest any distinct alternative. He would have preferred remaining at Ancona, brilliant in a gold coat trimmed with blue cloth, but that he was not allowed to do. And so, on the afternoon of July 16, in a state of hurry and flurry, he put to sea, having neither detailed charts, nor plans, nor information as to the defences of Lissa.[15]

12 Clowes, *Four Modern Campaigns*, p. 22.
13 Iachino, Lissa, p. 328.
14 Clowes, *Four Modern Campaigns*, p. 27.
15 Laughton, *Studies*, p. 172.

Reviewing the decision to attack Lissa, Admiral Iachino reflected on the only circumstances in which the mission could have been successfully undertaken:

> Only in the eventuality of Tegetthoff not taking up Persano's challenge, and remaining locked up at Pola, would our fleet have been able to proceed to the attack on Lissa with the object of a complete occupation of the island, having taken precautions against the possibility of a surprise appearance by the Austrian fleet by stationing a fast scout to monitor the exit from Fasana Roads. Instead, yielding to political pressure, however unofficial, Persano ended up going illogically to conquer Lissa with barely enough forces for a coup de main. That was a victory for political power, that is, for political incompetence over professional opinion.[16]

The decision to strike at Lissa has of course been roundly condemned by historians. It came about, as Iachino observed, because Depretis and the rest of the government were desperate to achieve a victory of some kind, somehow. They were entitled to regard Lissa as a worthwhile military objective, and perhaps, given the limited time available for the navy to chalk up a success without too great a risk, they might be said to have some justification for choosing it. But in doing so, there should have been proper consideration of the necessary precautions to be taken.

Depretis agreed to strengthen the proposed landing force by some 1,500 men, and to provide further reinforcements under General Fontana consisting of a battalion of marine infantry, two companies of engineers, and 1,500 chasseurs. With this having been agreed, Persano prepared to take his fleet out of the harbour of Ancona on the afternoon of July 16. He was very depressed about his situation, wailing to his friend Boggio: 'You do not think of the responsibility I have towards the country which entrusted me with this fleet, and the irreparable loss if we suffer a defeat.'[17]

Before putting to sea, Persano wrote a final letter to Depretis: 'Today at 3.00 pm with all the ships under my command I am going to take the offensive against the enemy. I wish to convey to your Excellency the commitment and satisfaction with which the officers of the fleet are preparing for departure.' He then issued the following order of the day:

> From the first opening of hostilities, the fleet was able to maintain its command of the Adriatic. Until now, particular circumstances have prevented us taking more action.
>
> Now the time has come to act.
>
> We sail to recover for Italy, against the arms of the enemy, the lands that belong to Italy. I am happy to announce this to you, and thus to satisfy your just impatience to fight. The King orders us to do so to the limit.
>
> Italy is watching us.
>
> We shall endeavour, in the way we know how, to do what is expected of us.
>
> Long live the King, long live Italy.[18]

16 Iachino, *Lissa*, p. 327.
17 Greene and Massignani, *Ironclads at War*, p. 222.
18 Iachino, *Lissa*, p. 324.

21

July 18

Lissa, known today as Vis, is a rugged mountainous island, heavily wooded, some eleven miles long and four miles wide. It lies about forty miles off the Dalmatian mainland at Split, from which it is separated by the islands of Lesina and Brazza. It is dominated at its western end by Monte Hum, some 2,000 feet high, which overlooks the bay of Comisa, formed by two promontories. The town of Comisa stands at the head of the bay. At the other end of the island, on its north-eastern coast, lies the excellent natural harbour of Porto San Giorgio, a mile and a half long and almost a mile wide, at the head of which is the town of Lissa. On the south eastern coast lies Porto Manego, an anchorage sheltered by the small island of Ravnik. The entire coastline is rocky, with many small inlets, and in many places the cliffs, overlooking the steeply shelving beaches, are as high as 500 feet. In 1866 the island had a population of about 4,200, and its economy was entirely agricultural, based on wine, olive oil, almonds, and figs, while its inhabitants also reared large numbers of bees, sheep, and goats.

It was, in time of war, thanks to its position a place of considerable strategic importance, and had been well fortified by the British when they had occupied it during the Napoleonic Wars. In 1860 it had been declared a military port, and with the imminent onset of hostilities the Austrians had extensively strengthened its fortifications. Particular attention had been paid to the forts defending Porto San Giorgio:

> On the north side, the approach was at the beginning of 1866 protected by Fort Georg and the smaller works Battery Mamula, Robertson Tower, Battery Zupparina, and Bentinck Tower, all of which stood on the small promontory which juts out between Porto San Giorgio and Porto Karober. On the south side, at the narrowest part of the entrance, stood Battery Schmid, with Wellington Tower above and behind it. At the head of the harbour was Battery Madonna. All the works, save Wellington Tower, which had fallen into decay, were in good order, though they were not modern, and had been constructed only to cope with wooden ships. In addition to them, upon the highest point of the road between Porto San Giorgio and Comisa, was a work known as Fort Max.[1]

1 Clowes, *Four Modern Campaigns*, p. 24.

The work put in hand to improve the defences in the period immediately before the war included the strengthening of Bentinck Tower and its outlying defences, and the repair of the Wellington Tower. In addition, a number of new works were added. On the north side of the entrance to Comisa Bay, Battery Magnaremi was erected, and on the south side of the bay a work was constructed on the slopes of Monte Perlic. New works were completed on the Vrani Kamic to dominate the north west coast of the island, while above Porto Manego the Battery Nadpostranje was constructed to protect the anchorage there. In what was seen as the most important sector of the defences, above Battery Madonna, seven new emplacements were made and armed on the hills of Andrea and Cosmo, at a height of about 800 feet. The island was linked to the mainland by a telegraph cable running to Lesina and Brazza, and there were also signal stations on the peaks to enable communication by semaphore.

Due to the mountainous nature of the island, most of the nine permanent works, and the eleven batteries, were located at a considerable height above sea level. They mounted in all some 88 guns, of which the heaviest were 24 pounder muzzleloading rifles, and 48 pounder and 60 pounder mortars and smoothbores. The garrison, commanded by Colonel Baron Urs de Margina, comprised a total of 1,833 men, of whom 1,200 were marine infantry, 562 were from the Coast Artillery Regiment, 27 were engineers and 44 were seamen. Albini's flag captain, Paulucci, was familiar with the island's defences, which he considered to be very strong, calling it the 'Gibraltar of the Adriatic.' His view may well have influenced Albini in his opposition to the projected attack.[2]

When Persano sailed from Ancona on the afternoon of July 16 he had with him a total of twenty four ships. This included eleven of the twelve ironclads possessed by the Italian Navy; only the *Affondatore* was missing, and she finally joined the fleet on July 19. His flagship was the *Re d'Italia*. There were four screw frigates: *Maria Adelaide, Gaeta, Duca di Genova*, and *Vittorio Emmanuele*; three corvettes, the paddle steamers *Guiscardo* and *Ettore Fieramosca* and the screw corvette *San Giovanni;* two armed dispatch vessels, the *Messaggiere* and *Esploratore*; two hired despatch vessels, *Flavio Gioia* and *Stella d'Italia*; the hospital ship *Washington*, and the store ship *Indipendenza*. Later on July 16 the three screw gunboats *Montebello*, *Vinzaglio*, and *Confienza*, with the unarmed despatch vessel *Giglio* sailed to join the fleet, as did the screw frigate *Garibaldi* on July 18.[3]

In order to conceal his objective, Persano first shaped his course from Ancona in the general direction of the island of Lussino in the Gulf of Quarnero, altering course during July 17 for Lissa, which he aimed to reach in time to launch an attack at dawn on July 18. Having no accurate maps of the island, he sent d'Amico on ahead in the *Messaggiere* to conduct a reconnaissance. For this purpose the vessel approached Lissa under British colours, and cruised around the island sufficiently closely for d'Amico to make a reasonably accurate map of its defences. When he rejoined the fleet at sunset on July 17 d'Amico reported that Porto San Giorgio, Porto Manego and Comisa were all defended by strong works. Although these were all located at a high elevation, he considered that they would be within range of the fleet's guns. With remarkable accuracy, he estimated the strength of the garrison to be approximately 2,000 men. Understandably, his depiction of Battery Madonna, at the head of the harbour of Porto San

2 Iachino, *Lissa*, p. 353.
3 Clowes, *Four Modern Campaigns*, p. 25.

Giorgio and hence further away from him, was less accurate. Otherwise, it was a successful reconnaissance, and d'Amico had a number of copies made of the map which he had prepared, which were distributed to the ships of the fleet.

The fleet arrived off the island during the night of July 17/18 and Persano made his plans for next morning's attack. He had with him only part of the landing force of 5,000 men for which he had asked; this consisted of 500 marines and 1,000 soldiers. The reinforcements which Depretis had promised had not yet arrived, but after all that had been said at Ancona after the fleets returned from its short training cruise, Persano did not believe that it was open to him to defer launching his attack until they arrived. His original intention had been to appear off Porto San Giorgio with the bulk of his fleet, and while he was engaging the forts there to send his troops to Comisa Bay to disembark there. Thereafter he planned for the troops to march across the island in order to take the garrison of Lissa and Porto San Giorgio in the rear. With d'Amico's report before him, however, he realised that a landing at Comisa might run into serious difficulties, and he came to the conclusion that Porto Manego might be a better place at which to disembark his landing force. In preparing his plans for the capture of the island, he did so in the belief that although this might not be completed before the reinforcements arrived, it was an operation which nonetheless was perfectly feasible, and he made his dispositions accordingly.

Vacca, with the ironclads *Principe di Carignano, Castelfidardo*, and *Ancona*, and the paddle corvette *Guiscardo* was to attack the fortifications at Comisa Bay, both as a feint and in order to destroy the enemy batteries to facilitate a landing there should this become necessary. Vacca's force carried a total of 82 guns. Albini, with the four screw frigates *Maria Adelaide*, *Gaeta, Duca di Genova*, and *Vittorio Emmanuele*, and the screw corvette *San Giovanni*, carrying in all 206 guns, was to silence Battery Nadpostranje, overlooking Porto Manego, in order to enable a landing to be effected there under Captain di Monale. Persano, with the bulk of the fleet, would attack the works protecting Porto San Giorgio. Four ships, under Captain Riboty, would attack the defences on the south and east side of the harbour mouth; he had the ironclads *Re di Portogallo, Maria Pia, Terribile* and *Varese* for this task. Persano himself, with the ironclads *Re d'Italia, San Martino, Formidabile*, the paddle corvette *Ettore Fieramosca* and the despatch vessel *Messaggiere* would attack the works from the front. The gunboat flotilla, which mounted 12 guns was to steam to Lesina, and cut the cable to the mainland, destroying also any other vessels and any other means of contact with the mainland. This was a task that should have been attempted sooner; messages had already been sent reporting d'Amico's reconnaissance cruise around the island. The *Indipendenza*, and *Washington* were to lie off the island of Busi, south west of Lissa, to await orders, while the *Esploratore* and *Stella d'Italia* were to cruise at a distance of some twenty miles from Lissa to watch for the approach of any enemy vessels.[4]

The Austrian garrison had been on the alert since d'Amico's reconnaissance of the previous day, and soon after the sun came up the lookout station on Monte Hum signalled that nine warships had been seen some twenty miles off. Flying no colours, they were steering a course for Lissa. As they neared the island, further ships were seen, until a total of twenty two were reported. By 9:00 a.m. they were visible from Battery Magnaremi. Although it had been Persano's intention that the attack should begin at dawn, the various units of his fleet were well behind schedule, and it was not until some time after 10:00 a.m. that the various squadrons

4 Clowes, *Four Modern Campaigns*, pp. 26-27.

began to reach their stations. At 9:00 a.m. the *Garibaldi* had joined the fleet, and had brought with her some additional troops, together with news that further reinforcements were following. Persano added her to Albini's squadron. He had given orders that for the bombardment of the island's fortifications, only the ordinary shot was to be fired; the use of steel projectiles was forbidden, as these were to be reserved for engaging enemy ironclads.[5]

Clowes considered that the plan adopted was inherently unsound:

> Persano's idea was with his ships to occupy attention at two distant points while a landing was being effected at a third and intermediate point. Ships do not necessarily occupy much of the attention of the garrisons of forts of elevated command. The forts may wholly or partially neglect the ships especially if there be no good landing place near. But an attempted landing is a real threat. Persano, therefore, should have concentrated his heavy ships and divided his landing parties … Moreover, Persano ought to have known the futility of expecting ships to deal successfully with works perched far above them.[6]

The first ships to get within gunshot of the island were the four ironclads of Riboty's division. Battery Magnaremi opened fire on these at about 11:00 a.m., upon which all the ships hoisted Italian colours and from a position to the northwest of the battery returned its fire, concentrating on the right flank of the works. Here, three rifled 24 pounders were heavily engaged; the officer commanding the battery then reinforced them by moving across the guns from the left flank. Riboty adjusted his position accordingly. At this point Albini's ships had come up within range, and engaged the left flank of the battery. Shortly after this Vacca arrived; Albini and Riboty got under way and steamed off to the positions which they had been ordered to take up, steering along the southern coast of the island. Vacca assumed command of all the ships remaining engaged at this point:

> Magnaremi, thus for a short time assailed by fourteen ships, behaved very creditably, and never slackened its fire; but the Italians had great difficulties to contend with, for the battery was not only small, but also about 500 feet above sea level. At first the projectiles did not reach the height; later they overshot it. Only two in all struck the scarp of the work. Whenever any ship moved within range of them, the two 6 pounder La Hitte guns, posted 800 feet high on Monte Perlic, were fired; but it cannot be supposed that such little weapons did much harm.[7]

Riboty led Albini as they made their way eastward; as he steamed past Battery Nadpostranje he briefly exchanged fire with it, but he then took his ships further out to sea, giving the island a wide berth as he made his way around its eastern end on his way to take up the position north east of the harbour mouth at Porto San Giorgio which had been assigned to him. Meanwhile Persano, with the rest of the fleet, was making his way along the northern coast towards the harbour.

5 Greene and Massignano, *Ironclads at War*, p 224.
6 Clowes, *Four Modern Campaigns*, p. 28.
7 Clowes, *Four Modern Campaigns*, p. 29.

Following Riboty, Albini arrived off Porto Manego and took up a position opposite Battery Nadpostranje. His flagship *Maria Adelaide*, together with the *Vittorio Emmanuele* moved within range, but it was soon found that the battery's position was so high that their shots were failing to reach it. The battery replied, firing twenty eight rounds, scoring a hit on the *Maria Adelaide* which killed two and wounded three of her crew. She had fired fourteen rounds and the *Vittorio Emmanuele* only one before Albini concluded that they were wasting their time to no purpose, and took them out of range. In fact, had they fired from a position further from the coast, the trajectory of their shells might well have enabled them to hit the battery. This was the subject of considerable enquiry at Persano's trial at the High Court, and di Monale, the commander of the landing force, was asked by the President of the court if it was merely the elevation of Battery Nadpostranje that led to the abandonment of the attempt on Porto Manego. He replied: 'Certainly it was for this reason, and it could not have been for anything else; if we had been more distant it would have been possible to send a few shells into the fortress, but we were at the preselected distance from the island, and it was impossible.'[8] What di Monale did not explain was why, the position having been badly chosen by Albini, the admiral did not change it when it was evident that the firing against the battery was so obviously ineffective.

As it was, Albini convened a council of war aboard the *Maria Adelaide* to discuss what to do next. This unanimously concluded that it was pointless to continue the engagement. Having been unable to silence the battery, it was felt doubtful of the wisdom of landing the troops in accordance with Persano's orders.

At this point Vacca appeared. The attack of his three ironclads in Comisa Bay had also been ineffective; the *Principe di Carignano* and *Castelfidardo* had begun shelling Battery Magnaremi, while the *Ancona* engaged Battery Perlic. Vacca soon reached the conclusion that the batteries were located at too great an elevation for him to damage them; he formed the impression that they were at 1,000 feet, twice their actual height, and suspended his bombardment at about 1:00 p.m.. As in Albini's case, his judgment might well have been wrong, had he engaged them from further out to sea. He, too, concluded that he could not achieve anything, and sent off the paddle corvette *Guiscardo* to Persano to tell him of the inaccessibility of the batteries which he faced, and that he was proceeding to Porto Manego to support Albini.

When Vacca arrived there he learned of the decision of the council of war. Albini had sent off the screw corvette *San Giovanni* to Persano to inform him what had occurred, and to seek further instructions. Vacca now offered to try his hand at engaging Battery Nadpostranje, but Albini declined; this may have been because his heart had never been in the operation at all. Wilson, referring to the Italian staff history, pointed out that Albini had nevertheless wasted an excellent opportunity by his decision not to carry out his orders, displaying 'a rare mixture of pusillanimity and disobedience:'

> If Albini, on finding that his ships could not attack Manego with any prospect of success, had taken the trouble to land detachments from his vessels, the work which only mounted two 12 pounder rifles and four 18 pounder smoothbores, and which was very weakly

8 Iachino, *Lissa*, p. 352.

> garrisoned, must have been carried. This would have been a serious embarrassment to the Austrian defenders of Porto San Giorgio.[9]

Vacca, his offer of help having been refused, steamed on and rounded the eastern end of the island to join Persano off Porto San Giorgio. When he arrived, he found the commander-in-chief to be utterly dismayed at the spineless performance of his two subordinate commanders:

> Admiral Persano was in no small degree surprised at the resultless nature of the operations of his subordinates, and made a communication in writing to that effect to Vice Admiral Albini. This was, perhaps, natural, for it is difficult to imagine that the small and loftily placed works dominating the south coast of the island could have been of sufficient force to prevent a seriously attempted landing of troops, or to bar their advance towards Lissa. It is disappointing, too, to any commander-in-chief that subordinates, instead of sending for fresh orders, should, on their own responsibility, abandon the position and duties assigned to them.[10]

At Porto San Giorgio the bulk of the Italian fleet had been much more vigorously engaged. The first of Persano's ironclads had come within range of Fort Georg at about 11:00 a.m.. The battery at once opened fire, but the ships did not reply, moving on to take up a position which almost surrounded the forts and then opened a heavy bombardment. They were soon joined by Riboty's division coming around from the eastward, and which stationed itself opposite Wellington Tower and Battery Schmid. These batteries were armed with guns of a lower calibre, and Riboty felt able to move his ships to a point within 1,000 yards of the defences. Persano's flag captain, Faa di Bruno, brought the *Re d'Italia* in still closer, to a range of 500 yards from Battery Schmid, which was soon overmatched by the ironclad's guns. At about 2:00 p.m. the flagship scored a lucky hit, and the battery's magazine blew up, burying some forty men in the ruins, to loud cheering from all the ships engaged at this point. Boggio wrote next day to Depretis with an enthusiastic account of his experiences:

> The noise was infernal. Your humble correspondent remained on the poop from eleven o'clock to half past six, exposed to a storm of shell … Persano is most unjustly accused; he deserves the perfect confidence of the government and the country. The heavy responsibility may have rendered him unduly careful; but now that the time of action has arrived, what a difference is there between him and others![11]

The bombardment by the fleet continued to take its toll of the defences; soon after the explosion in Battery Schmid other small magazines were destroyed in Fort Georg and Batteries Mamula and Zupparini, inflicting a number of casualties. Nevertheless, the defenders kept up a brisk fire, particularly those in Wellington Tower, and Persano ordered the *Maria Pia, San Martino* and *Formidabile* to close in to the fort, and subject it to the heaviest fire possible.

When the *Guiscardo* arrived with the news of Vacca's failure in Comisa Bay, Persano sent back an order that he should leave at least one of his ironclads there to occupy the attention of the

9 Wilson, *Ironclads in Action*, I, p. 222n.
10 Clowes, *Four Modern Campaigns*, p. 31.
11 Laughton, *Studies*, p. 175.

forts; but it was only shortly after sending this that Vacca himself arrived at Porto San Giorgio. Persano now ordered him to concentrate his fire on Wellington Tower and the inner defences of the harbour. Half an hour after Vacca arrived, Albini followed him; Persano instructed him to take his squadron to the inlet of Porto Karober to the west of the harbour entrance, and there disembark his landing force.

This Albini now prepared to do, taking up a position covered by the small promontory of Scoglio Ost, which forms the northernmost arm of the inlet at the head of which stands Porto Karober. Here, his squadron was largely shielded from the guns of Fort Georg. In any case, these did not offer much of a threat, the fort having suffered considerably from the bombardment during the course of the day. Having been under attack for some six hours, it had lost 20% of its garrison, half of its guns had been dismounted, and parts of the structure had been razed to the ground. It had been pounded incessantly by a force carrying 433 guns, and by 5:00 p.m. had for the moment been reduced to silence. Battery Mamula, which lay beneath the fort, had suffered similarly, losing its commander and a third of its garrison; it too had by now been silenced by the heavy fire poured upon it.[12]

Albini, however, did not land his troops. Given the firepower of the fleet, and its ability to suppress the defences that a landing at Porto Karober would have faced, Albini had plainly wasted another valuable opportunity, and his failure to carry out his orders was as inexcusable a dereliction of duty as his failure at Porto Manego.

Seeing the effect of the fleet's bombardment of the Austrian positions, Persano decided to follow it up by making an attempt to force the harbour, although since a landing had been ordered at Porto Karober, there was no reason for attempting to do all the work with the ships. The *Formidabile* was ordered to plant herself in the entrance, and the *Maria Pia* and *San Martino* were directed to steam into the bay and engage the batteries there. Several of the remaining ironclads approached the mouth of the port, and, with the paddle vessels, which up to that period had been kept at a distance but were now brought nearer, were instructed to throw their heaviest projectiles up harbour, while the *Re d'Italia* placed herself in front of the still almost undamaged Battery Zupparina.[13]

With this supporting fire, at about 4:30 p.m. the *Formidabile*, followed by the *Maria Pia* and *San Martino*, edged cautiously into the harbour, in the face of heavy fire from Wellington Tower and Bentinck Tower and, in particular, from Battery Zupparina. This last concentrated its fire exclusively on the ironclads endeavouring to make their way into the harbour, and was rewarded by hitting the *Formidabile* with a 24 pounder shell which exploded in her interior as she moved into a broadside position. Soon after this Battery Madonna, at the head of the harbour, joined in the action, and the three ironclads now began slowly to retreat. As the afternoon wore on, Colonel Martina had pulled back those of his troops that were occupying the town of Lissa to the heights of Andrea and Cosmo. At the same time he dug in all the available field guns behind the emplacements on those heights, in support of Battery Madonna.

During the course of the day Sandri's flotilla of gunboats had proceeded to the island of Lesina, and at about 4:00 p.m. entered the harbour there. Seizing the harbour officials, Sandri threatened to bombard the town unless he was at once informed of the position of the undersea

12 Clowes, *Four Modern Campaigns*, p. 32.
13 Clowes, *Four Modern Campaigns*, p. 32.

cable from Lissa. The threat was effective, and the cable was cut, although Sandri was not able to report this to Persano until about 10:00 p.m. that night. It has been said that before it was cut a message had been received from Tegetthoff: 'Hold out till the fleet can come to you.' This, it has been suggested is very doubtful; the only message recorded as having been sent by the admiral to Lissa was an enquiry at about 2:20 p.m. asking to know what was happening. At all events, when Sandri reported that he had been told this by an Austrian official, Persano disbelieved it; he considered it to be false information intended to put him off continuing his assault on the island on the following day.

By 6:00 p.m. all the Italian ironclads were concentrating their fire on Wellington Tower, which stood some 600 feet above sea level. With the nearby mortar battery, it was subjected to a fierce bombardment for two hours, to which it replied as well as it could; it was supported by Bentinck Tower and Battery Zupparina whenever any ironclad ventured within range. It is worth remarking that notwithstanding the elevation of Wellington Tower, the ironclads were able to reach it without difficulty.

At about 7:00 p.m. Persano began to withdraw his fleet in order to give his gunners some rest, though Vacca's division continued in action against Wellington Tower for another hour or so before rejoining the rest of the fleet, which anchored for the night eight miles off the coast of the island. Persano's plan for the following day was to keep the bulk of his fleet together in case Tegetthoff appeared, but would launch a further bombardment of the fortifications, and to carry out the landing at Porto Karober that Albini had so far failed to execute. He put this plan to Captain di Monale and those commanding the artillery and the engineers, who endorsed his proposal, but nevertheless believed that reinforcements were essential. Persano sent off the *Ettore Fieramosca* to Ancona with a report of the day's proceedings, and an urgent request for reinforcements.

With his report to Depretis he included copies of his letters to Albini and Vacca. He was thoroughly dissatisfied with their performance during the day, as well he might be, since they had failed to achieve anything much at all. His letter to Vacca ended by pointing out that the instructions which he had been given had authorised him to come to Albini's support only after the batteries at Comisa Bay had been silenced. He grandly termed his report to Depretis as his first 'War Bulletin,' and was at pains to talk up the fleet's success during the day, observing among other achievements that the so-called 'Gibraltar of the Adriatic' had been conquered. Admiral Iachino considered that the terms of his criticism of Albini and Vacca 'confirmed the pettifogging and exhibitionist aspect of Persano's character, which had already alienated him in the minds of most of his subordinates.' Bearing in mind the extent of their default, this seems a little harsh.[14]

During the day the Italian fleet had inflicted a good deal of damage on the fortifications, but Margina and his men were not downhearted. Throughout the night they laboured at their batteries, remounting guns which had been put out of action, and reconstructing embrasures. The garrison had, in spite of the ferocity of the bombardment, suffered remarkably few casualties.. As the sky lightened on the following morning, the Austrians stood to, ready to renew their contest with the Italian fleet.

14 Iachino, *Lissa*, pp. 377-378.

22

July 19

At Fasana Roads, Tegetthoff had spent the time since his foray to Ancona in continuing the preparation of his fleet. He took it out for a short cruise, but on this occasion did not approach the Italian fleet's base. He introduced a new signal code for the use of the fleet in battle; he ordered the ironclads to send ashore their upper masts and sails, and that their hulls be cleaned, a few ships at a time. The Austrian ships were all painted black; the Italian fleet was painted grey, so that in combat it was going to be relatively easy to know friend from foe. All this time Tegetthoff was anxiously waiting for news of the enemy. It finally came on July 17, when d'Amico's reconnaissance at Lissa under British colours was reported to him. Next day, there came a succession of telegrams:

> 'Nine ships of war without colours making for the island.'
> 'Ten warships advancing under the French flag.'
> 'Ships signalled are moving to the north west without colours; am alarming garrison.'
> 'Ships moving on Lissa, 10 miles distant; the attack imminent.'
> 'Comisa attacked by twelve ships; Sardinian *flag*.'
> 'Port of Lissa attacked.'
> 'Fierce cannonade of Lissa; no casualties.'[1]

Tegetthoff's first reaction to this information was extremely sceptical; he could not believe that Persano intended to make a serious assault on Lissa, and it seemed to him that it must be a feint intended to draw him away southward from Venice and Trieste. Rottauscher recalled that this was also the general belief in the fleet:

> Everyone drew a deep breath, for now we said we knew to a certainty that the very next telegram would announce the blockade of Trieste. The enemy's intention seemed quite clear; they wanted to decoy us away from Dalmatia by false reports so as to be able to attack the southern railway without hindrance. Thus we thought, and we waited excitedly for the moment when the fleet would be summoned north. Boat after boat sped here and there between the flagship and Brioni, and the telegraph operators of the forts were constantly

1 Wilson, *Ironclads in Action*, vol.1, p. 229.

> working. And always there came this strange report: Italian ships are bombarding Lissa. This was no trick; it came from the island's garrison. The entire enemy quadron was pounding the isle's feeble works.[2]

It was only during the morning of July 19 that Tegetthoff was finally persuaded that the attack on Lissa was no feint, and that it did indeed involve the whole of the Italian fleet, when he received a telegram from the governor of Dalmatia to the effect that the Italian assault on the island had been resumed. On the previous day the admiral had reported what he knew to the Archduke Albert at his headquarters at Codriopo in north east Italy, and had asked for orders; the response had been that he should not divide his fleet, and that he should prepare to defend Istria and Trieste. Now, with the latest news before him, Tegetthoff again telegraphed to the Archduke seeking instructions; this time, he telegraphed to the War Ministry in Vienna as well. Waiting for a response, he called together his senior officers to confirm his tactical intentions, and ordered all his ships to get up steam in their boilers, and as soon as they were under steam to assemble outside the harbour. Smoke poured from the tall funnels of the fleet as one by one the ships got under way. At 1:30 p.m. Tegetthoff, aboard his flagship *Erzherzog Ferdinand Max,* joined the rest of the fleet, and half an hour later he received confirmation that he could proceed against the Italian fleet. Rottauscher described the scene:

> Thus *Erzherzog Ferdinand Max* came pounding along, black as night, through the squadron from its tail to its head. Just now the colossus seems to me somewhat at variance with the grey used in modern times. Then all at once, without any order, all hatchways opened and a trampling mob rushed from the depth of the ships – the men ran onto the deck and stormed ever higher into the rigging ... On the ships which had bands, their members rushed together and played the national anthem. Tegetthoff took off his cap and waved it in wide circles. Sweeping by like a storm, inundated with jubilation, exposed to the utter discord of the confused music, the flagship rushed to the head of the squadron.[3]

Even allowing for a certain amount of hyperbole in which the response of the Austrian crew men was reported at the time, there is no doubt that Tegetthoff had inspired them to face the coming battle with remarkable enthusiasm. The Austrian official history described his frame of mind as his fleet steamed southward:

> With eyes only fixed on the target to be achieved; convinced that the undertaking, although difficult, was possible; firmly convinced that the power and prestige of his homeland, the salvation and reputation of the Imperial fleet depended, at that moment, on his firmness, and that the slightest hesitation would put everything in danger, he calmly continued to carry out his plan and to advance resolutely, trusting for success on the patriotism and high morale of his officers and crews.[4]

The instructions which Tegetthoff had issued to his captains were admirably clear and consistent:

2 Rottauscher, *With Tegetthoff*, p. 6.1
3 Rottauscher, *With Tegetthoff*, p. 63.
4 Iachino, *Lissa*, p. 364.

> The ironclad division was to break the Italian line, to strive to ram their ships, to fight at close quarters, and to concentrate its fire. The wooden ships, according to the enemy's order, were to attack one or other wing of the hostile line, or to be employed by Commodore Petz as he saw fit. The gunboats, small handy vessels, were to divide into three groups, and in the action to support the wooden ships, and strive to rake the enemy's ironclads.[5]

At Lissa, Persano had spent the night in an agony of indecision, fearing that the troops immediately on hand would be insufficient for his purpose. This was certainly the view of those around him; they doubted the wisdom of landing such a small force on an unknown shore. In the end Persano accepted this opinion, and decided to postpone the landing until the promised reinforcements arrived; but he ordered Albini and Vacca in the meantime to resume the bombardment of the Austrian fortifications. These, the defenders of Lissa had throughout the night laboured to repair with considerable success. For the Italians, a fresh attack on the morning of July 19 would mean the expenditure of a great deal of ammunition, and Persano can have had no idea of how and when he would be able to replenish it. But he could not simply wait for the arrival of further troops, and so at 7:00 a.m. the bombardment began again, with Vacca's division firing at Fort Georg and the adjoining works, and Albini's squadron firing on Wellington Tower. After an hour or so of this the bombardment ended, and the ironclads moved off to the north-west. Albini's squadron now steered towards Comisa before turning back. Then, at 9:30 a.m. it opened fire on Fort Georg, which was particularly vulnerable because its reserve magazine containing 55 tons of powder was very exposed. However, in this bout no great damage was done, and at 11:30 a.m. Albini withdrew out of range.

Meanwhile part of the expected reinforcements had arrived aboard the screw frigate *Principe Umberto*, which was accompanied by the *Carlo Alberto* and the paddle corvette *Governolo*. These were followed soon after by the long-awaited *Affondatore*. The new arrivals brought the landing party up to a strength of 2,600 men, and some of Persano's confidence returned. He resolved to make a determined effort to conquer the island, ordering Albini to take his squadron, supported by the four gunboats, to Porto Karober and at once put the troops ashore there. The *Terribile* and *Varese* were told off to Comisa Bay to occupy the attention of the forts there, while the *Formidabile* was to re-enter the harbour of Porto San Giorgio to silence the batteries there. Vacca, with the *Principe di Carignano*, *Castelfidardo* and *Ancona*, was to support this effort, while the *Re di Portogallo* and *Palestro* were to attack Wellington Tower. Persano, with the remaining four ironclads *Re d'Italia, San Martino, Maria Pia* and *Affondatore*, would support the landing at Porto Karober and suppress any batteries that sought to interfere with the operation.[6]

Although Persano had prescribed in some detail the tasks assigned to each group of ships, they did not, in the event, all comply with the orders which they had received. The *Terribile* and *Varese* did as they were told, and steamed round to Comisa Bay where, at 4:30 p.m. they opened fire on the northern face of Battery Magnaremi. Surprisingly, they were joined there by the *Re di Portogallo* and *Palestro*, which had proceeded there rather than, as ordered, carrying out the bombardment of Wellington Tower. Then, even more surprisingly, Albini's six wooden ships appeared in the bay. In spite of the large number of guns now firing on the defensive works, the

5 Wilson, *Ironclads in Action*, vol.1, p. 230.
6 Clowes, *Four Modern Campaigns*, p. 37.

batteries gave at least as good as they got. In particular, the Battery Perlic kept the wooden ships at a respectful distance, and out of effective range, by the accuracy of its fire. The bombardment achieved very little; after about half an hour the *Re di Portogallo* and *Palestro*, together with Albini's squadron steamed off. So little damage had been done to the forts that a large part of the garrison stationed there was now withdrawn and marched to reinforce the defenders of Porto San Giorgio.

There, the contest had been much livelier. At 4:30 p.m. the *Formidabile* had begun to discharge broadsides at Fort Georg, and, firing continuously, she went deep into the harbour to a point about a cable and a half from Battery Mamula. For her support Persano ordered the *Affondatore* to fire her 300 pounders up the harbour, and at 5:00 p.m. the admiral, with the ironclads *Re d'Italia, San Martino* and *Maria Pia*, took the station which had been occupied by the *Formidabile*, and got into hot action with Bentinck, Wellington and Zupparina. At 5:30 p.m. such of Albini's wooden ships as were off Porto Karober also became engaged.[7]

Throughout the day, the Austrian magazines had been especially at risk, in particular a large magazine located in the little village of Somogor, which had a series of narrow escapes when a number of shells landed close to it without exploding. The bombardment inflicted serious damage on all the fortifications, with the exception of Wellington Tower. Shells were bursting around all of the Austrian batteries, smashing down the embrasures and ploughing up the ground over a wide area. The exhausted gunners stuck to their task, however, continuing to suffer astonishingly few casualties considering the weight of the bombardment to which they were being subjected.

By 5:30 p.m., in addition to their destruction of Battery Schmid on the previous day, the Italians had succeeded in silencing almost all of the guns in the north west fortifications. Only a 30 pounder coast howitzer at the foot of Bentinck, and three 24 pounder breechloaders at Battery Zupparina remained in action. The task now was to destroy Battery Madonna, at the head of the harbour, to be followed by the landing of troops at Porto Karober. Once these were finally ashore they would advance to take what remained of the defence forces in the rear. Accordingly, the ironclads redoubled their fire, the *Re d'Italia* opposite Battery Zupparina, while the *Formidabile*, supported at a considerable distance of about two miles by Vacca's three ships, headed for Battery Madonna. This, with eight guns, was approximately equal in firepower to a broadside of the *Formidabile*. The defenders of Porto San Giorgio had now to face the most serious threat that the Italians had so far mounted:

> The garrison hastily placed its reserve artillery (in the shape of a few guns from the more remote emplacements) as near as possible to the harbour, and the 10th Company of Marine Infantry lined the slope on each side of Battery Madonna, and occupied the rows of houses; for the advancing vessels this time showed no hesitation, but a full determination to succeed.[8]

Dense clouds of smoke drifted across the harbour as Saint Bon brought the *Formidabile* to, at about three cables from Battery Madonna, taking up a position to discharge her broadside at

7 Clowes, *Four Modern Campaigns*, p. 38.
8 Clowes, *Four Modern Campaigns*, p. 39.

the battery. For the moment, this was largely unsupported, since only Battery Zupparina was able to direct its fire at the *Formidabile*, and was itself soon heavily engaged with the *Re d'Italia*. Vacca's ships had by now followed Saint Bon into the harbour but were, at first, entirely masked by the *Formidabile* until they swung clear, which enabled them to support her with their broadsides, which were concentrated on Battery Madonna. The Austrian 30 pounder shells did little damage when they scored hits on the armoured sides of the ironclads; but when, from time to time, they hit an open port, they caused fearful destruction between decks. Madonna was receiving support now from the field guns on Andrea and Cosmo, and also from the infantry.

Aboard the *Formidabile*, Saint Bon now executed what Clowes described as 'a brilliant and dangerous manoeuvre,' dropping anchor and letting the cable run out so that she went slowly astern towards San Girolamo. This further cleared the fields of fire of Vacca's ships, and put the *Formidabile* in a position from which she could enfilade Battery Madonna. However, Vacca did not remain to take advantage of this, and the *Principe di Carignano, Castelfidardo*, and *Ancona* turned, and began to withdraw towards the mouth of the harbour, pursued by shells from Madonna and Wellington Tower, leaving the *Formidabile* to continue the struggle by herself, exposed to the guns of Madonna and Cosmo. She had to stop firing, to close her ports, to steam up to her anchor and then to slip her cable. Twice, as she was doing this, her colours were shot away, but each time new colours were promptly run up.

Persano, seeing the extreme danger to which the *Formidabile* was exposed, ordered his flag captain, Faa di Bruno, to prepare to tow her out, but before this could be done Saint Bon managed to get his battered vessel under way and to steam slowly out of the harbour under fire from every Austrian gun that could bear. The ironclad had suffered badly, but Saint Bon's courage and skill had been outstanding:

> He came on board the flagship to make his report, and a melancholy report it was. More than fifty of the *Formidabile's* crew were *hors de combat*; her funnel, and her upperworks outside her armour, were riddled; rigging and bulwarks were cut to bits; and six port lids had been shot away. Persano's fleet had lost one of its best ships, for the crew was so worn and exhausted that nothing more could be expected from them, even if the ship herself had been in fighting trim. A single shell, bursting on one of her port sills, had filled her battery with smoke, so that the gunners were nearly choked. Her armour had not, however, been perforated. She retired to the west, intending to transfer her wounded to the hospital ship.[9]

In spite of all that Saint Bon had been able to do, Battery Madonna had suffered remarkably little damage; most of the Italian shells had either struck below or passed over the emplacements, and although the roof of the barracks was set on fire, the flames were promptly extinguished. Casualties here were particularly light, only one man being killed and one wounded.

While this was going on, Albini was supposed to be landing the troops at Porto Karober, and had he done so there would have been little chance that Margina could successfully have resisted their advance on what was left of his works. Albini, however, yet again entirely failed to carry out his mission, reporting that he had not attempted the disembarkation due to the surf at the landing place. Since Porto Karober opened to the north east, and the wind was from the south,

9 Wilson, *Ironclads in Action*, vol I, p. 223.

Persano was entitled to describe Albini's excuse for this further dereliction of duty as 'singular.' The sea was in fact perfectly calm, as Persano could testify, since the rest of the fleet had experienced nothing of the kind suggested by Albini. Even if there had been any considerable swell in the open sea, the inlet of Porto Karober was entirely sheltered.

Thus, once more, Albini had thrown away an opportunity. As night fell, at about 8:00 p.m., Persano withdrew his fleet to a position some eight miles from the island, and there dropped anchor. Conditions had now begun to deteriorate; a strong wind got up, and it would certainly no longer have been possible to put troops ashore that night. The admiral convened a council of war to discuss what action should be taken on the following day, having regard to what had so far been accomplished. Overall, considerable damage had been inflicted on the island's defence works:

> Fort Georg, Battery Mamula, and Robertson Tower had been effectually silenced. The scarp and counter scarp of Fort Georg had been knocked to pieces, the glacis was a series of pits, and the roof of the reserve magazine had been several times pierced. The barracks had escaped serious damage, but the breast work of the terrace on which the 18 pounders had been planted was completely razed. The open batteries had suffered most of all, and the carriages of every one of their guns were useless. Batteries Mamula and Zupparina had a few shell craters in the solid stonework of their scarps, but they would have received much worse damage had not several shells which struck near their magazines failed to burst. The hillside above Zupparina was ploughed up by the projectiles which, thrown from the direction of Novaposta, fell and burst there. A wooden building near the battery was burned to the ground. Robertson Tower had received few projectiles; Bentinck Tower, and the scarp of the work at its base, were marked with numerous small craters. One shot struck the powder magazine in the tower, but did not penetrate it. The right face of Battery Schmid was a mere heap of earth and stones, but the left half of the work was comparatively uninjured, though the guns were upset and their carriages smashed. Nadpostranje had not been touched. The marks of a few shells near the foot of the glacis were the only evidence that the place had undergone bombardment.[10]

During the first two days, the Austrians had fired a total of 2,733 rounds. Their total casualties had been twenty four men killed and seventy wounded. Aboard the Italian fleet, casualties on the first day amounted to a total of seven killed and forty one wounded, with a further nine killed and seventy three wounded on July 19. Apart from the *Formidabile*, which had sustained a large part of the casualties, a number of the ships had received some damage, although in no instance was this disabling. During the two days of the attack, however, the fleet had consumed a large part of its coal, having only about two days' steaming remaining.

Persano's essential dilemma had not been changed by the day's events. To return to Ancona with his tail between his legs would provoke an angry and contemptuous reaction from Depretis and the members of the government, for whom time was running out if they were to achieve the naval victory which they sought as a bargaining counter in negotiations. On the other hand, the longer he remained at Lissa, conducting an operation which had already taken longer than he

10 Clowes, *Four Modern Campaigns*, pp. 41-42.

had hoped, was to invite the Austrian fleet to interfere. With the numerical superiority which he possessed, he should have been able to face this with equanimity, but the performance of his subordinates thus far cannot have inspired much confidence in a personality that was it in any case far from resolute. The fleet's reserve of ammunition had been heavily depleted during the two days of fighting, in the course of which it had fired over 3,000 rounds; moreover, although all were perfectly seaworthy with the exception of the *Formidabile*, some of them had sustained damage which reduced their fighting efficiency.

The council of war which met that night aboard the *Re d'Italia* was, accordingly, a confused and rancorous affair. Vacca, it appears, strongly argued for a resumption of the attack on the island on the following day. Persano, on the other hand, had by now addressed his mind to the possibility that Tegetthoff might appear. What if he did? he asked. His captains responded confidently that if that should be the case they would sink him with their rams. Having pondered this, Persano finally decided to continue the attack next day, but to do so 'carefully and warily.' Albini was to land di Monale and his 2,600 troops, while Vacca cruised off the north of the island, and the *Terribile* and *Varese* once more attacked the batteries in Comisa Bay. With the rest of the fleet Persano would bombard the defence works at Porto San Giorgio. The operation was to commence as soon as the first guns were fired by the ironclads. That was the plan. It offered no indication of how the fleet should respond in the event of Tegetthoff's appearance, or what tactical instructions it would be expected to follow. After the war, Vacca was to write contemptuously of Persano: 'He never wished to talk about a battle plan, and he never discussed with his squadron commanders or anyone else the likelihood of an engagement. He never explained his ideas, nor the manoeuvres he intended to make, and he never prescribed any order of battle.'[11]

As July 20 dawned, the weather was, to Persano's dismay, dull and stormy. The wind was whipping up the surf along the intended points of disembarkation, raising fresh doubts as to whether it should go ahead. The optimistic Boggio urged the admiral to do so regardless. On the other hand, d'Amico was opposed. During the night he had been anxiously reviewing the fleet's situation. Both the shortage of coal, and the insufficient strength of the landing force, suggested to him that the better course would be to break off the attack on Lissa, and take up a position with the fleet off Lesina. He put this to Persano early in the morning, and the admiral promised to think about it, and to seek the views of Francisco Martini, the *Affondatore's* captain. Soon after this, Vacca came aboard the *Re d'Italia*. His belligerence of the previous evening had evidently faded. He now argued for the abandonment of the enterprise against Lissa, recommending that they should return to Ancona to refuel and resupply the fleet. This suggestion did not appeal to d'Amico.[12] The chief of staff's own suggestion had perhaps not been without merit. On the assumption that sooner rather than later Tegetthoff would put in an appearance, it would have given the fleet an opportunity to get into some sort of order for the approaching combat, in the course of which there was some reason to hope that it would be able to take advantage of its numerical superiority.

As Persano wrestled again with the possibility of breaking off the operation and returning to Ancona, at sunrise the paddle steamer *Piemonte* arrived, carrying a battalion of marine infantry,

11 Wilson, *Ironclads in Action*, vol.1, p. 224.
12 Iachino, *Lissa*, pp. 374-375.

which greatly emboldened the admiral. He immediately issued orders for Albini to proceed with the landing of the troops at Porto Karober, and by 8:00 a.m. preparations for this were well advanced. Troops were aboard boats heading for the shore, with their equipment and stores. The ironclads were, at this point, scattered around the coast. The *Terribile* and *Varese*, intending to enter Comisa Bay, were some nine miles off the island to the west; Vacca, with the *Principe di Carignano, Castelfidardo*, and *Ancona*, was cruising three miles to the north east; the first two of these had each just signalled that they were experiencing problems with their machinery. The *Formidabile* was alongside the *Washington* off Busi, transhipping her wounded; the swell here was so great that water was working in through her open ports. Persano, with the rest of the ironclads, was preparing to begin the bombardment of the works at Porto San Giorgio. A greater state of confusion can scarcely be imagined.

It was at this moment that the *Esploratore*, the only scout to the northwards, came in sight at her maximum speed, signalling 'Suspicious ships in sight.'

23

Opening Moves

After the Austrian fleet had left Fasana Roads, and was steaming south-east, the weather began to deteriorate:

> A fresh contrary wind and sea became ever more noticeable, making it harder for the wooden frigates, not just to maintain the prescribed speed of eight knots, but also to keep the distance between the ships, which was only two cables. Showers passed over us even more rapidly, and afternoon blended into night under dirty colours. Only deep in the west was there a lighter band above the horizon, and this followed us, even though in the meantime it became quite dark.[1]

The fleet was steaming in the order of battle in which it expected to encounter the enemy, in three wedge shaped divisions, one after another. The first, commanded by Tegetthoff, with the seven ironclads, was led by the *Erzherzog Ferdinand Max*; on the flagship's starboard quarter came the *Don Juan de Austria, Drache*, and *Prinz Eugen*, and on her port quarter the *Habsburg, Salamander*, and *Kaiser Max*. This division was accompanied by the despatch boat *Kaiserin Elisabeth*, and from about 5:00 p.m. was led by the *Stadion*, which joined the fleet from Pola and took up a scouting position. Next came the division of Commodore von Petz, consisting of wooden ships, with his flag in the *Kaiser*; on her starboard quarter came the *Radetzky, Donau*, and *Novara*, and to port the *Erzherzog Friedrich, Adria*, and *Schwartzenberg*, followed by the despatch vessel *Greif*. Finally there came the gunboats, under Commander Eberle, with his flag aboard the *Hum*; on her starboard quarter steamed the *Velebich, Wall*, and *Streiter*, and to port the *Seehund, Dalmat*, and *Reka*. This division was accompanied by the *Narenta, Kerka*, and *Andreas Hofer*. The smaller craft were in position to repeat signals.

The three divisions steamed at a distance from each other of 1,000 yards:

> Thus the formation adopted placed the strongest ships in front, covered in no small degree the weaker vessels, concentrated the maximum strength in the minimum space, gave scope for the employment of the ram, and yet did not mask the broadside fire of the ships. Tegetthoff's intention, when he met the Italians, was to break their line, and in the classic

1 Rottauscher, *With Tegetthoff*, p. 65.

> fashion to concentrate upon the weaker section of it. He did not altogether foresee the difficulty which would be experienced in keeping his ships together. But as they had orders to support each other, his captains could be trusted to do their best.[2]

It was in the detailed briefing which Tegetthoff had previously given to the Austrian captains that lay the single most crucial difference between the two fleets. The tactical reflections of Bouet-Willaumez stressed the importance of a commander giving his captains clear instructions before the start of an action, so that they should perfectly understand the meaning of his signals in the confusion of the fight. Given the disordered situation which would inevitably follow the first shock of combat, such a collective understanding was always going to be vital.[3] Tegetthoff had given instructions to Petz that once battle was joined he should act according to his own judgment, and that the third division, broken into three subdivisions, should stay in touch and be ready to support and assist the heavy wooden ships.

The deteriorating weather obliged Tegetthoff to slow his pace, and as evening fell he reduced speed to five and a half knots. Aboard the *Erzherzog Ferdinand Max* he held a conference with his flag captain, Maximilian von Sterneck, and the rest of his staff, to discuss the plans for the following day. In particular, it seemed to the admiral that by the time the fleet reached Lissa, it might be the case that the Italians had already taken possession of Porto San Giorgio. In this event, as would also be the case in the event of meeting the Italians in the open sea, it was decided that the ironclads should steam amongst the enemy at full speed and endeavour to ram, while firing concentrated broadsides at the shortest possible range. This had always been Tegetthoff's overriding intention; perhaps he placed more faith in the ram than was really justified, but it gave his captains unequivocal guidance as to the tactics to be employed, and took full account of his fleet's considerable inferiority in gun power.

During this meeting, the possibility that Tegetthoff might himself be killed or wounded was discussed; it was agreed that if this should happen, the news should not be signalled to the fleet until a suitable opportunity arose. It was felt wiser that, in the midst of battle, the flagship should continue to take the lead, regardless of her captain's seniority.

As the night wore on, the weather continued to worsen, so much so that the smaller ironclads, with their gun ports close to the water, were obliged to close their port lids. At about 7:00 a.m., through the murk, the *Stadion* reported sighting Italian vessels, though sight of them was soon after lost. At the relatively low speed at which the Austrian fleet was steaming, it would be some time before the fleets engaged, but Tegetthoff knew where his enemy was, and what he was going to do.

The same could not be said for Persano. The *Esploratore* had been hurrying back to the Italian fleet with her momentous signal flying, and Persano, if he used it wisely, still had time to put his fleet into some sort of order before the fleets came within range. A few minutes after reading the signal from the *Esploratore* he signalled to his whole fleet: 'Enemy in sight. Prepare for action.' He signalled to the *Terribile* and *Varese* to rejoin the fleet, and drew up his ironclads and those of Vacca and Riboty in a single line abreast, facing at first in the direction west south west. It soon became clear that this was wrong; realising this, Persano signalled 'Steer for a minute

2 Wilson, *Ironclads in Action*, vol.1, p 231.
3 Iachino, *Lissa*, p. 406.

to the north-east,' and then 'Close up' and 'Attack the enemy.' Almost at once both the *Re di Portogallo* and *Castelfidardo* signalled that they were suffering defects to their engines; it was some time before they were able to effect repairs, and until then the ironclad line could not be formed. The *Varese* made her way to join the end of the line; the *Terribile*, however, for reasons that were never explained, never did so, and merely joined Albini's squadron. At this point the *Formidabile* signalled that in her condition she was unable to fight, and would make her way to Ancona.

Persano simply acknowledged the signal, and did not indicate that he approved Saint Bon's decision, which later prompted an equivocal reaction, as Iachino explained: 'The conduct of Saint Bon on that crucial day for our navy has been variously judged by historians; Persano does not openly condemn it, some considered it justified by the condition of the *Formidabile*, others disapproved; but nobody wanted to take a clear position, probably because no one wished to criticise a commander who had conducted himself so bravely in the fighting at Porto San Giorgio.'[4] Persano himself observed without comment that at the time Saint Bon believed that, having regard to the condition of his vessel he could properly proceed to Ancona without waiting for permission to do so.

Persano ordered Albini to discontinue the landing of the troops, abandoning those already on shore and in the boats, leaving it to the gunboats and small vessels to pick them up; Albini was to form up his wooden ships behind the line of ironclads. This last was an order which Albini later claimed never to have received; as a result he remained off the island of Lissa, an almost stationary and entirely idle observer of the situation developing before him. Even if he had not received the order from Persano, Albini's failure was inexcusable, since it had previously been settled that in the event of an engagement the wooden ships were to form a second line parallel to the ironclads.

Tegetthoff, concerned that his crews should have the chance to have breakfast before going to quarters, made no immediate signal to the fleet reporting the sighting of Italian vessels, but continued steaming south east at the best pace he could in the conditions. It was 9:00 a.m. before the enemy were again briefly sighted, by which time the weather was clearing and the wind beginning to drop:

> A little before 9 o'clock the wind changed in a south westerly direction; the sea then began to go down, and in about an hour afterwards the sun's rays gradually pierced through the clouds, unveiling the bold outline of the coast of Lissa, and before them, as if by magic, the ships of their antagonists appeared looming in the offing. No one but a seaman can understand what must have been Tegetthoff's feelings during the bad weather, but his star was evidently in the ascendant, and fortune seemed undoubtedly to smile on the man who had so valiantly seized the opportunity which was destined to hand down his name to a distant posterity.[5]

Rottauscher recorded the feelings of the *Adria's* crew as the Italian fleet came into sight:

4 Iachino, *Lissa*, p. 391.
5 Wyatt, Captain W.J., *A Political and Military History of the Hanoverian and Italian War* (London: Macmillan, 1868) p. 317.

> As if the curtain of a theatre had parted, suddenly there opened from heaven to sea a gigantic fissure of the deepest blue. Dazzled, we saw in the distance the line of the Italian ironclads steaming off Lissa, looking like tiny light grey tin toys, running in a long line one after the other. But before we could count them, before the enemy's wooden ships could be made out, before the island's bare mountains were implanted on our eyes, the ray was covered by a cloud, which coming from behind rushed over us and enveloped us in darkness. The wind had veered round; a rainbow arched over us from the after deck to the foredeck. Covered by it, in blowing wind and water, the squadron hastened towards the enemy.[6]

When, at 10:00 a.m., the mist cleared away, Tegetthoff was able to see clearly the Italian fleet assembling off the coast of Lissa. In rapid succession, he made a series of signals that expressed, simply and clearly, his intentions: 'Clear for action;' 'Close order;' 'Lookout vessels to their stations;' Full speed.' Then, at 10:35 a.m. came the signal for which he was long remembered, and which Laughton described as amounting to his tactical legacy: 'Armoured ships will dash at the enemy and sink him.' (*Panzerschiffe den Feind anrennen und zum sinken bringen*). Tegetthoff had intended to make one further signal: 'This must be the victory of Lissa,' but the closing of the fleets meant that there was no time to display it.[7]

At about 9.00 a.m. Persano, who could not at that point make out the position of the Austrian fleet, but knew the direction from which they were coming, had decided to form his ironclads into a column of single line ahead. Vacca's three ships, the *Principe di Carignano, Castelfidardo* and *Ancona*, led the line followed by the division of three ships led by Persano in the *Re d'Italia*, with the *Palestro* and *San Martino*, and finally Riboty with the *Re di Portogallo, Maria Pia* and *Varese* (which was still some way astern). The *Affondatore* was steaming on the starboard beam of the column. Greene and Massignani reckoned that Persano's turn to the north east may have been prompted by a recollection of his experience on June 27:

> Such a quick turn ordered by Persano was probably due to his being criticised for his conduct on June 27 when the Austrians appeared off Ancona, when he waited too long to have all the ships disposed for combat, leaving time for the enemy to disengage. By advancing on the enemy he lost gunnery superiority because this advantage could be maintained by falling back from the Austrian fleet, and giving time for the wooden squadron to join the battle provided that Albini had any intention to do so.[8]

Persano later justified his hasty moves by saying that he intended to protect Albini's wooden squadron, still apparently trying to sort itself out, and also to prevent the Austrians from escaping and entering Porto San Giorgio or Cattaro on the Dalmatian coast to effect repairs.[9] Like a number of the explanations which he was later to put forward, this has the appearance of an afterthought, and not a very convincing one. If these had been considerations in his mind as he endeavoured to prepare for battle, it was not entirely unreasonable to conclude that, to make

6 Rottauscher, *With Tegetthoff*, p. 68.
7 Clowes, *Four Modern Campaigns*, p. 49.
8 Greene and Massignani, *Ironclads at War*, p. 231.
9 Iachino, *Lissa*, p. 395.

the most of their broadsides, his ironclads would be better disposed in line ahead to meet the oncoming Austrians.

However, it was at this point that he took a decision that has baffled historians, when he suddenly and unexpectedly resolved to transfer his flag from the *Re d'Italia* to the *Affondatore*. He ordered the flagship to stop engines to allow the *Affondatore* to come up alongside. He took with him d'Amico, his brother Enrico, a signals officer and a second pilot from his staff. His friend Boggio elected to remain aboard the *Re d'Italia*, apparently, according to a note among Persano's papers, because he did not like the look of the choppy sea across which he would have to make the transfer in a boat. Clowes observed:

> What possessed Persano to change his flagship at the last moment, in such haste, and without notifying the fact by signal to his fleet, has never been fully explained. He was, however, notoriously a great believer in the offensive and defensive powers of the ram *Affondatore*. Probably his besetting infirmity of purpose had prevented him from making up his mind at an earlier moment. The ship at that time had a speed of about 11 knots, but was very unhandy, and occupied eight and a half minutes in turning a complete circle.[10]

Whatever may have been Persano's principal object in making this sudden change, it was a lamentably unwise decision. The fact that the *Affondatore* was not a handy ship had been the subject of a complaint by her captain, Martini, on the previous day, and she had only pole masts and very little rigging, so that signals could only be made with difficulty; worst of all, none of his captains had any warning of what was intended, though doubtless the ships of Riboty's division would have been able to see what was going on.

The American Admiral Francis J. Higginson reflected on Persano's sudden decision, recalling how he had on June 27 at Ancona transferred his flag to a fast scout vessel:

> He seems to have been imbued with the military principle that a commander-in-chief should not be confined to the fighting line, but should be free to move to any point deemed best for directing operations, but he seems never to have discussed this idea with any of his subordinates, but to have set it aside, as he did all ideas of fleet combat, whenever the enemy was not actually upon him. As he waited in the gloom of the blanketing, sultry drizzle of that warm July day, the idea of betaking himself outside the line of battle, in order better to direct the operations, again came uppermost in his mind. 'I perceived,' he said afterwards, 'the convenience of taking up my position outside the line in an ironclad of great speed, to be able to dash into the heat of the battle, or carefully to convey the necessary orders to the different parts of the squadron, and direct their movements according to necessity.' The principle on which he was about to act is probably as applicable to a fleet action as to one on land, but the folly of applying it without the knowledge of his captains and squadron commanders, which should have impressed itself upon Persano by the consequences of doing so on a former occasion, seems never to have occurred to him.[11]

10 Clowes, *FourModern Campaigns*, p. 50.

11 Rear Admiral Francis J. Higginson, *Naval Battles in the Century* (Toronto: W & R Chambers, 1906), p. 191.

Others have chosen to see Persano's decision to transfer to the *Affondatore* as explained by a wish to be in a safer situation; Persano himself hinted that he had carried out the transfer at the last moment, and almost secretly, to prevent the enemy learning of it; it was believed for some reason that Tegetthoff had vowed to capture Persano alive or dead, which seems a highly improbable claim.

The transfer had been effected in the greatest hurry, so much so that the *Re d'Italia's* launch was unable to rejoin her ship, as the ironclads were again in motion. As soon as he and his party were aboard the *Affondatore*, Persano began to steam up and down the Italian line, making various signals which were either not seen or not understood, since his presence aboard her was not generally known, other than to the ships which had been immediately following the flagship; nobody seems to have paid any attention to him, and the Italian fleet was left to fight in isolated units against a combined force. Persano's own explanation for his curious decision might have had some force if he had signalled his intention to the fleet.

The immediate effect of the transfer was for a gap to be opened in the Italian line, since Vacca's three ships steamed on while the *Re d'Italia* was stopped; the distance between the flagship and the *Ancona* steadily increased, while all this time the Austrian fleet was approaching. The speed at which it did so has been put at 10 knots, but Laughton reckoned that it was probably not more than 8 knots; it may have seemed more, 'especially to the thunderstruck Italians.'[12]

At 10:43 a.m. the *Principe di Carignano* opened fire, at a range of about 1,000 yards. The Austrian ironclads did not begin to exchange fire with Vacca's ironclads until they had closed to a shorter range as they neared the gap, which they passed through about fifteen minutes after the *Re d'Italia* had again got underway. One of the first shots fired by an Italian ironclad hit the *Drache*, killing her captain Heinrich von Moll. As the leading Austrian ironclads went through the gap, Tegetthoff ordered them to form single line ahead on the *Erzherzog Ferdinand Max*; he then turned to attack the Italian centre group. At the same time Commodore Petz sent a similar signal to his division, and the *Kaiser*, at the head of the line thus formed, turned away to starboard. In each division the wings closed in and the ships took up their positions without regard to the regular order.

By now the leading Italian ships in each group were bearing towards the north. Vacca, edging towards the north west, was beginning to pass round the rear of the Austrian fleet, while the three ships of the centre division, now led by Faa di Bruno aboard the *Re d'Italia*, became involved in a melée with the Austrian ironclads. The situation was quickly becoming very confused; dense clouds of smoke covered the fleets, within which a number of unsuccessful attempts on both sides were made to ram the enemy. The *Affondatore* in particular tried many times to ram black painted ships; at one point, approaching the wooden *Kaiser*, she twice failed in her attempts to ram her. The ship of the line gave her the full force of her broadside before Petz headed southwards in the direction of Albini's squadron, but ran into Riboty's three ships, the *Re di Portogallo, Maria Pia* and, at some remove, the *Varese*. As the visibility decreased the confusion became still greater:

> Thereupon ensued a regular melée, which, from moment to moment, increased, both in complication and in magnitude, and which it is impossible to describe in detail. From that

12 Laughton, *Studies*, p. 180.

> time until the end of the engagement each ship manoeuvred independently, striving to ram, to escape the ram, or to interpose for the protection of a threatened consort. Vessels passed one another continually within pistol shot, emerging from one bank of obscurity to enter another, and often having barely time to discharge their concentrated broadsides into an enemy of whom they caught but vague and fleeting glimpses. The national ensigns were not distinguishable amid the rolling volumes of steam and smoke of powder and coal, and it was fortunate for both sides that all the Austrian ships were painted black and all the Italian grey. Tegetthoff's plans were of so simple and elementary character and they left so much to each captain's discretion after the first shock of action, that the Austrian commander-in-chief deliberately refrained from making any signals after the battle had begun. The smoke would have prevented signals from being taken in had he made them.[13]

The chaos into which the two fleets were now plunged created conditions which, as the Austrian official history pointed out, were new in naval warfare: 'There was therefore a confusion, a melée in every sense of the term, which rapidly increased, in which for the first time in naval combat, steam powered the ships and modern weapons of destruction were employed.'[14]

The various groups on each side had been able to retain some semblance of their previous formation only to a very limited extent. At this stage of the battle most of Petz's division had become engaged with Riboty's ironclads, while the right wing of the Austrian ironclads was locked in combat with the Italian centre. Those on the left were engaging Vacca's three ironclads. Persano, meanwhile, aboard the *Affondatore,* was, after the encounter with the *Kaiser*, pursuing an irregular course endeavouring to ram Austrian ships when he could while turning towards the south. It was at this stage of the battle, as the wooden ships of Petz's division passed by the Italian ironclads, that the *Adria* took a direct hit. Rottauscher described the scene aboard her:

> Between the crashing shots was the hubbub of the shouts of command, the rumbling of the guns as they rolled back, the hurrying of the ammunition numbers, and then all at once sounded a heavy bang, as if someone had thrown open a door. The deck trembled beneath our feet and seemed to rise, and the infantry lieutenant was thrown against me. Almost at the same time the air burst asunder with a shattering explosion – we had taken a direct hit. Pieces of the shattered chain armour rained through the scuppers, whizzing around; smoke the colour of manure climbed rapidly from the waterline, mingling with the smoke of the guns.[15]

It was the *Re d'Italia* that had hit the *Adria*, aboard which a fire broke out near the magazine. The pumps were working hard to put out the blaze as the *Re d'Italia* fired again, and missed, passing by with another vessel that did not immediately fire:

> Since we were then totally defenceless, we took her inaction as a real gift from heaven, and with satisfaction I saw them pass by. But then the silent one hesitated, steered up and

13 Clowes, *Four Modern Campaigns*, p. 51.
14 Iachino, *Lissa*, p. 424.
15 Rottauscher, *With Tegetthoff*, p. 74.

> posted herself so that she was eight cables off our stern, the crowned arms of Savoy plainly visible on her figurehead. I counted eight stubby, sinister barrels slowly swinging towards the *Adria*. They looked soulless and spiteful, iron fingers which halted their fumbling movement and pointed at our deck ... I would be lying if I did not say I was afraid. The disaster seemed inevitable, but only two of the enemy's guns were loaded. They flashed; one of the shells flew over the deck, the other hit the waterline and exploded.[16]

The *Kaiser* and the leading ships of Petz's division were coming under heavy fire from Riboty's three ships; the *Novara* was hit a number of times and her captain, the Swedish Erik af Klint was killed, while the *Erzherzog Friedrich* suffered serious damage below the waterline, causing her to make nineteen inches of water per hour, which was, however, kept under control by her steam pumps. In the dense smoke, the *Re di Portogallo* bore down on the *Kaiser*, unobserved until the last moment, with the intention of ramming:

> The two decker could have escaped the blow by making a quick movement of her helm, but, had she done so, she would have exposed to immediate destruction the *Kaiserin Elizabeth* and *Erzherzog Friedrich*, which were barely a cable's distance. Trusting, therefore, to the weight and structural strength of his ship, Commodore von Petz decided to attack his armoured foe. Turning first a little to starboard, and then hard to port, he placed his enemy's broadside fairly in front of him and rammed at full speed, striking the *Re di Portogallo* on the beam abreast of the machinery. It was exactly 11 o'clock, 17 minutes after the firing of the first shot by the Italians.[17]

Riboty, aware of what Petz intended, turned to port just before the moment of impact; he later admitted that if he had not done so, the *Kaiser* would certainly have sunk his ship. As it was, the *Kaiser* suffered terribly as she scraped alongside the Italian ironclad, losing first her bowsprit, then her entire stem, followed by her foremast. As this came down, it took with it the funnel. The imperial crown from the *Kaiser*'s figurehead was left on the *Re di Portogallo's* deck. The ironclad also had suffered considerable damage; she lost her anchor and several boats; one of the guns on her quarterdeck was knocked overboard; eleven of her port lids were smashed, and she lost more than sixty feet of her armour plating. As she swung round after the collision, the *Kaiser* was able to pour a heavy fire at short range from the forward guns of her main battery. Several hits were obtained on the ironclad below her armour plating, while a 24 pounder rifled shell exploded on her quarterdeck. The two ships exchanged repeated broadsides before the *Re di Portogallo* disappeared in the smoke.

Laughton, commenting on the discrepancy in fighting power between the two ships, thought it remarkable that the *Kaiser* should have survived the engagement:

> Between two such ships, the *Kaiser*, an old-fashioned line of battleship, and the *Re di Portogallo*, an ironclad of 5,700 tons, carrying amongst her 36 guns, all rifled, two 300 pounder Armstrongs, the word combat ought to be inapplicable. That the *Kaiser* even came

16 Rottauscher, *With Tegetthoff*, p. 75.
17 Clowes, *Four Modern Campaigns*, pp. 53-54.

> out of it, speaks, more positively than any detailed evidence, of the inefficiency of the Italians.[18]

The troubles of the *Kaiser* were not yet over. Suddenly, at a range of four cables, the *Maria Pia* appeared through the smoke. The wreckage that lay across the *Kaiser's* ruined funnel had now caught fire, but she nevertheless delivered a broadside at the *Maria Pia* which responded fiercely, hitting the *Kaiser* with two shells which burst between decks and put part of her main battery out of action. The steam pipe was shot through, and the quarterdeck swept clear, causing many casualties. The fire on the port side of the ship had now taken hold, and her engineer reported that the loss of the funnel meant that he could barely steam. Her condition worsened, and it was still impossible to extinguish the fire. Her forward batteries were out of action. Petz realised that she must be taken out of gunshot, and she began to limp in the direction of Porto San Giorgio.

The *Kaiser's* previous encounter with the *Affondatore* was not to be the last of her narrow escapes from disaster at the hands of the Italian ironclad. As she made her way slowly towards Porto San Giorgio, the *Affondatore* suddenly appeared out of the smoke heading straight for her. The ironclad's iron ram was no less than thirty feet long; if she rammed the wooden ship square on, the *Kaiser* must have been done for. In anticipation of the impact, Petz gave the order to his crew to throw themselves flat on deck:

> To his surprise, to the surprise of everybody who could see, her helm was put hard over, and she turned away to the right, receiving at a very close range the *Kaiser's* concentrated broadside on her thinly armoured deck. The true reason of the *Affondatore's* conduct will ever remain doubtful. It is certain that the order to turn to the right was given, and given with repeated emphasis, by Persano himself; but whether his doing so was a simple, well-meaning error of judgment, whether he was afraid of the effect of the shock on the exaggerated spur, or whether his humanity revolted from the idea of putting nine hundred Austrians into the water, cannot possibly be decided.[19]

Persano later offered an explanation. He had personally directed the commander of the *Affondatore*, Captain Martini, to ram the *Kaiser*; but when the ships were in close proximity, and only the order 'starboard your helm' was needed to produce the fatal result, he gave the word 'Port your helm,' and stuck to it in spite of the representations of those around him. He said that, chancing at that moment to observe for the first time how terribly the two decker had suffered, he had not deemed it proper further to concern himself with so helpless a foe.[20]

Admiral Iachino also gave some consideration to the incident:

> The fact that, as a result of Persano's order, the attempt to ram the *Kaiser* failed is not proof of an error of judgement, since during the battle many other ramming attempts failed, even when properly carried out. On the other hand, it must be observed that while Persano was a much more experienced seaman than d'Amico, Martini or any of the young officers present in the conning tower, he was the only one there to think that the correct move was to port

18 Laughton, *Studies*, p. 182.
19 Laughton, *Studies*, p. 183.
20 Clowes, *Four Modern Campaigns*, p. 63.

> rather than starboard. Giving that order, it cannot be ruled out that it was simply a mistake, which would be explained by accepting d'Amico's evidence that Persano misunderstood the orientation of the conning tower. In rejecting d'Amico's deposition on the point, he perhaps did so as he was already accused of so many other mistakes.[21]

After this encounter the *Kaiser* continued her slow progress towards Porto San Giorgio, and most of the rest of Petz's division followed, together with some of the gunboats which had been endeavouring to support the battered ship of the line. Several of Petz's ships had been much damaged:

> The *Schwartzenberg* had received seven shots in her rigging, besides one in her foremast and one below the waterline, and leaked so badly that all her pumps had to be kept at work. The *Adria* had suffered grave injuries to her rigging and boats, had had her ensign shot away, had been thrice set on fire, and had four men badly and two slightly wounded. Two dockyard labourers who were on board, and who were endeavouring to stop a hole which an 80 pounder shell had occasioned near the waterline, were struck by a second shell and blown to pieces, and the burning fragments caused by the explosion scattered themselves in the neighbourhood of the entrance to the magazine in such a manner that only by the coolness of the chief gunner, who promptly opened all the valves, was a terrible disaster averted. As for the *Novara*, besides her captain, she lost six killed and twenty wounded.[22]

Casualties were high aboard the *Kaiser*; she lost twenty four men killed and seventy five wounded. Among the latter was Petz. In the course of the battle she had fired 850 rounds, and had been hit no less than 80 times.[23]

21 Iachino, *Lissa*, pp. 433-435.
22 Clowes, *Four Modern Campaigns*, p. 55.
23 Custance, *Ship of the Line*, p. 67.

24

The Re d'Italia

While the *Kaiser* and her wooden consorts were engaged with Riboty, the Austrian ironclads were largely concentrating on those of the Italian centre division. Vacca's three ships, having drawn ahead, had turned to pass around the rear of the Austrian fleet, but for the moment were outside the confused melée in the centre. His two leading ships, the *Principe di Carignano* and *Castelfidardo,* exchanged a few shots with the left flank of Tegetthoff's ironclads, which consisted of the *Kaiser Max, Habsburg* and *Salamander.* They scored two hits on the *Salamander*; the first, on her conning tower, wounded her captain and two others and smashed the binnacle, while the other shattered the mizzen top.

In the dense smoke, individual ships engaged enemy targets as they came momentarily in sight of them. Not only were all the Austrian ships painted black and the Italians grey, which enabled rapid identification of an enemy, but the Austrian ships also had their funnels painted in different colours, so they could be individually identified. For the Austrians, the objective given by Tegetthoff to 'ram everything grey' was entirely straightforward, even if in practice carrying the order into effect was to prove extremely difficult:

> The Austrian ships ranged backwards and forwards in the smoke and uproar, always endeavouring to ram, and generally failing in their attempts. In particular they were directing their assaults upon the *Re d'Italia,* when the *Palestro* came up to her help. Concentrated broadsides, some of hot shot, were fired with the greatest rapidity into her stern, whilst her projectiles, as usual, went wide.[1]

Tegetthoff's flagship, the *Erzherzog Ferdinand Max*, had tried to ram two Italian ironclads but the angle of the impact was so acute that little was achieved. The second of these assaults, however, which was delivered on the starboard quarter of the enemy vessel, which was almost certainly the *Palestro*, brought down her mizzen top mast and gaff, the latter, carrying a gigantic Italian tricolor, falling on the forecastle of the *Erzherzog Ferdinand Max.* Aboard her, a quartermaster named Carcovich ran forward, and tore the flag clear under heavy small arms fire, and attached it to a stanchion.

1 Wilson, *Ironclads in Action*, vol.1, p. 235.

Meanwhile the principal target of the Austrian ironclads continued to be the *Re d'Italia*, which was surrounded by no less than four of them, one of which was the *Erzherzog Ferdinand Max*. The *Palestro* continued to assist her consort; her encounter with the Austrian flagship did not inflict any serious damage, and nor did the broadsides of two Austrian ironclads which barred her way. At this point, however, a shell hit the *Palestro's* unarmoured stern and burst in the wardroom, close to her magazine. An intense fire broke out, and the Italian ironclad was obliged to go about in an effort to get out of action in order to extinguish the blaze. The *Re d'Italia* was now unsupported, and at this crucial moment her steering gear was damaged. The *San Martino,* which had been following the *Palestro*, turned away to the south west, pursued by the *Don Juan d'Austria* and later by the *Kaiser Max*. The situation of the *Re d'Italia* was at once plain to the Austrian commander. As he gazed on the *Re d'Italia*, Tegetthoff could see that she was in difficulty, no longer obeying her helm and able to move only straight ahead or straight astern. She was firing both broadsides and had crowds of men ready on her deck to board if the opportunity arose.[2]

Sterneck, Tegetthoff's flag captain, was fighting his ship from a position halfway up the shrouds, and the situation of the *Re d'Italia* was equally clear to him. He ordered full speed as the *Erzherzog Ferdinand Max* headed for the port side of the Italian ironclad; at two thirds of a cable from her he ordered his engines stopped, knowing that the way upon her would carry her into her opponent. At this point, Faa di Bruno gave orders for the *Re d'Italia* to go astern, so that at this moment his ship was effectively dead in the water. Had he gone ahead, he might have avoided the blow, but at this moment, when the ship had ceased to forge ahead and had not begun to feel the effect of the reversed screw, and was practically stationary, she was struck full amidships by the Austrian flagship, which smashed into her with her whole weight of about 5,000 tons at a speed of eleven and a half knots. The blow was dealt over the engine room. Armour, backing, frames, beams, and planking all crumpled inwards. The breach that was made was estimated to have an opening 300 square feet in extent, half of it being below the waterline. Below decks in the *Erzherzog Ferdinand Max*, where no one expected the shock, crewmen were thrown violently forward. The chief engineer, in accordance with previous instructions, immediately reversed his engines, and withdrawing the ram, freed the flagship from her fatally injured adversary.[3]

The *Re d'Italia* heeled heavily to starboard as she took the blow; then, as the *Erzherzog Ferdinand Max* backed out, she lurched heavily to port, and at once began to go down. Aboard her, there were scenes of the highest drama; many of the incidents later described may well have been the product of journalistic licence. It was said, for instance, that Faa di Bruno, on seeing that his ship was doomed, drew his revolver and shot himself, a tale that was completely disposed of by the accounts given by Commander del Santo, Lieutenant Gualtieri, and Midshipman Orsini. Each of them was close to Faa di Bruno, and said that they saw the captain on the bridge preparing to jump overboard at the last moment, only to be dragged down by the suction of the ship's eddy. Boggio, who could not swim, was seen firing his revolver to the last as the ship went down. It does, though, seem to be true that as the doomed ship went under, her crew shouted 'Venezia e nostra.' There were other instances of courage at the last extremity; the chief gunner,

2 Clowes, *Four Modern Campaigns*, p. 57.
3 Clowes, *Four Modern Campaigns*, pp. 57-58.

Polito, as the ship was going down saw that one gun remained undischarged and ran to fire it, crying 'Just this one more.' When owing to the heel it was feared that the *Re d'Italia's* flag might be captured by the Austrians, an officer, Razzetti, caught it and fastened it firmly to the ship, firing his revolver at an Italian sailor who tried to strike the colours.[4]

Del Santo was with Razzetti as the latter prevented the striking of the colours. He later gave a deposition describing the sequence of events:

> Two or three times, our men were called to repel boarders, as the enemy threatened our stern or broadside, and once the division of firemen, to extinguish the fire which an enemy shell had kindled in the admiral's cabin. Our ship's company behaved splendidly, and especially those of them on the poop, where they were quite without shelter. Amongst these was Boggio, the deputy, who with his eye glass in his eye, was firing away with his revolver, determined to sell his life as dearly as possible. All at once, as the smoke slightly lifted, I saw the *Erzherzog Ferdinand Max* coming down against us on our port side. I rushed to warn the captain of it. As our rudder had been rendered almost unserviceable by the enemy's fire, he gave the order: 'Full speed astern!' But it was too late to prevent the enemy striking us just abreast the foremast. The ship did not feel any such shock as one would think the necessary consequences of the blow, but heeled over to port, very gradually, and sank.[5]

It was 11:20 a.m. when the *Re d'Italia* went down, just thirty seven minutes after the first shot was fired.

Lieutenant Gualtieri also gave an account of the vessel's sinking:

> About the sinking I think the main and lone cause was the fact that the rudder was exposed, therefore was blown off by enemy shots. Since we were steaming without steering, we were cut off from the fleet ... We tried at full speed to avoid the shock of the ironclad that headed toward our midships, but since we would have received those of another ship coming from bow, we reversed engines hoping to have as always some movement ... But the reverse movement stopped the ship. The ship sank with all the flags high, Officer Razzetti used his sabre to keep any sailor from taking down the flag. After being hit we fired a broadside and the men with boarding duty, along with those on the mast fired their small arms a last time. Then the crew threw themselves overboard into the sea without cries and confusion. When we were in the water we were targeted by some rifle shots from an Austrian gunboat which wounded two sailors and killed two others.[6]

Wilson doubted the last point, which he considered might 'probably be explained by the fact that, in the fury of the struggle, stray projectiles struck some of them.'

Where the *Re d'Italia* had gone down there remained only some fragments of wreckage and those struggling survivors who had gone overboard on the ship's starboard side; those who went over on her port side were mostly carried down and drowned as the ship went down. The

4 Wilson, *Ironclads in Action*, vol.1, p. 237.
5 Laughton, *Studies*, pp. 186-187.
6 Greene and Massignani, *Ironclads at War*, p. 232.

suddenness of the event for the moment stunned the Austrians; then, as the reality became clear, loud cheers rang out from the crews of all those Austrian ships within sight. The war diary of the *Erzherzog Ferdinand Max* laconically recorded the event: 'The engagement with the enemy ironclads was going on when at 11:30 am we succeeded, while steaming at full speed, to ram a large enemy ship that moved across, about on the quarter near the foremast. The enemy ship rolled back one time and sank a minute and a half after the shock.'[7]

Tegetthoff's immediate reaction was to do what he could to save the survivors of the *Re d'Italia*, and he ordered the paddle steamer *Kaiserin Elisabeth*, which had followed his flagship into the action, to pick up as many survivors as possible. She soon came under fire, however, from Italian ships unaware of what had occurred, and was obliged to retreat. The flagship did what she could; the only remaining seaworthy boat was ordered to be lowered, but before this could be done an Italian ironclad, obviously intending to attempt ramming, appeared on her port quarter. This was probably the *Ancona*, the third in line of Vacca's division. Sterneck deftly avoided the blow, but the two ships passed so close that the gunners serving the *Erzherzog Ferdinand Max's* port battery were unable to get their rammers into the muzzles of their guns. The *Ancona* fired a number of rounds, but no hits were made in spite of the close range, and it seems that in the confusion her guns were not shotted. An explanation of how this may have come about appeared in the report of *Ancona's* captain, which practically admitted that they were not. Captain Piola-Caselli told the commission of inquiry that 'since a commander had to wait until the moment to fire in order to choose to load the gun with wrought iron or steel shot (and to this last more powder must be added), it is possible that the chief gunner fired with powder alone, forgetting how the gun was loaded.'[8] This might also explain the previous escape from disaster recorded by Ensign Rottauscher aboard the *Adria*.

The loss of the *Re d'Italia*, the damage suffered by the *Palestro*, the timidity of the *Terribile* and the departure of the *Formidabile* meant that the Italian ironclad fleet had been reduced to eight. Then, while the *Ancona* was heading towards the *Re di Portogallo* in order to support her, she collided with the *Varese*, which had been somewhat astern of the other ships of Riboty's division, and was also endeavouring to come to the aid of his flagship. Both ships suffered damage, the *Varese* losing some of her armour plate. Their rigging had become so entangled that it was some time before they could be separated. The *Re di Portogallo*, temporarily without support, was making an attempt to effect repairs while turning away to starboard to evade the Austrian ironclads that threatened to surround her. She then found her way blocked by the wooden frigate *Schwartzenberg*. Riboty attempted to ram her, unsuccessfully, and his ship received a concentrated broadside which damaged both her hull and her masts.

Aboard the *Affondatore*, Persano was making an attempt to recover control of his fleet, signalling 'Surround enemy's rear,' followed by 'Fight at close quarters,' and finally 'The fleet is to follow freely the movements of the enemy.' None of these were of much effect. Vacca, having seen the *Re d'Italia* sink, did not know if Persano had been lost with her; he had apparently glimpsed something of the transfer to the *Affondatore*. Accordingly, he hoisted a signal for all the Italian ironclads nearby to form line on the *Principe di Carignano*, but there seems to be no evidence that any of them did so beyond his own division.[9]

7 Greene and Massignani, *Ironclads at War*, p. 233.
8 Greene and Massignani, *Ironclads at War*, p. 233.
9 Iachino, *Lissa*, p. 447.

Persano, seeing the *Palestro* on fire, steered to her assistance, interposing between the crippled ironclad and the *Kaiser Max*, which in accordance with a signal from Tegetthoff, was bearing down on her. Persano now ordered the *Governolo* to take the *Palestro* in tow, and signalled the unarmed *Indipendenza* to stand by her to take off her crew if necessary.

The *Maria Pia*, which had begun the battle on the extreme left of the Italian ironclads when they formed line abreast, had followed round the *Re di Portogallo*. In the confused fighting that ensued after Tegetthoff broke through the Italian line she had been obliged to take evasive action by steaming in a wide circle to avoid the entangled *Ancona* and *Varese*, and lost so much time in doing this that the *Re di Portogallo* had managed to disengage and no longer needed her help. Next, on seeing two Austrian ironclads which appeared to be bearing down on Albini's squadron, the *Maria Pia* turned to bar their way, but was then attacked by two other Austrian ships. She tried to ram one of these as it crossed her bow, but her target turned quickly to starboard and evaded the collision. Nevertheless, the *Maria Pia* was able to deliver a full broadside as the enemy ship swept past. She then steamed on to join the remaining Italian ironclads which were assembling, after a fashion, westward of the Austrian fleet. There was then a further collision, between the *Maria Pia* and the *San Martino*. The latter, having already suffered some damage, was now further damaged forward; her ram was twisted, some of her armour plating was bent or displaced, and she began taking on water. The *Maria Pia* lost one of her armour plates.

While the ironclads had been fighting it out, the *Adria* and the other wooden vessels had been escorting the battered *Kaiser* towards Porto San Giorgio and safety. Ensign Rottauscher described her condition following her narrow escape from the *Affondatore*:

> *Kaiser* looked horrible. Three times taller than her iron tormentor, she wobbled to starboard, and then to port, dragging herself slowly towards the harbour's shelter. A mast had fallen, the funnel had been destroyed and many small fires wrapped her hull in smoke from the deck to the waterline. In short, the battleship was nothing more than a gigantic burning cloud, over which improbably floated the huge red-white-red flag of the remaining mast. This mass of vapour, in which men wrestled with death and flames, wallowed towards the rocky island.[10]

Once the *Kaiser* neared the safety of Porto San Giorgio, the rest of Petz's division of wooden ships turned back towards the action in which the ironclads were still fighting:

> Tegetthoff's spirit had such a strong influence on the wills of the officers and on their speedy appraisal of the situation, that all at once all the frigates turned, as if in some mysterious manner they had received orders to leave the badly wounded vessel. As fast as we could, we steamed towards the ironclads, while *Kaiser* dragged herself towards the island. Although I have mentioned the inadequacy of the wooden frigates in modern times shortly before, although we could be hit over and over again and set on fire, although we had an

10 Rottauscher, *With Tegetthoff*, p. 76.

> opponent of like force (the Italian wooden ships which lay idly there off the island), in a trice we threw ourselves into the unequal contest, for there the battle was to be decided.[11]

At this point Persano, in the *Affondatore*, headed towards Albini's squadron, which had begun to open a distant fire on the Austrian fleet. It was his intention to order Albini to close with the enemy, and continue the battle. Albini's later claim, that he had three times attempted to join in the action, but that on each occasion he had been prevented from doing so by Austrian ironclads, could hardly be regarded as credible. Some of the Austrian ships at about 11:00 a.m. did notice a brief forward movement of the Italian wooden vessels, but they withdrew almost at once. Albini's squadron, which together with the ironclad *Terribile*, carried in all 400 guns, remained little more than spectators of the battle from start to finish, apart from a few ineffective rounds at great range. The comparison with the spirited behaviour of the Austrian wooden division was revealing.

Meanwhile at 12.10 p.m. Tegetthoff signalled his fleet to close on his flagship; then, 10 minutes later, he signalled 'Follow in wake of the admiral.' His ironclads were now joined by the wooden frigates of Petz's division, since it appeared that the *Kaiser* was no longer in need of their help. Tegetthoff now formed his fleet into three columns, each in line ahead, the ironclads forming the column nearest the enemy.

The battle was now effectively at an end. Tegetthoff, for his part, did not wish to resume it, seeing nothing to be gained by doing so:

> He was ready once more to meet his opponents, but he had no wish to provoke a second engagement. He had already scored heavily, and he did not want to imperil his success. He knew that his was much the weaker fleet, and that, if it was defeated, this was lost. His guns were useless against the Italian armour, and the ram, his only remaining weapon, had not proved so easy of employment as he had expected. If he had seen any reasonable chance of destroying the Italian fleet his determination to end the battle at this point would have been culpable, but as he had no chance of even catching his enemy, since his slowest ironclad was much slower than the slowest Italian, he can only be praised for his discrimination. Had he carried heavy Armstrong guns, or had his ships been a couple of knots faster, he could, and probably would, have made an end of Persano. But with his indifferent smoothbores and weak 24 pounders, with his eight or nine knot frigates, there was nothing to be done.[12]

Persano, on the other hand, had by the signals previously referred to, attempted to reform his fleet with the aim of renewing the engagement. His last signal had been effectively for a general chase. His intention had been apparently to interpose his fleet between Tegetthoff's ironclads and his wooden ships; but of the Italian ironclads only the *Re di Portogallo* heeded the signal, although the wooden frigate *Principe Umberto* did leave Albini's squadron and steer after the *Affondatore*, firing at the distant Austrians as she did so. Tegetthoff was comfortably able to complete the redeployment of his fleet. At 2:00 p.m. he sent the gunboats into Porto San Giorgio.

11 Rottauscher, *With Tegetthoff*, p. 78.
12 Wilson, *Ironclads in Action*, vol.1, p. 241.

Persano continued to fly the signals for a general chase and closer action, adding: 'The admiral reminds the fleet that the ship which is not in action is not in her station.' The two fleets exchanged a few rounds at long range, but it soon became clear to the Italian admiral that he had no hope of successfully renewing action. The *Palestro's* situation was perilous; the *San Martino* was now reporting that she could not maintain her station; and apart from the *Principe Umberto*, Albini's squadron, with the *Terribile,* remained more or less where it was. Accordingly, Persano led the fleet towards the channel between Lissa and Busi.

Meanwhile, before the fleet withdrew, the captain of the *Palestro*, Alfredo Cappellini, had declined the offer of a tow from the *Governolo* and of the boats sent by her and the *Indipendenza* to take off his crew. He declined to abandon ship, considering it a point of honour to remain to fight the blaze aboard his ship: 'Those who wish to go may go; for my part I remain,' he said:

> Following the example of their chief, the entire ship's company stuck to the *Palestro*, only the sick and wounded being removed to the *Governolo*. Every man went to his post and worked with the greatest devotion to combat the fire. The powder magazine was flooded, and danger from that quarter seemed no longer to be apprehended; but the conflagration reached a compartment where, during the battle, a number of filled shells had been placed. A great blaze of flame shot out from the ports on each broadside, a deafening report followed, wreckage and mangled corpses flew high in the air, and in an instant all was swallowed up by the waves. It was 2:30 pm when, in sight of both fleets, this final act closed the tragedy of the day.[13]

It must have been soon after this that d'Amico had a significant conversation with Persano. According to the evidence which he later gave at the admiral's trial, he said: 'I was convinced that the sinking of the *Re d'Italia* and the destruction of the *Palestro* had certainly affected the morale of our fleet, and I was convinced that a blow struck by the flagship pressing forward against the enemy would raise morale and would restore the state of things, probably to our advantage. It was at this point that I insisted that the admiral should inspire us by leading the *Affondatore* against the enemy.'[14] When during the trial, the President of the court asked d'Amico if the admiral had taken his advice, he said that Persano's reply was to the effect that he admired d'Amico's nerve, but that more important than his name and his glory was the interest of the country, and that if such a stroke failed it would only make matters worse. In this, Persano was almost certainly right; a single-handed effort by the *Affondatore* was, in the circumstances, an irrational thing to suggest.

Tegetthoff remained off the north coast of the island for some four hours, watchful lest the Italians did, after all, try to renew the battle, but it gradually became clear that this was not going to happen. He next sent the wooden ships of Petz's division to join the *Kaiser* and the gunboats in the harbour of Porto San Giorgio, following later with the ironclads. He left the *Habsburg* and *Prinz Eugen* with two gunboats to patrol outside the harbour, to serve not only as lookouts but also to rescue any survivors. The last to enter the harbour was the *Erzherzog Ferdinand Max*, which dropped anchor about sundown.

13 Clowes, *Four Modern Campaigns*, p. 67.
14 Iachino, *Lissa*, p. 453.

Meanwhile the Italian fleet, after cruising on and off the western end of Lissa for some hours, set off for Ancona at 10:30 p.m., arriving there on the morning of the following day. One proposal of what the fleet might have done, instead of retreating in this way, came from Albini. With good reason, he tended to keep a low profile after the battle, but at Persano's trial he put forward the suggestion that in the aftermath of the battle a very different outcome might have been achieved. Possibly in an effort to distract attention from the part which he had played, he offered the opinion that in going into Porto San Giorgio to anchor Tegetthoff had made a huge mistake, of which the Italian fleet had not been able to take advantage. The Austrian admiral, he suggested, had put himself in a position in which he might have been completely destroyed. In fact, if the Italians had really shown the slightest intention of renewing the engagement by approaching Porto San Giorgio, Tegetthoff would most certainly have emerged in time to meet them in combat outside the harbour, and having regard to the way in which the battle had gone, it seems entirely probable that he would have put the Italian fleet to the sword. In any event, as Admiral Iachino observed, quite apart from the lack of persuasiveness of such bold concepts emanating from Albini, after his lack of participation during the morning of July 20, it is very doubtful whether an attack by the Italian fleet on Porto San Giorgio would have been possible that evening or even on the following day.[15]

At 2:00 p.m. on July 21 the Austrian Lloyd steamer *Venezia* arrived at Lissa, bringing a telegram of congratulation from Emperor Franz Joseph, thanking the officers and men of the fleet and informing Tegetthoff of his immediate promotion to the rank of vice admiral. That evening, the dead were buried and the badly wounded were sent off to Split and Zara aboard the *Venezia*. At 8:30 p.m. the whole fleet, except the *Narenta* and *Kerka*, which were left to support the island's garrison, put to sea, and on the evening of July 22 anchored once more in Fasana Roads.

15 Iachino, *Lissa*, p. 479.

25

Aftermath

Due to the loss of the *Re d'Italia* and the *Palestro*, total Italian casualties were naturally much greater than the Austrian. 432 men died when the *Re d'Italia* went down, and another 230 perished when the *Palestro* blew up. There were remarkably few casualties on the other ships of the Italian fleet; only five were killed and thirty nine wounded, a testament to the protection given by the armour plating, as well as an indication of the relatively ineffective Austrian artillery. The total number of Austrian casualties was also surprisingly low; thirty eight had been killed and one hundred and thirty eight wounded, of which the greater part were aboard the *Kaiser*, which lost twenty four killed and seventy five wounded.[1]

According to Wilson, the surviving Italian ironclads fired some 1,452 rounds in the course the battle, of which rather less than a quarter were hits. The detailed record of the Austrian expenditure of ammunition is instructive. 4,356 rounds were fired altogether, of which the *Kaiser* fired 850; she of course carried many more guns than any other ship. But the *Novara*, *Schwartzenberg*, *Radetzky*, and *Donau* each fired more rounds than any of the ironclads, which is eloquent testimony to the major contribution which Petz's division of wooden ships made to the battle. So is the record of hits sustained by the Austrian ships; the *Kaiser* received 80 hits, far more than any other, but the *Novara* with 47 hits and the *Adria* with 27 also suffered a good deal of punishment.[2] The seven Austrian ironclads between them received 182 hits, but the actual damage inflicted was not great, demonstrating that their armour protection was also effective.

In fact, following the battle, the whole fleet remained fit for action, with the exception of the *Kaiser*, and even she required no more than twenty four hours' work before she was fit to sail with the fleet. Generally, the engines and steering gear had stood up well to the demands of battle, and the armour plating had suffered little damage. One of the plates in the bow of the *Erzherzog Ferdinand Max* had been beaten in by the force of the collision with the *Re d'Italia*; the *Don Juan d'Austria* was hit twice by 300 pounder projectiles, one between two ports and another below the waterline, each of which did some damage to her armour plating. Custance made a detailed analysis of the effect of the hits on the armour of the *Erzherzog Ferdinand Max*. She received a total of 42, of which 34 struck unprotected parts of the ship:

1 Clowes, *Four Modern Campaigns*, p. 68.
2 Iachino, *Lissa*, pp. 486-487.

> It will be noted that the armour kept out eight projectiles, of which five probably had some importance. The three in the wake of the guns might have produced casualties among the guns' crews; the two near the waterline might have caused leaks probably somewhat similar to those kept under by the pumps in the *Schwartzenberg* and *Erzherzog Friedrich.*[3]

Custance went on to consider why the number of hits was as small as it was:

> The tactics adopted were unfavourable to the use of the gun. To hit with the gun opportunity must be given to use it. The range must be kept short enough, and together with the bearing of the enemy, constant enough, for a time sufficient to make the hits required. This means that the ships heads must be laid in the same direction. This was not done at Lissa. The ships charged past each other, so that, except in the case of the *Kaiser- Re di Portogallo* incident, the opportunities to use the gun effectively were very short.[4]

The wooden ships, naturally, suffered greater damage; the *Schwartzenberg* and *Erzherzog Friedrich* were making water, while several had caught fire, particularly the *Adria*, although in every case except the *Kaiser* the blaze was quickly extinguished. This was so even aboard the *Adria*; she was the worst sufferer in this respect.

Of the Italian fleet, apart from the loss of the *Re d'Italia* and *Palestro*, the greatest damage sustained was to the *Formidabile*, during the operations in the harbour of Porto San Giorgio, and by the *San Martino* during the battle itself. Neither of them was fit for further action. Except for the *Terribile*, all the other ironclads suffered some damage; none of the wooden ships suffered any damage at all. The *Re di Portogallo* was the most seriously injured, principally as a result of her collision with the *Kaiser*. She lost 60 feet of her armoured protection, and although no plates were penetrated by shot, many were bent and forced inwards. The *Maria Pia* had one plate smashed; another projectile had become embedded in her armour. She had been struck by a number of shot, particularly aft, where she caught fire, seriously endangering her magazine. The other ironclads suffered variously:

> The *San Martino* had a projectile in her armour, another penetrated a plate nearly four inches thick and half the backing, and several plates were damaged. The ram was twisted to the left in consequence of the collision with the *Maria Pia*; and, although the ship was at once repaired, she continued to make water as late as September. She had been badly mauled; several shells had burst in her; and two fires which had broken out in her had been quenched with difficulty. Seven plates were removed from their places. In the *Castelfidardo* a shell, bursting in the captain's cabin, did much damage and occasioned a fire. The *Ancona* lost several plates; a shell burst between decks; another put fourteen men out of action; all the spars and rigging were rendered useless. The *Principe di Carignano* had a plate penetrated, and a shell burst beneath the conning tower. The *Varese* had only slight injuries … The *Maria Adelaide* received fourteen projectiles in her hull; a shell, entering underwater,

3 Custance, *Ship of the Line*, p. 71.
4 Custance, *Ship of the Line*, p. 71.

> penetrated to a coal bunker, but failed to kindle a fire there, and the masts and rigging were much knocked about.[5]

Finally the *Affondatore* had been hit a number of times, causing considerable damage to her upperworks.

As the Italian fleet made its way back to Ancona, Persano can have been under no illusion as to the nature of the reception he was likely to face. When the fleet came to anchor there on the morning of July 21, there seems to have been some attempt to represent the battle as having been some sort of victory, notwithstanding the loss of the *Re d'Italia* and *Palestro*. It was suggested that three Austrian ironclads had been sunk. But the falsity of this claim was soon exposed when news came from Pola that all the Austrian ships had returned safely.

In any case, an entirely different view of the battle was soon in the hands of Depretis. Entirely predictably, one of Vacca's first acts on returning to Ancona was to sit down and write a letter which was savagely critical of Persano, in terms which Admiral Iachino calls 'poisonous.' Vacca will have been confident that, in writing such a letter, he was pushing at an open door. It was accompanied by another letter, from his chief of staff Captain Bucchia. Taking advantage of his personal friendship with the minister, Bucchia wrote urging him to read and ponder carefully Vacca's 'beautiful' letter, in which there were 'great truths.' Persano was, he said, a coward, who in another navy would already be facing a courtmartial.[6]

Persano was not left long in doubt as to the way in which he was to be treated by the government. On July 27, Depretis, abandoning any pretence of concern or even simple courtesy, telegraphed Persano abruptly insisting that he send his report of the battle and accompanying documents immediately, adding that he was already late in doing so. When replying, Persano did not conceal the offence he felt at the tone in which Depretis was addressing him.[7]

As soon as the early claims of victory had been exposed as a sham, the furious outcry of the Italian Press and public at the disastrous outcome of the battle was intense. Even the *Gazzetta del Popolo*, a newspaper that had been previously a strong supporter of the admiral, thundered as early as July 25:

> The indignation against Persano, against Angioletti, against La Marmora is intense, profound and unquenchable throughout Italy. Everyone laments with anger and sorrow that La Marmora, under whose presidency Persano was appointed, did not consent to his removal, as Depretis had requested.[8]

The responsibility that was generally attached to La Marmora was entirely justified, since it had apparently been on July 14 that Depretis had expressly called for Persano's replacement, and La Marmora had refused it, and this had evidently become widely known; Depretis will have done nothing to conceal the fact that he made such a request at that time.

The report which Persano duly sent to the minister naturally put the best face it could on the battle and its outcome. Widely believed to have been drafted by the chief of staff, but bearing

5 Clowes, *Four Modern Campaigns*, pp. 69-70.
6 Iachino, *Lissa*, p. 502.
7 Iachino, *Lissa*, p. 508.
8 Iachino, *Lissa*, p. 507.

the commander-in-chief's signature, it accepted full responsibility for the way things had gone. However, it emphasised that the battle had not resulted in victory for the enemy, because he had captured neither ships nor prisoners but, on the contrary, had left the Italian fleet undisturbed until nightfall at the scene of the battle, and then made no attempt at pursuit. In essence, the report contended that the battle of Lissa had been indecisive in its outcome. It ended with the statement that Persano wished to refuel and resupply his ships, in order to put to sea to take revenge on the enemy, thereby implicitly confessing that the day had not resulted in success for Italian arms.

Depretis ordered both Albini and Persano ashore on July 28, and the fleet was divided into two operational squadrons. It was to be commanded by Vacca, who having been Persano's first accuser with his 'poisonous' letter of July 22, now saw his zeal rewarded. It appears that d'Amico, who like Vacca was a Neapolitan, contributed substantially to his appointment; in preparing the official report of the battle, the chief of staff had carefully refrained from any criticism of Vacca's part in it.[9]

Having removed both Persano and Albini, Depretis' choice of Vacca was no great surprise. It is not known what consideration he might have given to any other candidate, but in practice he probably had no alternative at that moment. In any case, it was not of great significance; the war obviously was nearing its end, and although Vacca was given orders to take the fleet to sea and to launch an attack on Pola, there was no time for such an operation to be mounted. Thereafter there would be plenty of time for reflection on the future structure of the Italian navy and the lessons to be learned from its defeat.

Negotiations to bring the war to an end had begun with the armistice concluded between Prussia and Austria at Nikolsburg. La Marmora wrote to the Archduke Albert, as the Austrian commander-in-chief, on July 23 indicating a willingness to agree to a suspension of hostilities between their countries. The truce began on July 25; intended to remain in force until August 2, it was extended until August 10. Discussions during this period failed to reach agreement. The Austrians were determined not to allow the Italians to prolong the talks, and were unwilling to make any further concessions. Accordingly, they made clear that if no terms could be agreed, operations would again commence, not only in the Tyrol, but also at sea; Tegetthoff was ordered to prepare to resume operations. The threat was enough: the Italians accepted the terms on the table, and the armistice was signed in August 12. The final political settlement did not come until October, with the conclusion of the Treaty of Vienna. The Italians gained Venetia, of course; but nothing else, and it may be said that Tegetthoff's victory at Lissa had ensured the ultimate abandonment by Italy of claims to any part of Dalmatia.

On the day after the armistice had been signed, Tegetthoff held a naval review at Trieste. The event was presided over by the Archduke Albert, who was generous in his praise for the achievements of the fleet. Tegetthoff accepted this graciously; but he was disappointed that the Emperor Franz Joseph had not come to Trieste to celebrate his navy's success. The admiral, and the rest of the navy, might reasonably look forward to the future with this success sufficient to ensure that it received a larger slice of the cake when future budgets were determined; but the

9 Iachino, *Lissa*, p. 511.

terms of the settlement excluded Austria from both Germany and Italy, and it was uncertain what would be the navy's strategic priorities in the future.[10]

While the negotiations for an armistice were going on, there was one ironic sequel to the battle of Lissa. On August 6 the *Affondatore* sank at her moorings in the harbour at Ancona, following a severe storm. It was suggested that she had succumbed to battle damage received on July 20, but this was not so; she went down because of her very low freeboard. She was salvaged, and remained a part of the Italian navy for nearly four decades.

Tegetthoff had naturally returned to a hero's welcome. Austria's crushing defeat at the hands of Prussia had been a stunning blow to national pride, and this rendered the moral effect of the battle of Lissa all the more important. Many decorations were awarded to him; one in particular will have given him particular satisfaction, which came with a letter from the Emperor Maximilian from Chapultepec on August 24. He wrote:

> The glorious victory you have gained over a brave enemy, vastly superior in numbers and nurtured in grand old naval traditions, has filled my heart with unmixed joy ... With the victory of Lissa your fleet becomes enrolled amongst those whose flag is the symbol of glory, and your name is added to the list of heroes of all time. To you, the officers, and the ships' companies, I send my heartfelt good wishes; and you, as a remembrance of your admiral and friend, and as a proof of my admiration, I invest with the Grand Cross of my Order of Guadelupe[11].

Historians have displayed a high regard for Tegetthoff's performance as a fighting admiral. William Laird Clowes wrote:

> The victorious admiral did not, I think, display tactical qualities of any exceptional brilliancy; for his attacking formation is never likely to be imitated; but he betrayed an intelligent grasp of the ruling principles of naval strategy and a consistent firmness and strength of character which cannot but favourably have influenced all who served under him.[12]

Reviewing Tegetthoff's tactics, H.W. Wilson wrote:

> His purpose was to throw a mass of ships on one point, and by superior handling of his inferior force to neutralise his opponent's predominance in strength. He decided to break the line near one or other extremity of it, and chose the van rather than the rear, because, had he attacked the latter, he would have been exposed to the crossfire of the wooden ships; perhaps also because he saw the gap between the *Ancona* and *Re d'Italia*. His force had a front of under one and a half miles. He sought to produce a general melée, partly because his fleet was the best trained and best disciplined, and therefore, he thought, would be less likely to fall into disorder or confusion, and partly because he had no long-range cannon, and if he had engaged at a distance the Italian heavy guns would have crushed him. His ironclads were to attack and ram the vessels in front of them, and thus to protect the feebler

10 Sondhaus, *Habsburg Empire*, p. 258.
11 Laughton, *Studies*, pp. 191-192.
12 Clowes, *Four Modern Campaigns*, p. 71.

> wooden ships. His formation was well adapted for the use of the ram, but was defective in two ways, it lacked elasticity, and there was some danger of friend firing into friend. He was, however, assailing a fleet in no order at all; a fleet so circumstanced as to give him the very best chance of using the ram; and yet he only succeeded in sinking one ship with this weapon.[13]

In 1867 Tegetthoff visited Britain, France, and the United States, and he was on his way back to Paris for the Great Exhibition there when he was recalled to Vienna. On arriving, he was ordered to undertake the melancholy task of travelling to Mexico aboard the *Novara* to recover the body of his late friend and mentor Maximilian, following the Emperor's execution by the Juarez government at Queretaro. Back in Austria, Tegetthoff was made *Marinoberkommandant* and head of the Navy Section of the War Office. In this post he was able to oversee the construction of new ironclads for the Austrian navy. He applied the conclusions which he drew from the battle of Lissa to the development of the navy's future shipbuilding policy. He called for new ironclads to have complete armour protection; to be powered by twin screws; and armed with the maximum number possible of heavy guns. The first of the new ironclads was the *Lissa*, of 7,086 tons, launched at Trieste in 1869 and completed in May 1871. She had armour of 5 to 6 inches; was designed for speed of 12.5 knots; and carried twelve 9 inch rifled breech loaders. She was followed by the *Custozza*, of 7,609 tons, with armour of between 6 and 9 inches. Her speed was to be 13.5 knots and her armament was eight 10.2 inch and six 3.5 inch rifled breech loaders. The slightly smaller *Erzherzog Albrecht*, of 5,980 tons, had a speed of 12.5 knots, with 7 to 8 inches of armour, and carried eight 9.4 inch and six 3.5 inch rifled breech loaders. In 1869 the *Kaiser* was taken in hand for conversion into a casemate ironclad; her hull was cut down and rebuilt with iron, but she retained her machinery. She carried ten 9 inch muzzleloading rifles in a two-tiered casemate, protected by 6 inch armour.[14]

Tegetthoff also succeeded in introducing a number of important reforms of the Navy's administration but, on April 7, 1871 he died suddenly in Vienna from pneumonia. He was still only 43 years of age. Many monuments were erected in his memory, and a large number of paintings made. Many of these depicted the dramatic highpoint of the battle of Lissa when the *Erzherzog Ferdinand Max* rammed and sank the *Re d'Italia*. The most famous painting of all, however, was the painting by Anton Romako of Tegetthoff on his bridge during the battle, Maximillian von Sterneck at his side with sabre in hand. It hugely reinforced the image of the admiral as one of Austria's most outstanding, if most surprising, national heroes.

Reflecting on the many portraits of Tegetthoff, Laughton wrote that they represented 'a hard Scotch type of face:'

> I do not know how far they are to be trusted, but they are not out of keeping with his recorded character. He is described as a man of few words, emphatically a man of action, one able to execute his meaning, but not always to tell it; at the same time ready to speak out, and sharply too, if occasion called for it or the good of the service required it.[15]

13 Wilson, *Ironclads in Action*, vol.1, pp. 247-248.
14 Greene and Massignani, *Ironclads at War*, p. 230; Konstam, *European Ironclads*, pp. 15-16.
15 Laughton, *Studies*, p. 193.

In Italy, the public rage against Persano continued. Since he was a senator, he could not, in accordance with the Italian constitution, be the subject of a naval court martial. Instead, the entire National Assembly was convened as a High Court to try him on a number of charges, including cowardice and treason as well as negligence and incapacity. He was represented by Avvocato Donato Sanminiatelli, who had an unenviable task, but who made as brave a defence of the admiral as possible in a climate of opinion that could not have been more hostile. The politicians that constituted the court which tried Persano cannot have been unmindful of the spirit in which their verdicts would be greeted by the press and public. Nevertheless, at the end of the first stage of the trial, the admiral was, on January 27, 1867 acquitted of the charges of cowardice and treason.

The trial continued with a detailed investigation of Persano's conduct as commander in chief. Sanminiatelli put up a defence which turned in part on the extent to which he had been let down by the ships of Albini's squadron:

> He had seen the inaction of the wooden fleet. His signals were not sufficient to overcome that inaction. His orders to the fleet as a whole had not been obeyed … Ultimately, he was responsible not for one ship, or a few, but for the entire fleet, subject to many hopes and fears, but which, on another day, could with better fortune have ended successfully.[16]

The trial continued until April. Sanminiatelli wound up his defence of Persano with a rhetorical flourish, which perhaps carried a reference to the discussion which d'Amico described as the battle came to an end:

> What was better: to leave the outcome in doubt or to precipitate a defeat? Who is it, gentlemen, that can, in such a case, reproach a man bearing such an immense responsibility, and apply to him the full rigour of the law, if on that day he no longer had faith in his star and in victory?[17]

The verdict was pronounced on April 15, 1867. Neither Persano nor his defence team were present, learning of it by a letter from the President of the court, Senator Celso Marzucchi. Persano was found guilty of disobedience to orders by 83 votes to 48, and of incapacity and negligence by 116 votes to 15. On the first charge, the court found:

> On June 27 he had manifestly disobeyed his instructions, which were to clear the Adriatic of enemy ships; on the cruise from July 8-13 he had equally violated his instructions by not seeking an opportunity to attack the enemy, or to blockade him in his harbours.

On the second charge, the court found:

> At Lissa he had let himself be surprised by the enemy, he had made no disposition for battle, had called no council of war, had gone without general intimation on board the

16 Iachino, *Lissa*, p. 475.
17 Iachino, *Lissa*, p. 554.

> *Affondatore*, had permitted the enemy to break his line, had managed the *Affondatore* badly and had left the battle to itself.[18]

The findings of the court were contained in a transcript of 300 pages. He was sentenced to be stripped of his rank as an admiral, dismissed the service, deprived of his pension and ordered to pay the costs of the trial. There can have been little surprise at the outcome, which was what the Press had been demanding.

According to Laughton, there were many in Britain who believed that 'Persano was a victim, sacrificed to the Italians wounded self-love.' Certainly there is a propensity on the part of a defeated nation to seek a scapegoat, and a defeated leader is frequently held to be largely if not wholly to blame for the misfortune. This was to be demonstrated a few years later when the French people seized on Marshal Francois Achille Bazaine as a scapegoat for the disastrous outcome of the Franco-Prussian war of 1870-1871, with rather less reason than the Italians had for treating Persano thus. Neither Laughton nor other British historians, such as H.W. Wilson and William Laird Clowes felt much sympathy with the admiral, Laughton observing that the court's decision was 'just and even lenient.' Wilson described Persano as 'an admiral of words, not deeds, playing only to the gallery, and obeying the orders of the gallery to 'do something' against his own intuitions,' adding that he was 'destitute of moral fibre, devoid of military qualities, though it would seem not altogether of courage.'[19]

Persano had certainly made a number of very poor decisions. One of the most obvious was to ignore his opponent. Admiral Philip Colomb likened this to that of Medina Sidonia and the Armada:

> The Italian government, or Persano for them, might have been justified in despising the Austrian force at Pola; but however little its strength might have been esteemed, it was an absolute necessity to paralyse its action if the capture of the island of Lissa was to be accomplished. If neither Medina Sidonia nor Persano had naval force enough for the double operation of paralysing the defending naval force, and covering the landing at the same time, and yet attempted to pursue the descent, they each courted the fate they met, and fully deserved it.[20]

Colomb went on to develop the point. No satisfactory explanation was ever put forward for the Italian failure to keep an eye on Tegetthoff:

> All the law that history had been so long in in elaborating was set at defiance. The Austrian force at Pola – supposed inferior – was unwatched by a single cruiser. Persano proceeded to bombard the forts of Lissa without a notion of what the Austrian movement might be. He had run counter to historical teaching in making bombardment the first and main attack on the island, instead of first landing the troops and making the ships play the subordinate part in cooperating with them.[21]

18 Laughton, *Studies*, p. 189.
19 Wilson, *Ironclads in Action*, vol.1, p. 249.
20 Vice Admiral Philip Colomb, *Naval Warfare* (London: W H Allen & Co, 1899), p. 244.
21 Colomb, *Naval Warfare*, p. 430.

Nineteenth century historians took their tone from the outraged public reaction and subsequent trial of Persano, and they found no extenuating circumstances to set against the unanswerable facts of what was seen as his undoubted incompetence and its consequences. Their review of that incompetence frequently extended to a florid condemnation of his general character. A century later Admiral Iachino, while not dismissing the allegations of incompetence against Persano, examined his conduct in more measured terms. A beaten commander can rarely put forward an explanation likely to satisfy his critics, and Persano's task in defending himself was harder than most.

And yet – he was the man he was. He was not the man to make good in a few months the failure to create a well trained and disciplined navy. He was not the man to overcome the dislike and contempt of his subordinates. Historians have certainly felt no pity for him, and if, as has been suggested, he actively sought the command, then perhaps he deserves none. But what if Countess Cesaresco was right, and he was put under pressure to accept it, and did so unwillingly? In choosing Persano it is said that the government did so because neither Albini nor Vacca would have been prepared to serve under the other; it is no more likely that either would have served under any other, more junior, officer, even if there was an individual who was seen to have the necessary qualifications.

Persano was certainly entitled to contend that he was not well supported by those under him, particularly by Albini. He was unfortunate in the way some of the events occurred, both before and during the battle. Notwithstanding his many errors, therefore, it is not unreasonable to suggest that his treatment was, indeed, harsher than was warranted. He always believed so; in January 1869 he wrote to the King appealing for justice; not to do so, he said in a humbly respectful letter, would be to fail in his duty to his family. The King's response was, through his personal adjutant, Marquis Spinola, to make Persano an offer of a private pension. To this, Persano wrote to a friend it was justice, not money, that he sought. In the end, however, he accepted the King's generous offer. Thereafter, he lived in obscurity, dying on July 28, 1883, at the age of 77.

As well as putting Persano on trial, the Italian government had, rather more constructively, on August 8, 1866 appointed a Commission of Inquiry with a brief to determine 'the state of the materials and the administration of the *Regia Marina*.' The commission reached a number of disturbing conclusions about the inefficiency of the navy's administration. Shipbuilding orders had been placed without regard to the contract rules; there was a lack of test minutes and, indeed, of many other important documents. Ships were completed with inherent defects requiring extensive and prolonged repair. Ships were delivered incapable of attaining their designed speeds. The *Affondatore* was in particular held up as an instance of design and construction failure.[22] The navy reacted strongly to the criticism, producing a booklet in its defence rejecting many of the commission's findings, pointing out factual errors in its conclusions. The professional evaluation of the Italian navy by its own officers remained upbeat, in spite of Lissa and in spite of its administrative failings, as Greene and Massignani noted:

22 Greene and Massignani, *Ironclads at War*, pp. 236-237.

> The general opinion of the Italian officers was that their navy was far superior to the Austrian one. This is reflected in all the testimony the commission took from various Italian officers appointed to different duties, and the commission's conclusions adhered to this statement.[23]

As for the Austrian navy, Lawrence Sondhaus has shown that in the aftermath of Lissa it became to a certain extent the victim of its own success: 'The heroes of Lissa soon found that their triumph had been too complete and that the navy would not be sharing the fruits of victory.' In the post-Königgrätz era, it was the army that plainly needed attention, and it largely received it. The fact that military expenditure was part of the common budget which, following the creation of the Dual Monarchy had to be approved by both the Austrian *Reichsrat* and the Hungarian Diet disadvantaged the navy, since many Hungarians believed that the navy was solely an Austrian interest, and that 'for most of its life under the Dual Monarchy, the navy would not receive the sort of attention it had received in the heyday of Erzherzog Ferdinand Max's time at the helm.'[24]

23 Greene and Massignani, *Ironclads at War*, p. 238.
24 Sondhaus, *Habsburg Empire*, p. 267.

26

Conclusion: the Decline and Fall of the Ram

Immediately following the battle of Lissa, warship designers and naval theorists carefully examined the incidents that had led to its outcome for indications as to the future of naval warfare. Although it had not been contested by any of the great naval Powers, as the first fleet to fleet encounter of the age of the ironclad its influence was considerable. Unfortunately, the most prominent signpost which it produced was pointing in entirely the wrong direction. The apparent success of the ram in justifying Tegetthoff's faith in it as his most powerful weapon was to shape warship design and tactical discussion for decades. The dramatic circumstances of the sinking of the *Re d'Italia*, and the suddenness of her doom, lent considerable weight to the belief that here was the weapon that would change naval warfare and with it the way in which warships must henceforth be designed.

As a result the ram remained a feature of warship design well after it had ceased to be the fearsome primary weapon that had been supposed. There was one curious aspect of the British Admiralty's approach to the question of the ram's potential. The members of the 1871 Committee on Designs, instead of looking at ways of developing the ram and ramming tactics, gave particular consideration to the best way to construct ships to resist ram attacks. Thus they put defence before offence, and hence did not reach a balanced conclusion. They seem to have taken for granted the efficacy of the ram as a weapon.[1]

The ram lingered on until the beginning of the twentieth century, even after the arrival of the *Dreadnought*, and battleships were still designed with bows that ended with a protruding ram. But it gradually got smaller, as Richard Humble observed: 'It took about ten years after 1906 to die out completely, like the shrinking vestigial tail of a metamorphosing frog.'[2]

Guns, armour, and speed, all the subject of rapid technological progress, would all influence the tactics to be adopted in the future; but for the moment it was the potential of the ram that dominated discussion of the lessons that could be learned from the battle of Lissa. Although before the battle such as Admirals Bouet-Willaumez and Boutakov had laid down some key principles, which had notionally at any rate been taken into account in both navies before the campaign began, there had not been a great deal of consideration of the tactics to be employed in a fleet action between ironclads. This continued to be the case in Britain, where naval theorists

1 Warren Berry, *The Predreadnought Revolution* (Stroud: The History Press, 2013), pp. 138-139.
2 Richard Humble, *Before the Dreadnought* (London: Macdonald & Janes, 1976), p. 113.

lamented the official failure to develop a coherent tactical system. Sir Cyprian Bridge wrote of the study of tactics in 1872: 'In the British Navy especially it has not been so much neglected as despised.' This he put down to the traditional opinion that a British admiral need only hope for 'plenty of sea room and a willing enemy.'[3]

And yet there were those who grasped that with the advent of steam everything had changed. One of these was General Sir Howard Douglas. He had for many years been an outstandingly influential influence in the development of naval gunnery. He had also been a determined opponent of iron hulls and armour. In 1858, at the age of 85, he produced a crucially important work when he published his *On Naval War with Steam*. In this, he pointed out that steam had removed the element of chance in naval warfare, so that fleets, free from dependence on variable winds, could manoeuvre just as their commander wished, concentrating on any given point of an enemy squadron. The effectiveness of bow and stern guns would come into its own, and an oblique formation would, he argued, replace the line ahead.[4]

After the battle of Lissa, one of the earliest and most influential voices to be heard on the conclusions to be drawn was Philip Colomb. For the next three decades he was to be one of the Royal Navy's most important and profound thinkers. In 1865 he had drawn attention to the potential of the ram; in 1867, in a paper put before the Royal United Services Institute, he returned to the subject and expressed forcefully his view that the ram had become the decisive weapon of future naval warfare:

> The power of the new weapon was conclusively proved, and it is henceforth impossible to doubt its practical value. The rise of the ram in foreign estimation is one of the most remarkable features of the age. Dating from the first utterances of our gallant Admiral of the Fleet Sir George Sartorius, the ram has carried all navies by storm, and, so far as I can gather, except in Russia, without enquiry. When I read my paper on modern naval tactics, here, in the year 1865, and acknowledged myself a complete convert to Sir George Sartorius' views, English naval opinion was incredulous. Admiral Boutakov had written ably on naval tactics, but had nowhere expressed a conviction that the ram governed the tactics of the future, although an enquirer so acute and unprejudiced could not avoid allusion to its growing importance. In France, a system of tactics based wholly on the supposed unrivalled empire of the gun existed, and there was only a faint glimmer of an idea that the old line of battle was about to fall from its high state. Now look at the change. Admiral Boutakov has worked at the ram question to an extent unattempted by us; and Russia has drawn up a scheme of naval evolutions on the avowed principle that the ram is the only weapon of value against a fleet. France has pushed her old system of evolutions into the background, in the firm belief that *the ram, and the ram only, need be feared at sea*.[5]

Edward Reed, the Admiralty's Chief Constructor from 1863 to 1870, like Colomb never afraid to express strong opinions, was equally emphatic. In *Our Ironclad Ships*, published in 1869, he

3 Stanley Sandler, *The Emergence of the Modern Capital Ship* (Newark, NJ: University of Delaware Press, 1979), p. 119.
4 Sandler, *Emergence*, p. 120.
5 Parkes, *British Battleships*, p. 176.

demonstrated his conversion to the ram, at a time when increases in the calibre of naval guns threatened the effectiveness of armour protection:

> While gunmakers and others therefore indulge in the complacent belief that armour is in vain and that the gun is all in all, I am obliged to maintain a wholly opposite position, and I assert with confidence that just as the *Hercules* is at this moment impregnable in the region of the waterline to the attack of any and every gun afloat in any part of the world, so the ships of the future may in like manner be endowed with a like impregnability against the guns of the future; and my conviction is that before armour ceases to be superseded as a defence against guns, guns will themselves be superseded as a means of attack and the ship itself – viewed as a steam projectile – possessing all the force of the most powerful shot, combined with the power of striking in various directions – *will be deemed the most formidable weapon of attack that man's ingenuity has devised.*[6]

Not all commentators were entirely persuaded that the ram had been shown to be the all-powerful naval weapon. H.W. Wilson quoted the opinion of Admiral Page, written soon after the battle of Lissa: 'Tegetthoff had a remarkable chance; the circumstances were extraordinary. In spite of the power of the ram, the gun is still the principal and dominating weapon of naval war.'[7]

Another writer to express some reservations about the effectiveness of the ram was Admiral Warden, writing after the 1868 trials of the Channel Fleet:

> The subject of ramming I approach with great diffidence. It is one which exists principally in the region of speculation. I am not one of those who think that in the next naval war ramming will rank before artillery as a mode of attack; but I believe firmly that it will play a very important and formidable part in all future engagements. Possibly some naval actions will be decided by the independent and energetic action of some individual captain seizing the fortunate moment and the right opportunity for running down his enemy at high speed. It is as clear as anything that can be that so long as a ship has good way on her, and a good command of steam to increase her speed at pleasure, that ship cannot be what is called 'rammed;' she cannot even be struck to any purpose so long as she has room and is properly handled. The use of rams, it appears to me, will only be called into play after action has commenced, when ships, of necessity, are reduced to a low rate of speed, probably their lowest. I therefore apprehend that it would be consistent with prudence and good tactics always, when going into action, to hold in reserve a portion of the squadron or fleet to act as rams; and that when action had commenced, and noise and smoke and fire were doing their work, the reserve to be brought into play, to act independently as circumstances might require. I believe also on this subject as well as on very many others connected with naval warfare, that the first great action which takes place at sea between ironclad squadrons will dissipate and cast to the winds many of our preconceived opinions and theories, disturb many of our prejudices, and throw an entirely new light on the whole subject.[8]

6 Parkes, *British Battleships*, p. 176.
7 Wilson, *Ironclads in Action*, vol.1, p. 248.
8 Parkes, *British Battleships*, p. 176.

The future First Sea Lord, Commander Jackie Fisher, was a contributor to the debate as to the tactical use of the ram. In a paper which he wrote in 1871, he asserted that there were only two tactical formations that a fleet required in the presence of the enemy. These were 'Line abreast – ready to attack and be attacked. That is, to ram or be rammed,' and 'Line ahead, from which in any required direction or situation the above formation can be attained.' The existing formations, he thought, were too numerous and unnecessary. He believed that in battle it would come to close-in fighting; and he saw the ram as a crucially important weapon.

At Lissa, Tegetthoff had approached the Italian fleet in a wedge shaped formation, which he chose because it maximised his chances of successfully employing the ram. All the ironclads on each side were broadside firing, save for the turret ship *Affondatore*. Persano altered his formation from line abreast to line ahead, though his abrupt decision to transfer to the *Affondatore* created a gap in his line. Analysing the tactical decisions made at Lissa, Colomb did not address any serious criticism of Persano, because he was so pleased to find that the views which he had previously expressed as to the potency of the ram had been so emphatically vindicated by the outcome of the battle. He saw it as demonstrating the value of fighting at short range; this, he felt, was 'more consistent with our English character, and more suited to it than fighting at range.'[9] This led him to conclude that the line ahead had ceased be a valid deployment; even though most ironclads still carried their guns on the broadside, the declining value of the gun meant that the exposure of the ship's side made it vulnerable to the ram.

Captain Wayne P. Hughes, writing in 1986, summarised the confusion of naval theorists at that time as to the proper tactical lessons that were to be learned from the battle of Lissa:

> After 1866 tactical debate threw the traditional column overboard, and chaos reigned amidst all manner of speculation about the best tactical course to take. Solutions broke the long column into small components. Some argued for short supporting columns, some for short lines abreast, some for units of two to five mutually supporting warships that could turn together as the unit commander dictated and that looked like a World War II circular formation – or the British infantry square. A melée was the logical consequence of each scheme, and tacticians despaired of finding any tactics that would give the fleet commander with a well drilled navy anything but the most fugitive advantage during the approach. Many plans of action were based on strong analogies with land combat. Some were so amateurish as to envision the attacker manoeuvring against a defending fleet that, like defending troops in ground battle, would be fixed in a stationary line.[10]

Had there been a fleet action based on such principles it would, he considered, have been chaotic; but although the new proposals were inadequate at best, at worst they did not lose sight of their aim to concentrate all forces without a reserve (unlike Admiral Warden) thanks to the manoeuvrability provided by steam propulsion.

The proponents of the ram had gained considerable support for their views from what was seen as the operational experience of the American Civil War. In any case, lengthy broadside ironclads such as the *Warrior* were unlikely ever to find themselves in a position to use

9 Sandler, *Emergence*, p. 134.
10 Captain Wayne P. Hughes, *Fleet Tactics: Theory and Practice* (Annapolis, Maryland: Naval Institute Press, 1986), p. 60.

the ram effectively, even if their bows had been designed accordingly; but the development of shorter ironclads, broader in the beam and more manoeuvrable made the adoption of ram tactics more viable. The French *Magenta* class, begun in 1859, were the first ironclads designed with ramming in mind.

Elsewhere, the Russian Admiral Boutakov had as Colomb noted become a strong advocate of the ram. The designs produced by Edward Reed reflected the growing belief that the ram would be the principal weapon of attack. In Germany, where the prevailing view was still that the gun was the dominant weapon, the potential of the ram was nevertheless acknowledged:

> Turning to the ram, it is an indisputable fact that the strongest ships, whether armoured or unarmoured, even those fitted with the most approved appliances which the science of construction has discovered, and subdivided into numerous compartments, would be disabled if rammed by an enemy on the broadside, at, or nearly at, right angles … The decisive effect of a well delivered blow with the ram is indeed indisputable.[11]

Greene and Massignani examined the case put forward by the proponents of the ram bearing in mind that, in hindsight, history had shown that it was, in tactical terms, a dead end. They reviewed the arguments put forward by David K. Brown and Philip Pugh that the ram would not in practice have been an effective weapon in the hands of the ironclad fleets of the decade following Lissa. They had contended that ramming was relatively ineffective 'especially when one ship was engaging one ship and both could manoeuvre,' and supported that case with detailed mathematical argument. Against this, Greene and Massignani offered another point of view, suggesting that the fewer and heavier guns with which ironclads were coming to be equipped would have resulted in a reduction in the volume of fire; the heaviest Italian guns after Lissa took a well-trained crew seven or eight minutes to fire just once, materially reducing the possibility of hits in a vital spot. They concluded:

> So while ramming may have been statistically a long shot, so to speak, so was gunnery in this period. And by ramming a vessel with a lucky and well directed blow an enemy would be more likely to disable or sink it. Equipping ships in this period with the ram made tactical sense and was a logical course of action. That it would be difficult to employ successfully, as Brown and Pugh point out, is also true.[12]

In April 1874 the Junior Naval Professional Association awarded its prize for the best essay on Naval Tactics to Commander Gerard Noel, later a distinguished admiral, in which he examined the influence of guns, rams and torpedoes on the outcome of fleet actions. He concluded that the well-worn controversy of guns versus armour had resulted in favour of guns. However, because of the reduction in the number of guns carried, and in the rate of firing, he suggested that 'the next general action will show that a larger number of guns of a lesser calibre will be of greater service.' He went on to observe that guns would not be the principal weapon, but would

11 Greene and Massignani, *Ironclads at War*, p. 119.
12 Greene and Massignani, *Ironclads at war*, p. 121.

become all-important if the engines of a ship or her steering gear was permanently or temporarily disabled.[13]

He went on to consider the ram. There was no doubt of its terrible and deadly effect when used as a weapon of offence, but opinions might, he considered, vary as to the possibility of its use and the method of attack to be adopted. There were obvious problems with its use by a fleet; if it intended to rely on this mode of attack, 'it must steer such a course, and be in such a formation is to facilitate the use of the ram on that course, or without diverging to any great degree from it.' A single ship action, on the other hand, was entirely different:

> What iron nerves, what cool-headed determination, what almost instinctive guidance will be required to steer one of our largest ironclads, moving at the rate of eight or ten knots, against one of another fleet approaching at the same rate, with the firm resolution of ramming her, should opportunity offer! There will be no prompting, no time to ask advice, no opportunity for further calculation than the eye and senses can command at the moment; the decision must be instantaneous, and immediately carried into effect; the only encouragement being, in the knowledge that the enemy's ship is commanded and guided by a man undergoing the same fearful test, and that the most determined man of the two, if sufficiently skilful, must secure his object.[14]

In his detailed review of the possible use of the ram in the next naval battle, Noel examined the opinions of leading naval theorists such as Captains Colomb, Dawson, and Pellew, and the French Admiral Touchard, and went on to conclude that all ships ought to be rams, and all officers ought to be practised in their employment. What is plain, he argued, was that ships of a steam fleet could not be handled so perfectly as those in the fleets of Nelson and Jervis. Much more manoeuvring would be required, and changes would succeed each other with much greater rapidity.

In one respect in particular Noel differed from Colomb as to a particular conclusion to be drawn from Lissa, and that was with regard to Persano's decision to forsake the *Re d'Italia* for the *Affondatore*. Colomb had argued that in future naval actions the commander-in-chief would not take a position in the line. Noel took a different view:

> I agree with Captain Colomb so far that it would be very desirable that an admiral should place himself where he could best see and be seen, but I am strongly of opinion that this place is at the head of his line. On land the general using signals would be on an elevation, looking down on the field before him; he would also have the enemy in a certain direction from him, his own army being immediately under his eye. After the first charge of the opposing fleets, how is the detached commander-in-chief to order the new formation? And on what bearings is it to be made, when possibly the enemy may be between him and his fleet? I hold that in future … The admiral should lead in his flagship.[15]

13 Commander Gerard H.U. Noel, 'Naval Tactics' in Unknown (ed.) *The Gun, Ram, and Torpedo* (London: J Griffin & Co, 1874), p. 5.
14 Noel, 'Naval Tactics', pp. 6-7.
15 Noel, 'Naval Tactics', pp. 48-49.

In awarding the prize to Commander Noel the judges, who were headed by Admiral Sir Alexander Milne, thought so highly of two other essays submitted that these were published with the Prize Essay. One of these was by John Knox Laughton. In his submission he argued that the gunners should not open fire until the range was very short indeed. What that range should be would depend on the particular circumstances: 'but I think that 400 yards ought not to be much exceeded.' This does appear to be a remarkably short range to suggest. It was Laughton's view that at such a range such a crushing fire might be achieved that the target ship ' ought to be sunk by the concentrated broadside, or be fatally rammed in consequence of it.'[16] Such a short range was perfectly consistent with current British naval thinking, as a foreign observer had remarked a few years before:

> All idea of firing at sea in iron cased ships at long range had been banished. The opinion of the most competent naval officers in England, with regard to the range with which fire can be opened at sea does not differ very much. The extreme limits lie between four hundred and at most one thousand yards, under favourable conditions.[17]

As to the effectiveness of the ram as a weapon, Laughton was in no doubt. Drawing in particular on the experiences of the *Erzherzog Ferdinand Max* at Lissa, but also several peacetime accidents, he was certain that an attacking ship would cut clean into her antagonist, and 'that the sinking of the vessel so struck would be the affair of a few seconds, or, at most, minutes; and that it is a question which only combat can decide, whether the striking ship would not pass through and over the shattered wreck.'[18]

Although the view of the ram propounded by Colomb and others was widely held, and its more extreme advocates like Sartorius even argued for ships to be designed as rams with little or no other armament, there was no immediate move to build such ships for the British navy. It had acquired almost by accident the two Laird rams originally built for the Confederacy. There were a number of possibly interesting warships designed during the course of the American Civil War that might have inspired such projects in Britain. Oscar Parkes considered that perhaps the most interesting of all of them was the little *Manassas*, a tugboat converted into an ironclad:

> She had the appearance of a floating cigar surmounted by two funnels abreast with a single 32 pounder carronade firing through a shuttered port up forward, the ram being a solid beak of 20 feet of wood. The whole hull was covered with a carapace of 12 inch oak enclosed in 1½ inch iron armour … Federal reports speak of her as 'the most troublesome vessel of them all.' Her chief claim to historical importance is that her exploits were to start a new vogue in warships having far-reaching consequences.[19]

In 1865 the French laid down the *Taureau*, designed by Dupuy de Lôme. She was a 2,718 ton turtle decked, spur bowed wooden vessel, armour plated and carrying one 9.5 inch gun, able

16 J.K. Laughton, 'Naval Tactics' in Unknown (ed.), *The Gun, Ram, and Torpedo* (London: J Griffin & Co, 1874) pp. 40-41.
17 M.H. Jansen, *The Revolution in Naval Warfare* (London: Publisher unknown, 1867), p. 144.
18 Laughton, 'Naval Tactics', p. 50.
19 Parkes, *British Battleships*, p. 175.

to make 12.5 knots. She was, though, no more than a harbour defence unit, and she and the four larger ships of the *Belier* class appear to have spent their whole lives in dockyard basins. In 1868 the British Admiralty laid down the *Hotspur*, the first British warship to be built as a fleet ram. As designed, she had a fixed turret mounting a 12 inch muzzleloading rifle. Of 4,010 tons, she had an 11 inch armoured belt carried down to reinforce her ram. She had a speed of 12.65 knots. She was completed in 1871, and was followed three years later by the somewhat larger *Rupert*. Of these two ships Sandler wrote that they were 'not only practically useless but a positive menace to their consorts.'[20] During the period of their construction the Admiralty's attention had become focused on the development of ships for coast defence, largely as a result of the French navy's experiences during the Franco-Prussian war, when its powerful oceangoing fleet of ironclads achieved nothing against the German coast defences.

Philip Colomb, meanwhile, had continued to be a staunch advocate of the ram, and at the beginning of the 1870s was strongly reiterating his belief in the reduction of the power of artillery. He contended that since the battle of Lissa it had declined to the point where it was now five times as inferior to armour as it had been in 1867: 'This seems to me to be a very startling conclusion to arrive at, and one which lies at the root of all construction and armament.'[21]

It was indeed very startling, and it reinforced his previous views as to the primacy of the ram as the only weapon that could be of decisive effect. There were few voices raised in opposition to this view. One was that of Commander Wallace B. Harding who wrote in 1873:

> Lissa itself, which is so often quoted by the advocates of the ram as an instance of its success, is, on the contrary, the best instance of its possible failure … Is this, we ask, the mode of attack which offers to the British navy the surest guarantee of success, the largest scope for our national characteristics of undoubted courage and coolness?[22]

For the moment it was believed that the battle of Lissa had demonstrated that the current armour plating had been shown to provide entirely adequate protection. The ironclads that contested the battle generally carried armour of 4.5 to 5 inches, and this had proved effective. This was, though, a temporary situation; the Italian gunnery at Lissa had been poor, while the guns carried by the Austrian ironclads were not as powerful as they might have been, because they had not been able to equip their ships with the new guns ordered from Krupp. The general change to rifled guns, and the design of larger and much more powerful guns, would soon increase the accuracy of fire and the destructive power of their shells. Warship designers accordingly began to increase the thickness of armour plating. The contest between offence and defence accelerated; as the years went by, larger and larger guns would be opposed by thicker and thicker armour. Since at the time of the battle of Lissa the balance favoured the defence, the suggestion that the primacy of the gun was no more carried considerable weight.

Thus the gunmakers resorted to the design of artillery of hugely increased size and power to meet the apparent dominance of armour protection:

20 Sandler, *Emergence*, p. 171.
21 Sandler, *Emergence*, p. 148.
22 Sandler, *Emergence*, p. 151.

> The main reason for the astronomical increase in gun size and power, therefore, was not the result of any objective study of foreign advances in ordnance or armour, nor, certainly, of the combat experiences of Britain, France, or America. Rather, one reason was an appreciation that armour, from the time of Hampton Roads through Lissa and even to the bombardment of Alexandria in 1882, clearly enjoyed (in battle) an ascendancy over the gun.[23]

The drive to increase the size and power of guns, with the necessary and corresponding increase in armour, owed a lot to the ceaseless sales pressure of gun manufacturers on the one hand, and the makers of armour on the other. It was a pressure which only clear-sighted designers and administrators were able to resist.

There was one other aspect of naval ordnance that would come to have a considerable effect on warship design, and with it on naval tactics, and that was the development of end-on fire. In June 1866 Captain Cooper Key, the captain of the gunnery establishment *Excellent*, and responsible for the oversight of all new naval armaments, produced a memorandum stressing the need for all-round fire with powerful arming of the bow and stern. Parkes described this paper as 'the principal influence for what were regarded as the most successful ships' of the following decade and a half. Key's arguments carried the navy with them. They naturally strengthened the hand of those advocating turrets; significantly, 'it was a very small step from these arguments to minimise the value of broadside guns altogether, and to exalt the value of end-on fire, as was done later in the *Inflexible*.'[24] Colomb, however, was sceptical, contending that such an important issue should not be raised without experiment. It was necessary, he said, that it be shown on paper that the positions of ships or fleets could be taken up in the manner suggested to use end-on fire and not be counteracted by enemy movements.

Sir William Armstrong, after his serious setback when his breech loading guns had to be abandoned in 1863 because of mechanical problems due to the design being too advanced for current technology, was leading the way to the production of larger guns. He developed a method of construction that enabled guns of increasing size to be built, and it was this that led to the reduction in the number carried by the latest ironclads. It was, however, the development of the turret ship that provided a platform for the heavier ordnance that could now be provided. The reintroduction of breech loaders, on the other hand, which were more accurate and had more penetrative power at longer ranges, was postponed for many years by the prevailing belief that naval battles would continue to be fought at short range.

It would be the best part of three decades before the efficacy of the ram was shown to be delusive. In that time there had been a considerable number of incidents in which the ram's lethal potential had been demonstrated in peace, not in war. Oscar Parkes listed the major accidents that had occurred during the period of 10 years after the *Hotspur* had been laid down in 1868:

> 1869: The Russian ironclad *Kreml* rammed the frigate *Oleg*, sinking her with a loss of 16 men.

23 Sandler, *Emergence*, p. 98.
24 Parkes, *British Battleships*, p. 118.

1871: The Russian ironclad *Admiral Spiridov* rammed her sister the *Admiral Lazarev,* which was only saved from sinking in Kronstadt harbour by the speedy arrival of pumps from the dockyard.
1873: The Spanish ironclad *Numancia* rammed the corvette *Fernando el Catolica* and sank her, all the crew except five being drowned.
1875: The French ironclad *Jeanne d'Arc* rammed the despatch vessel *Forfait* which was sunk but without loss of life.
1875:The British *Iron Duke* rammed and sank the *Vanguard,* but without loss of life.
1877: The French ironclad *Thetis* rammed the ironclad *Reine Blanche* which was run ashore to save her from sinking.
1878: The German ironclad *König Wilhelm* rammed and sank the turret ship *Grösser Kurfurst* with the loss of nearly all the officers and men.[25]

It was, though, the loss of the *Victoria* on June 22, 1893 that was perhaps the most spectacular instance of a battleship being destroyed by ramming in peacetime. The Mediterranean Fleet, commanded by Admiral Sir George Tryon, with his flag in the *Victoria,* was steaming from Beirut to Tripoli. It was proceeding in two columns when he signalled for a manoeuvre which would bring his flagship, then leading the starboard column, to a position at the head of the port column when the fleet arrived at its destination. He signalled for the two columns each to make an inward turn at a distance of only six cables, when the proper distance to effect this safely should have been ten cables, or 2,000 yards. This was self-evidently a most dangerous movement, and it was clearly a mistake. The *Camperdown,* at the head of the port column, struck the *Victoria* on the starboard bow ten feet above the anchor at an angle of about 68°, at a speed of 5 to 6 knots. The *Camperdown's* ram penetrated to nine feet at a depth of twelve feet below the waterline, smashing open a breach of between 100 and 110 square feet. As the *Victoria* steamed on, the forward battery door, two of the foremost ports and turret ports were still open, and when the ship lurched water poured into the battery. As her stern came up she fell slowly on to her side before capsizing. Some 400 of her complement, including Tryon, went down with the *Victoria*; the 173 survivors included Commander John Jellicoe, the future commander of the Grand Fleet during the First World War.

With this disaster fresh in the public mind, William Laird Clowes in the following year reviewed the history of the ram and its effects. He identified 74 instances in which the ram had been used in action between 1861 and 1879. Of these, 36 had caused no damage at all; 18 caused slight damage, and only 20 resulted in serious damage to either of the ships involved. His conclusion, which he found remarkable, was that ramming on the open sea was impossible unless the target ship was already disabled. The peacetime disasters, of which the *Victoria's* sinking was the most spectacular, showed that the ram had proved more dangerous to friend than to foe. Hindsight suggests, of course, that his findings ought to have been seen as overwhelmingly convincing; but the ram still had its adherents who argued for its value as a weapon in battle.

Stanley Sandler concluded that the reason for the belief in the ram was that in the Royal Navy in the 1860s and early 1870s 'the study and practice of tactics filled a distinctly subordinate role

25 Parkes, *British Battleships*, p. 285.

to design and construction,' and suggested that the erroneous conclusions reached were almost inevitable:

> Lacking battle experience, the British navy was compelled to rely upon Lissa, the more or less accurate accounts of the American Civil War, and theory. Furthermore, coal was too costly and engines too inefficient to permit the extensive and realistic battle manoeuvres necessary to test the validity of current tactical theory. Consequently, there was little agreement on the method of naval warfare for ironclads. These reasons, plus the lack of naval staff, go far toward explaining the great popularity of so untried a weapon as the ram.[26]

Having committed themselves so emphatically to the ram, its advocates were slow to change their minds. Philip Colomb, whose pre-eminent intellectual influence continued until the end of the century, appears never to have formally abandoned his belief in the ram, even though the major advances in ordnance technology, and in marine engines, as well as the coming of the torpedo, had put an end to the ram as a serious naval weapon.

In 1908 the French Captain Gabriel Darrieus pointed out the reasons why the ram had for so long been mistakenly supposed to be the key weapon for a battle fleet. He argued that 'weapons examined from the point of view of the real value of their action were inseparable one from the other,' and went on to explain how, without the benefit of reliable evidence, the ram's adherents had failed to apply this principle:

> No weapon has given occasion to overflowing enthusiasm more than this one; it has had and still has fervent and convinced advocates. And yet, to support such very strong convictions, there exist after all only very meagre experimental data, that is to say a few isolated scenes of the rather restricted theatre of the War of Secession, and the incident of the *Ferdinand Max* and the *Re d'Italia* at the battle of Lissa. In this almost general infatuation which still lasts, no voice of reason has been raised modestly to call attention to the fact that the gun in neither case took any part. It is therefore truly the separate examination of a weapon without connection with other weapons which has had such a remarkably lasting influence upon opinions.[27]

Four years later Admiral Custance could look back on the days when the ram was considered supreme, in the knowledge that its claim to primacy had now been completely exploded. He noted that for the Italians at Lissa to receive the Austrian end-on attack in line was to ensure that their guns would not be effective. American Civil War experience had shown that this was the case when ships approached end-on and with the range rapidly changing: 'This was the true objection to it, and not that usually given – viz, that the Italians were exposed to being rammed. On the contrary the line ahead was a favourable order in which to meet the ram attack, as the ships covered each other.' Thus he revived the doctrine of the line ahead so summarily dismissed by Colomb forty years earlier.[28]

26 Sandler, *Emergence*, p. 153.
27 Captain Gabriel Darrieus (translated by Philip R Alger), *War on the Sea: Strategy and Tactics* (Annapolis, Md: Naval Institute Press, 1908) p. 296.
28 Custance, *Ship of the Line*, p. 72.

Custance went on to restate the point that the gun was used improperly at Lissa:

> The battle did not prove that it was an ineffective weapon. The attack on the forts of San Giorgio, and the repulse of the *Formidabile* by the Battery Madonna, showed, on the contrary, that it could be very effective when given proper opportunity. Experience both before and since has confirmed this.

As for the ram, its success in the case of the *Re d'Italia* had caught both popular and professional imagination. It had not been the subject of sufficient enquiry as to the particular circumstances in which it had been employed:

> It was not noted that the *Re d'Italia* was not under command, which made the conditions exceptionally favourable, nor that the *Ferdinand Max* had previously made two unsuccessful attempts. It was not remarked that twice Italian ships had rammed each other, thus repeating the incident at Mobile Bay when the *Hartford* – Farragut's flagship – was nearly sunk by the *Lackawanna*, one of his own ships. Not until many years afterwards was the value of the ram as a weapon thoroughly examined. It was then proved to be entirely unreliable, and as dangerous to the one side as to the other when both are under way and under command. The conclusion drawn from the battle that the ram was a reliable weapon and superior to the gun was entirely wrong, misled professional thought for a generation, and seriously influenced the design of ships of war.[29]

As the first and only ironclad fleet to fleet action, the battle of Lissa could not fail to be enormously influential. In the end, however, the rapidly accelerating pace of technological advance soon began to make the lessons that it seemed to have provided, such as they were, obsolete, though it would not be until many erroneous decisions had been taken before this was evident. None of that, of course, detracts from the achievement of the brave and intelligent Wilhelm von Tegetthoff as the first fleet commander to win such a battle.

29 Custance, *Ship of the Line*, p. 72.

Bibliography

Part 1: Books

Anderson, R C, *Naval Wars in the Levant* (Liverpool: Liverpool University Press 1952)
Ballard, Admiral George A, *The Black Battlefleet* (Annapolis, Md: Naval Institute Press 1980)
Barnaby, Sir Nathaniel, *Naval Developments in the Century* (London: Publisher unknown 1904)
Barry, Quintin, *The Road to Königgrätz* (Solihull: Helion 2010)
Bartlett, C J, *Great Britain and Sea Power 1815-1853* (Oxford: Oxford University Press 1963)
Baxter, James P, *The Introduction of the Ironclad Warship* (Cambridge, Mass: Harvard College 1933)
Beeler, John F, *British Naval Policy in the Gladstone Era 1866-1880* (Stanford, Ca: Stanford University Press 1997)
Beeler, John F, (ed) *The Milne Papers 1820-1859* (2 vols) (Aldershot: Navy Records Society 2004)
Berry, Warren, *The Pre-Dreadnought Revolution* (Stroud: The History Press 2013)
Böhme, Helmut,(ed) *The Foundation of the German Empire* Oxford: Oxford University Press 1971)
Brown, David K, *Before the Ironclad* (Barnsley: Seaforth Publishing 1990)
Brodie, Bernard, *Sea Power in the Machine Age* (Princeton N J: Princeton University Press 1941)
Boynton, Charles B, *The History of the Navy in the Rebellion* New York: Publisher unknown 1867)
Callwell, Major C E, *The Effect of Maritime Command on Land Campaigns* (Edinburgh: William Blackwood and Sons 1897)
Cesaresco, Countess E Martinengo, *The Liberation of Italy* (London: Seeley& Co 1895)
Chatterton, E Keble, *Battles by Sea* (London: Sidgwick & Jackson 1925)
Clowes, Sir William L, *Four Modern Naval Campaigns* (London: Unit Library 1902)
Clowes, Sir William L, *The Royal Navy: A History from the Earliest Times to the Present* 6 vols (London: Sampson Low Marston 1901)
Colomb, Vice Admiral P H, *Naval Warfare* (London: W H Allen & Co 1899)
Courtemanche, Regis A, *No Need of Glory* (Annapolis, Md: Naval Institute Press 1977)
Cowburn, Philip, *The Warship in History* (London: Macmillan 1966)
Custance, Admiral Sir Reginald, *The Ship of the Line in Battle* (Edinburgh: William Blackwood & Sons 1912)
Dakin, D, *British and American Philhellenes during the War of Greek Independence* (Thessaloniki: Institute for Balkan Studies 1955)

Darrieus, Captain Gabriel, *War on the Sea* (trans P Alger) (Annapolis, Md: Naval Institute Press 1908)
Davis, William C, *Duel Between the First Ironclads* (Baton Rouge, La: Louisana State University Press 1975)
De Kay, James T, *Monitor* (London: Pimlico 1999)Dewar, Captain A C and Bonner-Smith, D (eds) *The Russian War, 1854, Baltic and Black Sea* (London: Navy Records Society 1943)
Donko, Wilhelm M, *A Land Power Goes to Sea* (Berlin: Holzbrinck 2017)
Duckers, Peter, *The Crimean War at Sea* (Barnsley: Pen & Sword 2011)
Durkin, Joseph T, *Confederate Navy Chief* (Colombia, South Carolina: University of South Carolina Press 1954)
Eardley-Wilmot, Captain S, *Life of Vice Admiral Edmund, Lord Lyons* (London: Sampson Low Marston 1898)
Elliott, Robert G, *Ironclad of the Roanoke* (Shippenburg, Pa: White Mane Publishing 1994)
Embree, Michael, *Bismarck's First War* (Solihull: Helion 2006)
Fioranzi, Giuseppe, *A History of Naval Tactical Thought* (Annapolis, Md: Naval Institute Press 1979)
Fuller, Howard J, *Clad in Iron* (Annapolis, Md: Naval Institute Press 2008)
Garrison, Captain Daniel J, *The Navy from Wood to Steel 1860-1890* (New York: Franklin Watts 1965)
George, James L, *History of Warships* (London: Constable 1999)
Greene, Jack and Massignani, Alessandro, *Ironclads at War* (Consohocken, Pa: Combined Publishing 1998)
Greenhill, Basil and Giffard, Ann, *Steam, Politics and Patronage* (London: Conway Maritime Press 1994)
Groener, Erich, *German Warships 1815-1945* (2 vols) (London: Conway Maritime Press 1990)
Hamilton, C I, *Anglo-French Naval Rivalry 1840-1870* (Oxford: Clarendon Press 1993)
Harris, Andrew, *Sir John Pakington: His Ministerial Career 1852-1868* Leominster: Harris 2013)
Higginson, Rear Admiral Francis J, *Naval Battles in the Century* (Toronto: W & R Chambers 1906)
Hilton, George W and others, *The Illustrated History of Paddle Steamers* (Lausanne: Patrick Stephens Ltd 1976)
Hogg, Ian and Batchelor, John, *Naval Guns* (Poole: Blandford 1978)
Hore, Captain Peter, *The Ironclads* (London: Southwater 2006)
Hovgaard, W, *Modern History of Warships* (London: Conway Maritime Press 1971)
Hozier, H M, *The Seven Weeks War* (London: Edward Stanford 1867)
Hughes, Captain Wayne P, *Fleet Tactics: Theory and Practice* (Annapolis, Md: Naval Institute Press 1986)
Humble, Richard, *Before the Dreadnought* (London: Macdonald & Janes 1976)
Hyde, H Montgomery, *Mexican Empire* (London: Macmillan 1946)
Iachino, Admiral Angelo, *La Campagna di Lissa 1866* (Milan: Il Saggiatore 1966)
James, William, *The Naval History of Great Britain* (6 vols) (London: Richard Bentley 1859)
Jane, Fred T, *The Imperial Russian Navy (*London: Conway Maritime Press 1983)
Jansen, M H, *The Revolution in Naval Warfare* (London: Publisher unknown 1867)
Jenkins, E H, *A History of the French Navy* (London: Macdonald & Janes 1973)
Jung,P and Winkler, D, *Rammkurs Lissa* (Vienna: Stohr n.d.)

Konstam, Angus, *European Ironclads 1860-1875*(Oxford: Osprey 2019)
Lambert, Andrew D, *Battleships in Transition* (London: Conway Maritime Press 1984)
Lambert, Andrew D, *The Crimean War: British Grand Strategy Against Russia 1853-56* (Manchester: Manchester University Press 1990)
Laughton,Sir John K, *Studies in Naval History* (London: Longmans Green 1887)
Levien, M, (ed) *The Cree Journals* (Exeter: Webb & Bower 1981)
Mack Smith, Denis, *Cavour* (London: Weidenfeld & Nicolson 1985)
Mack Smith, Denis, *Cavour and Garibaldi 1860* (Cambridge: Cambridge University Press 1985)
Marshall, Adrian G, *Nemesis* (Stroud: The History Press 2016)
Martin, George, *The Red Shirt and the Cross of Savoy* (London: Eyre & Spottiswood 1969)
Melton, Maurice, *The Confederate Ironclads* (New York: Thomas Yoseleff 1968)
Mitchell, Donald W, *A History of Russian and Soviet Sea Power* (London: Andre Deutsch 1974)
Mokin. Arthur, *Ironclad* (Novato, Ca: Presidio 1991)
Mordal, Jacques, *Twenty Five Centuries of Sea Warfare* (trans L Ortzen) (London: Abbey Library 1970)
Morriss, Roger, *Cockburn and the British Navy in Transition* (Exete: University of Exeter Press 1997)
Navy Records Society, *British Naval Documents 1204-1960* (London 1993)
Noel, Commander G and others, *The Gun, Ram and Torpedo* (London: J Griffin & Co 1874)
Palmer, Michael A, *Command at Sea* (Cambridge, Mass: Harvard University Press2005)
Parkes, Oscar, *British Battleships* (London: Seeley Service 1970)
Patterson, A Temple, 'Captain Cowper Coles and Palmerston's Folly' in *The Mariner's Mirror* (London 1965) 51:1 19-25
Pemsel, Helmut, 'Wilhelm von Tegetthoff: Admiral of the Unexpected' in *The Great Admirals*, ed Jack Sweetman (Annapolis, Md: Naval Institute Press 1997)
Peterson, Clarence S, *John A Dahlgren: Father of United States Naval Ordnance* (New York: Publisher unknown 1945)
Pocock, Tom, *Remember Nelson* (London: William Collins & Sons 1977)
Potter, E B and Nimitz, Fleet Admiral Chester W. (eds) *Sea Power: A History* (Englewood Cliffs, NJ: Prentice Hall 1960)
Ranfft, Bryan, ed, *Technical Change and British Naval Policy* (London: Hodder& Stoughton 1977)
Roberts, William H, *Civil War Ironclads* (Baltimore, Md: Johns Hopkins University Press 2002)
Rodger, N A M, *The Admiralty* (Lavenham: Terence Dalton Ltd 1979)
Ropp, Theodore, *The Development of a Modern Navy* (Annapolis, Md: Naval Institute Press 1987)
Rottauscher, Maximilian, *With Tegetthoff at Lissa* (Solihull: Helion 2010)
Sandler, Stanley, *The Emergence of the Modern Capital Ship* (Newark, NJ: University of Delaware Press 1979)
Scharf, J Thomas, *History of the Confederate States Navy* (New York: Roger & Sherwood 1894)
Simson, Jay W, *Naval Strategies of the Civil War* (Nashville, Tenn: Cumberland House Publishing 2001)
Sokol, Hans Hugo, *Des Kaisers Seemacht* (Vienna: Amalthea 2002)
Sondhaus, Lawrence, *Naval Warfare 1815-1914* (London: Routledge 2001)

Sondhaus, Lawrence, *The Habsburg Empire and the Sea* (West Lafayette, Ind: Purdue University Press 1994)

Sondhaus, Lawrence, *The Naval Policy of Austria-Hungary 1867-1918)* West Lafayette, Ind: Purdue University Press 1994)

Stillman, WJ, *The Union of Italy 1815-1895* (Cambridge: Cambridge University Press 1909)

Sulivan, Admiral Sir Bartholemew, *Life and Letters* (London: John Murray 1896)

Thayer, William Roscoe, *The Life and Times of Cavour* (2 vols) (London: Constable 1912)

Tracy, Nicholas,(ed), *The Naval Chronicle* (5 vols) (London: Chatham Publishing 1999)

Tritten, James J and Donolo, Vice Admiral Luigi, *A Doctrine Reader* (Newport, RI: Naval War College 1995)

Tucker, Spencer C, *Handbook of 19th Century Naval Warfare* (Stroud: Sutton 2000)

Wellesley, Sir Victor and Sencourt, Robert, *Conversations with Napoleon III* (London: Ernest Benn 1934)

Wells, Captain John, *The Immortal Warrior* (Emsworth: Kenneth Mason 1987)

Whyte, A J, *The Political Life and Letters of Cavour 1848-1861* ((Oxford: Oxford University Press 1930)

Wilson, H W, *Ironclads in Action*, 2 vols (London: Sampson Low & Co 1897)

Winfield, Raf and Roberts, Stephen S, *French Warships in the Age of Sail* (Barnsley: Seaforth Publishing 2015)

Wyatt, Captain W J, *The Hanoverian and Italian War* (London: Macmillan 1868)

Part 2: Articles

Ballard, Admiral G.A., 'Some Observations on Professor Baxter's book on *The Introduction of the Ironclad Warship*,' *The Mariner's Mirror*, 19.4 (1933) pp 404-416

Baxter, Colin F., 'The Duke of Somerset and the Creation of the British Ironclad Navy 1859-66,' *The Mariner's Mirror*, 63.3 (1977) pp 279-284

Bolander, Louis H., 'The Introduction of Shells and Shell-Guns in the United States Navy,' *The Mariner's Mirror*, 17.2 (1931) pp 105-112

Coutts-Smith, J.R., 'The Battle of Lissa 20 July 1866,' *The Mariner's Mirror*, 51.3 (1965) pp 265-269

Dakin, Douglas, 'Lord Cochrane's Greek Steam Fleet,' *The Mariner's Mirror*, 39.3 (1953) pp 211-219

Hore, Peter, 'Lord Melville, the Admiralty and the Coming of Steam Navigation,' *The Mariner's Mirror*, 86.2 (2000) pp 157-172

Laing, E.A,M., 'The Introduction of Paddle Frigates into the Royal Navy,' *The Mariner's Mirror*, 66.4 (1980) pp 331-334

Osbon, G.A., 'The First of the Ironclads. The Armoured Batteries of the 1850's,' *The Mariners Mirror*, 50.3 (1964) pp 189-198

A Temple Patterson, 'Captain Cowper Coles and Palmerston's Folly,' *The Mariner's Mirror*, 51.1 (1955) pp 24-25

Index

General Index

Index of ships

The period 1815-1914 is sometimes called the long century of peace. It was in reality very far from that. It was a century of civil wars, popular uprisings, and struggles for Independence. An era of colonial expansion, wars of Empire, and colonial campaigning, much of which was unconventional in nature. It was also an age of major conventional wars, in Europe that would see the Crimea campaign and the wars of German unification. Such conflicts, along with the American Civil War, foreshadowed the total war of the 20th century.

It was also a period of great technological advancement, which in time impacted the military and warfare in general. Steam power, electricity, the telegraph, the radio, the railway, all became tools of war. The century was one of dramatic change. Tactics altered, sometimes slowly, to meet the challenges of the new technology. The dramatic change in the technology of war in this period is reflected in the new title of this series: From Musket to Maxim.

The new title better reflects the fact that the series covers all nations and all conflict of the period between 1815-1914. Already the series has commissioned books that deal with matters outside the British experience. This is something that the series will endeavour to do more of in the future. At the same time there still remains an important place for the study of the British military during this period. It is one of fascination, with campaigns that capture the imagination, in which Britain although the world's predominant power, continues to field a relatively small army.

The aim of the series is to throw the spotlight on the conflicts of that century, which can often get overlooked, sandwiched as they are between two major conflicts, the French/Revolutionary/Napoleonic Wars and the First World War. The series will produced a variety of books and styles. Some will look simply at campaigns or battles. Others will concentrate on particular aspects of a war or campaign. There will also be books that look at wider concepts of warfare during this era. It is the intention that this series will present a platform for historians to present their work on an important but often overlooked century of warfare.

Submissions

The publishers would be pleased to receive submissions for this series. Please contact series editor Dr Christopher Brice via email (christopherbrice@helion.co.uk), or in writing to Helion & Company Limited, Unit 8, Amherst Business Centre, Budbrooke Road, Warwick, Warwickshire, CV34 5WE.

Books in this series:

1. *The Battle of Majuba Hill: The Transvaal Campaign 1880-1881* John Laband (ISBN 978-1-911512-38-7)
2. *For Queen and Company: Vignettes of the Irish Soldier in the Indian Mutiny* David Truesdale (ISBN 978-1-911512-79-0)
3. *The Furthest Garrison: Imperial Regiments in New Zealand 1840-1870* Adam Davis (ISBN 978-1-911628-29-3)
4. *Victory over Disease: Resolving The Medical Crisis In The Crimean War, 1854-1856* Michael Hinton (ISBN 978-1-911628-31-6)
5. *Journey Through the Wilderness: Garnet Wolseley's Canadian Red River Expedition of 1870* Paul McNicholls (ISBN 978-1-911628-30-9)
6. *Kitchener: The Man Not the Myth* Anne Samson (ISBN 978-1-912866-45-8)
7. *The British and the Sikhs: Discovery, Warfare and Friendship (c.1700–1900)* Gurinder Singh Mann (ISBN 978-1-911628-24-8)
8. *Bazaine 1870: Scapegoat for a Nation* Quintin Barry (ISBN 978-1-913336-08-0)
9. *Redcoats in the Classroom: The British Army's School for Soldiers and Their Children During the 19th Century* Howard R. Clarke (ISBN 978-1-912866-47-2)
10. *The Rescue They Called A Raid: The Jameson Raid 1895-96* David Snape (ISBN 978-1-913118-77-8)
11. *Hungary 1848: The Winter Campaign* Johann Nobili (ISBN 978-1-913118-78-5)
12. *The War of Two Brothers: The Portuguese Civil War 1828-1834* Sérgio Veludo Coelho (ISBN 978-1-914059-26-1)
14. *Forgotten Victorian Generals* Christopher Brice (editor) (ISBN 978-1-910777-20-6)
15. *The German War of 1866: The Bohemian and Moravian Campaign Theodor Fontane* (ISBN 978-1-914059-29-2)
16. *Dust of Glory: The First Anglo-Afghan War 1839-1842, its Causes and Course* (ISBN 978-1-914059-33-9)
17. *Saarbruck to Sedan: The Franco-German War 1870-71. Uniforms, Organisation and Weapons of the Armies of the Imperial Phase of the War* (ISBN 978-1-914059-88-9)
18. *The Battle of Lissa 1866: How the Industrial Revolution Changed the Face of Naval Warfare* (ISBN 978-1-914059-92-6)